The authors of *Lean Leadership BASICS*® have created a transformation model that gives leadership and influencers the ability to take a deep dive into the people side of Lean, enhancing the thinking behind the tools necessary to measure improvement in daily work; as it cascades to the orga goals. I recommend this book to all levels of lean learners out there wanting to understand and implement lean thinking on the shop floor for long-term growth and sustainability.

Tracey Richardson, co-owner of Teaching Lean Inc, and author of *The Toyota Engagement Equation*

The authors of *Lean Leadership BASICS*® have created a comprehensive guide for leaders at all levels to learn the principles, practices, and systems underlying a lean enterprise. Leaders' actions set the culture of an organization, and *Lean Leadership BASICS*® describes tangible practices and behaviors leaders can take to develop to create a learning organization. The BASIC® model and the authors' shared years of wisdom are a resource that will enable many more leaders to successfully create people-centered organizations that embrace continuous learning.

Katie Anderson, leadership and learning coach, and author of *Learning to Lead, Leading to Learn: Lessons from Toyota Leader Isao Yoshino on a Lifetime of Continuous Learning*

Many organizations attempt to apply continuous improvement tools only to be met with failure. *Lean Leadership BASICS*® is the missing link to the human aspect component necessary to sustain a continuous improvement culture. This book is the "go-to" guidebook for every leader. It not only answers the "why" but also drives the reader to daily execution of the right behavior. This book should be in the hands of every shop floor leader.

Patrick Adams, CEO, Patrick Adams Consulting

This book is a must read for any leader or aspiring leader in any type of organization, large or small! Many know the critical role of leaders in Lean systems and developing a Lean culture, but what are the specific behaviors and leadership practices which are required? And, how do you develop these desired leader behaviors throughout the organization, at every level? This book takes the reader on an enlightening journey to answer these vital questions. Due to the authors' direct experiences, the reader feels that he or she is walking side by side with the company leader and observing the activities of supporting and improving the process and developing people. At times, the reader actually feels like they are put into the shoes of the leader in the story, and directly learning! This book provides a detailed account of the hiring process at one of the Toyota facilities. This firsthand account not only describes their rigor in hiring an entry-level employee, but the story also details how the leadership development process begins early in the life of a Toyota employee . . . even before they are hired! I began by stating that this book should be read by any leader or aspiring leader. Actually, this book should be read by anyone who wants to learn about organizational excellence and how the Lean tools combine with the people development component to create an integrated system of continuous improvement.

David Rizzardo, Associate Director, The Maryland World Class Consortia

The authors have written a book that won't sit on the shelf but actually fills a much-needed gap and should be in continuous use. Charlie and the Team have many decades of experience that has been masterfully written and synchronized such that group leaders can use this book starting day one. The book, *Lean Leadership BASICS*®, is a very practical and useful book that reinforces the importance of Leadership and the human aspects of Lean Thinking. The tools that are used are described and integrated with the behaviors needed from implementation to sustaining. The book provides a clear view into the importance of Leadership, focusing on the Shop Floor and utilizes the BASICS® Lean Implementation Model as the primary foundation for the book. The group leader is a critical role and the book effectively describes the behaviors and processes needed to go beyond the traditional first line supervisor. Every Lean Leader, starting with the group leader should ensure they have a copy and embrace the learning as part of their Lean Journey.

Fred Whiton, BSME, MSME, MEA, MBA, PE, Chief Engineer, Raytheon Technologies, Former Commissioner, Maryland Advisory Commission on Manufacturing Competitiveness, Past Board Member, Regional Manufacturing Institute, Board Member, First Maryland Disability Trust

This is yet another book written by Charlie and his fellow Lean lovers that appeals to Lean experts as much as it does to those who are just beginning their Lean journey. This book is a collection of fascinating stories which make it easy to read, remember, and apply in everyday life. If you tried to "implement" Lean, "do" Lean, or "teach" the Lean tools and found it unsustainable, this book will take you back to the original premise of Lean: LEAN is all about the People. It's a mindset, a way of life, a culture, and vital behaviors—all described by the authors using real life examples and easy to follow tips. And while some may call it a "must-read," I think it is a "love to read" kind of book.

Evelina Edmundson, Healthcare Lean Coach

"The Magic Fix All" rarely exists. Why? Because everything is changing with time: markets, people's needs, people's skills, designs, supply chains, and the world around us. The 2nd law of thermodynamics sums it up quite nicely: entropy always increases. Therein lies the value in "Lean Leadership Basics®." It addresses the process of developing the positional leadership to remain flexible and driving for continuous improvement. This book emphasizes the importance of developing the mind set in the team around us to reflect on and to implement those tools and processes that create long term value. Of course, it begins with me. Temporary successes can be certainly be achieved with personal mastery of the tools and processes. However, entropy will win out much quicker with the absence of shop floor leadership development. Without it, there is no sustainable culture. If you do nothing else, post the "Ten Rules to Live By" at your desk and read them daily.

Joe McNamara, PE, President, Ttarp Co.

This book provides a breadth of knowledge that captures much of the authors' wealth of experience into a concise applicable source of knowledge that can be useful in all businesses. *Lean Leadership BASICS®* here will be useful in its application to develop the leadership in your organization maximizing performance in both productivity and employee involvement. The anecdotes and examples provide a link between the overall steps and application on the floor with individuals in specific circumstances. This book will be one we continue to reference in development of the next generation of company leaders.

Mike Bland, Senior Project Manager, Amsted Rail

The pages of *Lean Leadership BASICS®* are full of deep wisdom from many sources and are a joy to consume. The anecdotes and stories in this book are worth the read alone but combine them with the years of research and knowledge applied to the BASICS® Model approach proposed, and you will have the thinking to create an organization that will be distinguished as a great Lean company, and not just another poor copy of Toyota.

Nigel Thurlow, CEO, The FLOW Consortium, and author of *The FLOW System*

Lean Leadership BASICS®

Lean Leadership BASICS®

How To Develop And Empower Leaders To Sustain Continuous Improvement

Michael Meyers, Charles Protzman, Dan Protzman, Davide Barbon, William Keen, Cliff Owens

Foreword by Ritsuo Shingo
President, Institute of Management Improvement

Additional Foreword by Nigel Thurlow
CEO, The FLOW Consortium, Author of *The FLOW System*

Routledge
Taylor & Francis Group

A PRODUCTIVITY PRESS BOOK

First published 2022
by Routledge
605 Third Avenue, New York, NY 10158

and by Routledge
2 Park Square, Milton Park, Abingdon, Oxon, OX14 4RN

Routledge is an imprint of the Taylor & Francis Group, an informa business

ISBN: 978-1-032-12582-4 (hbk)
ISBN: 978-1-498-78095-7 (pbk)
ISBN: 978-1-315-15522-7 (ebk)

DOI: 10.4324/9781315155227

Typeset in Garamond
by Apex CoVantage, LLC

Contents

The authors are donating 15% of the royalties from this book to the University of North Texas to support the Managing Complexity Master's Degree Program.

Foreword

Culture

It is said that Toyota has a good culture (Toyota Culture).
The company name "Toyota" has a good culture?
No! It is Toyota *People* that have a good culture.
Suppose we change all people in Toyota to new people . . .
Then Toyota culture is gone . . .
We should have to create the new culture again from nothing.

Total Participation

One of the very important concepts of TPS (Toyota Production System) is total participation.
    Everybody (top management/middle management/staff/workers) should participate in these
    activities such as improvement activities.
Then everybody would have the ownership. Without ownership, it is very difficult to
implement the activities. This will create the sustainability of the activities.

People

Many of the concepts of TPS are related to the people. (Not the machines)
Visual Management, Hoshin Kanri (Objective Control), 4S, Standardization, Leadership,
    Teamwork, Gemba Walk, Continuous Improvement and so on.
You might understand how "People" is important. . . .
This book is focused on people.
You will be inspired.
Please enjoy.

Ritsuo Shingo
President, Institute of Management Improvement

Ritsuo Shingo

Foreword

My friend and recently departed "Godfather of Lean," Norman Bodek, was keenly focused during his last years with us on the human aspect of Lean and human advancement through Lean thinking. In conversations I had with him in the latter part of 2020, he talked to me about his desire to truly improve people through the application of Lean thinking. Norman and I shared many of the same beliefs.

Anyone who understands Lean knows it is about human factors, people, and behaviors and nothing really to do with the tools. Tools exist to be used and mastered by people, but without the respect for humanity and the respect for people that's all Lean is, a collection of tools with limited utility. When you look deeper into Lean, you also find that the tools are actually behaviors based on concepts or philosophies that people need to adopt, and there are actually few if any physical tools that you can pick up and use. Even if you describe some of them as a technique this requires discipline and skill and this comes from practice. Practice is a behavior.

Behaviors are what define us, and our culture is a product of our behaviors. Culture is emergent and cannot be planned or designed but will emerge based on how we behave. If you want to change your culture, and many Lean transformations start this way, then you need to change your behaviors, the way you do things, the way or act, the way you do what you do.

People overuse the phrase "Respect for People," which is a key tenet of "The Toyota Way 2001," originally published by Toyota as an internal document, and later the subject and title of the book *The Toyota Way* first published by Jeff Liker in 2003.

If we go back further to the Toyota Production System, we find the second core foundational principle of Respect for Humanity. The first is Customer First. You can find many references to this online, but I can say throughout my Toyota career the principles of TPS and The Toyota Way are taught differently. After all, TPS predates The Toyota Way by almost 60 years, and Customer First and Respect didn't first arrive in 2001. In the official Toyota Way, the statement "The Toyota Way 2001 defines how the people of Toyota perform and behave in order to deliver these values" reinforces that Lean thinking is about people and behaviors. The Toyota Way is described as "the beliefs and values shared by us all." It is not about tools.

Professor Yasuhiro Monden, in the 1983 publication "Toyota Production System," wrote,

> At Toyota, respect for humanity is a matter of allying human energy with meaningful, effective operations by abolishing wasteful operations. If a worker feels that his job is important and his work significant, his morale will be high; if he sees that his time is wasted on insignificant jobs, his morale will suffer as well as his work.

Toyota's continued success comes from a deeper philosophy based on its understanding of people and human motivation. The success comes from its ability to develop leadership, people, teams, and culture; to devise strategy; to build extended networks and foster supplier relationships; and to establish and maintain a learning organization.

Unfortunately, many attempts to implement Lean fail and are often superficial. The reason is that most companies focus too heavily on tools without understanding that Lean is a system that must permeate an organization's culture and emphasize respect for people. They copy the tools but not the behaviors. They continue to behave the way they always have and wonder why the tools aren't working. The tools are your behaviors and actions and so not changing your behaviors means you are using the tools incorrectly. Lean tools are not something you can buy at a do-it-yourself store.

In the approach proposed in this new book from Protzman et al., the BASICS® model embraces and brings these principles front and center, recognizing that without the behaviors I have spoken about true Lean leadership is not possible.

The statement "Constantly developing yourself through others to achieve competitive advantage while maximizing profitability" is a statement that needs greater inquiry. On the face of it, it reads like a focus on profits, but I urge you to look deeper. To achieve success, you must develop others through constantly developing yourself. There is nothing wrong with profit and a competitive advantage, but doing this ethically through the development of others is a phase shift in business thinking. Look deeper into the steps of the BASICS® model to discover they are all about developing people. Respect for People in the truest Toyota sense.

The focus on the human aspect is admirable and sorely needed in Lean thinking approaches and teaching outside of Toyota. The Protzmans have a family legacy that stretches back into the annals of time to the birth of Lean. In every chapter I read words that reiterate the language of Respect for People, from ex-Toyota leaders to others who have studied their methods and approaches.

The pages are full of deep wisdom from many sources and are a joy to consume. The anecdotes and stories in this book are worth the read alone but combine them with the years of research and knowledge applied to the BASICS® approach proposed, and you will have the thinking to create an organization that will be distinguished as a great Lean company, and not just another poor copy of Toyota.

Nigel Thurlow

Preface

Author Michael Meyers had the original idea for this book, which is based on his career at Donnelly Corporation. He said, "You know, Dan and Charlie, we should write a book on shop floor management. Most of our clients are struggling with their shop floors with so many baby boomers retiring." As such, the book is heavily influenced by Mike's past experiences and knowledge as well as the co-authors' experiences and research.

This book has been an interesting journey that started in 1985 with Bendix Communications Division in Towson, Maryland, and the "Hats" team. I have read probably over 400-plus books on Lean, including all the Ohno, Shingo, and Monden books and some excellent recent ones by Ritsuo Shingo, Nigel Thurlow, Tracey and Ernie Richardson, Katie Anderson and Isao Yoshino, which have influences in this book.

The Cynefin Framework, the Flow System, and the OODA Loop

The Cynefin Framework was conceived by Dave Snowden back in 1998. I spent the last couple of years learning about this framework after Nigel Thurlow introduced me to Brian (Ponch) Rivera, John Turner, Roger Venegas, Pam Dukes, Dan Offchinick, and many others at Toyota. In 2019, Nigel sent me in his place to a Whistler retreat in British Columbia, where I had the honor to meet Dave Snowden and his team while being instantly immersed in a master class, along with Brian Rivera and many others on the Cynefin Framework. As such, I would be remiss if I didn't put this book in context to the Cynefin Framework.

This book is written mostly within the context of both the Clear and Complicated Cynefin Domains (see Figure P.1). When we get into behaviors, culture, values, and the like, we venture into the complex and liminal domain. It is important to have the situational awareness to know which domain you are in when you are making decisions. The book has also been influenced by *The Flow System*[1] (see Figure P.2), written by Nigel Thurlow, John Turner, and Brian Rivera. It has also been influenced by fighter pilot Col. John Boyd's Observe–Orient–Decide–Act (OODA) loop (see Figure P.3), which was first introduced to me by Brian Rivera during a Toyota Scrum Master Training session conducted by Nigel Thurlow and subsequent conversations with Chet Richards and Don Vandergriff who worked with Boyd. OODA and the Toyota Production System (TPS) have much in common, and Boyd talked about TPS in his Conceptual Spiral briefings. Plan–Do–Check–Act (PDCA) is the non-implicit guidance and control path in the OODA loop.[2] PDCA is strongly linked to the Cynefin-ordered world of linear cause-and-effect-based problem-solving, and the OODA Loop. I personally feel PDSA fits more in the liminal area of Cynefin with Scrum and the Flow System.[3] We plan to go into much more detail in a future book in development for now titled "Drive Thru Parking."

We set out to write a book about shop floor management, but what emerged was a path to continuous leadership development at all levels and to sustainability of a Lean enterprise. Our last book, *The BASICS® Lean Implementation Model*[4] was primarily geared toward the "tools side" of

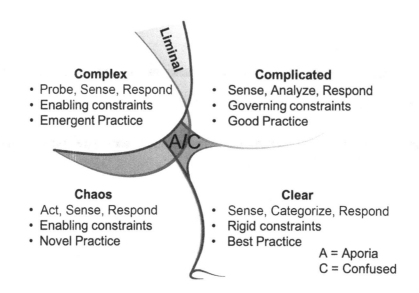

Figure P.1   Cynefin Framework with Liminal Domain.

Source: Used with permission from Cognitive Edge—cognitive-edge.com.

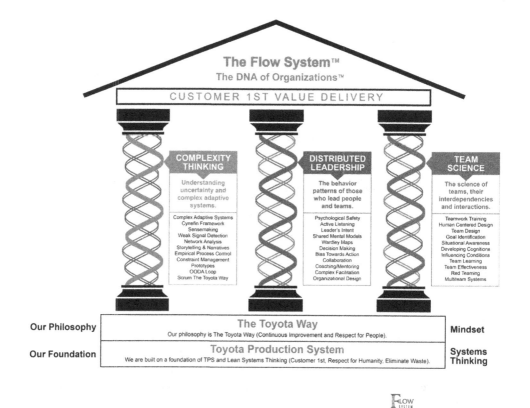

Figure P.2   The Flow System.

Source: Courtesy of Nigel Thurlow, CEO of The FLOW Consortium. This slide is part of the Flow System Foundations Course ©2019.

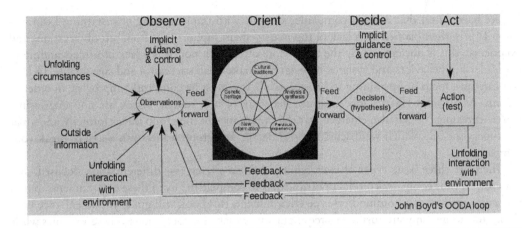

Figure P.3   The OODA Loop.

Source: Public domain.

Figure P.4   BASICS® Lean Leadership Development Path.

Source: BIG training materials.

Lean with some reference to the "people" side. Our goal with this book is to capture and focus on the importance of the "people" side of Lean and to show how the tools and the human aspect work together to form a cohesive system that will help not only sustain but drive continuous improvement. While we can't remove the entanglement inherent in a complex system, we have done our best to explain how the tools are intertwined.

Our experience has shown one needs to balance tools and people, or scientific management and respect for humanity, in order to implement and sustain Lean. Over the last four years, we developed a Path for Continuous Leadership Development (see Figure P.4), which has now become a part of our BASICS® Lean Model.

We have found that 80% of companies struggle with implementing or sustaining Lean systems. This is often blamed on a lack of top management support, but from our observations and experience, this is not necessarily the case. More often than not, it is a lack of understanding of the leadership behaviors and systems necessary to make Lean successful and sustainable. In fact, you can't just focus on sustaining to be successful. You must be constantly improving in order to sustain. As Sir John Harvey Jones, former chairman of ICI, stated, "If you are not progressing, you're regressing." What also emerged was the importance of the group leader formerly known as the supervisor role, which we discuss in great detail. The group leaders can make or break your company.

There are three basic types of overarching business strategies—differentiation, focused, and low cost.[5] If your company's product portfolio has to compete in any of these environments, but in particular the low-cost commodity–type environment, this book will guide you to enhance your ability to execute on your customer's requirements, which can continuously drive revenues while reducing costs, thus maximizing your competitiveness.

This book is about shifting an organization's leadership's behaviors starting with a focus on the group leader's role at the shop floor management level. Our Leadership Development Path prioritizes execution, meeting our customer's commitments, and delivering customer-focused results, which will require a significant change in thinking, recruitment, training skills, and on-the-job development.

This book is centered on the creation of a unique new leadership approach based on our BASICS® Lean Implementation Model.[6] The model is supported by over 35 years of empirical research and over 75 years of experience between the authors. This approach is geared toward any company, small and all the way to Fortune 500 companies. While the book explores and is fully aligned with Toyota's principles, we wrote the book so it could be applied by any company. It is based on our own experiences, with our own customers, whereby we have learned that just implementing Lean tools or trying to sustain is not enough. Implementing the Lean tools will not suffice unless you figure out how to simultaneously develop your team members and leaders. This won't be a simple overnight fix but, rather, a series of small, everlasting systemic changes nudging your organization in the right direction.

When Toyota entered into the joint venture with NUMMI between 1984 and 2010,[7] they sent Japanese Leaders to coach the American leaders for 3 years! When Charles Protzman asked a key leader during the NUMMI transition, Isao Yoshino, about this during a trip to Japan in 2017, Yoshino-san told him that not only was it true, "but it wasn't nearly long enough."[8]

While this book is geared toward the shop floor or office group leader, it can be applied to any leadership position in any profession. We prefer the term *group leader* because it has the connotation of teams and working together, whereas, opposingly, the word *supervisor* has the connotation of a taskmaster or a micromanager. A group leader is a salaried role similar to a supervisor in level and responsibility but significantly different in how they perform their job and how they lead their teams. A group leader is a leader of teams and expands on and includes a new set of duties and expectations when compared to that of what we consider a traditional supervisor today.

We also use the term *team leader* for an hourly role who runs the frontline cell or office team but does not have Human Resources (HR) responsibility for their team members. In addition, we typically will use the term *team members* in place of the word *operators*, that is, direct labor. However, team members, based on context, can be anyone in the organization.

Because many companies struggle with the human aspects of execution, this book is geared to how to create a successful and self-sustaining shop floor management environment. We explore the group leader's two primary roles:

1. Running the daily business by driving continuous daily improvement (through developing others)
2. Developing themselves by developing others

We put focus on the group leaders first because we need to evolve their skill sets before we can begin to develop others around them. It is the group leaders who need to ensure the execution of the daily plan with support of the senior leadership. We need to set a clear target or direction and continuously provide support and coaching for them through this process. Please note that developing your people should come before running the daily business. Running the business is accomplished by developing all your team members to become leaders and problem-solvers. Developing oneself includes building the knowledge, skills, routines, and abilities necessary to run the business, drive daily process improvement, and develop other people.

Please note that this approach is not for everyone, and you don't have to use this approach to become a successful company. Many companies are successful in spite of the way they treat their people or whether they implement Lean techniques. However . . . how much money are they leaving on the table? No one can know for sure as the accounting metrics don't exist!

A company will have difficulty surviving if a Lean competitor emerges that continuously reduces its costs, continuously develops and treats its people with respect, and not only sustains but also continues to grow market share or even disrupts it. Wouldn't you rather have an organization in which people look forward to Mondays and when you post a job you have a waiting list to join your company?

Do You Need to Read This Book?

The following are some warning signs for companies and group leaders. If you answer yes to any of these, then there is an explicit need for drastic action. Please check any of the following questions if they apply to you:

- Do you find yourself constantly fighting fires?
- Are you having trouble trying to manage the work in process (WIP) and statusing your customers on delivery?
- Do you find yourself physically checking on things so much so that it's impossible to even think about standardizing your workday?
- Have you recently been blamed for a problem or blamed someone else for a problem?
- Does your leadership use fear and/or intimidation tactics whether intentional, unintentional, or passive?
- Do you feel like you are just going through the motions and spinning your wheels but not actually getting anywhere?
- Are you spending large amounts of time in your office or in meetings all day?
- Do you have lots of "people problems" in your department?
- Are you spending overtime in order to just get the basic day-to-day activities done?
- Do the time standards (key performance indicators) you are required to meet seem too difficult?
- When was the last time the standards were updated? Three to five years ago?
- Do you have trouble keeping track of what your people are doing?

- Do you find yourself constantly barraged with questions from your team members? And from senior leadership?
- Do you lack the time to fix problems that arise each day?
- Do you find yourself throwing solutions at problems, but then they come back?
- Are you under constant pressure from a boss who is not a coach or mentor?
- When you look at your team, do you find there is no one ready to replace you?
- Have you been turned down for promotions?
- Have you implemented Lean but can't figure out why it doesn't sustain?

This book will answer all these questions and more. It is about evolving the thinking necessary for people who aspire to or are currently in a supervisory or even senior leadership role. If properly supported and prioritized, one can create an environment where the group leader's role is viewed as a highly sought after and respected role. This requires us to convert to a "growth mindset," shifting our behaviors from firefighting and managing problems to opening our minds towards fixing shop floor and administrative problems through daily management and execution so that they don't return. We hope to challenge many of your existing paradigms.

We are writing this book based on what we know to be a need by many companies to improve their ability to supervise at the frontline and the middle management levels. There seems to be a knowledge gap developing at many companies due to the retirement of workers, "brain drain," or where the supervisor role is not viewed as worth the investment in time and effort to promote from within. Once these key employees depart, we seem to lose the recipe for their jobs as much of their unwritten knowledge was only documented in their heads. New leaders are hired from the outside and often thrown into their position with little or no training, coaching, or mentoring and are left to their own devices in order to carry out their role. This is due to a lack of middle management leadership and coordination.

Inevitably, when they experience problems, it is the group leaders who were just thrown into that position, which are often criticized for how they performed their job. It is very stressful and unfair to anyone put in this position. As a result, many companies are losing their ability to manage on the front lines. This inability to effectively manage continues to spread, and if not corrected could end up crippling our factories, healthcare institutions, government agencies, and financial services. This gap is hidden within all the things we do not see on the factory floor or in the lack of desired team behaviors. However, like a heart attack or stroke, you must know the warning signs and know how to properly act when they arise.

This book will teach you an overview of the shop floor and overall management system which focuses on customer execution by teaching and developing others. The questions in the earlier list entail just a few of the typical warning signs or gaps we encounter. Gaps are referred to as mismatches in the OODA loop which create tension and a need for improvement. This need for ongoing improvement, along with systems that constantly inject and force quick responses to new information, is critical to organizations remaining open systems. When organizations become closed systems, they build entropy, which is equivalent to waste. Ever-increasing entropy (waste) threatens profitability, agility, and ultimately the very existence of organizations. We will show you how to identify and bridge the gaps which exist today and then how to overcome these gaps. The solutions must be balanced and integrated between people (behaviors) and tools application. First, we need to change our thinking and behaviors before we can start to administer the "Tools" or treatment to overcome the gaps and make the symptoms visible.

We start with an overview of the system. To date, Toyota[9] is still the benchmark for Lean management, but it is not called Lean at Toyota. Our system is loosely based on and refers to Toyota, but since we are not all Toyota, we put together an approach that any company can utilize.

The book starts with an overview of shop floor management and our BASICS® Lean implementation method. We then review some fundamental principles like batch versus flow thinking. We talk about the organizational structure that makes this system successful and review each of the new roles in this organization. Then we review the Lean tools followed by introducing our new Lean Continuous Leadership Development Path.

Our Leadership Development Path focuses on developing leaders that develop their people who turn into leaders. Mr. Yoshino, who is profiled in the book *Learning to Lead, Leading to Learn* by Katie Anderson,[10] is an example of this type of executive leader, as well as Ritsuo Shingo, who details this in his book *My Leadership, The China Years*.

On a final note, back when I read Henry Ford's, Shingo's, and Ohno's books I noticed they kept repeating certain things. It finally occurred to me that those things must be important. Please keep that in mind as you read this book.

Charles Protzman

Notes

1. The Flow System, Nigel Thurlow CEO of the Flow Consortium, John Tuner, Brain Rivera, Aquiline Books|UNT, November 19, 2020.
2. Based on Boyd's OODA Loop, Chet Richards, Necesse, VOL 5 Issue 1 © 2020.
3. The Flow System, Created by Nigel Thurlow, John Turner, Brian (Ponch) Rivera 2020 https://flow guides.org/, www.getflowtrained.com/
4. The BASICS® Lean Implementation Model, Protzman, Keen, Protzman, CRC Press, 2019.
5. Competitive Strategy, Michael Porter, New York Free Press, ©1980
6. The BASICS® model first appeared in print in the book *Leveraging Lean in Healthcare* and later explained in *The BASICS® Lean Implementation Model*.
7. www.popularmechanics.com/cars/a5514/4350856/
8. Personal conversation during the Toyota tour with Isao Yoshino in January 2017; Isao Yoshino-san coached John Shook.
9. This book is not specifically about Toyota but does refer quite a bit to their system known as the Toyota Production System (TPS).
10. *Learning to Lead, Leading to Learn*, Katie Anderson, Integrand Press, ©2020.

Acknowledgments

- This book is primarily based on the experiences and learnings of Michael Meyers, who had the idea for this book.
- We would like to formally acknowledge and thank this list of reviewers who read over early versions of the book and provided very valuable feedback: Dave Rizzardo, Jeremy Horn, Roger Venegas, Jonathan Peyton, Joe McNamara.
- Special thanks to Nigel Thurlow, who has been a good friend to Charlie and Dan Protzman and Bill Keen since we first met at the Lean Leadership Summit in Santorini Greece sponsored by George Trachilis and Paul Akers in 2017. Nigel has helped Charlie expand his learning with his suggestions for reading over 30 books on Lean design and subsequent teachings to one or more of the authors on High Performance Team Training, Scrum The Toyota Way, the inaugural training class for the Flow System, and the Advanced Cynefin and Complexity Training given at Toyota, along with the introductions to Brian (Ponch) Rivera, John Turner, Dirk Van Goubergen, and into the world of Complexity and Cynefin at Cognitive Edge—Dave Snowden, Michael Cheveldave, Gary Wong, and Zhen Goh.
- Thanks to Professor John Turner for comments on the book and allowing Charles Protzman to edit *The FLOW System* book, which was a tremendous learning experience and influence on this book. Also for John's teachings on Team Science, allowing us to collaborate on the Team Science Training.
- A special thanks to Roger Venegas, who worked many hours with us reviewing content and making suggestions which helped escalate the book to a new level, especially pertaining to the change equation and the OODA loop, which was moved to our future "Drive Thru Parking" book.
- Thanks to Tracey and Ernie Richardson for permission to share content from their new book *The Toyota Engagement Equation* as well as a personal conversation with Tracey during which she shared her Toyota-hiring story with us.
- Thanks to Katie Anderson and Isao Yoshino for allowing us to include content from their new book *Learning to Lead, Leading to Learn*. Also a note of thanks to Yoshino-san for his personal teachings during our trip to Japan in 2017 and subsequent correspondence.
- A very special thanks to Mike Riley, former BIG subcontractor, for sharing his Toyota-hiring story with us.
- Thanks to Jeremy Horn and Dan Protzman for their help with the graphics for the book.
- Thanks to Mark Jamrog, SMC Group, former sensei to Charles Protzman.
- Thanks to Evelina Edmunson for helping us perform some final detailed edits on the final book.

■ Thanks to MaryBeth Protzman who spent many hours going over various versions of the book.
■ Thanks to the AlliedSignal Bendix "Hats" group. You know who you are.
■ I would like to thank my wife Michelle Meyers and my five children for reviewing various versions of the book and being supportive of my Saturday and Sunday morning working in my office as well as the amount of time I spent away from home working.

Author Bios

Michael Meyers

Mike became a partner with Business Improvement Group in 2017, where he has used his abilities and past experience to help turn around businesses while supporting an international client base. Michael Meyers has over 25 years of operations leadership experience, filling a variety of leadership roles from the shop floor to executive vice president. For 17 years, Mike worked at Donnelly Corporation, where he focused on mastering and implementing Lean using the Donnelly Production System (DPS) company wide. The DPS system is a Lean philosophy modeled after the Toyota Production System. Mike worked his way up from production supervisor to the general manager of three plants. Mike managed the benchmark Donnelly plant that was awarded Toyota's coveted "Most Improved Supplier of the Year" award and was part of a worldwide benchmarking tour and video for Lean best practices by the Society of Manufacturing Engineers. Mike's comprehensive career experience also includes Vice President of Operations/Director of Lean Implementation at a Great Lakes Castings and Vice President of Operations for a Plasan Carbon Composites, where he was responsible for building a complete Lean Enterprise in a union environment. Under Mike's leadership, the company was awarded General Motors "Supplier Quality Excellence" award in recognition of its superior supplier teaming and outstanding customer satisfaction. As Vice President of Operations, Mike was involved in significant customer–board of directors' interface to ensure that objectives were aligned to secure investment in the company that enabled it to fund significant growth. Mike was certified by the Toyota Supplier Development Program and is certified as an instructor in Lean, KATA, Standard Work, Zenger Miller High Performance Work Teams, and Training Within Industry (TWI).

Charles Protzman

Charles Protzman is an internationally renowned author, speaker, trainer, and implementer of Lean and Agile improvements. Charlie started Business Improvement Group, LLC in 1997 and spent many years driving successful business transformations and Lean implementations across the United States, Europe, and China in all types of industries, government, and health care. He has taught Lean thinking principles to every level from executives to the team members on the shop floor and as well as physicians and hospital staff. His specialty is transforming Lean masters and experts into world-class Lean practitioners. He has been a keynote speaker in the United States, China, and Portugal. Charlie spent over 13 years with AlliedSignal (now Honeywell) and has been implementing Lean principles and thinking since 1985. He has published 12 books to date, receiving two Shingo Prizes. He was AlliedSignal's first Lean Master and Strategic Operations Manager, for the Government Electronic Systems Division, which was benchmarked by Harley Davidson for high-performance work teams. Charlie implemented Lean across eight US plants and received several special recognition and cost-reduction awards. Charlie, along with Vic

Chance and Jim Robinson, made a presentation in March 1996[1] that was instrumental in signing up over 60 companies to help Governor Glendening and Department of Business and Economic Development start the Maryland World Class Manufacturing Consortium, now MWCC, where he helped member companies develop their first Lean World Class Guidelines and led several assessments. Charlie has a BA and an MBA from Loyola College of Maryland and was a past member of Association of Manufacturing Excellence Champions Club.

Dan Protzman

Dan Protzman has spent the last 6 years as Director of Customer Solutions for Business Improvement Group LLC and, prior to that, 4 years with Maxim Healthcare. Daniel is an outgoing and charismatic leader and coach who has been implementing Lean in the United States, Europe, and the Caribbean. He completed two Japan study missions, one with Norman Bodek, and has conducted Lean workshops for Toyota, Under Armour, Abbott, Banco Popular and the State of Maryland's World Class Consortium. Daniel has consulted and conducted Lean and TWI training with numerous manufacturing companies as well as in the service and health care industries. Dan has conducted several hospital lean assessments and worked with GI clinics. Dan is a certified Lean Master Practitioner Level IV and has had the Shingo Organization Training Courses as well as training from Toyota's Dojo in Nagoya, Japan. Daniel is the co-author of the book One-Piece Flow vs Batching, Implementing Lean, and The BASICS® Lean Implementation Model. Dan is a certified MBTI instructor, Harada Method Coach, Lean Leadership Development Coach and TWI (JI) trainer. He has a BA from Virginia Tech.

William Keen

Bill has worked for several Fortune 500 companies and health care providers during his career—United Technologies, Atrium Health, Boulder Architects, Disney—and is currently working at Abbott Labs, where he led the COVID-19 rapid-testing manufacturing development and start-up. Bill Keen is a dynamic, energetic professional, with more than 20 years of professional experience in health care, manufacturing operations, construction operations, new-product design and launch, industrial engineering and maintenance management utilizing continuous improvement concepts. Bill brings a unique perspective to the application of continuous improvement through application while in the following roles: Vice President of Operations, Plant Manager, and Engineering Manager. Bill has consulted as a subcontractor for Business Improvement Group LLC all over the world. Bill holds numerous certifications such as Scrum Master, Lean Master (UTC), Pinnacle Assessor, Master Sensei (Atrium Health), Chief Industrial Engineer (Bach) and Divisional Strategy Director. Bill has been a Lean Instructor, has lead over 350 Lean and 3P implementations, and is certified as a coach in Team Development and Mentoring, Business Process Improvement, Safety and Environmental Programs, and Workstation Design. Bill is a dedicated continuous learner whose education includes undergraduate studies in Industrial Engineering (IE), Mechanical Engineering (ME), Electrical Engineering (EE), and Quality Systems; a master's focus in theology and business, and doctorate studies in IE, ergonomics, and logistics.

Davide Barbon

Davide is currently President for APAC (Asia Pacific) at a large US corporation. Over the past 25 years, he has led organizations globally across Europe, the United States, China, Latin America, and Asia. He focuses on elevating teams' performance by working with passion and strong commitment to challenge the status quo, with deep curiosity for acquiring new knowledge. He is a fond believer that listening and observing are critical to improvement. He finds that constant learning and actively participating in the line are the key for growing and driving progress while eliminating waste, challenging thinking and his own beliefs every day.

Cliff Owens

Cliff Owens has been in the automotive industry for over 30 years, during which he has held various leadership roles in new product and process engineering and the management of new program launches. He has also worked in manufacturing operations roles in Quality, Operations Excellence/Continuous Improvement, and Plant Management. He has lived and worked in multiple locations throughout the Americas, Europe, and Asia, spending significant time in India and China leading new-plant construction, as well as increasing commercial sales growth. He is currently leading Operational Excellence, which drives improvement to bottom-line financial metrics and customer satisfaction.

Note

1. www.bizjournals.com/baltimore/stories/1998/03/30/daily4.html

Contributing Authors

We would like to formally acknowledge and thank this list of contributing authors who provided either content editing assistance or inspirations for content for this book in no particular order: Ritsuo Shingo, Nigel Thurlow, Tracey and Ernie Richardson, Katie Anderson, Mike Riley, Patrick Adams, Michael Cheveldave, Melania Demartini, Dave Rizzardo, Jeremy Horn, Eric Ren Hui, Dominik Szozda, Professor Matthias Thurer, Jonathan Peyton, Brian (Ponch) Rivera, Justin Shang, Forest Sheng, Andy McDermott, John Turner, Danilo BrunoFranco, Roger Venegas, and Gary Wong.

Introduction

Even earlier than the beginning of my journey in 1985, as I mentioned in the preface, this book has its roots in teachings from post–World War II Japan. Following extensive research over the past 5 years, I have discovered that my grandfather, Charles W. Protzman, Sr., along with Homer Sarasohn and Frank Polkinghorn, (known as "the three wise men" in Kenneth and Will Hopper's book *The Puritan Gift*), was responsible for teaching what we now believe, became known as PDCA in Japan starting back in 1949 (pre-Deming) during their Civil Communications Section (CCS) Industrial Management Course.

PDSA and PDCA

PDSA (Plan–Do–Study–Act) came from Shewhart's 1939 book (see Figure I.1), which was edited by W. Edwards Deming. Deming modified the Shewhart cycle by adding a fourth step: Step 1—Design, Step 2—Produce, Step 3—Sell, Step 4—Redesign through marketing research (see Figure I.2). Deming stressed the importance of constant interaction among design, production, sales, and research and that the four steps should be rotated constantly, with quality of product and service as the aim. As stated in Tom Gilb's book *Competitive Engineering*,

> Deming taught that it did not matter where in the cycle one entered a PDSA process, nor where one exited, though Deming was not so concerned with the exit, as he viewed PDSA as an eternal process-control cycle, as long as there were competitive pressures to improve things.

PDSA was mainly focused on implementing improvements to design by getting customer feedback to make products that customers wanted to buy. Dr. Deming stated emphatically that "he didn't know where PDCA (Plan–Do–Check–Act) originated."[1] After switching from PDSA in the 1950s to PDCA, Deming switched back to PDSA in 1986. Moen references in his paper[2] that Imai[3] stated the Japanese executives recast the Deming wheel from the 1950 Japanese Union of Scientists and Engineers (JUSE) seminar into the PDCA cycle. With no intention of discrediting Deming's work, we believe Imai was actually referring to the CCS Seminars, which were held just prior to Deming's arrival.

CCS stood for the Civil Communications Section of MacArthur's occupation after World War II. Protzman and Sarasohn introduced the scientific method in a course called the CCS Industrial Management Course, which was taught to the senior leaders of all the Japanese communications companies, including the likes of what became Sony, Hitachi, Panasonic, Pioneer, Matsushita, and many more. This scientific method was introduced in the course as a tool for problem-solving for organizations, manufacturing, and improving quality and reliability.

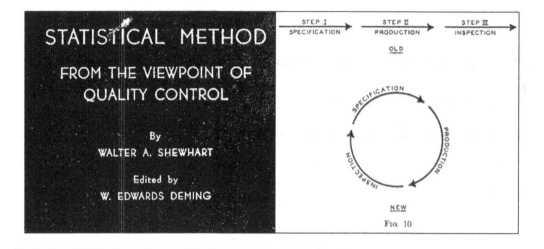

Figure I.1   Shewhart Wheel—Origin of Plan–Do–Study–Act.

Source: https://deming.org/wp-content/uploads/2020/06/PDSA_History_Ron_Moen.pdf—Foundation and History of the PDSA Cycle Ronald Moen Associates in Process Improvement-Detroit (USA) Graphics at top Courtesy of Nigel Thurlow, CEO, The Flow Consortium,

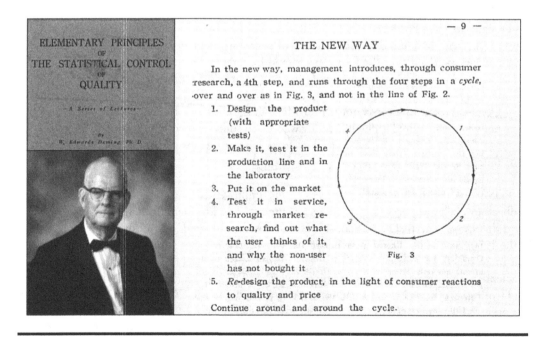

Figure I.2   Deming Wheel—Evolved Plan–Do–Study–Act.

Source: https://deming.org/wp-content/uploads/2020/06/PDSA_History_Ron_Moen.pdf—Foundation and History of the PDSA Cycle Ronald Moen Associates in Process Improvement-Detroit (USA)—Graphics at top Courtesy of Nigel Thurlow, CEO, The Flow Consortium.

In Toshio Goto's book *The Forgotten Origin of Japanese Management*[4] (see Figure I.3), he refers to this scientific method section of the CCS Course as PDCA. We believe that PDCA was taught in the CCS manual as a lighter-weight version of the scientific method at the same time as Deming's seminars. So when, for whatever reason, Deming went along with PDCA; this is what led to PDCA and PDSA getting confused. We are not sure why Deming switched over to PDCA while in Japan, but we know he acknowledged and was adamant that he did not know where it came from. Now we believe we know where it came from—the CCS teachings. According

As engineers and management people, we are convinced that the logical approach to determining what changes are needed and the benefits to be derived from them stems from the use of the Scientific Method. It merely involves careful, common sense, analytical thinking. Simply stated, the scientific method approach consists of five steps. They are:

1. Define the problem precisely.

2. Get the facts — all the facts.

3. Analyze those facts to decide upon a proper plan of action.

4. Put that plan of action into effect with the expected results identified.

5. Monitor the plan in process; make necessary timely adjustments.

The problem that we are dealing with in this course is quite easy to define. Manufacturing productivity and reliability is at an economically unacceptable low level. That calls into question the effectiveness of management organizations. We want to turn the situation around. In order to

称している。したがって経営管理における科学的アプローチとは、まさにCCS経営者講座の構成どおり、事業方針から始まって組織体制、各種の管理、運営という各要素が体系的に連動しており、全体を合理性が貫いていることを意味しているのである。

科学的アプローチについて、テキストでは次のような蓬のアクションと説明している。

（1）問題の設定

（2）問題に関するファクト・ファインディング

（3）事実にもとづく計画の立案

（4）計画の実施

（5）実施結果と計画のチェック

これは今日いわれているPDCAサイクル、すなわちプラン―ドゥ―チェック―アクションに他ならない。もちろん品質管理も科学的経営管理の一部分であることに相違ない。しかし、それは管理手法の一要素でしかない。もし科学的経営管理を品質管理に綾小化するとすれば、大きな誤りといわねばならない。

Figure I.3 **(Top) Plan–Do–Check–Act from the CCS Manual 1949; (Bottom) Plan–Do–Check–Act Japanese Edition of the Class.**

Source: Goto, Toshio. 1999. *Wasure Sarareta Keiei no Genten* (The Forgotten Origin of Japanese Management), Tokyo: Japan Productivity Center.

to Ken Hopper, those that took the CCS course and then Deming's seminars told him they didn't learn anything new. In fact, it was my grandfather and Sarasohn that recommended Dr. Deming to JUSE to continue their quality teachings when they had to return to the States in 1950. Sarasohn stated:

> Deming was actually our second choice, Sarasohn recalled. We wanted Walter Shewart from AT&T Bell Labs to be our quality guru, because he virtually invented statistical quality control in the 1930s, but Shewart wasn't available at the time—he was in poor health—so we settled for Deming. He's capitalized on it.[5]

To be clear, we still have more research to do, including another trip to Japan, before publishing a book on the history of the CCS. We still do not know the exact origin of the acronym PDCA in Japan, and it is not our intent to under-credit the Japanese. "Even before World War II, the Japanese made great progress in the sciences, medicine, technology, and other fields after the 1868 Meiji Restoration. Yukawa Hideki won a Nobel Prize in Physics in 1949."[6] However, after World War II, we believe, and have been told by US management historian Kenneth Hopper, as well as in conversations with Japanese professors and historians, that the CCS course had a big influence on the resulting Japanese economic miracle.

Our previously published and trademarked BASICS® Lean Implementation Model focuses on Lean tools and has its roots in PDCA. Dissatisfied with other problem-solving models at the time, I created BASICS®, a problem-solving model, in 1997 to help implement Lean processes and systems to assist with organizational transformations. Following in the footsteps of my grandfather, this book is focused on management and developing leadership within an organization, or the "people side of Lean." We will introduce and cover, in detail, our BASICS® Lean Leadership Development Path, of which many of the concepts have roots back to my grandfather's 1949 teachings.

Notes

1. https://deming.org/wp-content/uploads/2020/06/PDSA_History_Ron_Moen.pdf—Foundation and History of the PDSA Cycle Ronald Moen Associates in Process Improvement-Detroit (USA).
2. https://deming.org/wp-content/uploads/2020/06/PDSA_History_Ron_Moen.pdf—Foundation and History of the PDSA Cycle Ronald Moen Associates in Process Improvement-Detroit (USA).
3. Kaizen, Kaizen (Kyzen), the key to Japan's competitive success Imai, © 1986 by the Kaizen Institute, page 10, 60–63.
4. Goto, Toshio. 1999. Wasure Sarareta Keiei no Genten (The Forgotten Origin of Japanese Management), Tokyo, Japan Productivity Center.
5. Stranger in a Strange Land: How Homer Sarasohn Brought Industrial Quality to Japan and Why It Took Japan So Long to Learn By Robert X. Cringely, May 25, 2000.
6. Personal correspondence with Art Smalley 9/20/2019.

Chapter 1

The Leadership Development Path

Figure 1.1   BASICS® Lean Leadership Development Path.

Source: BIG training materials.

Our Leadership Development Path (see Figure 1.1) represents the human aspect, or the "people part," of our published *BASICS® Lean Implementation Model*. The Leadership Development Path encompasses both the execution and operational excellence of an overall business management and delivery system. The philosophy is deeply rooted in the belief that by developing others from head to heart, we, in turn, develop ourselves. It is only by developing ourselves that we will continuously improve our processes and constantly enable the business to maximize its competitiveness.

DOI: 10.4324/9781315155227-1

Our primary job should be to continuously develop our people using the BASICS® process-focused tools while treating profitability as the long-term measure of how we are performing. We start with learning the new thinking, tools, and interpersonal skills that we then deploy under the guidance of a coach. We follow up with practice, practice, and more practice, building it into "muscle memory" in order to sustain. This muscle memory is the intuitive and implicit guidance and control,[1] which starts with the individual and then needs to transcend to the organization.

The Leadership Development Path approach requires a major change in leadership behaviors and must be driven from the top. Even though the Leadership Development Path is a human-resource-based initiative, it is not necessary to be led by Human Resources (HR). In our years of experience, we've encountered many companies in which the HR Department seems to run independently from the rest of the business; in fact, sometimes we've seen the two actually working against each other. This misaligned "traditional HR Department structure" must evolve to play a more supportive role guided by the Executive Leadership Team to help develop this new system.

The thought process is, "We grow the business by *growing our people*," which is embedded in the tools we discuss throughout the book. The path starts with the mantra "Customer First," as well as Leadership's role in creating the new organizational structure, which fosters trust, teamwork, and self-reliance. This does not mean the traditional hierarchy is eliminated, as there is still a requirement for the "chain of command."

We use our BASICS® Lean Implementation Model toolset to develop the foundation to convert from batch production to one-piece flow wherever possible. The continuous leadership development "people piece" aligns with our BASICS® model (see Figure 1.2). Following are the four components of our Leadership Development Path, along with the corresponding step in our BASICS® model:

■ **B**aseline—Teaching our team members' self-reliance that is built on Learning to See Gaps and Waste.
■ **A**nalyze/**S**uggest—Teaching our team members accountability to improve business practices—which is based on Learning to Solve.

1.	**B**aseline	• Customer First
		• Constancy of purpose in your work
2.	**A**nalyze	• Take ownership and responsibility
		• Make everything visual (Mieruka)
3.	**S**uggest Solution	• Act on fact
		• Be persistent—never quit
4.	**I**mplement	• Bias for quick action
		• Follow each process with sincerity and commitment
5.	**C**heck	• Thorough communication
		• Involve everyone every day
6.	**S**ustain	

- *Continuously improve while never being satisfied—avoid complacency.*
- *Always strive for the most practical and effective solution—there is always a better way!*
- *Fully do the best for our stakeholders by driving our company's success through the development of our team members.*

Figure 1.2 BASICS® Principles and Goals.

Source: BIG training materials.

- **I**mplement/**C**heck—Developing our team members' skills and putting the systems in place, which is based on Learning to Share.
- **S**ustain—This is built on continuous leadership development whereby we are Learning to Teach others, which helps develop ourselves. You don't really learn it until you have to teach it.

This results in a highly efficient system whereby leaders develop leaders who deliver quality parts and services just in time to our customers at the lowest cost possible. The system is supported by the informal interconnections in the organizational structure and combined with leader standard work and what we call "scalable processes," which are not person-dependent but, instead, are customer—and process-focused, flexible, and adaptable. They are constantly improving and growing with the business over time.

Following the Leadership Development Path becomes part of the scaffolding and an enabling constraint for business growth that helps us run and sustain the business. Our BASICS® model requires the implementation of visual workplace management and organization including 5S, visual controls, visual displays, and mistake proofing (*poka yoke*) necessary to achieve top performance. It requires a new mental model with new leadership behaviors and tools as follows:[2]

1. Leader Standard Work: The structured daily routine that combines layered audits[3] with visualization. It includes the standard work necessary to achieve increased productivity and is designed to elevate the performance of leaders who now must enforce accountability and discipline through training, coaching, and mentoring.
2. Modeling Behaviors: The leader must role model the desired behaviors and lead by example in response to the needs of the situation.
3. Actively Addressing Issues: The leaders must respond and escalate as needed whatever countermeasures necessary to highlight and correct problems with a goal to fix them so they never come back.
4. Developing Others: It must become part of the day-to-day execution of their leadership tasks and leader standard work.

Continuous leadership development cannot be supported or sustained by using traditional management systems and behaviors, which are typically results-driven rather than process-focused and through which people become "assets" that are always considered replaceable.

Endlessly chasing results-oriented key performance indicators can drive some of the craziest behaviors and unpredictable results, which we can attest to seeing firsthand around the globe. Solely driving results from the leadership level robs any inherent motivation for the manager to improve the process. Instead, this feeds a reactive, "shoot from the hip" culture we all refer to as "firefighting." For most companies, the human aspect of the Leadership Development Path has not evolved; therefore, it requires the senior leadership to take the necessary steps to revamp or transform their culture to implement this type of behavioral change.

Customer First

Everything starts with the *external customer* (see Figure 1.3). The customer should be like the sun, the center of our universe,[4] because without the sun, we cannot survive. We must keep the customer at the forefront of everything we do, even when they seemingly are not involved. It is important to design the new system to get both positive and negative feedback from the customer often and quickly. This is called the voice of the customer. Peter Drucker said, "Leaders should be

Figure 1.3 Customer First.

Source: BIG training materials—Shutterstock.

asking five essential questions: What is our mission? Who is our customer? What does the customer value? What are our results? What is our plan?"[5]

We must design and build products and offerings the customers want to buy and sometimes don't even know they need. We call these "unarticulated needs."[6] The challenge is, "How do we get the customers what they want, exactly when they want it (even if it was yesterday), and make it at the desired quality level for the lowest cost possible?"

Objective of the Enterprise[7]

"Why does any company exist? What is the reason for being in any business enterprise? Many people would probably answer these questions by saying that the purpose of a company is to make a profit. In fact, if I were to ask you to write down right now the principal reason why your companies are in business, I suppose that most of the answers would be something of this sort. But such a statement is not a complete idea, nor is it a satisfactory answer because it does not clearly state the objective of the company, the principal goal that the company management is to strive for. A company's objective should be stated in a way which will not permit any uncertainty as to its real fundamental purpose.

For example, there are two ways of looking at that statement about profit. One is to make the product for a cost that is less than the price at which it is to be sold.

Selling Price – Cost = Profit

The other is to sell the product for a price higher than it costs to make.

Cost + Profit = Selling Price

These two views are almost the same—but not quite. The first implies a cost-conscious attitude on the part of the company. The second seems to say whatever the product costs, it will be sold at a higher price.

There is another fault that I would find in such a statement. It is entirely selfish and one—sided. It ignores entirely the sociological aspects that should be a part of a company's thinking. The business enterprise must be founded upon a sense of responsibility to the public and to its employees. Service to its customers, the wellbeing of its employees, good citizenship in the communities in which it operates—these are cardinal principles fundamental to any business. They provide the platform upon which a profitable company is built.

The founder of the Newport News Shipbuilding and Dry Dock Company, when he was starting his company, wrote down his idea of the objective—the purpose—of the enterprise. He put it this way. "We shall build good ships here; at a profit if we can—at a loss if we must—but, always good ships." This is the guiding principle of this company and its fundamental policy. And it is a good one too because in a very few words it tells the whole reason for the existence of the enterprise. And yet inherent in these few words there is a wealth of meaning. The determination to put quality ahead of profit. A promise to stay in business in spite of adversity. A determination to find the best production methods.

Every business enterprise should have as its very basic policy a simple clear statement, something of this nature, which will set forth its reason for being. In fact, it is imperative that it should have such a fundamental pronouncement because there are some very definite and important uses to which it can be put.

We can only make or increase our profit by focusing on what the customer wants and then reducing our costs.*"Reducing cost" does not mean "cutting costs"* (e.g., laying people off) Instead, reducing costs means reducing the wastes in our processes because, as my sensei used to say, "Waste threatens all our jobs."[8] If we do not make a profit, or make enough profit, we will have nothing left to invest in the business . . . and it will not survive. The way we ensure our job security is by getting everyone in the company engaged every day.[9]

Customer First Quality

The following is from the 1948 CCS Industrial Management Training Manual:[10]

Andrew Carnegie was one of the greatest business managers the world has ever known. As a boy he had no special advantages and, in fact, he had little school education. Very early in life he had to go out into the world to earn his own livelihood. But, from this poor beginning, he developed himself to the point where he became one of the richest men in the world owning one of the world's largest and wealthiest corporations—the United States Steel Company. In his autobiography, he wrote down what he believed was the secret of his success. He said: "Instead of objecting to inspectors, they should be welcomed by all manufacturing establishments. A high standard of excellence is easily maintained and men are educated in their effort to reach excellence. I have never known a concern to make a decided success that did not do good, honest work, and even in these days of the fiercest competition, when everything would seem to be a matter of price, there lies still at the root of great business success the very much more important factor of quality. The effect of attention to quality upon every man in the service, from the president of the concern down to the humblest laborer, cannot be overestimated. And bearing on the same question, clean, fine workshops and tools, well kept yards and surroundings, are of much greater importance than is usually supposed. But, the surest foundation of a business concern is quality. And after quality comes cost." This statement of Andrew Carnegie's emphasizes what is nowadays generally accepted by all companies. A company that does not base its operations on quality is a company that has no pride in its product. And further, it is generally to be expected that a company that cannot control its quality cannot keep in control any of its other functions and activities. In other words, the state of the quality of a company's products is a direct measure of the effectiveness of that company's management and operations.

In the 1960s, the Japanese were known for cheap toys and inferior electronics. The Japanese then surpassed the United States in quality in a relatively short amount of time as the result of two words: "Company Wide." Total quality management, or TQM as it was known in the United States back in the 1990s, was known as Total Company Wide Quality Control in Japan. In the United States, we missed the two words "company wide" and only applied it to the shop floor. The following is from the book *Company Wide Quality Control* by Yoshio Kondo:

> "Under Total Company Wide Quality Control, products have two specifications: "Must-Be" Quality and "Attractive" Quality[11] . . . thus they have a dualistic relationship with each other:
>
> ■ Some products sell well, even though they are the subject of many complaints, because they are highly attractive to Customers
> ■ While others that receive few complaints do not sell at all because they lack appeal.

Thus, to obtain positive Customer satisfaction, we must not only achieve "must-be" quality by eliminating defects and customer complaints, but we must also give our products "attractive" qualities which align with our Customer First Principle. Apple, Inc. is a good example of this.[12] Before beginning a quality initiative, companies must be sure the word "quality" is well defined and understood within the organization. Corporations need to concentrate on improving their processes to increase this attractive type of quality. The cost associated with this type of quality is not captured by Finance. The dollar amounts at stake here are just as large as the amounts at stake when we attempt to increase sales by developing new products.[13]

Customer Expectations

It is not enough anymore to just meet the customer specifications. Some customers, as they learn more and more about total company-wide quality and Lean, expect suppliers to be able to explain minor variations in their process, even though they meet the drawing specification. The real challenge is not just quality but control over your processes. This is known as Cpk, or process capability.[14]

A first-tier automotive component manufacturer was summoned to a Japanese customer to explain why the paint on their product looked different across a batch of parts. The thinking was that if all the parts went through the same process, then they should look the same. There was nothing wrong with the parts . . . but the customer rejected them because they looked a little bit different. What they were trying to ascertain was if their supplier really understood their processes, which in the end, they found the supplier did not. This forced their supplier to go back and truly study the process and start to identify what they didn't know. What they learned was astonishing, and in fact, they realized how lucky they had been not to have any major problems due to their lack of understanding the specifics of the process.

This component manufacturer learned the hard way that they needed to understand their processes better, as well as which parameters control what, as far as the form, fit, and function of the part as well as its aesthetics. In the end, their positive attitude toward their customer's feedback resulted in a 1-year study that significantly improved the capability of their painting process. Now they know what they still don't know, and they continue to study and improve the process.

How Do You Get the Most Out of Your Shop Floor and OfficeTeams?

We have a saying: "You can do it *to them* or do it *with them*." There are many successful companies "doing it *to them*" using the same old archaic traditional management styles, with batch manufacturing and lots of inventory. Many companies even tell their team members to "leave their brains at the door." While successful for some, the question is, How much money are they losing that their financial systems are not capturing? Companies do not have to follow the Leadership Development Path in order to be successful; however, implementing this approach and utilizing continuous leadership development can make you significantly more profitable and agile. *"How much money is your company leaving on the table every year?"*

We believe the contents of this book to be the missing link to sustaining Lean for most companies, as well as a real game changer for those companies willing to put these concepts into practice. Developing your team members, which includes your Leadership Team, is what it's all about, but it requires a totally different approach based on new shared mental models and sometimes using what's called "leaders' intent" versus a command-and-control style of management. This doesn't mean we do away with command and control, as it is still required. You also must create and instill a psychologically safe environment. It all starts with HR and the pre-hiring process, but at most companies, this particular HR role is nonexistent and severely misunderstood.

Shop Floor Management

We searched for a definition for *shop floor management* in books and online, only to find there was no true definition. There are definitions for *management* and *shop floor*, as well as links to all sorts of related pictures, software, and the like, but none on actual *shop floor management*. Even Wikipedia, as of the date of this publication, does not have a definition for it. This book describes how to create a shop floor management system with a strong execution focus. Execution means we deliver on our customer promises and our corporate goals.

While the principles and tools in this book are applicable to the overall organization, the foundation of this system starts with the critical role of the group leader, which ironically is seldom viewed this way. Our process to develop and revamp the group leader role will also influence your other leadership positions on and off the shop floor. The Leadership Development Path enables growing the business through continuous leadership development with an eye toward "Customer-Focused Execution." This means we are building a system of team member ownership designed to deliver on our customer promises of right quality, on time, at the lowest cost. It is based on fostering ongoing team member learning and development which does the following:

- Encompass the engagement of all team members
- Encourage daily improvements using ongoing PDCA problem-solving cycles
- Facilitate daily planning and development of process-focused alignment across the organization
- Manage the execution of continuously prioritized specific tasks, processes, and procedures necessary to implement the production plan to schedule and within budget
- Implemented on the shop floor or in the office with a goal of sustaining and ensuring ongoing daily improvement to the business

Implementing Process-Focused Leadership

We have discussed the importance to change our thinking and behaviors from results-focused to process-focused leadership. The following subsections are from Katie Anderson's blog[15] and describe some leadership lessons from Mr. Isao Yoshino,[16] a 40-year veteran of Toyota who is now retired.

Believe in Kaizen

The most important thing for a manager or leader to believe in is the importance of kaizen.[17] You don't have to be an expert in the actual work process, but you must be serious about how to appreciate the concept of kaizen, of change and continuous improvement. Create trust. Be consistent. Celebrate the attempt, not the outcome. Failure is the source of so much learning.

Be Persistent

When Mr. Yoshino went to the U.S. to train the General Motors managers as part of the Toyota-GM joint venture NUMMI, he was told often, "Yoshino-san, it's not easy to change culture." But NUMMI showed that you can. Be persistent. Keep doing it. Keep saying it.

Go to Gemba to Show You Care

One of the first things I was taught about the difference between Lean management and traditional management is that Lean managers "go to the Gemba" (the place work is done). I'd always thought that the primary purpose was to go collect facts and understand what is actually happening. However, Yoshino-san explained that his main purpose to go to Gemba is to show you care: "going to Gemba makes people feel like they are important." You then can see the facts as they actually are, but your primary purpose is to show you care about the people who do the work.

Teach the Process of HOW to Solve Problems

Managers first must set the target ("this is the result I'm expecting") and then teach the person how to achieve the goal. However, this is not about giving the person the manager's answer to the target, but rather show or explain the process by which the manger would go about achieving the goal. Training can provide knowledge and change your mindset, but knowledge is not enough. Yoshino-san and others put the GM managers at the NUMMI plant through an initial three-week training course, which helped shift their mindset. But the real learning only came when the leaders and trainers showed them on the shop floor how to manage and helped them practice and change their behaviors. The words you use are important—"Share" rather than "teach." Share your knowledge, experiences, and way of thinking. Don't set out to "teach" someone.

Be Patient

Sometimes people are not ready to hear your experiences or knowledge. You have to show them. Start acting the way you want them to act. Show the results of your actions. You will create interest (or "pull" in Lean terminology). They will likely then ask.

Find the Good

A good manager or coach finds the good in people—as a human and with their skills/thinking. Allow your team to have the experience of feeling good about their progress even if it's not how you would have done it.

Build Rapport and Trust

Take extra time to find out about someone. Be interested in them as people. You have to care. Respect is two ways. "Make a small effort to give a little bit extra every day." The human connection matters. Show that you care. Ask questions to find out where someone's skills or knowledge is at. Don't criticize the answers. Find the good in their thinking and ask "why" to learn more. A "yes" mode is so important.
  The preceding italicized section was contributed by Katie Anderson.

Notes

1. Implicit guidance and control are one of the paths in the OODA Loop by Col. John Boyd. The OODA loop has part of its roots in the Toyota Production System.
2. If the local leadership is not willing to put the time into the process, do not implement this concept.
3. Layered process audits (LPAs) are a quality technique that focuses on observing and validating how products are made, rather than inspecting finished products. LPAs are not confined to the Quality Department but involve all employees in the auditing process. Supervisors conduct frequent process audits in their own area, while higher-level managers conduct the same audits less frequently and over a broader range of areas. These audits also typically include integrated corrective and preventative actions taken either during or immediately after the audit. LPAs help manufacturers and service providers take control of processes, reduce mistakes, and improve both work quality and the bottom. line.www.ease.io/resources/what-are-layered-process-audits/
4. Quote by Nigel Thurlow, CEO of The Flow Consortium—used with permission.
5. www.inc.com/articles/2009/11/drucker.html
6. This unarticulated need was introduced to me by Dave Snowden, Cognitive Edge, and is part of his Apex Predator Theory.
7. From the *Fundamentals of Industrial Management—A Textbook for The Communications Manufacturing Industry of Japan*—by Charles Protzman and Homer Sarasohn, 1948.
8. Mark Jamrog, SMC Group

9. Inspired by Tracey and Ernie Richardson—The Toyota Engagement Equation, McGraw Hill, ©2019.

10. CCS Industrial Management Course ©1948.

11. Company Wide Quality Control, Yoshio Kondo, ©1993 JUSE Press pg 12–13.

12. Apple, Inc. is a good example of this. Their products are designed to be beautiful. www.washington post.com/news/wonk/wp/2016/04/08/how-silicon-valley-not-just-apple-became-obsessed-with-making-beautiful-objects/

13. Kondo Quality in Japan Section 41–20 QUALITY ASSURANCE AND NEW-PRODUCT DEVELOPMENT.

14. Process Capability Index (Cpk) www.whatissixsigma.net/process-capability-index-cpk/. Process capability index (Cpk) is a statistical tool to measure the ability of a process to produce output within customer's specification limits. In simple words, it measures the producer's capability to produce a product within the customer's tolerance range. Cpk is used to estimate how close you are to a given target and how consistent you are to around your average performance. Cpk gives you the best-case scenario for the existing process. It can also estimate future process performance, assuming performance is consistent over time.

15. This section was contributed and used with permission. It is a direct quote from a blog by Katie Anderson titled "Lean Leadership Lessons and Gemba Visit to Toyota City, Japan April 22, 2015/in Gemba/Site visit, Leadership, Lean" by Katie Anderson, consultant and author of *Learning to Lead, Leading to Learn: Lessons from Toyota Leader Isao Yoshino on a Lifetime of Continuous Learning*, Katie Anderson, Integrand Press, ©2020.
https://kbjanderson.com/lean-leadership-lessons-and-Gemba-visit-to-toyota-city-japan/https://kbjanderson.com/lean-leadership-lessons-and-Gemba-visit-to-toyota-city-japan/

16. Isao Yoshino is a lecturer at Nagoya Gakuin University of Japan. Prior to joining academia, he spent 40 years at Toyota working in a number of managerial roles in a variety of departments. Most notably, he was one of the main driving forces behind Toyota's little-known Kanri Nouryoku program, a development activity for knowledge-work managers that would instill the A3 as the go-to problem-solving process at Toyota. www.lean.org/WhoWeAre/LeanPerson.cfm?LeanPersonId=404

17. Kaizen here does not mean 5-day point kaizen events. It means ongoing small, daily improvements.

Chapter 2

The BASICS® Model Lean Overview

Figure 2.1 BASICS® Lean Leadership Development Path—The BASICS® Model.

Source: BIG training materials.

Our BASICS® model is composed of two parts which need to be integrated in order to sustain a Lean system (see Figure 2.1):

1. BASICS® Lean Tools[1]—Improving processes using both an individual, team, and company-wide-based scientific management approach
2. BASICS® Lean Continuous Leadership Development—Ingraining ownership for improving processes through the human aspects of developing people

DOI: 10.4324/9781315155227-2

Many companies have tried solely implementing the Lean tools and failed. This is because the human aspect necessary to sustain the new system was missing. Shigeo Shingo, consultant to Taiichi Ohno at Toyota, stated back in 1985 that "*no more than 30 to 40% of a successful Toyota Production System implementation is coming from the tools while 60 to 70% of the success is coming from the people.*"[2] We find this to still be true, yet most companies lack this "people piece" or what we call the human aspect.

BASICS® Lean Tools

The first step on the maturity path for developing a Lean system is to implement one-piece flow, or small-lot production. Wherever possible in our production and administrative systems whether it be manufacturing, government, health care, or service industries, we should be creating standard work prior to starting the Leadership Development Path. We use our BASICS® model to implement Lean and stabilize the process. We implement BASICS® tools using a team-based form of continuous improvement techniques and analysis that relies on scientific management[3] to identify and eliminate waste through a relentless focus on exactly what the customer wants (see Figure 2.2 the BASICS® Model).

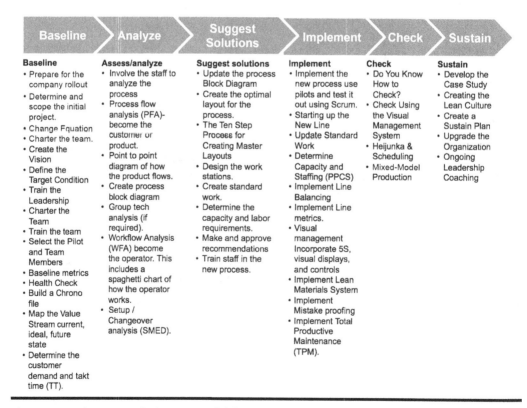

Baseline	Assess/analyze	Suggest solutions	Implement	Check	Sustain
• Prepare for the company rollout • Determine and scope the initial project. • Change Equation • Charter the team. • Create the Vision • Define the Target Condition • Train the Leadership • Charter the Team • Train the team • Select the Pilot and Team Members • Baseline metrics • Health Check • Build a Chrono file • Map the Value Stream current, ideal, future state • Determine the customer demand and takt time (TT).	• Involve the staff to analyze the process • Process flow analysis (PFA)-become the customer or product. • Point to point diagram of how the product flows. • Create process block diagram • Group tech analysis (if required). • Workflow Analysis (WFA) become the operator. This includes a spaghetti chart of how the operator works. • Setup / Changeover analysis (SMED).	• Update the process Block Diagram • Create the optimal layout for the process. • The Ten Step Process for Creating Master Layouts • Design the work stations. • Create standard work. • Determine the capacity and labor requirements. • Make and approve recommendations • Train staff in the new process.	• Implement the new process use pilots and test it out using Scrum. • Starting up the New Line • Update Standard Work • Determine Capacity and Staffing (PPCS) • Implement Line Balancing • Implement Line metrics. • Visual management Incorporate 5S, visual displays, and controls • Implement Lean Materials System • Implement Mistake proofing • Implement Total Productive Maintenance (TPM).	• Do You Know How to Check? • Check Using the Visual Management System • Heijunka & Scheduling • Mixed-Model Production	• Develop the Case Study • Creating the Lean Culture • Create a Sustain Plan • Upgrade the Organization • Ongoing Leadership Coaching

Figure 2.2   The BASICS® Six-Step Model for Lean Implementation.

Source: BIG training materials.

Our BASICS®[4] model is how we use scientific management for creating an environment that is optimized for the Leadership Development Path. Our goal with BASICS® is to create "continuous flow," wherever possible based on the takt time,[5] whereby the downstream operation "pulls" from the prior upstream operation in order to replenish just what is needed by the customer. It's very important for the group leader[6] and all the leadership to be trained in and understand the benefits of pull systems and one-piece flow. If not, the company will unintentionally undermine its opportunities for real everyday improvement.

We always coach the group leader to pursue perfection knowing we will never achieve it. We call this a stretch target, which is based on the company's strategic plan goals, or its "True North." The stretch targets create tension and ongoing dissatisfaction with "the gap" between where we are today and where we want to be (i.e., True North). Steve Spear referred to this a "Healthy Paranoia"[7] at Toyota.

This is how we begin to create the problem-solving culture. A Lean system is easy to remember by thinking . . . flow to a takt time . . . use a pull system . . . to stretch toward your True North goals: flow, takt, pull, then stretch to True North. The gaps between baseline and goal represent the gaps or opportunities for improvement. Sustaining Lean relies on creating a system to expose these gaps and find countermeasures. The gaps typically represent waste that is embedded in the system. The goal is to remove the waste. Waste is anything that doesn't add value for the customer. Before you can eliminate waste, you must first learn how to see through your waste lens and be able to identify it.

You cannot always just walk by a process and see waste. Yet this is what many leaders do on a daily basis. This is like walking through a park and missing all the wildlife camouflaged in the landscape (see Figure 2.3). You must stand and watch for minutes or sometimes hours to

Figure 2.3 Nature Blending with the Landscape—You don't see the squirrel when just walking by . . . you have to stop and look in order to see it.

Source: BIG training materials.

Figure 2.4 The Complacency Barrier.

Source: Used with permission https://txm.com/ tim.mclean@txm.com TXM Lean Solutions Pty. Ltd. Managing Director.

see and understand the waste. Then you must be willing to admit to yourself that what you're seeing is waste, especially if it was once hidden as "part of the process." The hardest waste to see is the waste created by your own past actions or improvements. Every action, process, and behavior you have modeled in the last two to three years has created the environment you have today. We council those we teach, not to get emotionally attached to any of their improvements. The best medicine is to create a mental model whereby you honestly believe that even though you just made an improvement yesterday, there is always a better way to do it. You only need to find it!

Over time, people become desensitized to the waste in their own process which leads to inattentional complacency (see Figure 2.4). We refer to this as the boiled frog syndrome. We need to implement discipline or what are called enabling constraints that help motivate the group leaders to continually question their processes, find waste, and encourage them to motivate their teams to improve every day. Only then will they become comfortable with making change.

5-Day Point Kaizen Events

Toyota does not use the words *Lean* or *Six Sigma*, and they don't have Six Sigma green belts, yellow belts, or black belts.[8] One of the thinking changes is realizing that a Lean culture encourages small, day-to-day, continuous improvement focused on improving quality and reducing cost. It doesn't rely just on 5-day point kaizen events. We have found most companies using point kaizen events rarely sustain even 50% of the improvements. Toyota uses kaizen events maybe 10% of the time and does not refer to them as that. Normally, these are the result of what they call quality-circle activities. Eighty percent of what Toyota uses is daily kaizen,[9] and this is the culture we strive to create. The other 10% comes from the Good Idea Club.[10]

Everyone making one small change a day, which we call the power of 15 minutes, over 240 working days will translate into much larger savings than just doing 5-day point kaizen events or only going after the big return-on-investment suggestions. Imagine what your company could achieve if you unleashed every employee, and they were empowered and inspired to improve their work area every day. Some tools critical for general or works managers, group leaders, and team leaders to learn are the following:[11]

1. One-piece flow for assembly or small-lot flow for machining based on group technology
2. How to calculate takt time
3. Process flow analysis to determine the percentage of value versus non-value-added in the product.[12]
4. Workflow analysis that equals differentiating the value versus non-value-added labor time for the team members[13]
5. Single-Minute Exchange of Dies (SMED)—setup or changeover reduction, which increases capacity and flexibility
6. Standard work—points out the current, best-known way to do the process
7. Layout principles—layouts are one of the biggest drivers of waste
8. Plan for every part[14]—material flow/kanbans and creating pull systems
9. Planning and scheduling systems—Level loading and synchronization
10. PPCS—Part Production Capacity Sheet—identifies the capacity based on headcount and shows the bottleneck and/or pacemaker
11. Line balancing—baton-zone balancing—bumping—which maximizes output
12. Leader standard work—standardizing the workday

Without these types of tools and thinking, there can be no process for daily improvement. Everything will just be reactive, and group leaders will end up firefighting and guessing where and how to focus their energy. The trick is to learn how and when to apply these tools that will help stabilize the processes. The team leader and group leader are responsible for driving continuous improvement for their specific area of responsibility. This is one of the secrets of continuous leadership development.

Batch Versus Flow

We find "batching" behaviors at some of the best, world-class manufacturing plants, even at Toyota in Japan. Unless the plant is totally automated for one-piece flow, we will always find some form of batching. Batching is the process of doing one step to an entire lot of parts and then moving the lot to the next step, where the next operation is done to the entire lot, and so on. If there is one thing you take away from this book, it should be that **batching is bad**, yet many of us believe it is the most efficient way to do everything. Batching creates excess materials that hide problems. Batching drives most of the Eight Wastes, especially the number one waste of overproduction. This results in excess inventory costs and a lack of production flexibility.

Many of you will argue with us because of your paradigms. We believe all of us are born convinced, or taught as a child that batching is the most efficient way to get things done. Batching thrives because it is a cognitive bias we all seem to share. Our minds perceive it as an easy way to handle problems. The extra material in the process, caused by batching (overproduction), covers up all the problems and removes any urgency to fix them. Batching gives us the illusion that it is an easier environment to manage. However, batching results in more cost and longer lead times to get the product to the customer.

Batching hides the underlying process issues and quality problems that will impact the entire production lot with no way to trace it back to the root cause. This is because the problem could have occurred hours, days, or, in some cases, weeks or months ago. How often have you found one part in a batch to be bad only to discover the entire batch is bad? We bet many of you can instantly think of processes in your mind which must be done in batches. You might be surprised to know we actually agree with you. However, we will follow up with the statement we must first eliminate the reasons that we batch; only then can we move toward the ultimate goal of one-piece flow. For more detail on this topic, see the book *Batching vs. One-Piece Flow.*[15]

When designed properly, one-piece flow systems are always more efficient than batching, but it may not always be possible without some major changes in your current process. Normally these changes, anything that is automated, high volume, production runs following one-piece flow, can be initially made for little or no cost. One-piece flow will always get the first piece completed significantly quicker than batching and reduces cycle times, inventory, and lead time.

> When faced with a new process challenge, always ask yourself—how do I get it to flow as close as possible to an assembly line?

The beauty of one-piece flow is that by removing the excess work in process (WIP), your problems and waste come immediately to the surface. However, you must have a system in place to be able to respond quickly to counter the problem(s) or you will revert to the old system. Leaders must learn to celebrate when our team members surface problems. This might sound strange, but if you do not recognize problems as positive, people will not feel encouraged to bring them to light, and if you cannot surface the problems, you certainly cannot fix them.

How Do We Define Waste?[16]

According to Shigeo Shingo, "[w]aste is any activity which does not contribute to operations."[17] Ultimately waste is determined by the customer. There are only two types of processes:

1. Value-added work
2. Non-value-added work

Some non-value-added work may be *necessary* but is still not considered value-added to the customer. Work advances a process and adds value whereas people just moving around quickly and efficiently may not accomplish anything.

Present Capacity = Realized Output + Waste

Declining productivity + Increased waste = Perceived need to increase people

Rituso Shingo warns that thinking there is no problem is the worst problem.[18] When your organization becomes literally obsessed with the total elimination of waste in everything it does and is never satisfied with the current state, then your organization will be well on its way to embedding the new culture.

Value-Added Versus Non-Value-Added

When observing a manufacturing process, all activities can be identified as either value-added or non-value-added. (See Figure 2.5.) For an activity to be considered value-added, it must meet all three of the following criteria:[19]

1. The customer cares.
2. There is a physical change made to the product or thing going through the system. (In health care, we say physically or mentally changes the patient for the better.)
3. The step is done correctly the first time.

In a typical manufacturing environment, only 1% to 3% of all activities are value-added. This does not mean 97% of all the other activities can just be removed from the process. These steps were probably needed for some reason in the past. The current way of doing things may rely on some of those other activities which we refer to as non-value-added but are necessary or required work.[20] This is the work that needs to be done in the current system but is not considered to meet all three of the previous criteria. Both value-added and non-value-added work can be targeted for elimination, rearrangement, combination, or simplification.

Waste Characteristics

Waste is like a disease. It hides underlying problems, and if we do not treat it or eradicate it, it gets worse. Waste creates workarounds to our processes and results in poor staff and customer satisfaction because we are constantly searching for or reworking things, which then delay our products and services. Ultimately, waste decreases our ability to compete in the marketplace and, as we stated before, threatens all our jobs.[21] Waste causes variation and imperfection in our

Value-Added

1. Customer Cares
2. Physical Change to the Product
3. Done Right the First Time

Required Work or Non-Value-Added

It must be done based on our current processes TODAY but does not meet all three (3) criteria above.

"VALUE" is what the customer is buying.

Figure 2.5   Value-Added Work Must Meet All Three Criteria—For health care, we say physical or emotional change for the better.

Source: BIG training materials.

processes. The big question is, Are we dissatisfied enough with the waste to create a compelling need to change the system, and rid ourselves of the waste? We have a saying we tell our customers: *"Minutes Count but Seconds Rule!"—Shawn Nosewothy.*[22]

The Eight Wastes[23]

While waste may be difficult to see, it first helps to know what type of waste you are looking for. The following are the Eight Wastes using the acronym DOWNTIME (see Figure 2.6):

1. *Waste of Making Defective Products*—This is making products that do not meet the customer's specifications or perceived quality characteristics.
2. *Waste of Overproduction*—This is making more than the customer demands. (This is the number one waste in the Toyota Production System that Taiichi Ohno worked on the most, and we find it is the hardest to remove.)
3. *Waste of Waiting* (idle time)—This is anyone who is idle or people trying to look busy.
4. *Waste of Non-Utilized Talent* (an organization's most valuable asset)—This waste is the waste of underutilizing and not developing or engaging your team's brainpower, ideas, and experiences.
5. *Waste in Transportation*—This is parts or paperwork being transported from one place to another.
6. *Waste of Inventory* (stock on hand)—This includes excess stock and WIP between processes or team members.
7. *Waste of Excess Motion* (worker movement)—This occurs whenever someone has to reach outside their normal path of motion while sitting or standing, including having to get their own parts or supplies.
8. *Waste of Excess Processing*—We define this as doing more to a part or paperwork (electronic or paper) than necessary to meet the customer-defined specifications or perceived customer quality needs.

Ohno was very clear that this is not a comprehensive list of wastes. There are many more.

As the preliminary step toward the application of Toyota production system, all wastes must be identified completely.

1. Waste of making too many
2. Waste of waiting
3. Waste in carrying
4. Waste of machining itself
5. Waste of inventory
6. Waste of movement
7. Waste of making defective products

Figure 2.6 The Original Seven Wastes—Number one is overproduction. But Ohno did not say this was inclusive of all the wastes.

Source: Ohno's The "Bible" of the Toyota Production System manuscript.

The Levels of Waste

When looking for and identifying waste, it's not always easy to know where to look. Here, we have listed what we call the "five levels of waste":

1. **Obvious Waste**—low-hanging fruit—The easiest waste to spot is referred to as "low-hanging fruit" because it is easy to see and very obvious to anyone looking at the area.
2. **5S Wastes**—These are the wastes that have to do with organization, housekeeping, and discipline.
3. **The Eight Wastes**—See the previous section.
4. **Boiled Frog Waste**—This is waste that is hard to notice after a while because we pass by it every day. We have seen it so long it now is just part of the process with little notice. New team members and outsiders, customers or suppliers, can see this waste.
5. **Hidden Unseen Waste**—Ohno said the worst waste is the waste we do not see. We typically cannot see hidden wastes because they are hiding behind or are masked by other wastes. You really must hunt for them! These are the hardest wastes to find and yet the most dangerous. Reviewing videos and asking simple questions like "Why do you do this?" is the best way to discover hidden waste.

How Do You Find Waste?

If unable to see and find the waste on your own using the five levels and the Eight Wastes, we recommend inviting outsiders into your area. Many times, outsiders help show us the waste we do not see whether it's intentional or unintentional. A fresh set of eyes will see things we do not because we are too close to it. Here are some examples:

Shigeo Shingo Famous Banana Example—When you go to the register, you pay for the banana by weight, but Shingo points out most of the weight is in the peel, which you discard.

Cucumber Story by Ritsuo Shingo[24]

"When I visited one of my clients' plants, I heard that they throw away products which have a slightly different color. So, I bought two cucumbers, straight and curved. I showed them to the plant people and said to them. . . . If you cut them the taste is the same (function is the same). Please ask your customer if they will accept a slightly different color with the same function or not. Then we can avoid waste."

The 2 × 4 Waste Story—Consider the 2 × 4 story. A 2 × 4 is a piece of wood used for framing walls, which is 2 inches by 4 inches. However, the sawmill cuts it to a size of 1.5 by 3.5 inches, so we end up having to pay for the sawdust.

The Three As

To find waste, you have to go to the Gemba and look for it, and then recognize it. Honda does this with an exercise it calls the three As:[25]

1. Go to the **A**ctual Place and
2. See the **A**ctual Part
3. In the **A**ctual Situation.

We have to learn to train ourselves to see this waste and then commit to getting rid of it. It sounds easy, but it's very difficult to do. The most difficult waste to see is the waste that occurs in processes we have created or already improved ourselves. When these wastes are pointed out, we tend to be defensive. After all, this puts the blame on us. This is normal behavior and justified as it shows our ownership over the process, which is good because we should take pride in everything we do. But because we take pride in our areas, we should be willing to expose the waste or be grateful when others point it out to us.

How to Eliminate Waste—The 5 Whys, Because, and Therefore[26]

The best way to eliminate waste is to figure out why it is there and how to get rid of it. We do this by constantly asking, "Why?" Asking "Why?" a minimum of five times and adding in the words *because* and *therefore* (see Figure 2.7) allows the opportunity to start searching for root causes and begin to identify opportunities for improvement. Here is a 5 Whys example:

A part was installed in the wrong (reversed) position:

1. **Why?** The worker was not sure of the correct part orientation; Therefore . . . he put the part in backward.
2. **Why?** The worker was not sure of the part orientation—point cause.
   Because . . . the part was not marked properly to show which side went where.
3. **Why?** Engineering designed it that way. Therefore . . . the vendor marked it that way—point cause.
4. **Why?** The vendor marked it according to the print. Therefore . . . the part had no orientation specified, which led to the error—point cause.

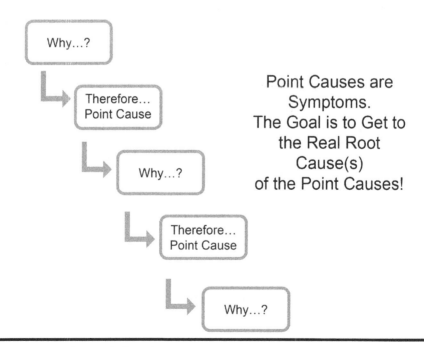

Point Causes are Symptoms.
The Goal is to Get to the Real Root Cause(s) of the Point Causes!

Figure 2.7 The 5 Whys and Therefore.

Source: BIG Training Archives—inspired by Scrum The Toyota Way Training by Nigel Thurlow.

5. **Why** didn't engineering note the proper orientation in the part marking on the print? Because . . . the engineering design process did not account for possible manufacturing gaps even though they did a PFMEA[27] in their conference room—point cause.
6. **Why?** The engineer had never been to the floor, assembled the product, or talked to the operators. It turns out this is the *root cause* and real problem to be solved.

In the end, research and development engineering should own quality results and production throughput time because these are the processes they created.

The most important thing is to act on the waste. Just being able to identify it and give it a name does not improve the process. The courage to actually change the behavior or process is the only way to eliminate or improve the condition.

How Designing a One-Piece Flow System Can Help a Group Leader Be Successful

One time I[28] was working on a project for a client in the medical device field aimed to help them increase capacity to satisfy growing demand. Here is a little background: This company was a very traditional batch company. They had 42 separate processes taking place on 42 different workstations. Their takt time was 95 seconds. Each workstation did a specific process with a cycle time ranging from 3 seconds to 145 seconds. With the cycle times that ran much faster than takt time, they would run for a day and build up a large amount of inventory and then the group leader would count inventory every day and move people to different workstations to perform the next process steps.

The main role of the group leader was counting inventory and moving people to other processes. A minimal amount of time was spent trying to problem-solve and drive continuous improvement. The product did not flow in natural directions, so it went back and forth, and process cycle times were not matched with takt time. This company did a really nice job with maximizing the cycle time of the individual stations and coming up with right-sized equipment. The manufacturing manager was a brilliant engineer and did a really good job. When we first started talking about one-piece flow and the concepts of Lean, they were skeptical that it would work in their environment because their process was unique.

Our strategy was to create a work cell in which work-balanced product flowed in a natural direction across the entire value stream. We combined processes to create operator cycle times that were balanced with customer demand. The product had a natural starting point and ending point where a part never moved backward. In this environment, the group leader was able to manage one value stream instead of 42 individual processes.

The assembly line was developed to exit a part every 90 seconds to support customer demand. As we worked to transform from theory to working functioning value streams, we had our moments of struggles and spirited discussions, but we successfully transformed the production process to where a finished good was exiting the work cell under takt time. As we were nearing the completion of the project, the group leader approached me and shared the following comments, which were very impactful to me. The following was our conversation:

FRANK: Mike, when we started this project I believed that it would not really change very much. I figured we would make some small improvements but didn't think it would work for us. I have been here for 15 years and this is always the way we did it. We have been working with a different consulting company, and yet, this way of doing it was never talked about. We were always trying to optimize the individual process steps instead of the entire value stream.

MIKE: Frank, the reason this was successful was because you guys were very open to making changes and not stuck in the traditional way of doing things.

FRANK: When you told me that it would make my job easier I really didn't believe you but it has completely changed the way I do my job. I now go to the end of the production line every hour and can evaluate how we are doing against our customer demand using the day-by-hour boards we put in place. If we are off our target I can walk the production line and easily spot where our problems are by simply looking at the WIP and flow of the product. We can always see if we are not hitting our targeted cycle time. If the product isn't flowing I know I have a problem and I can work with the team to fix it. My job has completely changed from counting parts and moving people from station to station to really feeling like I own and am managing this department now.

As I was writing this book, the memory came to me as I was talking with a client earlier in the week about the benefits of one-piece flow. My takeaway from the conversation with Frank was that companies are realizing one-piece flow puts their group leaders in a position to be successful because now they can manage one value stream instead of 42 individual processes. Creating the environment for them to flourish is more than training and providing good support teams; it's also how your value streams are designed. Designing your value streams as close as you can to one-piece flow not only eliminates a great deal of non-value-added work from a production stand-point but also makes running and managing operations easier from a leadership viewpoint. This is an example of how to realign the thinking and behaviors necessary to create an environment to enable the group leader to perform the job they were meant to do.

Notes

1. The BASICS® Lean Implementation Model, Protzman, Keen, Protzman, CRC Press, 2019.
2. www.kaizen.com/blog/post/2018/07/05/why-are-most-companies-failing-with-lean-implementation.html
3. Scientific management has been around for a long time in one form or another. It can be traced back to the Babylonians and the Chinese.
4. The BASICS® Lean Implementation Model Routledge, Protzman, Keen, Protzman, 1 edition (September 7, 2018).
5. *Takt* means "beat" in German. Takt time is available time divided by customer demand. We design output to meet customer demand, no more, no less.
6. The group leader at Toyota is a supervising position that has the HR responsibilities of hiring, firing, grievances, and the like.
7. The Lean Practitioner's Field Book: Proven, Practical, Profitable and Powerful Techniques for Making Lean Really Work, Productivity Press; 1 edition (April 4, 2016) Protzman, et al.
8. www.qimacros.com/lean-six-sigma-blog/how-many-green-and-black-belts-do-you-need/
9. The word *kaizen* causes much confusion and has many contexts. Kaizen in Japan is everywhere. It simply means change for the better. In the United States, kaizen is typically associated with 5-day or shorter-length point kaizen events. In Japan, it equates to small improvements every day.
10. The Lean Practitioner Fieldbook by Charles Protzman., Fred Whiton, Joyce Kerpchar, Christopher Lewandowski, Steve Stenberg, Patrick Grounds, CRC Press, © 2016. and 40 Years, 20 Million Ideas: The Toyota Suggestion System, Yuzo Yasuda, Productivity press (c)1990

11. These tools are explained in detail in The Basics® TPS Implementation Model and The Lean Practitioner's Field Book.
12. Improving the process flow is equal to increasing the velocity of the material flow in your company. This yields the overall throughput time or lead time improvement, which is the time it takes from the start to the end of the process. The quicker the velocity, the more agile and flexible we become to satisfy our customer's demand.
13. Here we work to reduce team member motions which makes them faster by making their job easier. This yields the total labor time required to produce one piece.
14. PFEP is plan for every part—Making Materials Flow by Rick Harris, Chris Harris, Earl Wilson, Lean Enterprises Inst Inc; September 2003, version 1.0 edition (September 1, 2003).
15. Batching vs. One-Piece Flow, Protzman, McNamara, Protzman, CRC Press, 2016.
16. The Lean Practitioner's Field Book: Proven, Practical, Profitable and Powerful Techniques for Making Lean Really Work, Productivity Press; 1 edition (April 4, 2016) Protzman, et al.
17. *The Lean Practitioner's Field Book: Proven, Practical, Profitable and Powerful Techniques for Making Lean Really Work*, Productivity Press; 1 edition (April 4, 2016) Protzman, et al.
18. Ritsuo Shingo taught at the Lean Leadership Institute (LLI) conference, August 2017, hosted by George Trachilis in Santorini, Greece.
19. AMA video, Time is the Next Dimension of Quality, Start Thrower Production.
20. Some companies refer to necessary work as business value-added.
21. Mark Jamrog SMC Group—The Lean Practitioner's Field Book: Proven, Practical, Profitable and Powerful Techniques for Making Lean Really Work, Productivity Press; 1 edition (April 4, 2016) Protzman, et al. The BASICS® Lean Implementation Model Routledge, Protzman, Keen, Protzman, 1 edition (September 7, 2018).
22. The Lean Practitioner's Field Book: Proven, Practical, Profitable and Powerful Techniques for Making Lean Really Work, Productivity Press; 1 edition (April 4, 2016) Protzman, et al. The BASICS® Lean Implementation Model Routledge, Protzman, Keen, Protzman, 1 edition (September 7, 2018).
23. The first seven wastes came from Taiichi Ohno—The Root Cause of Most of These Wastes Is Batching! Ohno stated these were not the only wastes! The Eight Wastes, here the fourth waste of talent, was added by Charles Protzman back in 1997 and has since been accepted by most.
24. The Cucumber Story was created by me. My father created the very famous Banana Story, so I created cucumber. Why I created the "Cucumber Story"? When I visited my client, I stayed at the hotel where they served iced water with sliced cucumber in it. I could not tell whether the original cucumber was straight or curved. Then I created the Cucumber Story, which is not famous at all. Personal correspondence with Ritsuo Shingo 6–12–2020.
25. Powered by Honda, Book Given to me by Tom Chickerella, R. Dave Nelson, Patricia Moody, and Rick B. Mayo, Hoboken, NJ: John Wiley & Sons, 1998, p. 101.
26. This concept was introduced to me by Nigel Thurlow, former Toyota Exec. and CEO of the Flow System.
27. Process Failure Modes Effects Analysis (PFMEA) is a methodical approach used for identifying risks on process changes. The PFMEA initially identifies process functions, failure modes their effects on the process. https://quality-one.com/pfmea/
28. Michael Meyers.

Chapter 3

The BASICS® Model Methodology[1]

Figure 3.1 BASICS® Lean Leadership Development Path—Implement BASICS® tools first to create the standards.

Source: BIG training materials.

The BASICS® Lean Leadership Development Path (see Figure 3.1) starts with using the BASICS® model to create the standards for our processes. We are only going to cover small portions of the BASICS® tools model in this book. The book *BASICS® Lean Implementation Model* (see Figure 3.2) is a must-read for leaders and describes in detail how to implement one-piece flow or small-lot

DOI:10.4324/9781315155227-3

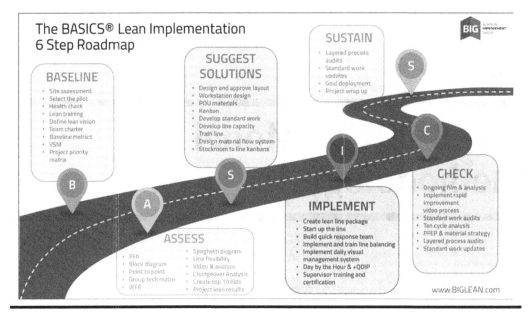

Figure 3.2 BASICS® Road Map.

Source: BIG training materials.

production lines. We use BASICS® for any type of process from high-mix, low-volume to low-mix, high-volume lines. Lean was originally designed for high-mix, low-volume lines.

When we convert lines from batch to flow, we attack the entire process or value stream as one Lean implementation project over 4 to 6 weeks, depending on the total labor content of the end product. This makes the projects significantly faster and more sustainable compared to point kaizen events which can take years.[2] We also spend a lot of time working on changing team members' mindsets and hearts by involving everyone in the conversion process. An overview of the BASICS® model steps is provided in the following sections.

1. BASICS®—Baseline

The first step in any improvement activity is to baseline the current state of the process. One cannot know if or how much one improved if there is no starting point. Value stream mapping is one tool we use to baseline the process and track our improvements over time.

Value Stream Maps

Value stream maps (VSMs; see Figure 3.3) documents the process from beginning to end, including gathering data and soliciting ideas and suggestions for improvement from everyone involved inside and outside the process. The map is created by going to the floor, or *Gemba*, to observe the process and interact with the team members. The book *Learning to See*[3] explains VSMs in detail.

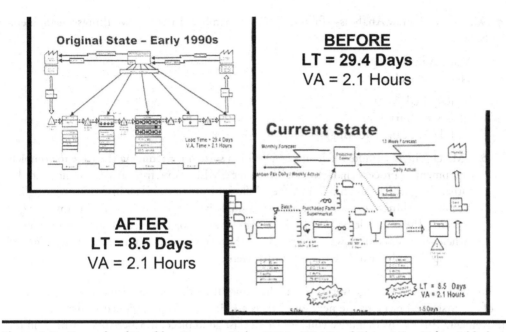

Figure 3.3 Example of Tracking Progress Using VSMs. LT = Lead Time; VA = Value Added.

Source: SME Value Stream Mapping Video, Donnelly Mirrors portion of the video.

2. B̲A̲SICS®—The Analysis Process[4]

There are three things we analyze when improving a process. First, we follow the product (part, transaction, or person) in the process; then, we follow the team member; and, finally, we analyze the setup or changeover. We video[5] each of these separately and analyze them, accompanied by the frontline team members who do the work, and we analyze them down to the second. We help stimulate their minds with questions and get their ideas on how to improve the processes and what the standard could be or even should be. Imagine walking the value stream with a cross-functional team filling out this sheet and really having this level of understanding of your process.

- PFA—Process Flow Analysis—follows the product. There are four things the product can do:
  1. Transport
  2. Inspect
  3. Process
     a. Value-Added
     b. Non-Value-Added
  4. Store
     a. Raw Material
     b. Work in Process (progress)
        i. Lot Delay (Batch Delay)
        ii. Between-Process Delay
        iii. Within-Process Delay
     c. Finished Goods

- WFA—Work Flow Analysis—follows the team member. There are two things a team member can do:

1. Value-Added
2. Non-Value-Added

   a. Required Work
   b. Unnecessary Work
   c. Idle Time (not working)

3. **SMED** (Single-Minute Exchange of Dies) is a system for reducing the time to complete equipment or process changeovers. The name SMED came from Ritsuo Shingo, not his father, Shigeo; Ritsuo Shingo told me, "When I tried to translate his book into English, he [Shigeo Shingo] explained to me that a single handicap was great for an amateur golf player."[6] The principle of SMED[7] is to convert setup or changeover steps from internal (when the machine is down) to external (performed while the equipment is running) and to simplify and streamline the remaining steps.

Our definition for "changeover" is from the removal of the last good piece to the completion of the first good piece of the next lot. This is a strict definition designed to drive the most improvement. This means that once you remove the last good piece, if paperwork, turning off the machine, or moving the job in the material requirements planning system is required, it all counts as part of the internal changeover time. We make a distinction between *clock time* and *labor time*: Clock time is the internal time it takes for the changeover. Labor time is the total amount of labor involved in the changeover. The four components of setup are as follows:

1. Preparation and organization
2. Removing and mounting
3. Calibration, centering, dimensioning, aligning, measurement, and testing
4. Trial runs and adjustment

3. BA_SICS® Suggest Solutions[8]—Standard Work

Standardized work in the context of the Toyota Way refers to the most efficient and effective combination of people, material, and equipment to perform the work that is presently possible. "Presently possible" means it is today's best-known way, which can be improved. Leader standard work is the repetitive pattern of activities which represents the least wasteful method of planning and controlling a business process. The repetitive activities are designed to identify abnormal situations.

—Dr. Jeffrey Liker[9]

During the BASICS® video analysis process, we break down the job and involve the team members by using their ideas to eliminate wasted motions with the overarching goal to make their job easier. This helps reduce or eliminate any resistance to change. The steps left after those omitted in the analysis become the basis for the standard work. This technique is described in detail in our BASICS® book.[10] Standard work is the foundation of every Lean system and is made up of three elements:[11]

1. Cycle Time—This is the approximate time or, if it is a robot, the exact time, in which each step should be performed.
2. Work Sequence—These are the sequence of steps in which an operation is to be completed. They include the key points and reasons for key points for each process step.
3. Standard Inventory—This is the amount of inventory required to do a job safely and hit the cycle time.

The standard work should include all elements of the work including inspection, packing, paperwork, computer work, and so on. In order to have standard work, we must have the basics required to support the standard work. These include repeatable one-piece flow, parts, tools, machines, and the like in the order the product flows (physical or transactional) and must be produced with sufficient raw material and work in progress (WIP) along with a TPM[12] system to keep the machines running during the scheduled available time.

It also means the team leader, group leader, manager, director, and so on are also following the standard work, when it makes sense. This creates a disciplined system with accountability which ensures the system sustains and continues to improve. The standard work must be "built into" the quality system, that is, the company's infrastructure or muscle memory. Please keep in mind it is not enough just to sustain our current processes. Sir John Harvey Jones said, "*If you are not progressing, then you are regressing, because the whole world is moving against you.*"[13] These words could not be truer.

Why Is Standard Work Important?

Most team members will do the best job they can with the process, tools, and training provided by management. If they do not have the right tools to safely do the job, they will find other typically non-safe tools to do the job. It is also not uncommon when rolling out standard work to hear, "Oh, you just want us to be robots." We confront the perceptions of standard work directly. All team members from the executive level to the frontline staff must understand that the goal of standard work is not to make team members into robots but to improve the quality of the work and allow for the implementation of continuous improvement. We find that most team members really want to do a good job and want to be appreciated for their work.

If we do not standardize the work, then everyone does the job differently and quality suffers. We also lose our chance to improve the process. For example, let's say we have a process with four steps, but all the team members do the steps in a different order. We review the process and find a way to eliminate Step 2. What will happen when we tell everyone to eliminate Step 2? Everyone will eliminate a different step. This leads to inconsistencies in quality, flow, and delivery. If we have process-focused leadership and standard work in place at every level and for every person and machine, then there is nothing that should be able to stop us from producing the necessary good parts per day.

Granted, standard work is not any CEO's top priority today. Growth is normally the top priority, but one cannot sustain growth if their people and processes are not stable and capable of supporting it. Standard work is the foundation for all continuous improvement and one-piece flow, or small lot production is the foundation for standard work. Without standard work, there is nothing to update when making improvements. Standard work must become part of the fabric of the workplace, which means it should be part of International Organization for Standardization or other quality or process standards that apply to your business. *Standard work should be written for processes you need to control, are repeatable, and be value-added.*[14] By ingraining the processes in your formal policy and procedures, it will be much more difficult to revert to the way it was before.

> If you think of standardization as the best you know today, but which is to be improved tomorrow—you get somewhere. If you think of standards as confining, then progress stops.
>
> **—Henry Ford**

4. BAS<u>I</u>CS® Implement—How to Create Standard Work

There are two tools used for standard work. One is what we call the Standard Work Form (see Figure 3.4); the other is called the Standard Operation Routine Sheet (SORS) aka Standard Work Combination Sheet (see Figure 3.5). The next step is to create standard work for any other value-added process or job such as indirect labor positions like floaters, material handlers, and the like. Then we create standard work for the changeover or setup team members. It is extremely important to have the team members involved in creating the standard work since it is going to be part of their

Operator Standard Work Form 1.0 Cell

PART NUMBER:	PART NAME:	No. People Needed	TOTAL LABOR TIME:		Available Time	Daily Demand			HEAD COUNT:	1	2
OEM 1.0 with Button	Adjustable	3.38	304		54,000	600			CYCLE TIME:	304.0	152.0
									CYCLE TIME MIN:	5.1	2.5
									HOURLY OUTPUT:	11.8	23.7
									DAILY OUTPUT:	177.6	355.3

Standard Work Area:

Baton Zone Map — Layout Area and Walk Patterns

Job Step #	Operation Description (what they do)	Key Points and Quality Notes (how they do it)	Reasons for Key Points	Time	Cum Time	1	2	3	4	5
1	Assemble shock tube and cylinder end assembly.			11.0	11.0					
2	Install Shock Tube Assembly into Cylinder	Flat side of Retaining Ring faces outward	Retaining ring can jump out of groove	16.0	27.0					
3	Assemble Piston Head Assy and drop in unit.	Throw out ball used to form seat	Ball can be damaged by Mecco press	40.0	67.0					
4	Assemble Piston Rod, Bearing, and Wiper Retainer Assembly	Cup side of Rod Seal faces down,	Unit will leak.	33.0	100.0					
5	Install Bearing Assembly into unit.	Don't fold or twist foam while inserting in Cylinder	Unit will not stroke properly.	25.0	125.0					
6	Oil unit, assemble/install Fill Plug, set unit on "lockout", and wash unit.	Verify unit was not oiled on "lockout"	Unit will not fill properly on "lockout".	60.0	185.0					
7	Paint, assemble/install knob, verify "lock out", install setting locking set screw, and torque fill plug..			50.0	235.0					
8	Mark unit on Propen	Make sure unit sits flat in collet before clamping.	Unit will not mark peroperly if sitting crooked.	5.0	240.0					
9	Install Piston Cap and Cap Pad			14.0	254.0					
10	Test in Functional Test Stand			12.0	266.0					
11	Install red ball, gage threads, and crimp Bearing.			19.0	285.0					
12	Roll unit in instruction sheet, bag unit, label, and box.			19.0	304.0					

OEM WITH A BUTTON

QUALITY CHECK	SAFETY CHECK	AIR CHECK	CLEAN HANDS		STANDARD WORK IN PROCESS		TAKT TIME	CYCLE TIME	HEAD COUNT
★	✓						90	76.00	4.0

Figure 3.4 Standard Work Sheet Example.

Source: BIG training materials.

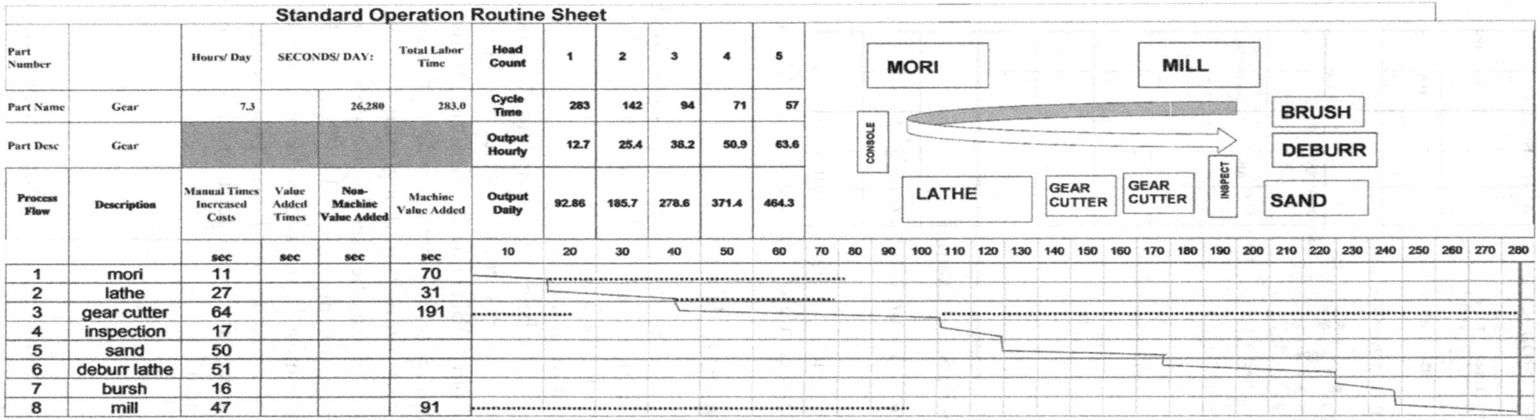

Standard Operation Routine Sheet

Part Number		Hours/ Day	SECONDS/ DAY:	Total Labor Time	Head Count	1	2	3	4	5
Part Name	Gear	7.3			Cycle Time	283	142	94	71	57
					Output Hourly	12.7	25.4	38.2	50.9	63.6
Part Desc	Gear		26,280	283.0	Output Daily	92.86	185.7	278.6	371.4	464.3

Process Flow	Description	Manual Times Increased Costs	Value Added Times	Non-Machine Value Added	Machine Value Added
		sec	sec	sec	sec
1	mori	11			70
2	lathe	27			31
3	gear cutter	64			191
4	inspection	17			
5	sand	50			
6	deburr lathe	51			
7	bursh	16			
8	mill	47			91

MORI | MILL | BRUSH

CONSOLE | INSPECT | DEBURR

LATHE | GEAR CUTTER | GEAR CUTTER | SAND

Figure 3.5 Standard Operation Routine Sheet (SORS) aka Standard Work Combination Sheet.

Source: Courtesy of Joe Markiewicz, Ancon Gear, Long Island NY.

PART PRODUCTION CAPACITY SHEET

Part No	Gear #12345	Hours/Day	SECOND S/DAY:		Total Labor Time	Takt Time (sec):				Head Count	1	2	3	4	5
Part Name	Gear	7.3	26,280		283	275				Cycle Time	283	142	94	71	57
Desc.	Gear	TIME DISTRIBUTION								Output Hourly	12.72	14.12	14.12	14.12	14.12
Job Step	Process Step	Labor Non Value Added	Labor Value Added	Machine Non Value Added	Machine Value Added	Complete Time	Bottle Neck	Tool Exchange Time		Output Daily	92.86	103.06	103.06	103.06	103.06
		(sec)	(sec)	(sec)	(sec)	(sec)		Units	Sec	Time Allocated	Prod Cap (units/day)	Comments			
	Cumulative Times:	283	0	0	383	666									
1	Mori	11			70	81					324.44				
2	Lathe	27			31	58					453.10				
3	Gear Cutter	64			191	255					103.06				
4	Inspection	17				17					1545.88				
5	Sand	50				50					525.60				
6	Deburr Lathe	51				51					515.29				
7	Brush	16				16					1642.50				
8	Mill	47			91	138					190.43				

Figure 3.6   Part Production Capacity Sheet Example.

Source: Courtesy of Joe Markiewicz, Ancon Gear, Long Island NY.

job to sustain it. You cannot sustain standard work without constantly improving it; otherwise, you will go backward. We have a saying: Even a bad standard is better than no standard.

PPCS—Part Production Capacity Sheet

We then develop the layout and determine the capacity of the operation based on the headcount. We have two main rules: no isolated islands and make the layout flexible. Layouts are one of the biggest drivers of waste in any operation or office. It is important to spend time on the layout to get it right by utilizing point-to-point diagrams.

The PPCS is a form (see Figure 3.6) to help you understand the process flow, output by headcount, and where the bottleneck and pacemaker are located. The PPCS is an important link to daily management and the day-by-hour (DBH) boards. This form is easy to create[15] and gives the group leader or team leader the knowledge they need to determine their capacity and staff their line properly to meet the required cycle time. Even though this form was originally designed for manufacturing, it is a powerful form that can be used for any process from banking to insurance to hospital laboratories to landscaping, among others. The PPCS is a sheet that is rarely used by companies. We have found that even most Lean experts do not know about it or do not understand how to use it properly. It is a phenomenal tool for the group leader or team leader to have at their disposal. Now they have all the data at their fingertips to answer any questions regarding the output of their lines from management.

5. BASIC̲S® Check

Check means to audit to see if we are following the implemented process and identifying where we can improve the process. Wherever we have gaps, we need to implement countermeasures, identify the root cause and check to see if we fixed the gap.

JIT and Jidoka

There are two main pillars that support the Toyota production system: just in time (JIT) and *jidoka*. Ritsuo Shingo explained in his TPS Masterclass that this pillar was originally called built-in quality which he preferred. JIT means we received what is needed, when it is needed, and in the amount needed. It consists of establishing a takt time to meet the customer's demand. The original purpose of JIT was to remove the excess inventory in order to expose the underlying problems. JIT is synchronized production and, when combined with jidoka, means never passing on a bad part. It requires constant communication and job rotation between teams, which encourages good teamwork.

Jidoka (see Figure 3.7) is the concept of automation with a human touch. This means the machine can stop by itself before producing a bad part. It can also be using an Andon signal,

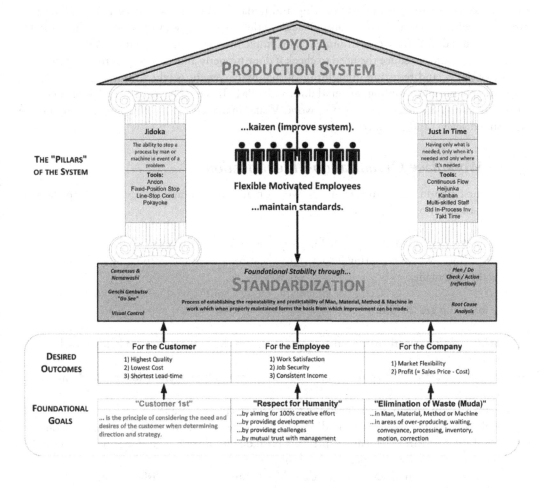

Figure 3.7   The Toyota House.

Source: Courtesy of Nigel Thurlow, CEO, The FLOW Consortium, Copyright Nigel Thurlow ©2006.

that is, light, sound, or both, to stop the production line whenever an abnormality occurs. Jidoka prevents defective parts from being transferred to the next machine, process, or team. The cause of the defect can then be investigated, and countermeasures taken against recurrence. Jidoka frees up workers from watching the machine and allows for one team member to oversee several processes or machines, thus improving efficiency. In the Toyota House analogy, these pillars support the overall house, which is built on a good foundation of standard work, *heijunka*, and so on. Yet, from a big-picture view, we find most companies focus 80% to 95% of their effort on JIT and virtually none on jidoka. In most cases, it is because they are not familiar with or do not truly understand jidoka.

6. BASIC<u>S</u>® Sustain—Visual Management—*Mieruka*

Sustain means we are constantly improving and updating standard work with the countermeasures that addressed the gap's root cause to achieve the desired target. One way we help to sustain the factory or administrative environment is to implement visual management. Visual management can eliminate or reduce the need to check if done properly and is the key to running, sustaining the business, and reducing firefighting. Visual management is where we end up integrating layout design, mistake proofing, material flow, and TPM. This is why you can't just implement one aspect of Lean and expect the system to work. Visual management has three main components: 5S, visual displays, and visual controls.

1. 5S—Workplace Organization—Identification

5S is the first step in visual management. We normally incorporate 5S as we bring up the new lines. 5S is about two main principles:

1. Housekeeping—which is a place for everything and everything in its place
2. Discipline—which is putting it back in its place every time and keeping up with the changes as they are made.

The following are the 5Ss:

1. Seiri—sorting (clearly distinguish the needed items from the unneeded items and eliminate the latter.)
2. Seiton—straighten (keep needed items in the correct place to allow for easy and immediate retrieval).
3. Seiso—scrub, sweep, shine (keep the work area swept and clean).
4. Seiketsu—systemize and standardize (establish systems and procedures that ensure continuity of the first three elements. It prevents breakdown of work conditions and reduces muda (non-value-added work) spent maintaining the work area).
5. Shitsuke—sustain, discipline (make a habit of maintaining established procedures).

In conversations with Ritsuo Shingo, son of the famous Shigeo Shingo and 40-year Toyota veteran, he notes that he was always taught and always used a different sequence. The fifth S added in the west being unused, and not even recognized by him, or by those colleagues we know in Toyota in Japan. The sequence they are more familiar with is:

1. Seiri—sort, arrange, organize.
2. Seiton—tidy, orderliness, arranging neatly.
3. Seiketsu—cleanliness or hygiene.
4. Seiso—shine, neat and clean.

The most difficult part of 5S in our culture is the discipline necessary to maintain good house-keeping and worker attire. Another difficult part of 5S is letting go and getting rid of those things no longer needed. In her book,[16] *The Life-Changing Magic of Tidying Up*, Marie Kondō suggests the following:

> Visible mess helps distract us from the true source of the disorder. By acknowledg-ing their contribution and letting them go with gratitude, you will be able to truly put the things you own, and your life, in order. There are three approaches we can take toward our possessions: face them now, face them sometime, or avoid them until the day we die. To truly cherish the things that are important to you, you must first discard those that have outlived their purpose. To throw away what you no longer need is neither wasteful nor shameful. Can you truthfully say that you trea-sure something buried so deeply in a closet or drawer that you have forgotten its existence? If things had feelings, they would certainly not be happy. Free them from the prison to which you have relegated them. Help them leave that deserted isle to which you have exiled them.

2. Visual Displays—Information

Visual displays are the second component of visual management and all about improving communication. The idea is to make the factory, laboratory, or office area speak to you. There are endless examples of visual displays, but the key is they help you understand what's going on . . . even something as simple as visual displays in a furniture salesroom can help you out with what specific details you may like on a couch, as opposed to simply reading the catalog (see Figure 3.8). Their purpose is to identify important equipment or necessary informa-tion, that is, safety, instructions, and the like, but do not necessarily control what people or machines do. It could be the name of a line, machine, process step, department metrics board, and so on. Visual displays such as signs and bulletin boards do not suggest or enforce any action. Their purpose is to identify and inform to help you know what something has hap-pened or to label something. They can also be informative to provide important information in one area or to update a status or situation. Their sole purpose is to communicate informa-tion. The menu shown in Figure 3.9 from a restaurant is very visual. This is a common visual display in Japan and other countries whereby the diner can simply point to what they would like to order.

3. Visual Controls—Instructional

Visual controls are instructional. They communicate instructions or tell you how to perform a task. The idea is they trigger you to do something. They could be DBH boards, statistical process control charts, work instructions, planning documents (if updated in real time), Andon, lines on floors, directional signs, and the like.

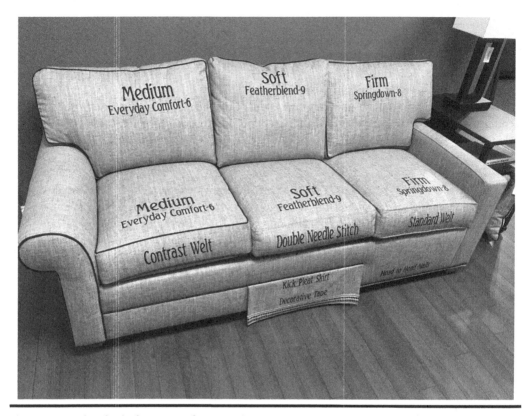

Figure 3.8 Visual Display—Couch at Furniture Store.

Source: BIG training materials.

4. Visual Management—Daily Management Planning

Visual management combines the first three along with mistake proofing, total productivity maintenance, material flow, and so on. We discuss this more later in the book as it is linked to other aspects of the Leadership Development Path.

Notes

1. www.amazon.com/BASICS-Lean-Implementation-Model-Profitability-ebook/dp/B07JVDN6YN The BASICS® Lean Implementation Model Routledge, Protzman, Keen, Protzman, 1 edition (September 7, 2018).
2. We have participated in many BASICS® Lean conversions that realized better results and a much higher sustain rate than 5-day point kaizen events that spanned months or years. Some projects can be implemented in less than four weeks if there is very low labor content or we are switching from station-balanced lines to baton zone–balanced lines.
3. Learning to See Rother and Shook—Lean Enterprise Institute; 1 edition (June 1, 1999).
4. The BASICS® Lean Implementation Model Routledge, Protzman, Keen, Protzman, 1 edition (September 7, 2018).
5. LeanEdit is a great tool to use with videoing a process. https://leanedit.com/

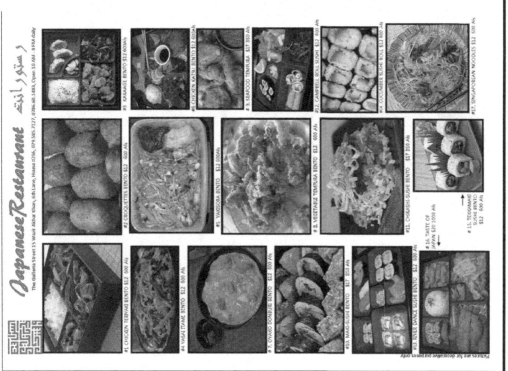

Figure 3.9 Japanese and Czech Republic Restaurant Menus Visual Display.

Source: BIG training materials.

6. Dan Protzman talking—The name SMED comes from Ritsuo Shingo, who coined the term for his father's, Shigeo Shingo's, golf score. The name of SMED was by me. When I tried to translate his book into English, he explained to me that a single handicap was great for an amateur golf player. Personal correspondence 6–9–2020.
7. We now say the goal of reducing changeover times is to reduce it to single digits (i.e., less than 10 minutes).
8. The BASICS® Lean Implementation Model Routledge, Protzman, Keen, Protzman, 1 edition (September 7, 2018).
9. Dr. Jeffrey Liker—used with permission The Toyota Way to Lean Leadership, Keynote, The Toyota Way, 2nd Edition, Jeffrey Liker, McGraw-Hill Education; 2nd edition (December 1, 2020).
10. The Lean Practitioner's Field Book: Proven, Practical, Profitable and Powerful Techniques for Making Lean Really Work, Productivity Press; 1 edition (April 4, 2016) Protzman, et al.
11. Toyota Production System, Productivity Press, Ohno, 1988 page 22.
12. TPM is total productivity maintenance.
13. Chairman of ICI—the late and great British industrialist and star of the *Troubleshooter* series back in 1989 to 1999.
14. Webinar with Ernie and Tracey Richardson 5–1–20.
15. To Learn how to create a PPCS see The BASICS® Lean Implementation Model, Protzman, Keen, Protzman, CRC Press, 2019.
16. *The Life-Changing Magic of Tidying Up: The Japanese Art of Decluttering and Organizing*, Hardcover—October 14, 2014 by (Author).

Chapter 4

BASICS® Baseline—Introducing Team Member Self-Reliance

Figure 4.1   BASICS® Lean Leadership Development Path—Baseline.

Source: BIG Training Materials

Now we introduce you to the Leadership Development Path (see Figure 4.1), which is the people or human aspect part of the BASICS® Lean Model (see Figure 4.2). The developmental part of the Leadership Development Path breaks down into the following four components:

DOI: 10.4324/9781315155227-4

Figure 4.2 BASICS® Lean Tools Foundation.

Source: BIG training materials.

1. **Learning to See—Team Member Self-Reliance (TSR)**—Teaches team members how to see waste, break down the job, and be responsible and accountable to perform and improve their job
2. **Learning to Solve—Improving Business Practices**—Teaches leaders how to problem solve and continuously improve the way jobs are performed
3. **Learning to Share—Skills and System Deployment**—Teaches leaders how to quickly train team members to do a job correctly, safely, and conscientiously; teaches Leaders how to evaluate and take proper actions to handle and prevent people problems
4. **Learning to Teach—Continuous Leadership Development**—Teaches leaders how to manage for daily improvement

Step 1—TSR

TSR is the first step in the BASICS® Leadership Development path, which falls under "Baseline." This philosophy means that it is every manager's main job to develop, engage, and challenge their team members in learning to see the waste and gaps in their processes and constantly think about improving their work and making things better.

There Are Six Steps to TSR

These six steps (see Figure 4.3) are accomplished in learning how to breakdown down the job and creating standard work and include the following:

1. Create accountability for the job
2. Instill ownership for improving the job
3. Having the discipline to create, follow, and improve standard work
4. Have a bias for action and continuous improvement
5. Learn a variety of Lean technical skills
6. Create baseline metrics to measure improvements

Figure 4.3   Team Member Self-Reliance.

Source: BIG training materials

TSR Is Based on New Thinking and Behaviors

Your training program may be in trouble if you must ask your group leaders how they know if a new team member is trained properly, and you get these types of responses:

- We just told or showed them how to do it.
- We ask them if they got good training.
- We watch them if we have time.
- We see if they achieve the rate.
- They sign themselves off on the training form.

If these responses sound familiar, you may be placing new team members, and your organization, in a position that will eventually lead to failure.

TSR is the missing sustain piece for just about every company in developing a daily improvement culture.[1] The original idea of TSR came from a book called *Self-Help*[2] by Samuel Smiles, written in 1859, which sold over 250,000 copies all over the world before he died. It extolled the virtues of hard work, thrift, self-improvement, and perseverance. TSR is about transforming the organization from a "Do as you're told" to a "What do you think?" culture.[3] It is about transferring the ownership from the leader to the frontline team member. These are the people who get the work done and make the money for your company. The role of the Leadership Team is to keep their team members for life versus putting all that money into training only to have them leave.

TSR Is about Job Ownership[4]

A high-level outline is as follows:

> Before you say you can't do something, try it.
>
> **—Sakichi and Kiichiro Toyoda[5]**

TSR is about creating team member ownership for both the job and improvement of the job. Toyota calls this method Ji Koutei Kanketsu. We have found that all companies have extremely knowledgeable people but struggle to pass on the unwritten knowledge to new team members. We use TSR as a tool to extract that unwritten know-how from experienced team members and decrease the learning curve for new team members. This tool is part of the foundation for TSR. It is designed to teach the leaders how to train team members to perform a quality job by following the standard and working as safely and quickly as possible.[6] During the training sessions, these two important concepts are repeated numerous times, so the instructors are clear on two important points:

1. It is the responsibility of the group leader and team leader to be able to teach workers how to do and improve their jobs.[7]
2. The group leader must develop their skills in how to share their knowledge.

The team member is taught how to reduce or break down each job to the most basic and fundamental steps along with key points (see Figure 4.4). Key points, that is, quality, safety,

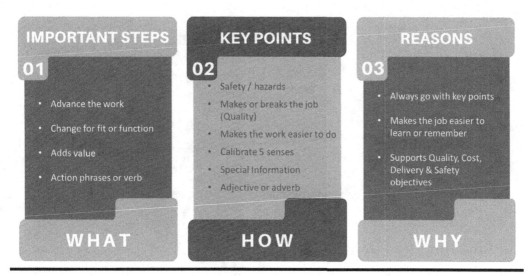

Figure 4.4 Job Breakdown of Key Steps, Key Points, and Reasons for Key Points.

Source: TWI JI public domain.

or a knack of how to do something, among others, and reasons for these key points.[8] This way the team member learns not only what the step is and how to do it but also why it's important. These key points become the focus of the training. Each person must keep in mind improving the entire process, not just their step in the process. Therefore, cross-training and job rotation are important.

Needs of a Leader

There are five basic needs of a leader (see Figure 4.5):[9]

1. *Knowledge of the work*—Refers to the kind of information which makes your business different from all other businesses: material, tools, operations machines, processes, and technical skills. Some people have spent their lifetimes at work and are still acquiring knowledge of their work. If they move to another industry, brand-new knowledge of work must be learned.

2. *Knowledge of responsibilities*—Refers to the company situation regarding policies, safety, interdepartmental agreements, rules, mental regulations, schedules, and relationships. These are different in every company or plant. Every group leader must have a clear understanding of their authority and responsibilities as a part of management.

3. *Skill in improving methods*—Deals with utilizing materials, machines, and personnel more effectively by having group leaders study each operation to eliminate, rearrange, simplify, and combine steps of the job.

4. *Skill in leading*—Helps the group leader to improve their ability to work with people. There are basic principles that, when applied day in and day out, will tend to keep relations smooth and prevent problems from arising.

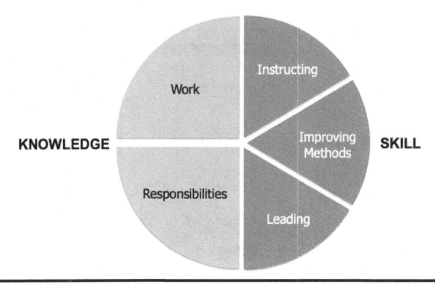

Figure 4.5 Five Needs of Group Leaders.

Source: TWI public domain.

5. *Skill in instructing*—Helps group leaders develop a well-trained workforce, resulting in less scrap, rework, and rejects; having fewer accidents; and having less tool and equipment damage. The group leader is not necessarily born with these skills and must acquire them by actual individual practice.

TSR—How to Achieve a 90% Skill Retention Rate

Job instruction[10] is a short program that introduces group leaders to a few aspects of the art and science of teaching. Job instruction is broken down into four steps:

1. *Prepare the worker.* This means creating a well-thought-out and documented plan before starting the training, this includes putting the worker at ease, stating the job, and getting them interested in doing the job.
2. *Present the job.* This teaches the group leader that all people learn differently. We demonstrate during the training how just showing, telling, or using visual displays by themselves are poor methods of instruction with very poor retention rates.
3. *The Job Breakdown sheet* (see Figure 4.6). This sheet becomes the basis for standard work. We explain how to properly instruct the worker, combining these methods with an overall picture of the job, how to break down the job, how to discover key points, and reasons for key points along with repetition.
4. *Practice.* This is based on learning by doing and takes advantage of the fact that this method of learning has a > 75% retention rate. The follow-up is the coaching and mentoring required to obtain a 90% retention rate. We live by the motto "If the student hasn't learned, the teacher hasn't taught."[11]

JOB BREAKDOWN SHEET

Operation :	
Parts :	
Tools & Materials :	
Safety Equipment :	

MAJOR STEPS	KEY POINTS	REASONS
What: A logical segment of the operation when something happens to advance the work	How: Anything in a step that might — 1. Make or break the job 2. Injure the worker 3. Make the work easier	Why: Reasons for the key points
1.		
2.		
3.		
4.		

Figure 4.6 Job Breakdown Sheet.

Source: TWI JI public domain.

Job Breakdown[12,13]

A critical component of TSR is learning how to break down processes routinely performed, which eventually leads to the creation of standard work (see Figure 4.7). The steps include the following:

■ Break down the job
■ Question every detail
■ Develop a new method
■ Apply the new method

Standard work helps eliminate errors, provides role and task clarity, and decreases variation within an activity, task, or process. TSR teaches scientific management to the team members using video and motion-study techniques. Team members learn to question everything, use creative thinking, and never assume one cannot make more improvements. The training instills a continuous improvement mindset and stresses the importance of being action oriented. We call it having "a bias for action."

Figure 4.7 Four Steps to Team Member Self-Reliance.

Source: BIG training materials.

When Do You Need Standard Work?[14]

Every company has numerous problems with production, scrap, and accidents. While these problems may vary in accordance with the production load, the plant facilities, and employee turnover, all of them can be helped through better methods of training. The creation of a company training representative role may be necessary. We find that ongoing training and development help a company training representative to both

1. identify the immediate training needs of their organization and
2. develop plans to meet them.

If this is a full-time job, we may designate someone part- or full-time in Human Resources, Finance, or Operations as a training director. We use a four-step method of identifying training needs and in developing plans to meet them:

1. **Spot a Production Problem**—Get supervisors and workers to tell us about their current problems. Uncover problems by reviewing records for performance, cost, turnover, rejects, and accidents. Anticipate problems resulting from changes—organization, production, or policies. Analyze this evidence. Identify the training needed and tackle one specific need at a time.

2. **Develop a Specific Plan**—Who will be trained? What content? Who can help determine? How can it be done best? Who should do the training? When should it be done, and how long will it take? Where should it be done?

3. **Turn plans into action**—Stress to management evidence of need using facts and figures. Discuss the plan, content, and methods and submit or update an existing training time-table. Present the expected results. Secure understanding and acceptance by those affected. Train those who do the training. Fix responsibility for continuing. Be sure management participates.

4. **Check Results**—How can results be checked? Against what evidence? What results will be looked for? Is management being kept informed? Is the plan being followed? How is it being sustained? Are any changes necessary? The line organization has the responsibility for making continued use of the knowledge and skills acquired through training as a regular part of the operating job. The staff organization provides plans and technical know-how and usually works through the line organization.

The Standard Work Paradox

The glue that holds the system together is the combination of the standard work paradox and developing your people. The paradox is that standard work is rigid, in that everyone must follow it, yet flexible in that everyone, and this is the developing-people part, is constantly trying to improve every operation every day and then updating the standard work. Toyota embodies the standard work paradox to the point if you asked one of their team members, we bet they would tell you they are still working on the system and have not yet discovered all its secrets. If Toyota feels they still have a long way to go, what does that say for the rest of us? The tools to sustain Lean are not new, but they are very difficult to implement because human nature is always working against you. If it wasn't difficult, every company would already be Lean. It's much easier to ignore a gap (problem) or just throw a solution at it versus making the effort of getting to the root cause.

Leadership behaviors at all levels must change for this system to work. Standard work must be built into the company's business system, starting at the foundation. Without making standard work part of the quality system, there is no way to ensure the standard work gets into muscle memory. All appropriate people should sign off daily improvements for each shift. We recommend the Quality Department be responsible for storing, approving, and auditing the documentation.

Cross-Training: Multiskilled Team Members

A team member cross-training matrix (see Figure 4.8) is not only important but is also a great visual that shows the overall skills required to perform a particular job and the progression being made over time to learn those skills. This tool provides team members opportunities for flexibility as well as professional growth. Every team member knows where they stand at all times. The cross-training table (see Figure 4.9) should be posted and shows the planned schedule for team members to be trained. The performance levels vary by company but generally include the following (see Figure 4.10):

1. In training
2. Can follow the standard at 50% of the cycle time
3. Can follow the standard and hit the cycle times 100% and suggest improvement ideas
4. Qualified as a trainer[15]

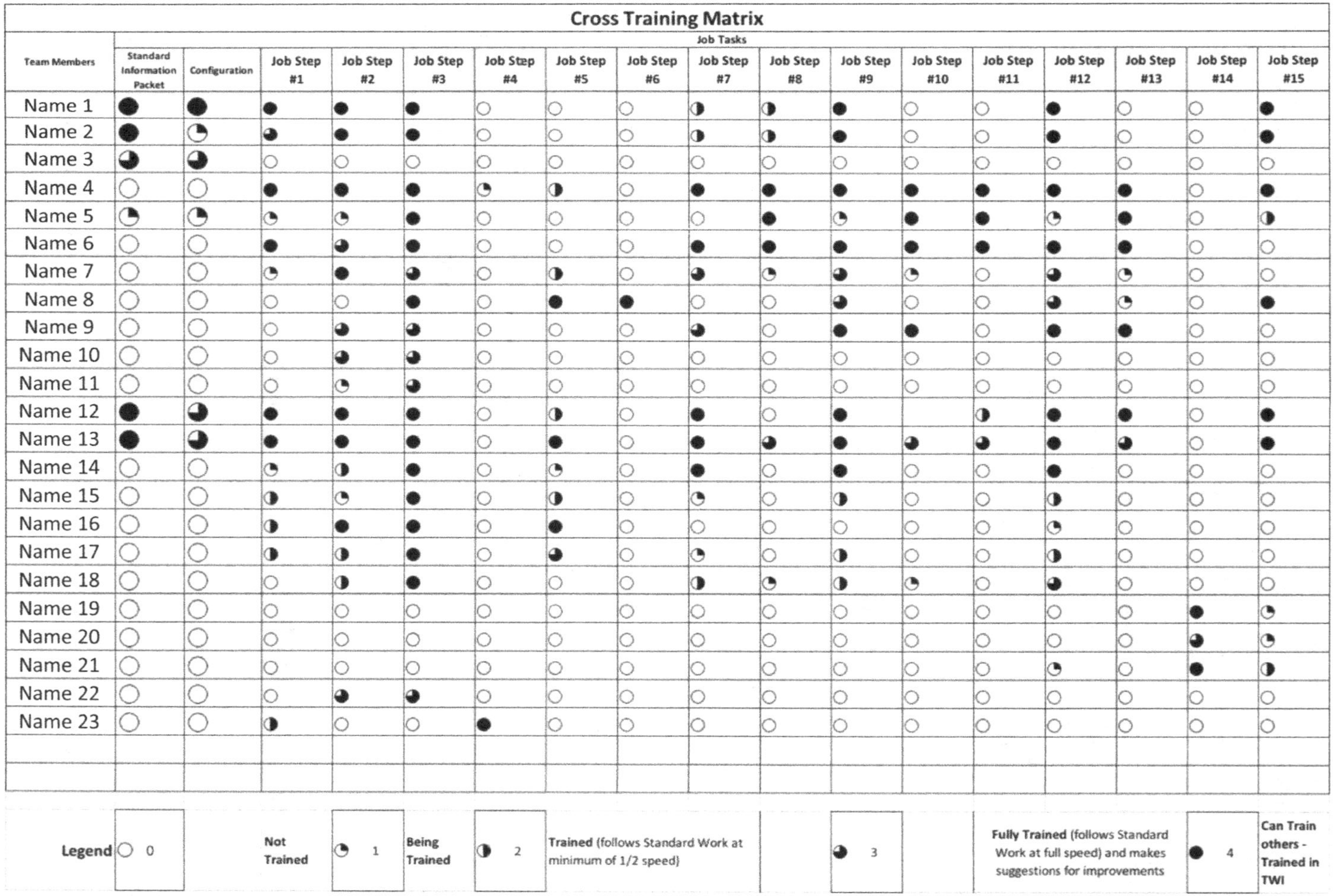
Cross Training Matrix
Job Tasks
Team Members
Standard Information Packet
Configuration
Job Step #1
Job Step #2
Job Step #3
Job Step #4
Job Step #5
Job Step #6
Job Step #7
Job Step #8
Job Step #9
Job Step #10
Job Step #11
Job Step #12
Job Step #13
Job Step #14
Job Step #15
Name 1
Name 2
Name 3
Name 4
Name 5
Name 6
Name 7
Name 8
Name 9
Name 10
Name 11
Name 12
Name 13
Name 14
Name 15
Name 16
Name 17
Name 18
Name 19
Name 20
Name 21
Name 22
Name 23
Legend
0
Not Trained
1
Being Trained
2
Trained (follows Standard Work at minimum of 1/2 speed)
3
Fully Trained (follows Standard Work at full speed) and makes suggestions for improvements
4
Can Train others - Trained in TWI

Figure 4.8 Cross-Training Matrix Example. 1 = in training, 2 = can follow standard work at 50% speed, 3 = can follow standard work at 100% speed, 4 = can train others/suggests improvement ideas.

Source: BIG training materials.

2017 Training Plan

Name / Trainer

Department: Training

Date: 24-Sep

Legend circle:
- 1 — In Train, use Job Breakdown Sheet
- 2 — Can follow work at 50%, Use Standard Work Sheet
- 3 — Can follow standard work at 100% speed and suggest ideas, Use Standard Work Sheet
- 4 — Can Train Others, Certified Trip Trainer

Job to be trained	Finishing Unloading		Area 1 C/O		Finishing Loading		Area 2 C/O		Area 3 C/O		Area 4 C/O		TPM AM		Reason for Training
	Status	Date to Reach the Next Level	Status	Date to Reach the Next Level	Status	Date to Reach the Next Level	Status	Date to Reach the Next Level	Status	Date to Reach the Next Level	Status	Date to Reach the Next Level	Status	Date to Reach the Next Level	
Total Number to be trained to Level 3 or above	9		2		5		5		5		5		3		
Job Breakdown Number	1		2		3		4		5		6		7		
Person 1		10/5/16		12/1/16		11/1/16		11/1/16		11/1/16		11/1/16		11/1/16	To replace another employee leaving
Person 2															New Employee
Person 3								12/1/16							Ongoing training in changeover
Person 4				1/1/17		12/1/16				12/1/16		12/1/16		12/1/16	Ongoing training in changeover
Person 5						12/2/16									Complete Finishing unloading and loading
Person 6						2/1/17				2/1/17		2/1/17		2/1/17	Continue training
Person 7		10/1/16													cross training mechanic
Person 8		1/1/17						1/2/17							Ongoing training in changeover
Person 9		6/1/17													poor performance - was a 3 for Finishing UL
Current Status 3 or 4s	5		0		1		2		2		4		1		

Figure 4.9 Cross-Training Plan.

Source: BIG training materials.

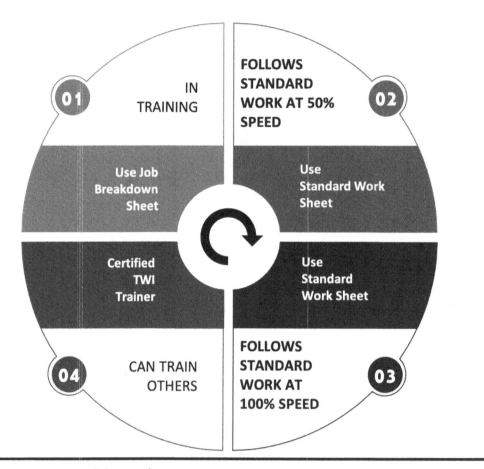

Figure 4.10 Cross-Training Levels.

Source: BIG training materials.

The group leader is responsible, with the participation of the team leader, for creating and updating the cross-training plan each year. The responsibility to define this type of goal would be with executive management, and it should be part of the strategic and the more detailed goal deployment plan. We want to ensure the maximum number of team members are cross-trained to offer both flexibility and staff availability to flex to customer demand changes.

Job Rotation

Job rotation (see Figure 4.11) allows for team members on the shop floor or in the office to swap jobs for a designated period. Individuals gain the experience of sharing and learning simultaneously as they experience the other's position. This option has a real win–win approach, and it's important that these types of activities be treated as learning experiences with good planning and preparation prior to the rotation. This not only provides some satisfaction in terms of new knowledge, but this knowledge and skill can also be leveraged to assist an organization as it experiences abnormalities. This applies to all levels of the organization.

5S Job Cycle Chart			Entered by :	Jakicic		Date :	3/19/2020				
			Department :	BV Assembly & Test							
			5S's					Job Frequency				
No.	**5S Job**	Responsible	Sort	Set-In-Place	Shine	Standardize	Sustain	Daily	Weekly	Bi-Weekly	Monthly	Quarterly
1	Consolidate Carts to 3 Staged	Valve Technician		X				X				
2	Maintain Assembly Tables	Valve Technician		X				X				
3	Maintain Teststands	Valve Technician		X	X			X				
4	Clean Washtanks	Valve Technician			X				X			
5	Recharge Lifts	Valve Technician			X				X			
6	Clean Personal Fans	Valve Technician		X								X
7	Sweep Floors	Valve Technician			X			X				
8	Evaluate Inventory	Valve Technician	X	X							X	

Figure 4.11   Job Rotation.

Source: Courtesy of Joe McNamara and BIG training materials.

Job rotation can be done each hour, after breaks, or after lunch, based on whatever makes sense for the business. It gives the workers a sense of accomplishment, and by learning new skills, they become more marketable. Additionally, it can break down silos, help with ergonomics, and provide a better understanding of the whole process. Maybe, more important, students learn to be teachers, because the planning requires them to develop the material, including the standard work used to train the participants.

Do You Know What You Do Not Know?

Think about this question: "Do you know what you don't know?" Seems like kind of a strange question, doesn't it? Yet, you would be surprised how often we find that people, simply put, do not know all that's "necessary" about their own processes. The worst effect of this conundrum is that those doing the work are not aware of the importance of the facts that they're missing.

Col. John Boyd, a famous fighter pilot, said, "*You gotta challenge assumptions. If you don't, what is doctrine on day one becomes dogma forever after.*"[16] We utilize the team member's talent and experience in every step of our BASICS® improvement process methodology. While many times we hear, "The team members are the experts," we find this may be true sometimes but not always. Team members only know what they *know* based on how they were trained and who trained them. Sometimes, they do not know or understand everything the machine can do or what the final product looks like or even how it works. We have created the following diagram which divides knowledge into four quadrants (see Figure 4.12):

- *You know you know:* The meaning behind this one is obvious.
- *You know you do not know:* The meaning behind this one is also obvious.
- *You do not know you know:* Many times, we realize we knew something that at first, we did not think we knew. For instance, we may improve things without realizing it, or sometimes, just thinking about a problem or using deductive logic, we can sort it out.
- *You do not know you do not know:* This is the most dangerous quadrant. Many times, we think we know things, or we know everything, which, of course, we really don't. We call this "knowing enough to be dangerous." The other interpretation is we don't know what we don't know in which case, it behooves us to find an expert or continue to dig and research a problem, so we get to a point of finding out what we still don't know.

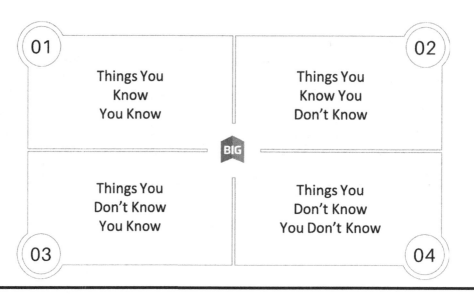

Figure 4.12   The Four Quadrants of Do You Know What You Do Not Know.

Source: BIG training materials.

Example

At a first-tier automotive company, we asked them about the static-value readout on an electrostatic painting machine and why they recorded it every 2 hours. They thought they were having a lot of quality issues with the machine. To make a long story short, the machine wasn't the problem. The problem was that no one knew, not even the head of quality or process engineering, what the static-value readout meant or how to set it properly. They were constantly setting this value to some arbitrary number that someone in the past thought was the right number, which was unwritten knowledge for many years, and we subsequently found out to be wrong. What we discovered after reading the manuals and talking with the company's painting expert was that the value should have never been changed once it was making a good product. It was standard operating procedure and Quality Department requirements driving the constant changing of the value that was creating the process problem. In addition, the length of the hoses from the paint-loading station to the machine played a role in the static-value readout. Over time, maintenance was moving the equipment and would extend the hoses, which then changed the static value of the paint. Because we did not know what we did not know, we always had increasing common cause variation. After a year of study, we discovered what we knew and we still did not know.

"Know How" Versus "Know Why"

How often have you had a problem in which you just went and fixed several things all at once and, suddenly, it works? But which change fixed the problem? How do you know? Alternatively, when we have a problem with testing equipment on the shop floor, we tap it (or hit it with a hammer) and it suddenly works. Sometimes we know *how* to fix things, but we do not know *why* it's suddenly fixed. Eventually, we find the tapping or hammering does not work anymore. We must learn the *know why* in addition to the *know how* to truly fix the root causes of problems.

Do You Know How to Check?

At a first-tier automotive company, we asked the inspectors about two separate inspections performed to check a heating device used in an automated process. The first question we asked was, "Why do you perform the inspection?" They told us it was because the documents told them to do it. We said, "Is that a good reason? Shouldn't you know why the document tells you to do it?" When I asked how the test worked, they said, "We wipe it with a cloth that contains a special liquid and then watch to see how long it takes to disappear." We discovered that they didn't even time it, nor did they know what the definition of the unit of measure was. When we asked, "What is the standard?" we discovered there was no standard to set the temperature. This whole inspection process drove the production people crazy because they never knew how to set the temperature properly. Every inspector literally told them something different! Then the inspector told us to increase the temperature on the heating element. We asked why. He said that based on his test result, it wasn't hot enough. After we increased it, I asked him, "What about all the parts we have done so far? Do we need to scrap them?" "No," he responded, "they are still good!" My thought was, "How can this be?"

This was a good news, bad news story. The bad news is they had no idea what they were doing. The good news was, if they were this clueless, think of the opportunities to make ongoing future improvements.

TSR Is about Accountability

One fundamental and extremely challenging problem we often encounter early in most organizations is a lack of accountability throughout the organization. We must establish an organization where the entire chain of command is accountable. The senior Leadership Team must drive accountability through their line organization and continue to coach and develop their leaders. If there is no accountability at the leadership level, it won't take root at the shop floor level. If accountabilities are not in place and understood early on, then you will not change the culture and continuous leadership development will become a flavor of the month. Through the TSR process, we begin to build this accountability starting with the team members *even before they are hired*. There are typically four kinds of people:

1. People who wait for things to happen
2. People who watch things happen
3. People who wonder what happened
4. People who make things happen and do not need to be followed up

We must supply initial and ongoing training on how to manage in this new environment. It is an interesting side note that most other languages don't seem to have a word that describes accountability. Most translate it as responsibility. Accountability means that people say what and when they are going to do something and then do what they say and when without being followed up. If they are going to miss a promise, they notify the proper person, their internal customer, at the time they discover the gap and suggest a recommendation for how to proceed. This system needs both positive and negative consequences[17] in place to work.

We stress accountability to team members starting in the hiring process. For example, if you are going to work here you must learn to take ownership and constantly look for better ways to do things and encourage others to do the same. We do not expect to have to follow up on your commitments.

This creates a fun, participative work environment where we all trust each other to get the job done right. We coach team members, when working on an improvement, not try to get it perfect the first time. Implement something and see if it works. Check the results against the standard to see if it improved. If you use these mini Plan–Do–Check–Act (PDCA) loops and take a small step every day, you will be amazed at how much you have improved over the course of a year. Make taking action, or what we call a bias for action, a daily goal. The following is an excellent excerpt from Fred Lee, written in his book *If Disney Ran Your Hospital*:[18]

> Accountabilities drive structure and structure drives culture . . . Any leader who is striving to change the culture . . . would do well to ponder this key principle: You cannot change the fruits of a tree without changing the roots . . . but here is where I want to indicate how powerful Disney's simple principle of making courtesy more important than efficiency. It strikes at a cultural root. Do you have a tree rooted in structures that support this rule, or do you have a tree rooted in structures that support primarily the fruits of unit efficiency?
>
> But now we come to a surprising paradox: by putting courtesy and service first, our problem with phony efficiency virtually disappears. So do problems with communication and teamwork between departments. [See Figure 4.13.] One rule, if followed by all departments, aligns the entire culture. Talk about an elegant model! This means that we can actually get the fruits of overall corporate efficiency when we subordinate departmental efficiency for the sake of courtesy and responsiveness (the most important aspects of service). [The Disney Paradox: Focusing on Customer First (Figure 4.14)] is more efficient and demonstrates the line of thinking behind this paradox. The ultimate

We Need Trust & Teamwork Across All Departments

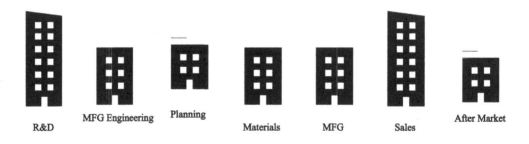

R&D MFG Engineering Planning Materials MFG Sales After Market

Enterprise Value Stream

Figure 4.13 Teamwork across Departments. R&D = Research and Development; Mfg = Manufacturing.

Source: BIG training materials.

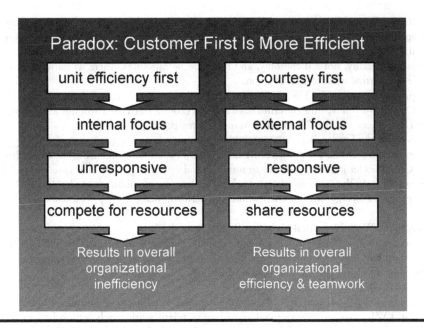

Figure 4.14   Line of Thinking behind the Efficiency Paradox.

Source: If Disney Ran Your Hospital: 9 1/2 Things You Would Do Differently [Kindle Locations 765–770], Fred Lee, 2004. Second River Healthcare: Bozeman, MT. Kindle Edition, with permission.) If Disney Ran Your Hospital: 9 1/2 Things You Would Do Differently (Kindle Locations 765–770), Fred Lee, 2004. Second River Healthcare: Bozeman, MT. Kindle Edition. With permission.

shortcut to getting the best overall efficiency is to focus on service and make it more important than efficiency.

As long as department directors have to answer only for their own labor costs, cross-functional savings and teamwork are not likely to happen. And the waste will go unmeasured and unnoticed as it gets invisibly absorbed by the organization. Placing service above efficiency, however, and the internal Customer will speak up and document the waste caused by poor service delivery. Working together as an internal service provider and Customer department, these inefficiencies would be identified and addressed in a culture of teamwork and responsiveness instead of competition. Again, this one rule may help change the entire management culture more dramatically than twenty team-building retreats. What top management needs to figure out is how to foster a climate in which departments and their managers are held accountable and rewarded for service instead of being punished for it, as they would be under conventional budget monitoring and accountability systems.

Notes

1. You will hear similar things about Toyota Kata and Training Within Industry (TWI). But TSR includes TWI, other aspects of Toyota's group leader training and development, and Toyota Kata, but it is much more than any of these separately.

2. *Self-Help* by Samuel Smiles was written in 1859 and has been translated into many languages, including Japanese, Dutch, French German, Danish. Croatian, Czech, Arabic, Turkish, and several dialects in India.

3. This is a generality, not a dichotomy, and there are no absolutes. There will always be times when people will be told what to do and so on.

4. This process is inspired by TWI public domain but has some inherent differences.

5. Emi Osono, Norihiko Shimizu, Hirotaka Takeuchi (2008), Extreme Toyota: Radical Contradictions That Drive Success at the World's Best Manufacturer. p. 86

6. This is called the Leader as Teacher method of training.

7. Of course, this assumes the group leader can do the job. In many large US companies, this is not the case. Group leader jobs are positions to rotate in and out of as part of their career path. This means they cannot train the team members and therefore have no credibility with their team. We have seen some group leaders literally beg their workers to perform, make more pieces, work overtime, and the like.

8. This is called Work Flow Analysis in our BASICS® model.

9. These come from a World War II program called Training Within Industry TWI JI, JR, JM, PR, public domain.

10. Inspired by TWI Job Instruction—public domain.

11. TWI JI Training Motto—public domain.

12. Inspired by TWI JI Manual War Manpower Commission's Bureau of Training 1944.

13. All four TWI programs are adamant regarding standard work. Each session had to be presented exactly as described and within the time elements designated for each section. The actual sessions are highly participative and have each participant describe how they would handle a problem with the rest of the group engaged in a dialog concerning whether the participant is following the process. An important point is the instructor is coached to make sure that the participants' concern is for following the process more so than the actual result of the individual problems. The problems are not the primary issue to be taught; the process is being taught and needs to be followed.

14. Taken directly from TWI Program Development—public domain.

15. Some companies have the following categories: 25% Performance, 50% Performance, 75% Performance, 100% Performance.

16. Boyd, The Fighter Pilot Who Changed the Art of War, Robert Coram, Hachette Book Group, 2002. Boyd was known as "40-Second Boyd," who could beat any challenger in 40 seconds and never lost a bet, also creator of the OODA (Observer–Orient–Decide–Act) loop. John Boyd prolifically studied the Toyota Production System and included it in his briefings.

17. For more on this, see the book *Bringing Out the Best in People* by Aubrey Daniels.

18. The Lean Practitioner's Field Book: Proven, Practical, Profitable and Powerful Techniques for Making Lean Really Work, Productivity Press; 1 edition (April 4, 2016) Protzman, et al. Lee, Fred. If Disney Ran Your Hospital: 9 1/2 Things You Would Do Differently (Kindle Locations 765–770). Second River Healthcare. Kindle Edition. with permission

Chapter 5

BASICS® Analyze and Suggest for Improving Business Practices

Figure 5.1   BASICS® Lean Leadership Development Path—Analyze/Suggest.

Source: BIG training materials.

After "Baseline," is Step 2, which is "Analyze" and "Suggest Solutions" in the BASICS® Leadership Development Path (see Figure 5.1). During this section, there is a concentration on "Learning to Solve." This is where our team members and leaders learn to solve by analyzing and suggesting solutions to close gaps as they arise throughout our business practices whether on the shop floor or in administrative areas and is composed of the following (see Figure 5.2):

DOI: 10.4324/9781315155227-5

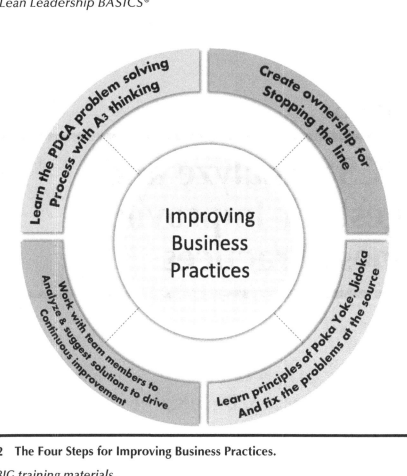

Figure 5.2 The Four Steps for Improving Business Practices.

Source: BIG training materials.

- Learn the Plan–Do–Check–Act (PDCA) problem-solving process with A3 thinking
- Create ownership for stopping the line
- Learn principles of mistake proofing, poka yoke, jidoka, and fixing problems at the source
- Work with team members to analyze and synthesize root causes and suggest solutions to drive continuous improvement

Analyze and Suggest are at the heart of developing a problem-solving culture. The idea is that team members are taught the concepts and tools to learn how to analyze and synthesize ideas and then implement them while on the job. This is how we learn and then deploy problem-solving and develop ownership with the team members for fixing problems using PDCA with A3 thinking.

Develop a Company-Wide Standard Problem-Solving Model

Companies should have a standard problem-solving method in which everyone is trained. This seems self-explanatory, but we normally find one of two cases:

1. There is no standard problem-solving model, and in some cases, the organization is not trained on how to solve problems.

2. There is a standard problem-solving model, but people do not understand it or choose not to follow it.

Our recommendation is to train everyone in the company on PDCA or whichever problem-solving model you choose out of the many that exist.

Key Points about Problem-Solving

- What type of problem is it?
- Do you understand the knowledge and skills behind your job? There must be a standard before you can problem-solve.
- Do you understand the purpose of your work? When was the last time you reviewed the standard?
- Always question: Is this work value-added from the customer's viewpoint?
- Be attuned to external and internal environment changes and always question what you are doing; that is, Has technology changed? Always work on reducing costs and look for value engineering suggestions.

Introducing PDCA and A3 Thinking

At the core of the BASICS® model is the problem-solving method of PDCA. PDCA had its roots in the scientific method and is based on current research popularized in Japan as part of a course in American industrial management conducted by Charles Protzman's grandfather, Charles Protzman Sr., and Homer Sarasohn as part of the Civil Communications Section (CCS) in 1948 and 1949. The CCS course, as it became known, was taught to the heads of all the major Japanese communications companies during the American occupation after World War II.[1] (See Figure 5.3.) The original text from the manual which became known as PDCA in Japan is as follows:

> As engineers and management people, we are convinced that the logical approach to determining what changes are needed and the benefits to be derived from them, stems from the use of the Scientific Method. It merely involves careful, common sense, and analytical thinking. Simply stated, the scientific method approach consists of five steps. They are listed below with their equivalents in the BASICS® Model and PDCA Model:
>
> 1. Define the problem precisely and get the facts—all the facts. (Baseline—Plan)
> 2. Analyze those facts to decide upon a proper plan of action. (Analyze/Suggest Solutions—Plan)
> 3. Put that plan of action into effect with the expected results identified. (Implement—Do)
> 4. Monitor the plan in process. (Check—Check)
> 5. Make necessary timely adjustments. (Sustain—Act)
>
> The problem we are dealing with in this course (CCS) is quite easy to define— manufacturing productivity and reliability is at an economically unacceptable low level. That calls into question the effectiveness of management organizations. We want to turn the situation around. . . .[2]

Graduates of the Civil Communications Section's management course, Osaka, 1950
The Americans (front row center, left to right): *Homer Sarasohn, Frank Polkinghorn, Charles Protzman.*

Figure 5.3 The CCS Taught PDCA as Part of the Industrial Management Course in American Management in Japan in 1949–1950.

Source: BIG archives.

These five steps perfectly align with BASICS® and PDCA as seen earlier. There is a built-in assumption here that PDCA starts typically with an improvement idea or gap found by checking or the discovery of a gap between the current state and desired state. This gap launches us into the PDCA cycle. Some gaps may be so large that they need continuous small PDCA cycles. In the following subsections, the original PDCA steps are connected to what is today known as an A3 format.

Step 1 (Plan): Define the Problem Precisely[3]

In order to define the problem precisely you must go and see the problem for yourself. You cannot solve the problem sitting in your office. Next you need to understand the situation and clarify the problem (see Figure 5.4[4]). Engaging in a continuous improvement initiative means that everyone must learn how to problem-solve. Problem-solving starts with understanding and being able to write down the problem or gap. Steve Jobs said, "If you define the problem correctly, you almost have the solution."

Title of this A3

Who needs to approve any measures to solve problem?

Name/Position	Name/Position	Name/Position	Name/Position	Name/Position
Signature	Signature	Signature	Signature	Signature

0. Background

1. Clarify the Problem

2. Break Down the Problem

What?

Who?

Where?

When?

3. Target Setting

4. Root Cause Analysis

5. Define Countermeasures & Plan

6. Monitor & Review

7. Standardize and Yokoten

8. Further Actions

Figure 5.4 A3 Template—It's Just a Guide. Every A3 is unique and tells a story.

Source: Courtesy of Nigel Thurlow, The Toyota Way Scrum Training Course©2017 Part of the Flow System.

Get the Facts—All the Facts

Next, break down the problem into questioning what happened, where it happens, who it happened to, and when it happened. Sometimes we add how it happened and how much. The purpose is to get to why it happened. This is known as the 5Ws and 2Hs (see Figure 5.5). Honda's Golden Triangle keeps in mind that data can be interpreted or skewed, so they don't always represent facts. The purpose of questioning "the who" is not to blame but to identify who to talk to in order to understand the facts and where it happened to cause the gap. We need to understand the data and context of the current state and then set the target condition. The gap can come from anywhere, but by getting baseline metrics in place we can understand the current state and develop our target. In some cases, management may set the new improvement target in their strategic plan, or we find a need (mandated or innate) to do something better than it is today. We may solicit people's ideas, whether it be from a team member, customer, supplier, patient, and the like (see Figure 5.6).

Standardized Management

5 Ws 2 Hs

➢ Knowing WHAT to do
➢ Knowing WHEN to perform the activity
➢ Knowing WHY it needs to be done
➢ Knowing WHO should do it
➢ Knowing WHERE the activity should take place
➢ Knowing HOW to perform the activity
➢ Knowing HOW MUCH is required

Figure 5.5 Honda's Golden Triangle.

Source: Tom Chickerella—V.P. Process Improvement Ohio Health.

Setting the Target Alignment

The target (see Figure 5.7) of setting stretch targets should have a desired outcome and should also have a designated time frame. The target provides a basis against which to measure your progress. This target should be realistic and may take anywhere from 2 seconds to years to realize (see Figure 5.8).

Figure 5.6   Setting the Target Alignment with a Clear Line of Sight.

Source: BIG training materials.

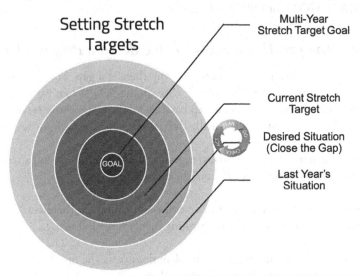

Figure 5.7   Setting the Target.

Source: BIG Training Materials

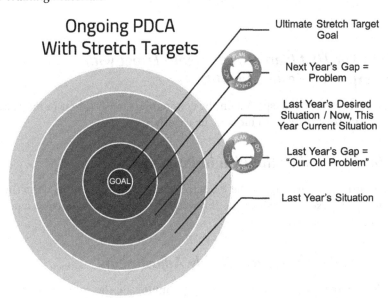

Figure 5.8   Ongoing Plan–Do–Check–Act for Setting the Stretch Target.

Source: BIG training materials.

Next record the problem statement. Ritsuo Shingo defines a problem as any "deviation from the standard. Without the standard you cannot find the problem."[5] The problem statement should identify what is wrong (as compared to a standard or expectation), where and when it is occurring, the baseline or magnitude at which it is occurring, and what it is costing us. We refer to this as creating the business case. The business case should be such that it justifies us spending the time to root cause and solve the problem. Once that is done, then the objective problem statement can be written as follows: Improve some METRIC from some BASELINE level to some (stretch target) GOAL, by some TIME FRAME, to achieve some BENEFIT, and improve on some CORPORATE GOAL or OBJECTIVE.[6]

Step 2 (Plan): Analyze Those Facts to Decide on a Proper Plan of Action

Once we identify the gap, we need to figure out why there is a gap. For this, we use something called "root-cause analysis" or "A3" thinking."[7] (See Figure 5.9.) When we are faced with a new problem, our first step should be to take a step back and look at the entire system that is at work. Ask yourself the following question: Is it really the person who is at fault, or is it the system?

1. Analyze the problem; identify all the symptoms. We call these "point causes."
2. Find the root cause or causes for the point causes.

In some cases, one root cause may solve several point causes, or there could be multiple root causes tied to one point cause. Root-cause thinking involves the following:

◼ Fixing the symptom just manages the problem doesn't fix the problem.
◼ Blame gets in the way of finding the real problem.
◼ Use poka yoke (mistake proofing) to make sure the problem never comes back.
◼ If you cannot prevent it, use jidoka to inspect it 100% by machine or sensors. The best solution is to design it up front with built-in quality.

Step 3 (Do): Put That Plan of Action into Effect with the Expected Results Identified

Next, implement the plan and keep data on the countermeasure. It is best to implement only one countermeasure at a time in order to measure its effectiveness.

Step 4 (Check): Monitor the Plan in Process

Check to see that it fixed the gap to the expected level. Also understand what time horizon is necessary to ensure we fixed the root cause. If it wasn't fixed, then it is probably a point cause and the PDCA process must be repeated.

Step 5 (Act): Make Necessary, Timely Adjustments

The last step is to update the standard work and communicate the countermeasure to any other group that may be affected by the same or similar gap. It should also be analyzed to see if it can be applied to other plants or processes. PDCA is not a difficult concept; however, PDCA thinking is

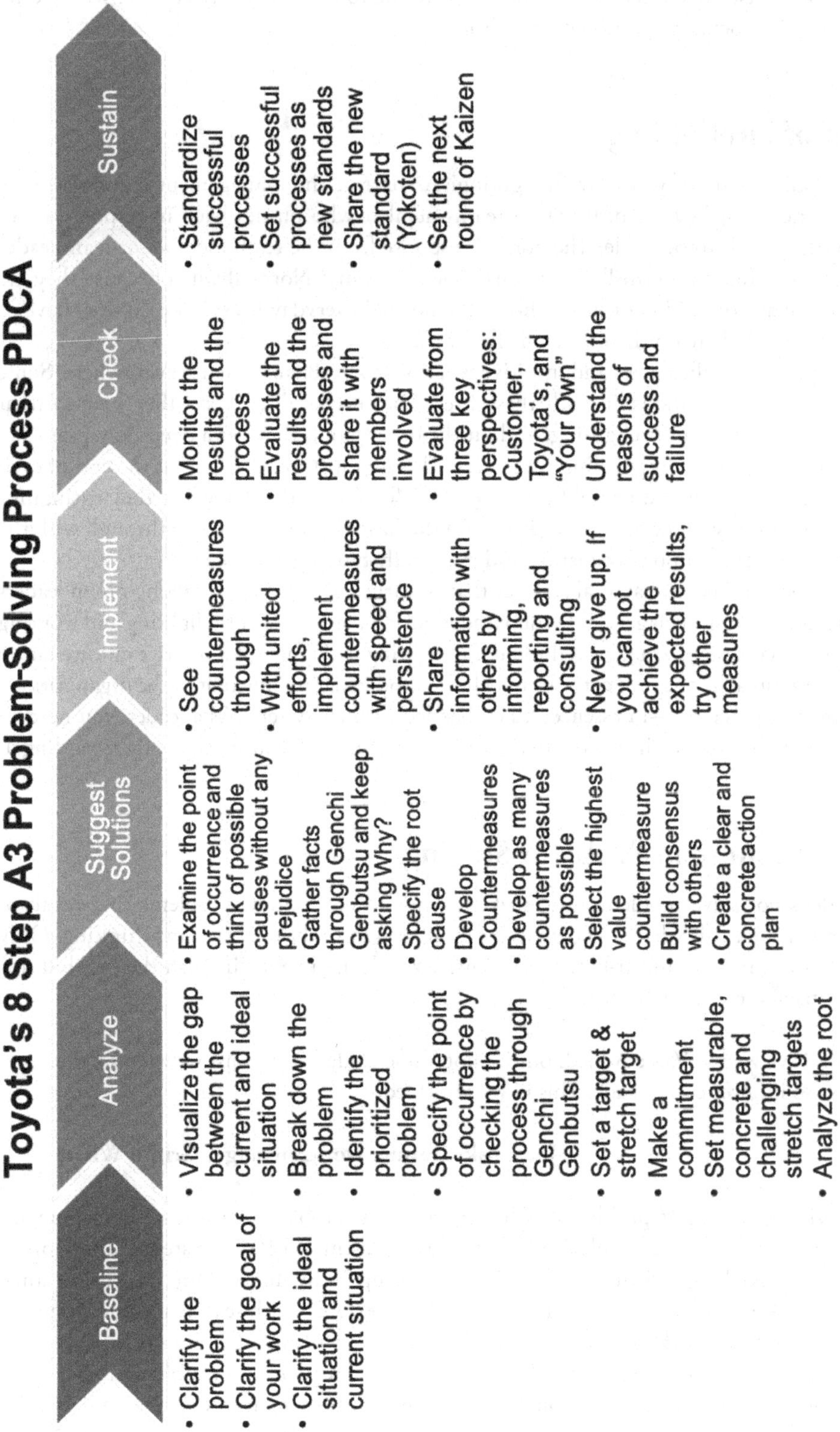

Toyota's 8 Step A3 Problem-Solving Process PDCA

Baseline	Analyze	Suggest Solutions	Implement	Check	Sustain
• Clarify the problem	• Visualize the gap between the current and ideal situation	• Examine the point of occurrence and think of possible causes without any prejudice	• See countermeasures through	• Monitor the results and the process	• Standardize successful processes
• Clarify the goal of your work	• Break down the problem	• Gather facts through Genchi Genbutsu and keep asking Why?	• With united efforts, implement countermeasures with speed and persistence	• Evaluate the results and the processes and share it with members involved	• Set successful processes as new standards
• Clarify the ideal situation and current situation	• Identify the prioritized problem	• Specify the root cause	• Share information with others by informing, reporting and consulting	• Evaluate from three key perspectives: Customer, Toyota's, and "Your Own"	• Share the new standard (Yokoten)
	• Specify the point of occurrence by checking the process through Genchi Genbutsu	• Develop Countermeasures	• Never give up. If you cannot achieve the expected results, try other measures	• Understand the reasons of success and failure	• Set the next round of Kaizen
	• Set a target & stretch target	• Develop as many countermeasures as possible			
	• Make a commitment	• Select the highest value countermeasure			
	• Set measurable, concrete and challenging stretch targets	• Build consensus with others			
	• Analyze the root cause	• Create a clear and concrete action plan			

Figure 5.9   Toyota's 8 Step A3 Problem-Solving Process and BASICS®.

Source: BIG training materials.

very difficult. We must force ourselves to work to solve the root cause; otherwise, we will end up spending all our time being reactive and firefighting.

Inception of Firefighting

Do you spend all or part of your day firefighting? As part of the management team, you may personally experience or have to deal with a team member who pushes back in response to an improvement that needs to be made. The normal response from the team member or team leader is "We do not have time to do this!" Why don't they have time? Normally, it is because they are too busy doing their normal job or just fighting the normal everyday fires. Why do they have to fight fires every day? Where do the fires come from?

The fires represent inefficiencies and intuitive reactions to problems that are everywhere. Some people have a love/hate relationship with these fires. On one hand, they say they hate to fight fires and will complain about firefighting, and on the other hand, they get a deep-down satisfaction from conquering and extinguishing these fires. This is your typical "hero" at the end of each month. Most staff are rewarded or publicly recognized for saving the day when they extinguish these fires. They typically know how to work around the formal systems to come through with the impossible; however, this can be exhausting and eventually burns people out.

Firefighting is an inherent, habitual skill set that is learned and rewarded among group leaders and managers today. Most managers and group leaders are all competent at firefighting and working through the informal systems, many need to be. Firefighting is the sign of a reactive culture rather than a proactive approach. The fires come from behavior and variation inherent in the organization's current culture and processes—in essence, it's embedded in their system. As a leader, you need to come to terms with the fact that if you are firefighting, then somehow, you are currently rewarding it.

The Role of Blame in Problem-Solving

Firefighting does not solve problems and, in fact, tends to create more problems that result in even more firefighting. It is what is known as a causal loop in traditional systems thinking. Only root cause analysis can solve linear-based problems. Firefighting may extinguish the fire, but it is almost guaranteed to come back.

> Reaction is viewed as Value Added, but it's not Value Added. You must strive to fix the problem so it never comes back. This is Value-Added.
>
> **—Joe Cuske, former works manager Griffin Wheel**

Thus, think of the fires as problems with the processes, problems with time management, or problems with behaviors of people, and ultimately problems with our systems. These problems cannot be solved by writing people up or blaming individuals. This creates an anti-psychologically safe environment. Blaming people interferes with exposing the inherent problems in the system. *Problem* is not a bad word; however, *blame* is. Humans seem to have an innate need to find someone or something to blame when there is a problem, and the last person we typically will ever blame is ourselves. In the continuous improvement (CI) world, blame always gets in the way of solving the problem. Whenever we blame someone, we lose sight of the bigger picture. This is characteristic of non-systemic thinking. One must remove the blame and place themselves into the situation and go and see where the problem is occurring, and if it is repeatable or intermittent. Intermittent problems are more difficult to solve as they may be troublesome to diagnose.

How to Slowly Transition from Firefighting to Problem-Solving

We must replace our firefighting skills with problem-solving skills. We must ask if the problem is really the person or the system.[8] Dr. Deming always said that 90% to 95% of the time the system was to blame. This means that if a person can, they will make a mistake. Humans are only 1 to 2 sigma[9] at best. So, we must figure out how to take the human out of the equation so they cannot make the error that leads to the defect (mistake). Systemic problems need systemic solutions. Managers and group leaders need to gain a solid understanding of these Leadership Development Path concepts, principles, and tools so that when changes are made and the staff poses questions and concerns, they can be addressed with confidence. To implement continuous leadership development, we need to change the systems so that fires eventually go away and managing becomes easier.

> As to methods, there may be a million and then some, but principles are few. The man who grasps principles can successfully select his own methods. The man who tries methods, ignoring principles, is sure to have trouble.
>
> **—Harrington Emerson**

PDCA Requires a Conscious Mindset Change—What Do We as Humans Normally Do?

We have found 80% of the time, unless it's a crisis, most of us want to ignore or bury the problem and hope it goes away. If we can't do that, we tend to throw a solution at it with little to no investigation. Throwing a solution at the problem requires our intuition based on our past experience. If we have a good orientation,[10] that is, past experience and knowledge with the particular problem (gap) at hand, then this makes sense. However, all too often, we don't have this knowledge or experience and we guess as to what's the cause. Guessing may result in fixing the gap, but more often than not, it fixes a symptom of the problem (point cause); in which case it eventually comes back and typically at the worst time possible; or makes the original gap even worse than it was before. Since we didn't take the time to measure it before or after, this all becomes part of the hidden factory. We have no idea if we are helping overcome the gap or not. There are many words and phrases for firefighting, like "just make it happen"; check, rework, recheck; design loop; hidden factory; and so on.

We tend to throw solutions at gaps, that is, firefight, because we all believe we are too busy and don't perceive we have the time to follow the PDCA thinking process. Yet, ironically, we all seem to have time to rework it when it goes wrong. This means we are normally just reacting with thoughts like "I need to make this go away. . . . I need to fix it right away, or I am going to get yelled at or get in trouble or get fired if I don't get this fixed now!" When we purely react quickly, or when we throw a solution without the proper past experience, we are not doing PDCA.

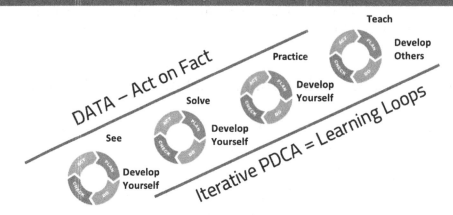

Figure 5.10 Ongoing Mini PDCA Cycles.

Source: BIG training materials.

Firefighting + Ignoring or Throwing a Solution at the Problem = More Firefighting

A mini PDCA cycle requires a behavioral change (see Figure 5.10). It drives a different way of thinking, and for most of you reading this book, it is a huge paradigm shift.

High-Level Company Target

1. Baseline is three turns.—Goal is 20 turns in next 5 years.

   - Establish the systematic inventory management that can respond quickly to all changes (such as order variance, project postpone, urgent requirement, production nonconfirmed performance, and so on.)

     - Break down the inventory plan target by raw material, raw material in transit, work in progress (WIP), self-manufacturing finished goods (FG), trade FG, trade FG in transit, and revise the plan every month end.
     - The inventory plan rule follows the PFEP (plan for every path) concept.
     - Specify the inventory day for each inventory to further understand the inventory impact in order to clarify the inventory control method.
     - Monthly, reflect the inventory performance and countermeasure to the deviation (separate report).

Figure 5.11 High-Level Goal Deployment (*Hoshin*) Target.

Source: BIG training materials.

You must always ask yourself . . . "Are you managing the problem or fixing the problem? You cannot manage a problem—you have to solve the problem. . . . Once you
identify it you have a big responsibility. . . . You must fix it."[11]

It can take years to truly learn how to problem-solve (larger-scale problems) in the true spirit of
PDCA (see Figure 5.11). Many old and even recent books have been written on it,[12] but most
companies and Lean experts do not really understand that PDCA, or what is also known as A3
root-cause thinking, requires a culture change (see Figure 5.12). Leaders must first create a culture
where it is safe to fail in order to encourage problem-solving. Daily continuous improvement is, by
its nature, derived from continuous A3 thinking.

Think–Write–Share[13]

A great tool for the Suggest phase of BASICS® is in a category called liberating structures. A
liberating structure is designed to generate unbiased feedback and is taken from the Red Team
Handbook. This handbook has many useful tools and thinking to surface ideas in a psychologically safe fashion. Think–Write–Share (T-W-S) is designed to mitigate fast thinking, grandstand-
ing, thinking aloud, spot-light rangers, and the highest-paid person's opinion.

It supports reflection, increases reasoning, understanding, and creates new ideas. The tool
allows time to create space between a question being asked and the time an individual needs
to think about them. Too often when collaborating with others, groups are challenged with
dynamics that stifle the emergence of valuable ideas. Introverts usually develop better thoughts
on their own, while extroverts synthesize the dialog from others to create their improved ideas.
T-W-S is the tool often used to foster critical and creative thinking for all group activities, no
matter the size.

The T-W-S Method

Facilitator: Before utilizing the T-W-S tool, the facilitator is responsible for developing a priming
question for the group to answer. The question needs to target key concepts of what the group is
focusing on—demonstrating understanding, solving problems, building knowledge, examining
information, or making recommendations. Consider allowing the participants only six words to
get at the core of their ideas. For example, clearly state the question—"What are the key issues or
challenges within your organization?"

THINK Provide a specific amount of time to the group; that is, "THINK for 5 minutes . . ."
about the question. This engages individual thinking.
WRITE down your ideas, as many ideas as you can. Do not self-censor. Do not share ideas or
look at others' ideas.
Facilitator: ELABORATE: "Keep an open mind and withhold judgment." Continue to write
and revise to develop and refine your ideas. Transferring thoughts by writing them down
forces the mind to engage in slow thinking and reflection of your thoughts.
SHARE the ideas.
Facilitator: SELECT the appropriate tool (Affinity Tool, Circle of Voices, 1–2–4–Whole
Group, Circular Response, etc.) that supports the outcome the group is trying to create.
"We will SHARE our ideas with a Circle of Voices."

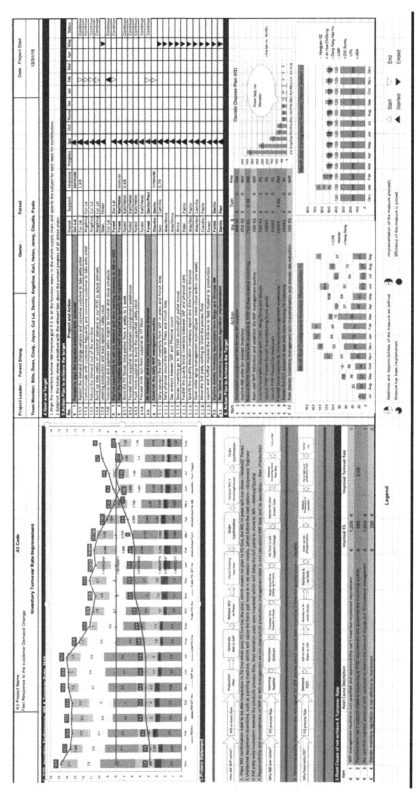

Figure 5.12 Actual A3 Inventory Turns—Over 3 years, turns increased from 3 to 14, freeing up millions in cash flow and working capital. Colors show linkage throughout.

Source: BIG training materials.

VARIATION: Facilitator can interchange T-W-S with Think–Draw–Share. If you are trying to get participants to visualize the desired end state or complex ideas, drawing a diagram, model, or illustration can clarify ideas the participants are not able to express in words.

Leading and Learning—by Tracey and Ernie Richardson[14]

A phrase often repeated at TMK was "Leading and Learning." The idea was that people should always be learning and improving their thinking as they go, but at the same time developing others. This way of managing, along with a relative lack of a command and control hierarchy, will sound paradoxical to a student of traditional top-down management. If workers aren't told what to do, how can we ensure that they will put in their best efforts? And how can we ensure that they will work toward results that align with the company's goals? The short answer is that in Toyota's workplace culture, team members not only manage themselves, but work in autonomous teams to help the company move forward toward its goals and toward the interests of the Customer. Creating that culture is the primary focus of Toyota's philosophy and the precepts behind the phrase "Toyota develops people who happen to build cars." This culture has, in our view, two pillars: The discipline to follow a path of continuous problem solving and self-improvement and accountability to work standards, fellow team members, company goals, and the Customer Experience.

However, we did not see these as two separate elements. Somehow, they were both interwoven as a single entity that pervaded our daily work. For us, they represented the feeling of the Toyota culture that was atmospheric. Therefore, we like to speak of discipline and accountability as one, and we have labeled the concept DnA. In our years of training, DnA has been our brass ring. Every year, we try to get better at helping companies grasp and attain DnA, which in our view is the key to Toyota's phenomenal achievements. And that is our goal with this book as well. The leaders at TMK brought this mindset to the workplace in two ways: They ensured that every worker learned and internalized both the skill set and the thinking for uncovering and addressing problems and improvement opportunities. They made sure every worker was engaged throughout the organization. To reflect this, we organize our training programs around a simple learning equation, which is designed to help learners remember and internalize the essential elements that took us years of practice to assimilate.

$GTS6 + E3 = DnA$

- **GTS6** *represents six competencies required by every worker to identify and correct problems.*
- **E3** *is short for Everybody Everyday Engaged, represents the role of leaders in motivating and serving the workforce.*

GTS

1. *Go to See*
2. *Grasp the Situation*

   a. *What is an ideal state?*
   b. *What is the current state?*
   c. *What is a measurable gap?*

3. *Get to Solution*

4. Get to Standard
5. Get to Sustainability
6. Get to Stretch (goal—new standard)

This sequential thinking process not only takes you through problem solving, but it takes you around the continuous improvement "kanri cycle" of defining a standard through problem solving and working to continue raising the bar to the next level. In between you see questions that leaders should be asking themselves and their team members at the Gemba, involving and engaging people in dialogue about what should be, what is actually happening, and how to measure the difference. These questions encourage leaders to be present, giving them real actions they can practice (as well as replicate by teaching to others).

E3

Everybody Engaged Every-day in problem solving and continuous improvement. As a leader and a coach, whatever level you are in the organization, this is what you want to focus on and encourage in others. This creates actions and habits that give people a line of sight to how they're contributing to the company, its True North and business goals. Put these things together and what does this create?

DnA

Or rather, Discipline 'and' Accountability (DnA). Both are necessary for any organizational culture to progress. And not just progress in any fashion, but progress in such a way that again, the organization is building and improving upon standards. People often ask me, how did you do it every day at Toyota? My answer is always some version of the equation above. We had an infrastructure in place that required us to practice GTS6 by all levels and functional areas (silos), so everyone was engaged every day and we all knew the expectations. If you did not follow the standard, there was a possibility you could have a conference with Human Resources.

I often use the example of our strict attendance policy. So, our shift start was 6:30 a.m. and the assembly line started to move at that time. With our production takt time being 57 seconds per car (meaning a car was produced off the line every 57 seconds), if you were 30 seconds late to your job (process) then you were considered "late." Why so rigid you may ask? Well, in an organization that relies upon teamwork, it makes it a little more difficult to run the line if people aren't in their appointed positions. A team leader (line leader) would have to take their place which often shifted the group leader to cover the team leader role and so on. So, attendance is very important not just for the team, but holistically, for the company to learn and improve.

Our managers recognized the strict standard, but at the TMK plant there was also a flipside to the rigidity, a little incentive if you will. If you attained perfect attendance (specific criteria) at the TMK plant, you had your name placed in a bin and every year they drew 15 names for 15 cars (different model mix: Camry, Avalon, Venza) to be given out as a reward for having perfect attendance. It's a great program, it generates tons of morale, and it always brings out some friendly competition among workers. During my time at TMK I had several years of perfect attendance before moving into a salary role. (It was a great "edge-of-your-seat" feeling to think you may get a set of keys handed to you for coming to work every day on time!)

Does this GTS6 + E3 = DNA equation for TPS [Toyota Production System] leadership solve every problem for your organization? No. But it does describe at a high level of all actions leaders must take if they want to support a long-term, sustainable culture of problem solving. A culture where people feel empowered to make a difference for their organization and have a stake in the company's overall success.

Job security = problems solved.

    I cannot tell you how many times I have been asked, "What did you have to go through to get hired at Toyota?" The result is DnA. The formula should not lead one to believe that we are presenting instant answers. On the contrary, this book is about recapturing the thinking behind the tools that we feel often gets lost when people pursue a TPS agenda. That is why it has been so important for us to try to replicate the voices of our trainers, and to try to put you, the reader, in the same frame of mind we were in when we learned these lessons for the first time. I try really hard to practice what I teach. One of the key concepts of TPS transformation is the repetition of continuous improvement cycles. As many already know, without standards there cannot actually be continuous improvement, otherwise how do you know what you're improving upon? So, you must have a baseline standard against which to measure your successful practices.

    I remind you (and myself) of this because I have actually practiced some continuous improvement thinking in how I teach and explain TPS concepts across industries and in my writing. TPS concepts can be difficult to explain in a one or two-day workshop session or short articles, which is why it's important to track how well I am doing."

    The preceding section was contributed by Tracey Richardson.

Notes

1. PDCA was taught to the Japanese in a course called the CCS course (Civil Communications Section parts of SCAP in World War II), which was developed and taught originally by Charles W. Protzman Sr. and Homer Sarasohn in 1948 and 1949. The CCS course was then translated into Japanese and taught by Japanese Union of Scientists and Engineers until 1976 and at some Japanese companies until 1993. PDCA is different from PDSA (Plan–Do–Study–Act), which comes from Walter A. Shewhart and was later revised by W. Edwards Deming and the Japanese. Dr. Deming wrote his famous 14 points. PDCA and PDSA were taught during the same period in Japan, and as a result, there is some confusion as to how these two relate. Original Inspiration?: Principles of Industrial Organization, Kimball, McGrawHill (c)1947 pages 150–154.
2. The CCS Manual was written by Charles Protzman Sr. and Homer Sarasohn while in Japan in 1949.
3. PDCA based on the CCS Manual—Fundamentals of Industrial Management—A textbook for The Communications Manufacturing Industry of Japan—by Charles Protzman and Homer Sarasohn—1948.
4. Used with permission of Nigel Thurlow is CEO of the Flow Consortium, co-creator of the Flow System, and former Chief of Agile at Toyota.
5. Toyota Masterclass Seminar June 25, 2021.
6. Contributed by Jane Fitzpatrick, Executive Consultant, Success Staging International, and LLC.
7. Understanding A3 Thinking, Art Smalley, Durward Sobek Productivity Press, (C)2008.
8. System within the context of the ordered domain.
9. Based on a Six Sigma scale with a 1.5 sigma shift.
10. Orientation here is in reference to the OODA loop by Col. John Boyd.
11. Danilo BrunoFranco, Executive Director, Global Railway Segment, ITT Corporation.
12. Guide to quality control, Total Company Wide Quality Control, Managing to Learn, A3 Thinking, to name a few.
13. Red Team Handbook ver. 9.0 pg. 202 This publication is available at https://usacac.army.mil/organizations/ufmcs-red-teaming/ and for registered All Partners Access Network users at https://community.apan.org/wg/tradoc-g2/ufmcs-red-team-central/.
14. Richardson, Tracey and Ernie Richardson. The Toyota Engagement Equation: How to Understand and Implement Continuous Improvement Thinking in Any Organization. McGraw-Hill Education. 2020 Kindle Edition. Used with permission.

Chapter 6

Jidoka—The Logical Extension of Improving Business Practices

Figure 6.1 BASICS® Lean Leadership Development Path—Analyze/Suggest.

Source: BIG training materials.

We are still in Step 2 of our Leadership Development Path (see Figure 6.1). On the shop floor or in an office environment, abnormalities should be clearly and immediately visible in the workplace and fixed in real time. This requires defect-free processes to support a one-piece flow (or just-in-time, JIT) system; thus, our number one goal is built-in quality at the design stage. If this is not possible, then

DOI: 10.4324/9781315155227-6

we need 100% defect prevention at the source. If this is not the case, then the system breaks down and delays occur. The only way to prevent defects from escaping to the customer is to inspect 100% of the parts at each operation by a machine, not a human, which leads to the concept of jidoka.

Common-Cause Versus Special-Cause Variation

Let's start with the difference between an error and a defect. An error is a mistake that is made; a defect is a problem that occurs because of the error. Dr. Shingo often referred to this as the importance of separating cause from effect. An example would be as follows:

> *(Cause) Error—leaving the lights on in the car*
> *(Effect) Defect—the car battery died.*

When dealing with cause and effect, it is important to understand the difference between common-cause and special-cause variation. For example, if one were to drop a penny onto the table, it will end up in a particular spot on the table. If you drop it again from the same location, it will end up in a different spot. As this process is repeated, a circle will form encompassing these spots. We can now predict the penny is going to land within the range of this circle, but we can't predict exactly where. This circle is an example of common-cause variation. If, however, an abnormal condition occurs, like I get bumped while dropping the penny or a huge wind comes out of nowhere, the penny will land outside our normal range in a different spot. This is called special-cause variation and requires a special-cause action (see Figure 6.2).

Many times, in a process, we will see a result that is not the norm and assume it is a special cause when in fact it is within the normal range of variation. If we then take a special-cause action, we will most probably upset the norm.

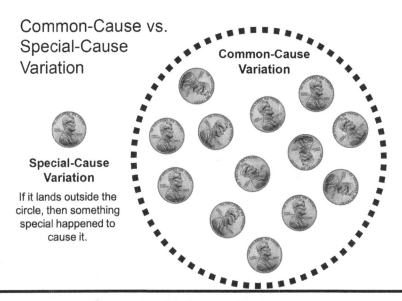

Figure 6.2   Common-Cause Versus Special-Cause Variation.

Source: BIG training materials.

Engineering Should Design in Mistake Proofing

There are two types of mistake proofing: *baka yoke* (person-focused) and poka yoke (process-focused; see Figure 6.3). The only way to mistake proof people is to take people out of the equation. People make mistakes! Poka yoke provides a mechanism to eliminate the errors so defects won't occur. There are three different classifications of defects: Materials, Processing, and Design. If we can mistake proof (see Figure 6.4) at the design phase, we wouldn't have

Poka yoke
Preventing errors caused
by absentmindedness

Baka yoke
Preventing errors when the standard is
beyond human ability

Figure 6.3   Poka Yoke Versus Baka Yoke.

Source: www.linkedin.com/pulse/re-translating-lean-from-its-origin-jun-nakamuro#a11y-content (public domain).

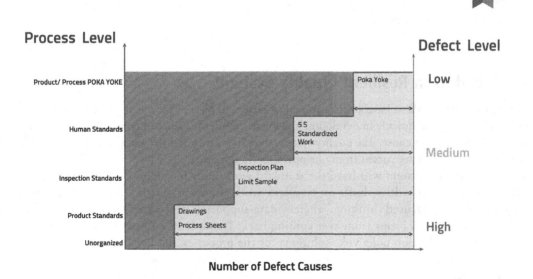

Figure 6.4   BASICS® Lean Hierarchy of Process Control.

Source: BIG training materials.

to do a PFEMA.[1] This is another example of new thinking we need to get in place. While it may sound simple, we have never seen it documented anywhere. We have learned through our experience the following is a hierarchy for mistake proofing from most desired to least desired:

1. Research and development engineers design in mistake proofing, whereby it is physically impossible for humans to make a mistake.
2. Technology engineers design mistake proofing into automated or semi-automated machines—the machine stops before it can make a mistake. This is jidoka.
3. Manufacturing engineers design mistake proofing into workstation via tooling and fixtures, whereby some may have visual notifications of gaps—poka yoke.
4. 100% inspection by machine at the source or at the end (goal is digital readouts with go/no-go results). The machine stops immediately after it makes a mistake. Team members should not have to interact with software. Results should automatically go into the quality data or electronic manufacturing system collection system. Abnormalities/gaps should be immediately visible (Andon, light, and sound).
5. The product is released, and team members design ways to mistake proof their operations. Human inspection is 1 to 2 sigma, approximately 93% effective:

    a. Baka yoke—simple operator-created visual controls or displays
    b. Successive checks—team members inspect the prior step before starting their operation and then inspect their operation when complete
    c. Inspection by quality department—sample to 100%—visual or with tool
    d. Inspection or testing by instrument or team member
    e. Visual inspection by one team member

Once you start inspections, it means you do not trust the process. Theoretically, if we designed in mistake proofing for every product, we wouldn't need a Quality Department. When you change your mind, the mind changes your actions, and your actions change the results.

The Need for a Resilient Quality System

The organization needs to have a resilient quality system in place. This means the organization is agile and can respond quickly in developing the initial countermeasures or containment plans and quickly get to the root cause. The quality system should ensure good parts are always being made and that no bad parts are passed from one operation to the next.

A good quality system will have the standard work built into its infrastructure and the quality system itself will be built on standard work. In addition, the quality system will encourage process-focused thinking, whereby data-supported, fact-based solutions are implemented to prevent problems from ever coming back. If you have a Quality Department, its job should be to develop poka yoke solutions for the processes and help to root-cause problems so they do not come back. Remember if we have to inspect it, we fundamentally do not trust the process.

The Jidoka Process

One certain indicator jidoka is needed is when you hear a team member on the line or in the office say, "I cannot leave the machine." When we ask why, the team member says that it might crash, produce a bad part, or have some type of problem. They also typically add that when it does have a problem, "It's a mess." We always ask the same question when met with this scenario, "How often does it have a problem or break down?" The team member usually doesn't know, or they have to think back to an episode years ago. In the majority of companies worldwide, we find team members spend most of their time monitoring the machines, whereby the company pays the team member to stand idly by "just in case" the machine breaks down or has a problem.

We like to relate this occurrence to an example. We ask the operators in these scenarios if they go home and watch their dishwasher or washing machine . . . just in case it were to break. Usually met with a blank stare, followed by a chuckle and then an obvious, "No," we say, "Then why sit and watch a machine at work." The truth is nobody should have to sit and watch a machine, but many machines have not been designed or applied the right protections to free these people up from having to watch them.

Many times, when we tell team members that they no longer need to watch the machine, they think we are sacrificing quality by removing their human inspection. We are actually doing the opposite by building the quality into the system. The machine should be trained or designed to catch mistakes before they happen, if not while they happen, to prevent passing on a bad part. Figure 6.5 shows the steps for the jidoka process.

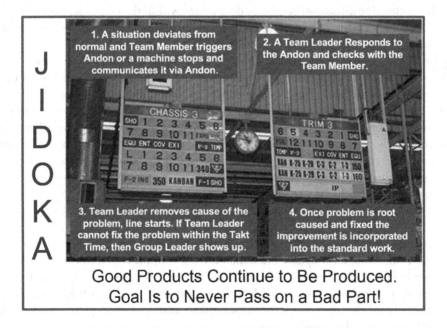

Figure 6.5   The Jidoka Process—If a team member must babysit a machine, then you need jidoka.

Source: BIG training materials.

Step 1: The process begins with an abnormality being detected. The Andon light goes yellow. It is interesting to note that if there are no visual controls or triggers for the abnormality, the process will continue to go unchecked and produce bad parts until someone discovers them and eventually stops the process. The objective is to detect the abnormality at the source or as near as possible to its occurrence, so it doesn't progress forward to the next step and, in the worst case, reach the customer.

Step 2: A standard work process must exist documenting this system for it to work and sustain. Many companies put in Andon lights with no standard work or system behind it. If the team member turns on the Andon light and no one shows up, your system is now dead. If the team leader is in meetings all day or constantly pulled off the floor, what are the chances for this system to work? We have seen Andon lights turn into holiday decorations at some companies.

    The team leader must respond immediately to the Andon and check with the team member to understand the abnormality that has occurred. The team leader must ask the team member to explain their problem in detail and ask the team member what they would do to fix the problem. Note: If the team leader just solves the problem, they have missed a wonderful coaching opportunity (*Kata*) for the team member to learn and develop their problem-solving skills. Together, the team leader (coach) and team member (student) discuss the problem and see if they can determine the root cause. If so, they discuss possible solutions. If they can come up with a countermeasure, they implement the solution as soon as possible. If the root cause cannot be discovered, they brainstorm a temporary fix (containment measure) and again implement only one at a time until the problem is solved (the Andon returns to green) so they can continue to meet the takt time, or the cycle time at which the line is running.

Step 3: If a containment action cannot be determined within the takt time, the line is stopped, and the Andon goes to red. In some cases, the product might be flagged and fixed at the next station or at the end of the line.

Step 4: As soon as the line is stopped, the group leader should immediately show up at the line. Once again, an opportunity for Kata exists and the group leader will discuss the problem with the team leader and team members and ask for ideas. If containment is needed or a countermeasure is determined, it is implemented, and the Andon returns to green. If it cannot be implemented within the takt time, the light stays red. If a solution cannot be determined within the next 15 minutes, the group leader's boss shows up and repeats the process. This continues until the plant manager shows up because the assumption is that at this point, they are the only ones able to and responsible for solving the problem. Therefore, promotion from within is a crucial part of the process.

Step 5: Once the line restarts, the team leader has several duties:

- ■ The team leader must continue to check to make sure the problem has been solved.
- ■ The team leader must update the standard work with the countermeasure (this is the act step in Plan–Do–Check–Act [PDCA]) and the cycle time for the step, as well as any key points on how to do the step safely and reasons why the step must be done. Of course, this assumes that there is a standard work document already in place and that everyone follows the standard work.
- ■ If a containment action was put in place, then, by definition, we have not discovered the root cause. The next step would be to work with the team members at lunch or off shift to continue the PDCA process (plan) and work to determine the root cause. Once the root cause is determined (this process could take hours to months), a countermeasure can be

implemented, and the containment plan removed. The solution must be checked short term and long term (6 months later) to make sure the problem does not return.

■ Once the problem has a solution and the countermeasure has been implemented successfully, the team leader must once again update the standard work with the countermeasure and the cycle time for the step as well as any key points on how to do the step safely and why the step must be done. They must also put a check card into the tickler file (file organized by date) to remind them when to come back to check to make sure the problem has still not returned and validate that the root cause was indeed fixed. Part of the standard work for this process must dictate the conditions for when to stop the line and how the Andon light system is supposed to work.

Step 6: Reflect and *Yokoten*—It is best to keep a log of the activity and lessons learned as they occur. Our memories are not what they were several days or even a day later. Ask, what could we have done to improve the overall problem-solving process? Can we cascade the improvements to other lines, departments, or plants?

Person-to-Machine Ratios

What is your person-to-machine ratio? Do you currently measure it? Is it a key performance indicator (KPI) for your company? We find this a great way to measure your long-term progress with jidoka. It is also a respect for people's concern. As we stated before, having people stand at a machine all day with much of their time idle watching the machine is not fair to them and affects the company's profitability. Most companies around the world think they are world class if they have one team member for two or even three machines. However, these pale in comparison to Toyota's statistics:

■ In 1896, Toyoda Loom Works averaged 30 to 40 machines per team member.
■ In the 1940s, Toyota Motors averaged five machines per team member.
■ In 1993, Toyota Motors averaged 16 machines per team member.

Jidoka is the tool that makes these types of ratios possible.

The Magic Fix-All

The magic root cause solution that leads to a permanent solution rarely exists. More important, the problem-solvers need to develop a resilient culture that realizes there is no permanent solution or single root cause. Dr. Deming was opposed to the concept of a permanent corrective action because the concept of permanent was contrary to the concept of continuous improvement. It also meant too much time wasted trying to find the perfect solution.

This doesn't mean we can't work to mistake proof the gap. But we must learn how to be agile in our responsiveness and build systems that can get countermeasures in place quickly until the problem can be solved. The team must be focused on realizing that improvements can always be found. *Thomas Edison stated, "There is always a better way; find it."* Even if you find the root cause, we must work to find ways that will prevent the root cause from ever coming back. This is one of the most difficult things to do as it takes a totally different mindset for most people.

Leaders' Intent

Don Vandergriff discusses a concept called leaders' intent in his book *Adopting Mission Command*.[2] The idea behind leaders' intent is for the Executive Team to communicate where they want to go and why they want to go there. It is then up to the rest of the organization to figure out how to get there without interference from the top. Guidance is okay; interference slows you down. Don discusses in his book how the Germans, during World War II, were initially winning most of the battles because the decisions were left up to the commanding officer in the field. It was okay, and even encouraged, to not follow direct orders if they felt they had a better way to get it done. The United States was exactly the opposite. Leaders in the field waited for orders from on high—those farthest away from the battlefield.

The concepts in this book parallel US factories and their leaders. Orders come from on high to tell the team member what to do and how to think. The team leader's job is just to show up every day and get the work done. Don explains how this is due to the influence and teachings of Frederick Taylor during the end of the 19th century and the beginning of the 20th when Taylor benchmarked the railroads and developed the manufacturing, accounting systems, and what we know today as command-and-control style of leadership. Taylor's teachings have influenced the military ever since. It is just now, through Don's and others' work, that the military decision-making process is beginning to change.

It is important to note that there is not necessarily a one-size-fits-all approach to leadership as seen from the following excerpt from an interview with Norman Bodek, where Ohno is using leaders' intent and Shingo is using more of a Socratic style. It depends on the context as Shingo and Ohno played different roles.

> "*Strategos*: What were the key personality characteristics that Shingo and Ohno brought together that provided so much success? *Bodek*: They were both like tigers, fiercely aggressive, neither would accept the idea that something could not be done. They gave you the concept and told you to do it. Ohno would simply say, "I want you to change this warehouse into a machine shop and I want everyone working there to be retrained. I will come back in one year to see it done." He did not tell them how to do it. Ohno had the power, as chairman of Toyota Gosei at the time, and was "ruthless." You had very little choice with him. Dr. Shingo was also a tiger, but a gentle tiger. He was absolutely brilliant, probably the greatest manufacturing genius of our time, able to solve every manufacturing problem presented to him. His way was different. He was a teacher. He would help you by asking you questions and encouraging you to experiment. He knew you had the answers within you. He would teach you about waste and give you guidance on how to eliminate that waste."[3]

Discipline

Many companies are seriously lacking in frontline leadership and management skills. We are not sure why this is, but it seems to be more and more prevalent in recent years. Group leaders and team leaders seem to spend their time in meetings all day or at their desk versus being on the floor 100% of the time. Factories appear to have self-managing teams when, in reality, they are the opposite. There is a serious lack of discipline up and down the chain of command. It is like the plants or offices are set on autopilot. No one pays any attention to metrics or tracks their output or knows what output they should be getting. Even if they do know what they should be getting, few actually understand, in the moment, why they are not getting the desired output. Usually, at the end of the day, they'll say that "things ran slower today" or that they "had that period of unexpected downtime," but usually this only accounts for a fraction of the parts or products that they don't complete.

According to the *Merriam-Webster Dictionary*, discipline means

> [c]ontrol that is gained by requiring that rules or orders be obeyed and punishing bad behavior, or a way of behaving that shows a willingness to obey rules or orders, or behavior that is judged by how well it follows a set of rules or orders.

The word *discipline* generally conjures up the idea of some sort of punishment from an external standpoint, which is why it tends to carry a negative connotation. We often struggle when an organization talks about discipline or the lack of it. It usually means that they are blaming their team members when something goes wrong:

- *Make a bad part*—"Write them up."
- *Did not hit the rate*—"Write them up."
- *Disagree with their group leader*—"Write them up."
- *Missed work*—"Write them up."

Oftentimes, if people will not follow the standard, it's due to one of two things: (1) The standard is wrong or there is a better way to do it, or (2) the person doesn't care and will do whatever they want. Both reasons need to be researched as to "Why?" We must not jump to the conclusion that it's the team member's fault.

Ritsuo Shingo says: "Never blame the worker. It's your fault not theirs. Figure it out!"

In our new environment, accountability starts at the top, and discipline is not a bad word. We as leaders need to look at the system surrounding the team members and always be considering how we can improve the system and make our team members successful. In this new culture, discipline should be an enabling constraint and should be viewed positively as a quality for each of us to develop.

Discipline can be external or internal. From an external standpoint, it is following the rules and, if not, being subjected to some type of negative reinforcement. However, internal discipline is the ability we develop in ourselves to take the initiative, stick to a plan, follow the rules, get to meetings on time, adhere to standard work, meet our deadlines, and so on.

Discipline is a key ingredient in the recipe for continuous leadership development. Without discipline, there is chaos. We need people to have the discipline to follow standard work, put things back where they belong, get back from breaks on time, start on time, follow through on audits, conduct root cause analysis, and create the continuous improvement environment. If they have a suggestion or better idea . . . great! Then let's try it out, video it, and find out if it really is a better way. If so, then we can update the standard work.

As a leader, we have a responsibility to follow our own "leader standard work." We must role model discipline through our behavior. If team members do not follow the standard work, we need to coach them to follow it and may have to show them how to do it. The best way to train team members is using the Team Member Self-Reliance system, which puts accountability on the trainers to teach the student and then for the student to be accountable for ongoing improvement.

Remember, if the student has not learned . . . the teacher has not taught.

Notes

1. Product failure mode effects analysis.
2. Adopting Mission Command, Don Vandergriff MA RSA, Naval Institute Press, ©2019 Don is the Academic Officer and Chief Trainer for Special Tactics LLC. He is an author and speaker, https:// specialtactics.me/ email: Vandergriffdonald@usa.net.
3. Strategos, Inc. Pioneers of Lean Manufacturing—Taiichi Ohno & Shigeo Shingo, Featuring an Interview With Norman Bodek, Author of Kaikaku: The Magic and Power of Lean. 2004.

Chapter 7

BASICS® Implement—Skills and System Deployment

Figure 7.1   BASICS® Lean Leadership Development Path Implement/Check.

Source: BIG training materials.

> *A company's senior leadership must take on the mission to create and reinforce such a "self-educating" culture. Like so many cultural attributes, this is best done first through example and then by promoting the careers of subordinates who practice it.[1]*

> —**Chet Richards**

To quickly review, Step 1 was Baseline, which covered Team Member Self-Reliance (TSR). Step 2 was to Analyze and Suggest Solutions, which we did by studying how to improve business practices.

DOI: 10.4324/9781315155227-7

Implement and Check is Step 3 in our BASICS® Leadership Development Path (see Figure 7.1), which we call Skills and System Deployment. We discuss Step 3 over the next few chapters in this book, combining various pieces of the people and tools implementation of the BASICS® model. Team members learn to implement and check results by practicing their training on the job, which was learned in the self-reliance and business practice teachings.

The idea behind Skills and System Deployment is to take the tools learned earlier, TSR and Improving Business Practices, in the classroom and apply them to the physical job at hand. You are taught in the classroom, but the training really starts on the shop floor. This is also known as the apprentice/journeyman approach. This practice on the shop floor (or in the office) is intertwined with a focus on delivering to the production schedule and meeting our Customer First commitment, that is, high quality, lowest cost, and delivered just in time. The coaching, whenever possible, involves asking thoughtful questions to the group leaders. It means giving them clues but not the answer, challenging them to grow by sometimes letting them fail, and providing feedback including correcting, praising, and motivating them.

The other goal is gaining this experience in a safe environment where it is okay to make mistakes. More exposure to increased skills across the organization helps build a person's orientation repertoire[2] or knowledge, skills, and ability repository.[3] This increases the individual's trust and the capability to make faster intuitive judgments when needed. We often tell group leaders they should be able to "feel" how the machine or production area is doing like you can feel when your car will shift into the next gear. One needs to strive to become adept and the master of their area(s) of responsibility. This gets back to do you know what you don't know. This will lead to optimizing the people development cycle.

On-the-Job Development

Toyota considers human resource development (see Figure 7.2), that is, developing and growing their employees, to be indispensable to maintaining the drive for continuous improvement. Practicing the actual work is the most effective way of learning, because adults learn

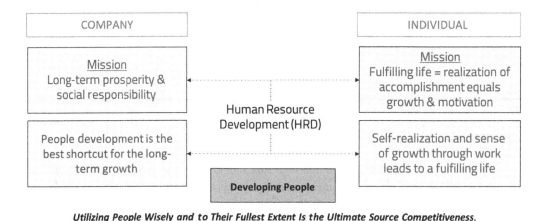

Utilizing People Wisely and to Their Fullest Extent Is the Ultimate Source Competitiveness.

Figure 7.2 Human Resource Development—Linkage from Individual to Company.

Source: BIG training materials.

best by doing. Toyota's philosophy is that by growing their people, they are also growing the company. This process is viewed as an investment, not a cost. The theory behind it is that employees will appreciate the value gained through their personal growth while at the same time their accomplishments will contribute to the company's continuous development, thus reducing turnover.

The other theory behind it is that if you can hire someone to fill a position from the outside then a competitor can do the same. At Toyota, there are things that team members learn from apprenticeship while moving up through the ranks that is knowledge that cannot be obtained outside Toyota. It is the same philosophy behind jidoka. If you can custom design and build machines that stop before it makes a mistake, it is something your competition does not have access to in the market. This becomes a barrier to entry for the competitor. In the same way, one could view Toyota's human resource development program as a barrier to entry.

If a company starts with the premise that everyone is replaceable, then they probably have a low employee retention rate, high training costs, and lots of firefighting. These areas are not easily measured and where executives tend not to focus, but it impacts the company's overall competitiveness. If your company has a low retention rate, what does it say about your on-the-job human resource development program? What is the incentive for company loyalty or retention? It is Toyota's policy to use human resource development as a foundation for people's trust, ability to think, teamwork, and respect for each individual. As a leader, developing people becomes your full-time job, not a part-time job.

Being satisfied with the status quo means you are not making progress.

—**Katsuaki Watanabe**[4]

On-the-Job Development

Four steps compose the on-the-job development process.

1. *Knowledge, Skills, and Abilities*

   a. Understand the jobs within your workplace.
   b. Understand your team members' knowledge, skills, and abilities.
   c. Team members are selected for the job based on their cross-training table.

2. *Interpersonal Relations and Self Awareness*

   a. Motivate your team members and provide a fun and learning atmosphere.
   b. Challenge team members to think and perform.
   c. Follow up, and share your feedback.

3. *Group Leader and Team Leader Roles*

   a. Audit your team members' daily work and understand their situation and concerns.
   b. If your team member is not meeting expectations, let them know and work together to identify the root cause.
   c. Work with your team members to coach and motivate them to follow and improve the standards.

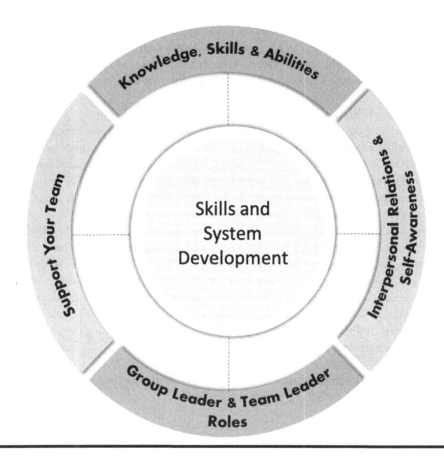

Figure 7.3   Skills and Systems Deployment (On-the-Job Development).

Source: BIG training materials.

4. *Support Your Teams*
   a. Evaluate their work.
   b. Provide constructive feedback.
   c. Recognize their efforts
   d. Evaluate yourself as a leader. Did you lead your team, follow the standards, and hit/improve the targets?

1. Knowledge Skills and Abilities

It is important to understand the jobs within your workplace and your team members' knowledge, skills, and abilities. Team members should be selected for the job not just based on their experience but also based on their strengths and weaknesses and then added to the cross-training table. There has to be an overlap between work that needs to be done, should be done, and team members that have the ability and want to do it.[5] "Use me wisely . . . is what most team members want." Every employee wants to feel like they accomplished something at the end of the day. This means we give them work with a challenge to always be thinking about how we can do it better. We need to come up with ways to motivate the person doing the work based on the company's purpose and values and show how their work links to customer value.

Leadership and leadership style is situational. The more advanced the team, the more the leader will be required to eventually evolve from just a disciplinarian to the role of internal consultant and coach to the team. The knowledge, skills, and abilities[6] of the team determine the role of the leader. In addition, the leaders must continually transfer their knowledge, skills, and abilities to enable their team to evolve. The organization needs a system to create, store, and transfer knowledge to its team members.

The group leader role can chew you up and spit you out if you do not thrive in an ever-changing environment. Many times, we put people in these roles because they were the best team members or had excellent attendance; however, those reasons alone are not a good enough reason to put someone in that position.

The group leader needs to be the face of the company. Your team members will watch their team leader and group leaders and will march to their beat. I often tell companies that the first-line leaders will make or break your company.[7] They typically are the heartbeat of your organization. As they go, you will go, and they can take you places you never thought you could go. The way they are developed and mentored is critical to your organization's success.

The group leader must constantly focus on their own development as a leader and as a continuous improvement implementer. They require formal classroom training and need day-to-day management, coaching, and guidance on the shop floor. They require established routines in their place of work. We call this leader standard work. Acquiring knowledge should not be considered the only goal; we must also practice the new skills and develop ourselves while developing our people. Do not just train . . . coach and develop continuously using the following equation:

Learn (Acquire new job *Knowledge*) + *Improve* (add new problem-solving *Skills*) + *Practice* (On-the-job skills development becomes *Abilities*) = *Sustain*.

The group leaders must watch the processes with their team leaders and team members and ask questions to make them see the waste and learn how to improve the process. They need to allow their team leaders and team members to teach back the process as the group leader is teaching them. This not only promotes active listening,[8] it allows the team member, team leader, and group leader to see the process differently. This is essential to how leaders develop while they are developing leaders.

2. Interpersonal Relations

The interpersonal relations training (see Figure 7.4) is targeted to the foundations of participative management and is part of the skills development and implementation portion of the Leadership Development Path. A group leader must get results through people. The training is broken down into good team member relations[9] and how to handle team member situational type problems described as follows:

1. Let each team member know how they are getting along.
2. Give credit when due. Course correct when required.

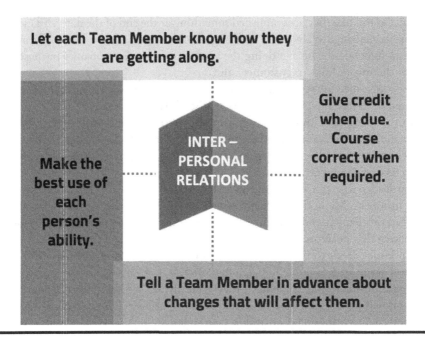

Figure 7.4 Skills and Systems Development (On-the-Job Development).

Source: BIG training materials.

3. Tell a team member in advance about changes that will affect them.
4. Make the best use of each person's ability.

Some benefits of creating a good development process are seen in Figure 7.5.

"I¹⁰remember sending a manufacturing manager to train on changeover reduction (how to reduce setup times) as part of his development plan. He went to the training with the understanding that he had to use his new knowledge on a regular basis when he returns. The next week we met to discuss the project to develop a new changeover for a particular model. He started the meeting telling me how much he learned and how excited he was to use his newfound knowledge. I asked him if he had selected a product line and team of cross-functional team members to participate. He told me he did not but would work on it over the next couple days.

We set a time to review his progress a few days later, and again I received similar responses. This happened for the next two weeks. It was evident to him that I was now frustrated with the lack of progress. He said to me, 'I am not sure you understand how busy I am, but I really do not know if I can spare the time to work on special projects'. Please keep in mind that I was a newly hired Vice President of Operations for this company and the mission was trying to change the culture and implement the Lean systems.

I discussed with the manufacturing manager the following: "Jim, I think it's really important that you and I have a very clear understanding of the roles and the responsibilities and how we need to perform the role." I went on to say that implementing Lean systems is not a special project or something on the side that you try to fit into your job. It is the job! I then went on to talk with him about evaluating the things he is doing on a daily basis and determine what he shouldn't be doing to allocate time for the

Benefits of Human Resource Development for Group Leaders

Productivity

- Organization's productivity is the summation of an individual's accomplishments. With individual capability improvement, the organization's productivity increases.

Mutual Trust and Respect

- People feel grateful to the supervisor who encourages them to grow. Throughout the development processes, values are shared trust solidifies. This increases motivation with team members who try their best to contribute to the organization's goals.

Goal Deployment Time Management

- With the improvement of team members' abilities, supervisors can delegate more work, leaving themselves with more time to spend on higher-level tasks such as continuous improvement. This enables supervisors to lead the organization more efficiently and effectively toward accomplishing targets.

Personal Growth

- By teaching team members, group leaders increase their personal and professional growth.
- Development is a two-way activity.

Figure 7.5   Benefits of Human Resource Development to Group Leaders.

Source: BIG training materials.

important things, not just the urgent. This is where we began to create a common understanding of the role and used leader standard work to capture our agreements. We would develop a routine whereby weekly we would review performance against our agreements.

It was a moment where he and I had a crucial conversation, but it laid the groundwork for how we continued to evolve his role and how he performed his role. We needed that conversation to create alignment for the work to be done and he needed to have that same conversation with his team. Having ongoing dialogue with your team members will start creating alignment. They need to take place daily and your actions as leader are far more important than the words you say. In the balance of this section, we explore the tools, roles and responsibilities that go with skills and systems deployment. "The following contains the Toyota website's definitions for respect and teamwork.

Respect

In our relationships with our colleagues and with others, it is important everyone is respected both for what they contribute and for who they are. That includes their ideas and their cultural and personal beliefs. Through Respect we accept personal responsibility for what we do and build mutual trust and understanding with those around us. It is also central to our mission to build a diverse and sustainable workforce that reflects society around us and our changing customer base.[11]

Teamwork

Successful teamwork is about everyone understanding our goals and working together to achieve them. Every member of a team is given the opportunity to do their best and the accountability to achieve results. That is true throughout our business, from the boardroom to the production line. We recognize that our people are our greatest asset. We strive to give them stable employment and, with the Toyota Way, the opportunities to develop their skills, responsibilities and commitment as individuals and committed team members.[12]

How do these definitions from Toyota's website compare to the actions and behaviors one might observe in your culture?

Importance of the Leader Needing to Be Self-Aware
by Jonathan Peyton[13]

> *Until you make the unconscious conscious, it will direct your life and you will call it fate.*

—**Carl Jung**

While it is possible to be a good manager without a high degree of self-awareness, the benefits of understanding yourself and how you affect others, cannot be overstated. When you practice self-awareness, you will be able to create a culture where people do not fear repercussions when sharing an idea or giving feedback. This is how you tap into one of the most underutilized resources on earth, the minds of the people. When you are open and engaged, your people will be as well. Self-awareness works in different contexts:

- In the Personal Context—What I See is Self-Awareness. What I Do is Self-Management.
- In the Social Context—What I See is Social Awareness. What I Do is Relationship Management.[14]

My journey toward self-awareness began when I received feedback from my wife. She had an intuitive feeling based on witnessing my interactions with other individuals that I was not making any friends. She started giving me good, yet unsolicited, feedback. I did not appreciate the feedback initially; I thought she was too sensitive and making way too much out of nothing, hence part of my problem right there. The truth is that I was damaging relationships and limiting my opportunities with my "cutting" words and constant criticism of others. This began to change after I was passed over for a promotion.

I asked the people that interviewed me what I needed to work on to move up in the organization. They mentioned a few things but not enough to act on in a meaningful way. At the time I was reading lots of books on leadership and personal development. I needed a way to understand what was holding me back so I would know what to work on. I read about the 360-degree review (asking people from all the areas of your life for feedback on you) and decided to put one together for myself. I used a simple format in an email in which I asked about 15 people for feedback. I explained why I was asking for feedback and that I genuinely wanted to know what they thought.[15] I also included a few people that I knew did not like me.

I made it clear that I would not hold anything against them for answering candidly. I asked two simple questions:

- What are 3 things I do well?
- What are 3 things I need to improve?

Upon getting the feedback I was surprised both positively and negatively with the feedback, I synthesized the feedback so I could make a plan that would fundamentally change the way I interact with people. Now I smile more, ask more questions, do not make as many jokes about people, limit my interaction with digital devices when I have a person in front of me, and listen to understand not just to think of a response.

Implementing these concepts is a work in progress that I am aware of every day. There was much more that went into my journey toward self-awareness than I have room to write. The point is that no matter where you are on this journey, it's never too late to start asking the people around you about how they see you and what you should work on. The benefits are that it lets people know that you are open to feedback and that you want to do better. It helps people on your team trust you, be more open, and be willing to really engage. When it comes to changing leadership behaviors we need to really focus on our interactions with others.

Team Leader Versus Group Leader

There is a significant difference between a team leader and a group leader. Very simply put, the group leader is responsible for the people and a team leader is responsible for the process. The group leader has the responsibilities of hiring, selecting their team, terminating team members, develop, monitoring performance, and driving accountability and discipline. They are responsible for creating a culture of teamwork, trust, and participation.

3. Todays' Team Leader Role

The team leader is a key focus of the group leader. For our purposes, the term *team leader* refers to either the working team leader of a self-directed team and or the leader of an office area. The team leader is ultimately responsible for spending 50% of their time focusing on meeting the production plan requirements by supporting their teammates and 50% of the time spent on continuous improvement. Some will scoff at this, but if you are unable to spend this percentage of time on improvement, you are probably spending it on firefighting. The goal is to convert firefighting to ongoing improvement.

The team leader is an hourly team member and part of the production team. The role of a team leader is to manage hour to hour and day to day. They are key to the group leader's ability to be effective. The team leader is not the group leader's backup and does not manage people or performance issues. That boundary can never be crossed because that's the group leader's role. But they play a key role in the performance of the production team. Once they are trained, a team leader should be able to facilitate a point kaizen event or rapid improvement kaizen activity without outside assistance.

The team leaders do not have hiring or firing or disciplinary authority. They normally work in the cell or office area and are responsible for training and making sure their team members follow their standard work. They are responsible for hitting the hourly performance targets and surface and fix problems, "gaps," and ideas. If the identified gaps are beyond their control, they are responsible for escalating them to the group leader. The team leader is normally promoted from a team member or frontline office position.

To be successful these team members need a strong leader, stable infrastructure, process-focused goals, well-defined and robust measurement systems and standards, and staunch accountability for the achievement of those goals. The group leader must have the ability to guide the work team's performance on a daily basis. The group leader is ultimately accountable for the achievement of the goals and actions of their team leaders, teams, and their overall department.

Team Leaders' Responsibilities

1. Be the first responder to problems in your assigned area.
2. Manage the process not the people.
3. Provide team member training.
4. Be on the production floor at least 90% to 100% of the time.
5. Spend very limited time in meetings other than daily huddles.
6. Manage day-by-hour boards and documents when additional problem-solving is needed for temporarily implemented countermeasures.
7. Be able to perform all jobs in a team and fills in if someone is sick or on break.
8. Monitor adherence to schedule, quality, ergonomics, and safety.
9. Make sure standard work is available and adhered to.
10. Be extremely process-focused and encourage engagement of every team member in daily improvement.

Team Leaders' Daily Jobs

The team leader role is to be the expert trainer and monitor hour to hour performance. They fill out the day-by-hour charts, do standard work audits, 10-cycle analysis (see Figure 7.6), update standard work, and complete time-study analysis. A team leader on average should have four to six people, but the maximum can vary depending on the structure, individual roles, and geography. Toyota is a good example of leaders' intent. Their production teams are typically composed of four to six members, including the team leader. The group leader teams then have four to six members. Having a larger team will generally lead to teams not being managed properly. They need to be very well versed in all the Lean tools, but most important, they are responsible to set the tone and expectation of the team.

In a Toyota factory in Princeton, Indiana, highlighted during a CNN interview,[16] Don Dees said,

> We have 15 managers and 3 general managers. The people on the shop floor run the day to day operations. 2,000 people, making improvements every day, it's a dynamo. Every day you come out to the shop floor and something's changed, something's made better.

Ten Cycle Analysis Form

Video Name		Process Description	
Person Conductin 10 Cycle		Process Input Boundary	
Date		Process Output Boundary	

You can choose how many cycles you wish to run

Step No.	Description		Cycle 1	Cycle 2	Cycle 3	Cycle 4	Cycle 5	Cycle 6	Cycle 7	Cycle 8	Cycle 9	Cycle 10
		Cycle Time Min	1.60	1.90	2.12	2.55	1.90	1.85	1.98	1.95	2.08	2.05
		Cycle Time Secs	96	114	127	153.00	114.00	111.00	119.00	117.00	125.00	123.00
1	Step 1	At. Start Time (optional)	0	0	0	0	0	0	0	0	0	0
		Cum	10	11	14	11	12	13	15	16	16	10
		Split Time	10	11	14	11	12	13	15	16	16	10
2	Step 2	At. Start Time (optional)										
		Cum	16	15	15	16	16	17	35	20	20	15
		Split Time	6	4	1	5	4	4	20	4	4	5
3	Step 3	At. Start Time (optional)										
		Cum	30	32	27	41	40	43	44	41	45	47
		Split Time	14	16	12	25	24	26	9	23	25	32
4	Step 4	At. Start Time (optional)										
		Cum	54	59	107	123	115	117	120	119	125	126
		Split Time	24	27	40	42	35	34	36	38	40	39
5	Step 5	At. Start Time (optional)										
		Cum	101	105	120	154	127	125	130	129	135	133
		Split Time	7	6	13	31	12	8	10	10	10	7
6	Step 6	At. Start Time (optional)										
		Cum	121	122	129	206	135	133	140	139	147	145
		Split Time	20	17	9	12	8	8	10	10	12	12
7	Step 7	At. Start Time (optional)										
		Cum	136	154	207	233	154	151	159	157	205	203
		Split Time	15	32	38	27	19	18	19	18	18	18

Figure 7.6 10-Cycle Analysis.

Source: BIG training materials.

In order for a team leader to be effective, they need to have well-written leader standard-work sheets. These sheets are an agreement between the group leader and the team leader as to where their focus should be. The team leader does not write their own leader standard-work sheets; they are done in conjunction with or under the direction of their group leader who is aligned with middle management.

Without leader standard work, this position often turns into endless random checking, aimless wandering, firefighting, and being the gofer, break giver, garbage dumper, pop and potty break giver. Many organizations fail to realize the benefit of this role. Generally speaking, in well-run organizations that have this role, it's very well defined, and the team leader is a dedicated position that may substitute for breaks, absence, or team member improvement time but, otherwise, does not work on the line. Fifty percent of their time should be working on root-cause analysis and implementing team member suggestions.

How to Create the Team Leader Role[17]

The team leader role is an hourly position. The company at which I spent the first 17 years of my career made a very large investment in developing this team leader role. We called it a learning plan versus a training plan, and we called the team leader a team facilitator. The learning plan consisted of training including the following:

1. Standard work
2. Self-reliance and supervisor interpersonal relations
3. Problem-solving (Plan–Do–Check–Act [PDCA]) and the introduction to A3 thinking
4. The 5 Whys and the 5Ws and 2Hs
5. Process capability and in-station process control
6. Level 1 project management
7. 5S training
8. How to conduct time studies and fill in a part production capacity sheet
9. Value-stream mapping
10. Rapid improvement process

Well over 120 hours of training was completed before anyone was accepted in this role within the first year. It required demonstrated skill over time and ownership of the process and owner-ship for improvement of the process. We now call this the Skills and System Deployment part our Leadership Development Path.

Standard Work Audits—BASICS® Check

Just because people are meeting or exceeding the cycle times or metrics does not mean they are following the standard work. The only way one can know is to audit. This ties into the CHECK part of our BASICS® model (see Figure 7.7) and TSR. Every day, one of the primary group leader and team leader jobs is to audit their team members' standard work, not only to see if it is followed in the right sequence of steps but also to always look for and solicit improvement ideas from the team members. Challenging your team members to think is a way to get them engaged every day.

When the team leader audit is completed, any gaps should be brought to the attention of the person performing the job, so corrective action coaching can take place immediately. If the group leader is in the area, coaching should take place with the group leader present. If not, still do the coaching and contact the group leader so they can reinforce the coaching, monitor the operation,

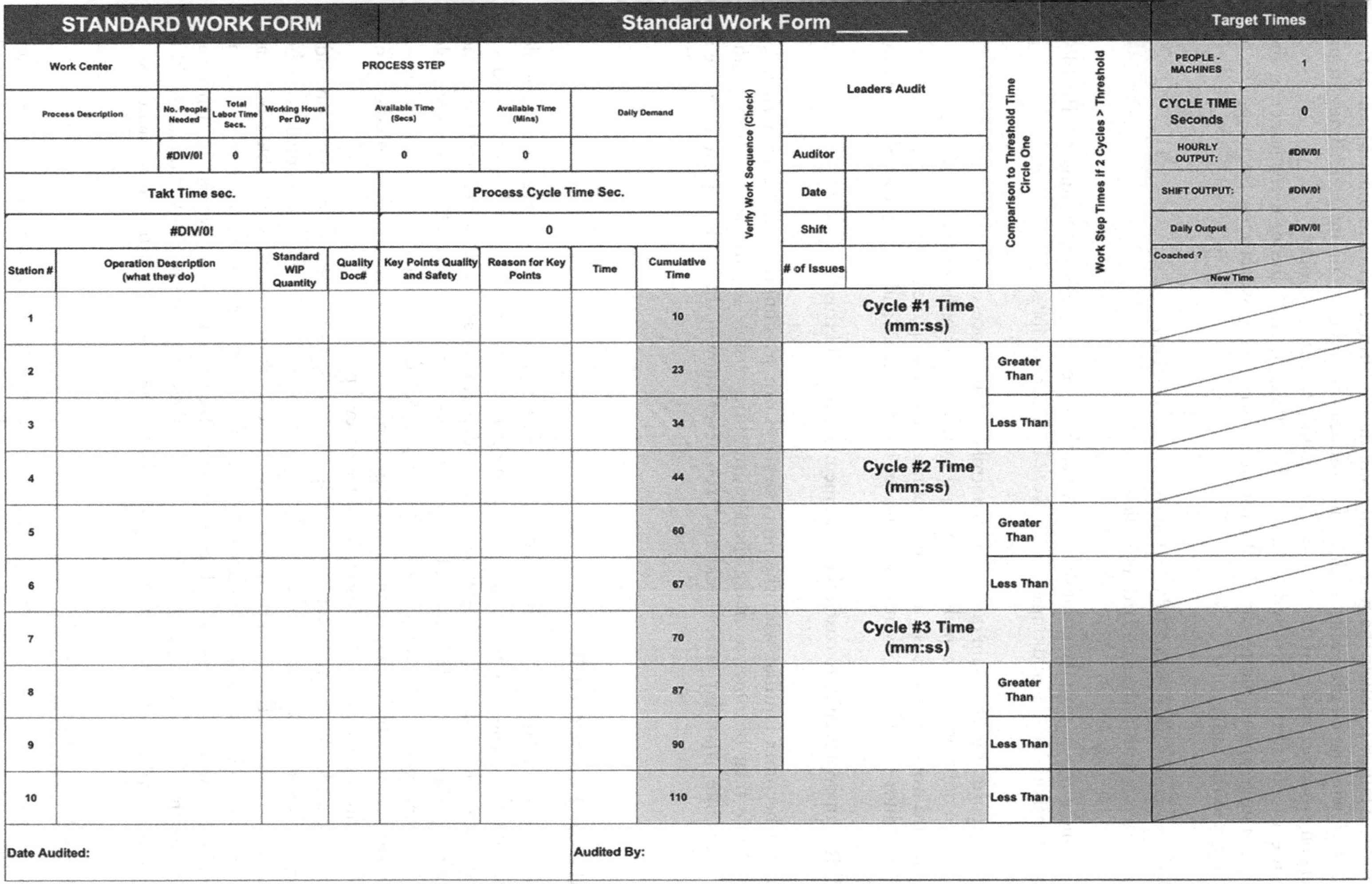

STANDARD WORK FORM

Standard Work Form

Target Times

PEOPLE-MACHINES	1
CYCLE TIME Seconds	0
HOURLY OUTPUT:	#DIV/0!
SHIFT OUTPUT:	#DIV/0!
Daily Output	#DIV/0!

Coached ?   New Time

Work Step Times if 2 Cycles > Threshold

Comparison to Threshold Time — Circle One

Leaders Audit — Auditor / Date / Shift / # of Issues

Verify Work Sequence (Check)

Work Center

Process Description	No. People Needed	Total Labor Time Secs.	Working Hours Per Day	**PROCESS STEP** Available Time (Secs)	Available Time (Mins)	Daily Demand
	#DIV/0!	0		0	0	

Takt Time sec.   #DIV/0!

Process Cycle Time Sec.   0

Station #	Operation Description (what they do)	Standard WIP Quantity	Quality Doc#	Key Points Quality and Safety	Reason for Key Points	Time	Cumulative Time		Cycle #1 Time (mm:ss)		Cycle #2 Time (mm:ss)		Cycle #3 Time (mm:ss)	
1							10							
2							23			Greater Than				
3							34			Less Than				
4							44							
5							60					Greater Than		
6							67					Less Than		
7							70							
8							87							Greater Than
9							90							Less Than
10							110							

Date Audited: Audited By:

Figure 7.7 Standard Work Audit Form.

Source: BIG training materials.

and evaluate if failure to follow the system will result in instituting short-term containment of the product. Following up on the audits is critical for reeducating and/or retaining (recertifying) team members on processes or identifying areas for improving the current process.

We use a tool called the Layered Process Audit (LPA). The LPA means every leader in the organization up to and including the CEO must audit various processes at some frequency. There are two steps to the audit:

1. The standard-work steps are followed in the proper sequence.
2. Each step is within the standard time allowed.

If we can find a way to mistake proof the problems, then the need to audit diminishes. The LPA frequency is negotiable, but auditing standard work is important for several reasons:

- It is important to maintain quality and control over the process.
- One can only sustain the quality if standard work exists, is audited, and is updated.
- Standard work is key to sustaining and maintaining a disciplined environment.
- The auditor should be constantly looking for improvements and asking team members for ideas.
- This is an opportunity to coach the team members to build trust and respect.

The auditor becomes familiar with the processes and can see abnormalities as they surface. The challenge then becomes to make the abnormalities visible to anyone. "Auditing standard work is like balancing your checkbook. You never know if the bank is going to make a mistake."[18]

4. Group Leader Role

The group leader can be over the shop floor or an office department. This person is responsible for hiring and firing and for disciplinary action. This person may sometimes do "hands-on work" in the area but is located on the shop floor or in the department area, not in a cozy office in the next building. The group leader is normally responsible for four to six teams. They are responsible for the achievement of their team's goals, which are inextricably linked to the company's strategic goals and are accountable to management. Management, in this case, is typically a middle manager, a plant manager, a general manager, or a director-level person.

The group leader is responsible for Step 3, Skills and System Development, for their team leaders. They should be promoted from the team leader position, which should be promoted from the team member position. They are responsible to plan the work by identifying suitable work that needs to be carried out while understanding their team's skill and grasp of the current condition, cross-training, and development plan. They are responsible to identify work worthy of their team members and maximize their team's motivation by challenging them to think thoroughly. The group leader determines the way to follow up and share observations with their team members.

Today's Group Leader Role

Today's group leader is considered a coach, similar to an athletic coach, who can help guide, correct, and show their team leader how to perform. They keep score on how the team is doing and can help correct their team's performance. Like a football coach, they watch videos of past games, which allows team members to see their performance and provides a basis for continuous and participatory improvement. The focus is on connecting the thought process of the individual with their performance within the system.

Group leaders not only have to be an inspiring individual that can foster continuous improvement; they also need to understand the BASICS® model and problem-solving tools and be the chief driver, promotor, and implementer of the overall improvement system. When we work with companies, we always tell them that their first-line leadership will be the main focus for implementation. It's critical that they have the desire and be open-minded. They can be taught the tools, but the leadership portion, if they are not born with it, must be developed, refined, and managed. To make it in this role, you have to have to be genuine, care about people, and have a bias for action and implementation. An effective group leader does not have to be followed up to see if they have completed their actions. They should be developed to an overall empowerment Level 4 or 5. This is discussed in more detail later.

If you want to be an effective first-line leader, you must be thirsty for knowledge and have the courage to make physical improvements in your environment. The more open to change you are, the more open to change your team will be. As a trainer, you must be able to know the job and be able to educate and train on the job. You are responsible to foster the learning environment. If you want to make it in this role, you must be the following:

1. Open to change and encourage risk.
2. Enjoy trying and experimenting
3. Be okay with failure as long as you and your team are learning.
4. Give credit away freely.
5. Enjoy the journey. It's about the process which leads to the results.
6. Be a people person first. Ritsuo Shingo says, "Lead with your heart."
7. Focus on the process.
8. Coach the thinking process, not the outcome you want, and find someone to coach you.
9. Understand your success is tied to the success of your team.
10. Reinvent yourself daily and never be satisfied with where you are today.

We like to say BASICS® creates the foundation by providing the tools and behaviors leaders need to be successful. The plant's current situation directly reflects the role of its past and current leadership.

Group Leader Responsibilities

The group leader should work to improve safety, quality, and eliminate waste. To be effective, they need to develop standard routines. Structured routines create an environment of daily tasks that are agreed on between group leaders and management. These routines include the seven general duties of a group leader. The duties start with safety and teamwork that will help make the numbers. If you focus just on the results, you will normally kill teamwork. The harder you work to make it simple, the more people will follow it.

1. Safety

    a. Be the advocate for safety and ergonomics by training and observing teams on the process and evaluate conformance with standardized work.

    b. Lead the safety talks and document team participation. Ensure the teams have safety training specific to their areas, lock-out tag-out, hazardous waste, materials safety data sheets, and so on.

    c. Implement and support the early safety investigation. Help the team leaders document accidents and near misses by going to the accident site and collecting team members' and the team leader's input on accident details. Help the team fill out the report and countermeasures and send documentation to Safety.

    d. Post and communicate accident and countermeasures to all teams and management and record all accidents in the team's file and on safety boards.

    e. Be responsible for training the evacuation plan and coordinate team evacuation and confirm all teams present and report to evacuation coordinators.

2. Daily Improvement and Teamwork

    a. Create the compelling need for change and ongoing improvement.

    b. Develop a vision for the team consistent with upper management.

    c. Encourage trust and good teamwork in your group and develop close working relationships with other group leaders.

    d. Resolve daily problems within the group, that is, production, safety quality, human resource problems, and so on.

    e. Create future leaders—Develop your teams and your people. Be the most knowledgeable of the work and become an expert on the machines.

        i. Utilize and improve your own skills.

        ii. Be able to actively listen—do not think of what to respond as the person is talking.

        iii. Do not tell but ask insightful questions.

        iv. Learn to manage conflict.

    f. Foster both mentor and mentee relationships—Kata is built on this.

3. Leader Standard Work

    a. Ensure your teammates are meeting customer quality specifications via hourly checks. Create and respond to visual controls.

    b. Conduct audits and drive continuous improvement.

    c. Establish regular daily interactions at the Gemba. This relationship is critical to develop the next level of learners.

4. Visual Management

    a. Make sure the 5S plan is implemented and sustained and evaluated daily.

    b. Use visual controls everywhere to expose problems and improve the team's understanding of the group's goals.

    c. Implement visual management everywhere possible—eliminate the need to physically check. This ensures that goals and actions are being managed versus firefighting and visually shows any abnormal conditions immediately.

5. Accountability—Make the numbers by supervising team leaders and team members.

    a. Be an advocate for the company and their teammates.

    b. Understand company policies and practice them.

    c. Understand the standards and standard work.

6. Discipline—Clear goals and process-focused key performance indicators with structured problem-solving.
7. Create a challenging environment with accountability while enforcing discipline to follow standard work and meet commitments.

   a. Run effective team meetings—first-line leadership needs a clear definition of deliverables that are reviewed daily.
   b. Get teams' input on processes and support teams in solving problems.
   c. Improve the efficiency of your group—use structured problem-solving like A3 to eliminate issues.
   d. Escalate problems as needed—communicate effectively from management to teams and from teams to management.

8. Maximize profitability through daily cost reduction

   a. Establish one-piece flow and eliminate overproduction wherever possible.
   b. Increase Productivity—Labor team reduction (indirect labor and direct labor).
   c. Reduce throughput time and minimize work in process (WIP).
   d. Run the lines:

      i. Ensure materials are available when required to feed the line.
      ii. Focus on meeting the takt time.
      iii. Manage the bottlenecks.
      iv. Utilize process and 24-hour boards.

   e. Track, record, and reduce changeover times.

Group Leader Daily Jobs

The group leader must convey that continuous improvement and problem-solving are the responsibilities of everyone. This means the system is constantly being improved by everyone's daily engagement working together to achieve the company goals. The group leaders must verify their lines are using the proper torques, quality checks, exchanges, temporary quality standards, and reworked or retrofitted parts are documented and communicated to the managers on other shifts. They are responsible for updating the standard work by observing and documenting their teams' compliance. They support and help coordinate the training plan, support their team's development, and ensure all documentation is accurate and signed off. They observe the Andon board and are part of the response team. They respond as secondary support to the team leader and help evaluate and countermeasure the line stops.

The group leader develops their team's awareness to look for different types of possible defects with an emphasis on future avoidance. They train their team members on the standard procedure to follow when a defect occurs. This helps get the line running and ensures quality.

The group leader trains their teams on the kanban and milk-run systems to make sure the work is pulled from the next station downstream. They observe team members handling of parts, monitor inventory levels, and report any discrepancies. They make sure that any part that does not meet the company's quality standards and cannot be repaired to meet standards is rejected.

They monitor scrap levels and report situations with root causes and countermeasures, ensure accuracy of scrap documents and verify with accounting reports, support problem-solving activity, and place hold tags on all parts as needed with necessary data. They monitor the plan for every part (PFEP; see Figure 7.8) reports to compare current usage and replenishment frequency and work with the Materials Department to establish and maintain a minimum and maximum amount for team supplies. They manage the correct handling of waste to make sure it is labeled correctly, monitor waste usage, and look for ways to reduce solid, liquid, and hazardous waste.

They support and coach teams in improving business practices using PDCA and A3 thinking, help document the gaps, support their team with developing short- and long-term countermeasures, evaluate the countermeasures' effectiveness, and verify updates to the job instruction training and standard work. They work with the quality circle[19] leader(s) to teach problem-solving when needed, advise the circle of potential problems (themes) to work on, and promote participation. They encourage and stress the importance of daily continuous improvement, ensure the process is stable beforehand, get baseline metrics, evaluate the effectiveness of the improvement activity, and help support it. They also pass along the improvements to the other shifts and evaluate the effectiveness with daily follow-up.

They maintain all documentation, that is, attendance records, vacation requests, absence reports, attendance calendar, add records, and the like; administer attendance policy consistently in all instances; maintain the supply of all attendance-related forms; and ensure the correct routing of all documents. They track attendance and sign all requisitions for overtime. They continually look for ways to reduce overtime and get prior approval if needed. They also plan major overtime activities to increase group efficiency.

The daily paperwork role of group leaders includes shift-to-shift and direct runs; quality, safety, productivity charts, attendance, suggestion forms; quality awards; scrap reports; build-ahead status; and all teams' evaluations. They document team performance in quality, following standardized work, teamwork, human relations items, and so on, including both positive and negative information. They file all required documentation, organize files, and purge all outdated files.

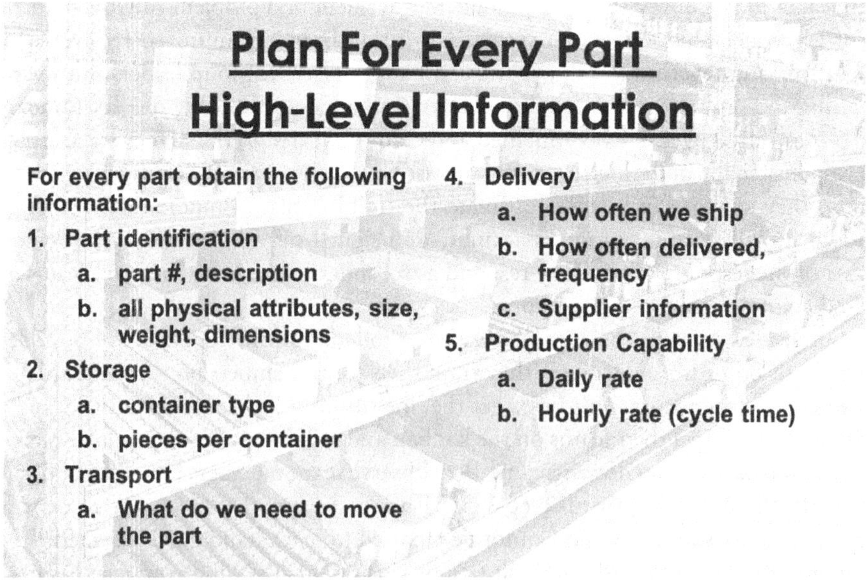

Plan For Every Part
High-Level Information

For every part obtain the following information:

1. Part identification
   a. part #, description
   b. all physical attributes, size, weight, dimensions
2. Storage
   a. container type
   b. pieces per container
3. Transport
   a. What do we need to move the part

4. Delivery
   a. How often we ship
   b. How often delivered, frequency
   c. Supplier information
5. Production Capability
   a. Daily rate
   b. Hourly rate (cycle time)

Figure 7.8 Plan for Every Part Example.

Source: BIG training materials.

They keep all confidential files secured from all others. They document specific positive or negative actions with problem individuals, being careful to deal with only the facts and document all discussions supporting team members' development. The most critical aspect of addressing performance is to act fairly and strive to achieve the best solution for both the company and the team member.

A group leader is to develop his or her teams until they reach the next level. This requires the group leader effectively teach their team all the knowledge they have obtained through the continuous learning process. This shared knowledge enables all teams the opportunity and direction for growth and advancement to the next level, which is directly linked to the group leader's ability to advance. They must be able to communicate effectively with all levels of the organization, and all teams should be treated with fairness, equality, dignity, and respect.

Group Leaders and Standardization

As stated, several times, without standards there can be no quality. Imagine if a dollar bill could be any varying amounts of cents or an inch could be any length. This is a central theme for the group leader and they must live for it. The group leaders should implement one-piece flow wherever possible and manage and standardize their equipment, materials, and time in the most efficient manner to produce the highest-quality product at the lowest possible cost for the customer in the shortest possible lead time while paying the utmost respect to the teams who make the system work. Without a standard, there can be no improvement.[20] The group leader should design the work in the best sequence for each assembly and machining process and ensure it is always repeated the same way. This avoids excess motion and wasted effort while maintaining safety, quality, and preventing equipment damage.

The Trust Triangle

A group leader needs to be able to earn the trust of their team members. There are many models of trust out there. . . . Just google it. We like the following discussion from Frances Fei and Anne Morris:[21]

> So how do you build up stores of this foundational leadership capital? In our experience, trust has three core drivers: authenticity, logic, and empathy. People tend to trust you when they believe they are interacting with the real you (authenticity), when they have faith in your judgment and competence (logic), and when they feel that you care about them (empathy). When trust is lost, it can almost always be traced back to a breakdown in one of these three drivers.

(See Figure 7.9.)

"In order to build trust as a leader, you first need to figure out which of the three drivers you "wobble" on. People don't always realize how the information (or, more often, the misinformation) that they're broadcasting may undermine their own trustworthiness. What's worse, stress tends to amplify the problem, causing people to double down on behaviors that make others skeptical. For example, they might unconsciously mask their true selves during a job interview, even though that's precisely the type of less-than-fully-authentic behavior that reduces their chance of being hired.

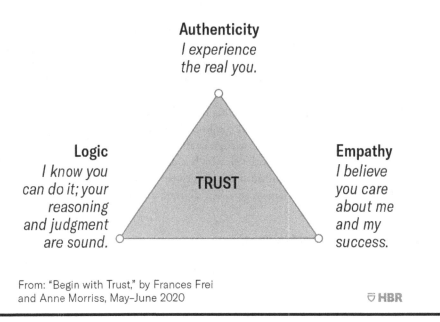

From: "Begin with Trust," by Frances Frei
and Anne Morriss, May–June 2020

Figure 7.9   The Trust Model.

Source: HBR Begin with Trust, by Frances X. Frei and Anne Morriss, From the May–June 2020 issue, used with permission.

The good news is that most of us generate a stable pattern of trust signals, which means a small change in behavior can go a long way. In moments when trust is broken or fails to get any real traction, it's usually the same driver that has gone wobbly on us—authenticity, empathy, or logic. We call this driver your "trust wobble." In simple terms, it's the driver that's most likely to fail you. Everybody, it turns out, has a trust wobble. To build trust as a leader, you first need to figure out what yours is."[22]

5. Support Your Teams and Create a Good Work Environment

The group leader should always support their teams. In just about every company at which we have worked, people like to complain about other people. They may work for them, with them, or even above them, but in the end, it is very unproductive and creates bad morale and an unpleasant workplace. We train the group leaders how to handle this situation, as we do not tolerate this behavior in the organization and quickly escalate to the executive leadership when necessary.

A large part of creating support for your teams begins with developing and fostering empowerment for the people in your group or organization. One of the best things you can do as a manager is empowering those below you in order to develop them to their fullest potential. Different people will be at different levels of empowerment based on their past performance, behavior, and mindset. It's important that you recognize the different levels of empowerment to help you determine what level your people should be at. Once you determine their level of empowerment, the goal is to continue to work with them and move them up to the next level once they're ready.

Empowerment—Freedom Scale[23]

Team member empowerment and participation are central tenets to the foundation of leadership development. Empowerment includes acknowledging the freedom scale (see Figure 7.10) level for the team leader and their team. Team member participation means that we are constantly striving to get ideas from our team members on how we can improve the processes. It can be in the form of a suggestion system (but not suggestion boxes) as part of a daily huddle meeting, quality control circles, or gemba walk inquiries. If we are not tapping into our team members' brain power, we are missing a valuable component of the Leadership Development Path. The freedom scale represents the comfort levels between a manager/group leader and their direct reports or teams they are championing. The scale can be utilized for empowering individual tasks, job descriptions, and team projects. Let us discuss each of these five levels listed from low to high:

1. Told What to Do
2. Ask What to Do
3. Recommend, Then Take Action
4. Take Action, Notify at Once
5. Take Action, Notify Periodically

Level 1: Told What to Do

The Level 1 team member begins on the first day of work or when the team or staff member is presented with a new task. The staff member is so new that they may not even know how to answer the phone. For example, most companies have a specific way they would like their employees to

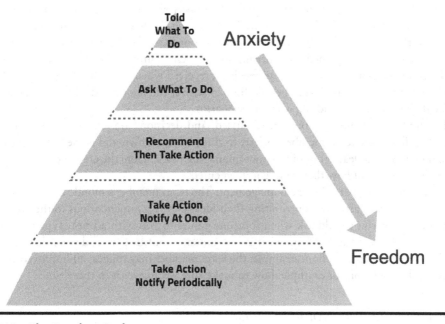

Figure 7.10   The Freedom Scale.

Source: BIG training materials.

answer the phone. If you are new, you are probably just going to answer the phone the way you would normally at home, "Hello, how can I help you?" instead of the standard, which is "Hello, thank you for calling the Business Improvement Group, how may we assist you?"

At which level will they be working? The answer is Level 1. Team members do specifically what they are told, normally nothing more or less. In this mode, one may find the team member standing around with nothing to do because they have completed their assigned task. If asked why they did not tell someone they were idle, they will usually respond with a version of "I wasn't told to do that!"

Level 2: Ask What to Do

As team members progress through the freedom scale, for each task, job, or decision they must gain a better understanding of the task along with their manager's acceptance or comfort level with the team member or team and the like. For example, someone can be proficient at a task but not necessarily have good people skills. So, there must be some level of comfort involved as well when empowering on a task. Additionally, the team member, in turn, must feel they have the proficiency and comfort level to perform the task.

The managers will now tell the team member to start asking what to do next. At Level 2, the employee no longer asks if they should answer the phone but is taught and guided by the standard work on how to answer the phone and the expectation to answer it within so many rings. In some cases, Levels 1 and 2 are good opportunities to ask the team member if they see any waste or "stupid things" being done in the plant or process that could be improved as they are not yet "boiled frogs."

Level 3: Recommend, Then Take Action

At this level, managers are much more comfortable with the team member, and the team member is much more confident and competent with their tasks or decisions. Now the team member is told to recommend what they think should be done next. If they present a problem, they should be asked to think about what the answer might be prior to providing the answer.

At Level 3, they have gained more orientation in their environment and are able to make decisions based on previous experiences and feedback received when answering the phone. They now have the "intent" from their leader behind how to answer the phone and what to say, gained over time by their experience handling different scenarios.

The problem and the solutions are discussed, and decisions are jointly made on a course of action. This forces the team member to start to think on their own and is the first step to moving the team member and leader out of the micromanaging mode. Here the employee starts to identify reasons for change and how they can be implemented.

This is the start of participative management. The team member's morale and motivation will increase because they are now contributing their ideas and recommendations to the organization. The first question you should ask when someone comes to you with a linear type of problem is, "Can you clearly state the problem, what is the standard and the gap, and what do you think we should do about it?" In our phone example, the team member may suggest an improvement to how we answer the phone or, for example, how to make sure we answer it in three rings.

Level 4: Take Action, Notify at Once

At this level, managers are very comfortable with the team member, and the team member or team is totally competent with the task(s) and decisions. Team members are told, "From this point on,

I am going to trust you to take the appropriate action and implement the solution to solve the problem or complete the particular job or task at hand."

We have shifted the authority now from the phone call example to where the information resides, and at Level 4, the team member can fully initiate phone calls and even incorporate an andon cord scenario in which they feel comfortable enough to raise any red flags, or make real-time adjustments, because a psychologically safe environment has been established by shifting from a delegation to an intent-based leadership. At this point, the team member may be requested to start training others in the phone call process.

The manager, however, also tells the team member(s) to notify them immediately of the actions taken. This is just in case they missed a step or did not totally think things through for mitigating risk. Team members are trusted, but managers may want to make sure things were done properly or provide damage control if necessary. We call this "trust but verify." Managers must make sure that team members at this level are on a professional growth plan to move up within the organization so team members can develop to their full potential.

Level 5: Take Action, Notify Periodically

At this level, the manager and their team member are extremely comfortable with each other and the process; the team member is competent and can be trusted implicitly. Team members are told to make whatever decisions are necessary and report back via a weekly, monthly, or quarterly report. In this case, our team member can work to improve the phone call process or make any changes they deem necessary which support the Customer First principle.

Every team member should be moved to Level 3 as quickly as possible. This requires ongoing training and mentoring (Kata) to be successful. Managers who have trouble with this level stick out once you know the tell signs.

When a team member comes to a manager with a problem and does not come prepared with a solution, recommendation, or prepared to have a discussion and the manager simply answers the question or provides the solution, they force their team members to stay at Level 2, and they have impeded their ability to grow.

A leader with all their team members always below Level 3 can be classified as a micromanager. The micromanager has an ever-increasing desire for control that results in destroying trust in the team and slowing everything down, sometimes to a stop, because they are not available to give the requested direction. This is why we maintain that leadership is situational and not one size fits all. Level 1 and 2 employees need to be told what to do. As they progress, you can move toward more of a leader's intent environment.

Delegation Should Be Based on the Leaders' Intent Whenever Possible

We should strive to shift authority to where the information resides. Leading requires a level of comfort with delegation. Delegating is not something we learn in school, but it is a powerful tool that, when done correctly, implies the delegate to follow the intent of the leaders who gave the command. Managers or group leaders may typically resist delegating a task or project because they do not think anyone else is as qualified to do it as well or as fast as they could. Engaging frontline staff in problem-solving and supporting them require managers to be able to empower and delegate activities, but there is an understood agreement that they will do these tasks with the best interest of the company in mind.

Some managers are not as proficient in coaching or mentoring. Many times, it is because based on their past experiences, they like to have total control and simply do not trust other people. They have almost an innate comfort in knowing and managing every detail and making every decision, micromanaging, as it were. However, these managers seldom advance far in their careers. They do fine until the number of decisions that must be made outstrips the time they have available to make them. Then their team members start waiting hours, days, weeks or even months before they get a decision.

We are not saying that there aren't decisions a leader must always make, but by always making the decision or giving them the answer, you are, in fact, not developing your people or really encouraging them to think. What will happen the next time they encounter a problem? The managers will be asked again for the answer. Some managers relish being the "be all and end all," the person who always saves the day and provides all the answers. Some team members enjoy this, as it keeps them from ever taking any accountability or responsibility for their actions and they will always be able to blame the manager because they made the decision. Many actually see this as job security because if they never make a mistake, they can never be blamed for making a bad decision. As a result, they are never afforded an opportunity to make a mistake and therefore never forced to learn from a bad decision.

We always tell managers that if you cannot learn to delegate and develop your people, you will never have a successor because no one will ever be ready to take your place, which means you cannot advance in the organization. Once you have identified where your members are on the freedom scale, it will also help in determining what level of tasks you ought to be delegating. Not knowing where someone is on the freedom scale could be a contributing factor to a previous time when someone wasn't able to accomplish what you delegated.

A Freedom Scale Example

During our initial journey,[24] I remember facilitating my first point kaizen event. Nobody in the company even knew I was doing it. I only did it because I was witnessing another work area doing point kaizen with a consultant and was watching to see what they were doing.

1. They were moving from batch to one-piece flow.
2. They were doing time studies.
3. They were moving workstations around in the form of a U.
4. They were developing standard work.

I really did not understand what they were doing or why they were doing it. I just knew they were doing it and we were just communicating that we were on a path of this Lean stuff—whatever that was. I was a production group leader, and we were told they wanted us to be mini plant managers so that is what I thought we were supposed to do. So, we started doing the following:

1. Video
2. Time study
3. Develop standard work
4. Balance the line
5. Prepare for implementation

This is where one of my biggest learning comes from that I still remember almost every day. The production line we were working on went through a major transformation three months prior.

One hundred fifty thousand dollars' worth of turntables were purchased and installed by the equipment facilities engineer, let's call him Doug. He never consulted us, just put them in over a weekend. The turntables did what they were intended to do, but it did not fit our new one-piece-flow process directive. Doug forced us to go back to batching with quality problems everywhere.

So, I decided to do my own point kaizen event where we were going to remove them and simply use standard WIP (SWIP) to provide time for the parts to cure. We tore the new turntables out on Saturday, moved workstations around, did our standard work, and were ready for Monday production. As we were getting the shift ready to start up, Doug came flying down the aisle, livid, and asked me what the hell we did. I simply said we did a point kaizen event. He looked at me with steam coming out his ears, his face was red, and he was visibly upset and said "I am going to get the plant manager," let's call him Pete.

Now I barely knew Pete. He was probably four or five levels removed, and this was a big plant. I only knew him from when he told us we needed to be mini plant managers, whatever that meant. Five minutes later, I see Doug and Pete walking down the aisle toward our new improved one-piece-flow work cell. Pete had only been in his job for a few weeks at the time, so I had no idea what to expect. He walked up to me and asked what I was working on. I told him we did a point kaizen event. He asked how it was working. I said, "Good, but we still have some bugs to work out." He asked, "What did we do with the big new turntables?" I told him we removed them and threw them outside. He asked why we did that, and I said they did not fit with one-piece flow. He asked who gave me permission to do a point kaizen on this line. I told him that I was operating under his direction, that we were responsible for our work cell, and that I just did it. He said, "Okay, thanks for the update," and if I needed anything to please let him know. Doug had big disappointment showing in his eyes as they both walked away.

I really never gave it another thought for years until I was in a position in which I had to empower people to make decisions and give them the latitude to make them. I am sure Pete was processing thousands of things in his mind on how to handle this. If he got upset, he would have stifled me and others from taking a chance in the future. If he told me that I should have asked permission to do the event, he would have really stripped me of acting like a mini plant manager. If he disciplined me or scolded me, it would have told all the other team members that they really weren't empowered.

Small acts like this can really shape people's careers. I called Pete as I was writing this book, and oddly enough, he doesn't even remember this event while for me, it is something I'll never forget. We influence people every day and often without knowing it. I also called Doug. He's still pissed off about it, lol. I did tell Doug it's been 20 years now, so he can let it go. As a group leaders, we want to provide an environment to fail safely and learn through the process of failure. This will encourage them and challenge them to think outside the box. It will push their comfort zone and threshold of knowledge. If you allow experimenting and pushing the threshold of knowledge, you will find the percentage of time it fails will decrease.

There is no one-size-fits-all solution. We are providing examples of what we and others have done to highlight options one can consider in making leadership decisions. If leadership was clear cut, there wouldn't be so many books on it. You must be situationally aware and understand the context before you act. To not only make it in this role but to also thrive in this role, you have to wear many hats, including mentor, counselor, friend, teacher, principal, judge, juror, bartender, scientist, engineer, industrial engineer, safety person, material manager, Lean expert, scheduler, maintenance leader, statistician, and quality person.

While you cannot be all those things, all the time, you must be knowledgeable and able to coach and develop those roles within your teams. This is your job as the group leader. To be an effective leader, you have to have a genuine concern for both people and the business.

When I was first starting out, one former manager used to always say, "All your decisions need to be taken into consideration; both the needs of the people and the needs of the business." Trying to balance those two needs seems simple and basic in nature, but it's an extremely difficult balancing act.[25]

Types of Leaders We Don't Want to Role Model

- The Politician/Career Manager—This leader is self-centered and only cares about one thing: managing their career and getting to the next rung on the ladder. They will say or do anything, throw anyone under the bus, and so on to achieve their goals even if it means a negative impact to the company or customer. They are typically good schmoozers and will say anything they think their boss wants to hear. This leader will only develop people if they see it as a way to advance.
- The Superman Manager—This leader believes no one else can do as good a job as themselves and as a result never delegates or develops their people.
- The Flowery Leader—This leader only focuses on the positives and never provides negative feedback. As a result, people only develop based on their strengths but never develop their weaknesses.
- The Hands-Off Leader—This leader has no time for details and never visits the floor or talks to the people that do the job. This leader, when asked for a report from upper management, immediately delegates it. When the person they delegate it to asks for help the leader responds: "Well if you can't do it, I can find someone else that can." There is no coaching or mentoring for their people. It's sink or swim.
- The Blind Delegator—This leader blindly empowers their subordinates regardless of their knowledge skills and abilities. This hurts the development of their people who already know the job and hinders those who do not yet have the skills to do the job.
- The Puppet Leader—this leader agrees to any request above them regardless of how it will impact their people. Team members end up confused with multiple priorities and no direction.
- The Micro Leader—This leader always keeps their people in a freedom scale Level 1 (told) or 2 (ask what to do next) state. They never develop their people to think for themselves.

Participative Versus Permissive Management

Be careful to not confuse the difference between participative management and permissive management. Participative management is a key to the implementation of any Lean organization as well as developing a strong culture that thrives on incremental changes and where ideas are freely exchanged to improve the process as well as organization where to be good overall is the priority. Everybody needs to participate. But participation is not the same for everybody in every situation. Participation can come in the following levels:

1. Designing the new process
2. Improving the process
3. Adhering to the process

Each of these levels is critical to not only the success of any organization but also understanding that everybody is participating by performing within these three levels. Every change isn't going to be universally supported or agreed on by everybody. This is where leadership has to lead by making sure people understand what level of participation or empowerment individuals are going to have.

Permissive management is where one tries to make everybody happy and one who constantly changes their position on an issue or decision based on who they are speaking to at the time. If everybody doesn't agree with the direction or the new process, it's decided not to move forward with the new or variety of scenarios.

As an example, a team suggested redistributing the workload based on data and participation from selected team members. The team then developed standard work for the new process and presented it to the operations manager. The operations manager really liked the new design and said, "Great job; now let's meet with the group leaders on the other shift to get their buy-in because if we don't, it will fail." The core team met with the off-shift group leaders and gained their support and buy-in. They left the meeting by saying, "Now we need to meet with the team members on each shift to get their buy in or it won't work." The team broke up into three groups, and the representatives from each shift met with their present shifts to present to the teams. All three team members reported back that 90% of the team members were fully supportive and thought it would work really well.

In the end, it turned out that one team member who didn't think it would work complained so much and so loud that they ended up blocking the entire process because leadership was hesitant to move forward. This individual didn't provide any additional suggestions or other options; they just didn't like the new process and were very vocal about it but would give no objection other than it was different.

After the team presented to the operations manager, they were not allowed to move forward with the changes. They were told to take three weeks to go back and reanalyze the process. They came back with the same conclusion and suggestions, and the operations manager finally granted authorization to move forward with the new process. This is an example of permissive management in which the leader wants to move forward but is afraid of upsetting one or some of the team members. This is different from someone having a valid objection, safety issue, or the like. This is just because someone is very vocal and the leader is afraid to upset the apple cart. Typically, these types of leaders waffle on decision-making. You can probably identify with this scenario: The leader will tell one of their subordinates they agree with them, and then when another subordinate disagrees, the leader will waffle and agree with the other subordinate as well but not tell the first one. Now the two subordinates are at odds because the leader is afraid to decide for fear of upsetting one of them.

When you are a change agent, it's important to get participation, but you need to be strong enough to implement a change or make a decision even though there will be some struggles along the way. The team members who spent the week working on the new process felt let down by the leadership team because they allowed one individual to derail the work of an entire team. Be participative, not permissive. Be persistent and persevere. Give people the opportunity to participate. The following are some ways for team members to participate:

1. Continuous improvement events/quality circles
2. Task forces/tiger teams
3. Daily shop floor management meetings

Allowing people to be part of the process will provide a smoother path to implementation but won't eliminate all the challenges and the requirements for leaders to lead. Always remember leaders need to lead.

Failure Is a Part of Leadership

Failure is only the opportunity to begin again more intelligently.

—Henry Ford[26]

Creating a "safe to fail" environment will encourage your team to experiment with new ideas. An excellent book for this is *The Fearless Organization* by Amy Edmonson.[27] When we work in a safe environment, we are more willing to try new things and are not satisfied with the current condition. Failure is part of the learning process. We all need to embrace the idea that experiments won't work all the time, and if it doesn't work, it will push our knowledge and lead us closer to solving the problem. However, every experiment needs to be done in a safe and controlled environment.

If you are coaching interpersonal skills, there needs to be a target condition to which we are attempting to nudge their behavior and a way to evaluate it. There is a tool called sensemaking that can help with this.[28] We do not need a team full of knob turners who are constantly changing processes. It is important to know and understand the process you are trying to change. Sometimes, trials are quick while others take time to evaluate results.

I worked for a leader whose motto was "Fail, but fail fast."[29] It's a simple saying, but without really listening, people do not understand it. What he was saying was take your best shot and do *something* instead of analyzing over and over before trying something. We should embrace experiments within the confines of PDCA[30] and utilize total quality tools to make sure we do not create another problem while trying to solve the one you're working on.

By implementing experiments, you will learn and be able to adjust quickly to the results. We have another saying: Don't let perfect get in the way of good! Perfection takes too long. Do not get into analysis paralysis. Capture just enough baseline information to make a decision and then *act* on it. This means you must have before and after metrics and video where applicable. Many times, you will see things on video you will never see by direct observation. Video can be reviewed with the team members and others to get their improvement ideas. When it's their idea, it makes it much simpler to implement as it lowers the energy gradient to resistance to change.

Learning to Share

For leaders, learning to share their learnings with their teammates and cascading across their sphere of influence includes

- Developing coaching skills and learning by sharing,
- Taking learning and spreading to their other areas of responsibility,
- Co-leading rapid improvements with their coach or mentor, and
- Developing presentation skills by teaching and reflecting on rapid improvement activities.

We use the word *share* purposefully instead of *teach* as this connotes more of a teamwork and trust environment. This step is where the team member practices the tools of self-reliance, process ownership, problem-solving, and ongoing business practice improvement that we discussed in the earlier chapters. We also teach them intangibles such as business acumen, teamwork, interpersonal skills, and empowerment. This is where we coach the group leaders[31] on how to share what they have learned. By coaching their team members, they also learn and develop. We have a saying: You don't really learn it until you have to teach it! This is a training method known as Leader as Teacher.

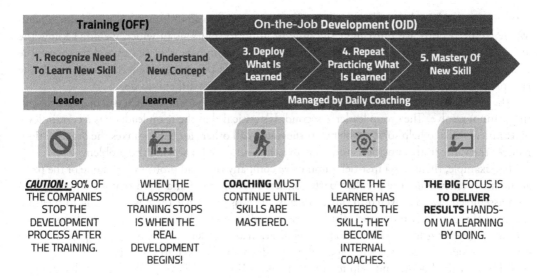

This Is Continuous Leadership Development!

Figure 7.11   Learning to Share Steps.

Source: BIG training materials.

Learning to Share Steps

Do you have a culture in which people want to join and remain in your company? As you evolve your development program, remember that just sending somebody to a conference or a two-day training is great but not enough to be considered development. Development happens through on-the-job training and coaching. It helps to bring new knowledge to someone or teach them a new skill but following up and making sure the new skill becomes part of the job and is properly used, requires practice and routines not only by the learner but also by the leader as they help teach the learner. This is called Learning to Lead. (See Figure 7.11.)

Most companies stop at the second step and do not understand why the training was inadequate. This was the problem with Six Sigma black belts at many companies. We spent $10,000 or more to train them, they did one project, and then they went back to their regular jobs.

The manager requesting the new skill or training needs to take the time to mentor the group leader or trainee through the entire process. Acquiring new knowledge is easy compared to doing something until it becomes a habit or mastering the skill. We call this getting the skill into "muscle memory." When you are working on your development plans make sure you include the practice portion, which is the only way it turns into "muscle memory" or whereby these new skills turn into routines and those routines turn into habits.

Avoid the Work-Around Solution

The team leader must encourage trust and teamwork and have a "process-focused" mindset. This is not easy and foremost requires ongoing training to change their mindset. What makes this even more difficult is that management in most companies is "results-focused" rather than "process-focused." In these cultures, the temptation to jump to an unknown solution is imminent. While we need both, we must fight the urge to jump to solutions in which we don't know the answer and work first to expose the problems and then to find the root causes and fix them. The only way to do this is by focusing on the process. If you get the process right, the results will take care of themselves. Again, this sounds easy to say, but it is very difficult to do.

The team leader position is the first level of escalation when a team member discovers a problem they cannot resolve. The group leader is second. It's critical that the team leader has a certain level of technical skills to help solve problems. If they only call others for help, it taxes the organization, reduces the value in this position, and increases the lead time for solving the problem.

For example, there was a first-tier automotive company that had problems with one of the parts at the final test station. The problem parts consisted of a housing and a pin that were pressed and then assembled. We discovered in our root-cause investigation that there was no way to measure the force of the press or the proper distance the pins should have been pressed into the housing. As a result, engineering added Loctite® to the specification as a workaround to secure the pins. Because there was sometimes excess Loctite applied, they added another step to wash the parts, which also served to heat the Loctite and help to cure it quicker. This created overprocessing and batching at the washer. It also resulted in constant frustration for the team members and was a difficult process to control that created defects and firefighting. All this chaos was due to a results-based solution.

To solve this problem, we changed the focus back to the original process. Modifications were made to the press to ensure the proper depth, and we standardized, measured, and recorded the force for the pins electronically. This prevented the variation and resulting defects and eliminated the need for the Loctite® and the wash step. By studying and focusing on the process we found root-cause solutions versus just throwing a work-around solution at the problem, which in the end made the problem even worse. By eliminating the need for the wash step, we also eliminated the need for the washer equipment and the need for SWIP created by the batch washer. By focusing on the process and fixing problems at the source, it helps mistake proof the process and makes everyone's job and life a little bit easier. This eventually led to an error-proofing system being implemented on the entire line.

People-Dependent Processes

People-dependent processes cannot scale or can only scale up to the limit of a person's 24 hours in a day. When the person leaves, the system dies. We created a new tool to highlight this issue called the *"Informal Responsibility Wall Map"* (see Figure 7.12).

This tool is intended to show the informal networks within a small-medium sized organization ($20 to $60 million[32] or up to 200 people) or within larger organization departments. Typically, we find that there tends to be a built-in dependency on three to six "key people" in the system. These people quite literally have their hands in everything. On one hand, they may complain about being too busy, but many learn to love the power and control it gives them. This is the environment that facilitates the hero complex.[33]

We find it important to note that each wall map has the propensity to tell a story about the informal interconnections of the company. What you will typically find is that there seems to be repeated names involved in each department or process-based columns. Work your way across your wall map and, once complete, step back and look at how involved these three to six people are in multiple tasks across multiple departments. Note we say "involved," not owned. Each wall map will contain different results, but we find it important to encourage you to "listen" to your map and really understand the "why" behind this breakdown of responsibilities.

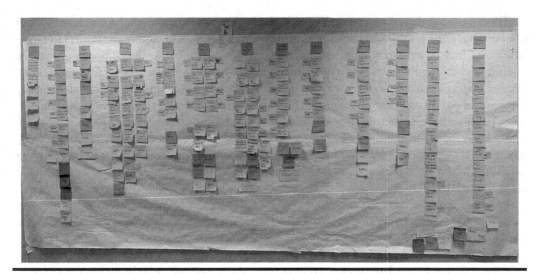

Figure 7.12   Diagramming the Informal Responsibility Wall Map.

Source: BIG training materials.

If something happens to any of these three to six people, the company will be in trouble. These types of processes are normal with start-up companies, but once the company reaches a certain size, these people-dependent processes start breaking down. Over time, if not addressed, as new highly skilled and talented people are brought into this people-centric model, they will start to push back on the three to six people who are still trying to micromanage the organization. If the micromanagers don't let go, they will lose their new highly skilled and talented managers. We need to create processes that are not dependent on a specific person(s). The processes need to be scalable and can be flexible or even designed to break if certain thresholds are reached. The processes should be standardized wherever it makes sense, that is, ordered domain and built into the organization's muscle memory.

The irony is that "developing people" is not considered a priority at most companies. They may talk about it, but have no true systems in place to support it, they rely on experience alone to develop those in the company. For many, it is viewed as a cost rather than a way of life. How many of you reading this have ever had to try to justify a request for training? But this sense of training and developing must become part of the culture. Otherwise, you end up with processes and systems that are dependent on specific people.

The *Informal Responsibility Wall Map* is a powerful realization tool and can be utilized in many ways. We find that a company wishing to realign tasks and responsibilities into the departments where it makes most sense can use this tool as an introduction to cross-training.

Scalable, Flexible Process Definition

The goal in any system[34] is to create scalable processes to the extent it makes sense based on this broad context. As a group leader, you will be creating and improving processes. It is very important that you create processes that are scalable. Scalable processes can absorb the company's growth without major changes and should be flexible and adaptable. The process doesn't have to be modified or take more people or more time as the company grows.

These processes do not rely on the group leader having to physically go and check the area or micromanage their team leaders or team members. Processes that do require the leaders to physically check may be easy to sustain when the company is small, but as the company grows, the amount of checking increases, and the leader no longer has the time to absorb all the checking. Micromanagers eventually run out of time as the company grows. This becomes evident as key decisions get put off until the micromanager has the time to deal with them. Eventually, the processes fall apart because there is just not enough time in the day for the micromanager to keep up.

Some decisions can and should be intuitive based on your experience, but others should be run through PDCA. How do you know? If you don't know how to proceed, you have no expert you can ask, you have no experience with the decision, and it is not complex or chaotic, you should run it through the PDCA cycle.

Processes must be designed to empower and challenge the team members to continuously improve to be scalable. For example, your leader's standard work says each hour you need to check a machine to make sure it's running okay and not producing defects. This may be fine when you have just one machine but at a brake plant I worked with, they went from one very large press machine to 14 machines. This means that now, 80% of the day you are walking from machine to machine, checking. This is a waste of time and easily puts one into firefighting mode. What if we modify the machine to let us know when it is having a problem or makes a mistake and shuts itself down (jidoka). Now, you only check the machine for total productivity maintenance, and when it has a problem, it lets you know. This makes your job easier and frees up 70% of your time.

Problem-Solving Teams—Quality Circles[35]

Many companies have a weekly continuous improvement meeting for their groups that work together. These are like the quality circles introduced in the 1960s. A key part of the concept was continuous learning of PDCA and basic statistical concepts like the seven basic total-quality quality tools, creative thinking, data analysis, and problem-solving tools. These can all be covered in short 20- to 30-minute sessions combined with practice using current problems facing the team. Group leaders and team leaders need to coordinate these sessions with a skilled mentor or coach who can help them plan which topics to cover and provide training material appropriate for the knowledge level of the students and the time available.

Rapid Improvements: Using the Power of 15 Minutes

The rapid improvement process consists of a structured approach incorporating short PDCA cycles whereby we break down the problems into small pieces and manage the improvements daily. This gives team members the ability to see daily continuous improvement and will build momentum.

How to Facilitate

1. First 5 Minutes—Find an operator and ask the question, "What bugs you?" and work with them to form a problem statement. It should be quantifiable and time-bound with a gap to target.
2. Second 5 Minutes—Go down and talk with the operator and review the metrics and the root cause. (Most simple problems don't require an analytical tool). Ask the operator what

they want to do to make it better. This becomes your hypothesis. If you do this, you will achieve this target. Simple motion and transportation wastes don't normally need fancy problem-solving tools.

3. Third 5 Minutes—Implement the solution with the operators and then watch for 10 cycles and record results (PDCA).

Small improvement after small improvement accumulates over time, which grows to be very significant and motivational. We don't need to solve every problem to make a major improvement or to even get to the desired condition. Do not waste your time with developing an action list with hundreds of problems.

I often hear a manager ask the group leader the status of a project to which the reply is "The team is working on it." When they give me this answer, I question the framework they are working in and the process they use for daily follow-up. Developing a daily routine based on a standard schedule with standard questions aligns us on the deliverables. This is what we mean by developing a standard repeatable process. It's where the teacher and the learner can develop an agreement on deliverables. Yes, teams and leaders need to lead, but it's critical that they are part of the process. This is the only way the process will sustain and people will feel valued. The ability to identify a problem is easy. Solving the problem is hard. As a leader, you should make sure the team is progressing and guiding the problem-solving process. The results of your team are your results. You cannot blame the team. The team reflects your leadership skills. We have a saying, "with the right to criticize comes the responsibility to recommend."[36] This doesn't mean you have the solution or are expected to have the solution, but it does mean you are thinking about the situation and developing some ideas on how to move forward. Remember, when making changes, just try it! But keep in mind that it is much easier to sell ideas if you can make them "their" ideas.

Notes

1. Richards, Chet. Certain to Win: The Strategy of John Boyd, Applied to Business. Xlibris US. Kindle Edition.
2. Reference to Col John Boyd's OODA (Observe–Orient–Decide–Act) loop.
3. Reference to the Flow System, Nigel Thurlow, John Tuner, Brain Rivera, Aquiline Books|UNT, November 19, 2020.
4. https://quotefancy.com/quote/1670535/Katsuaki-Watanabe-Being-satisfied-with-the-status-quo-means-you-are-not-making-progress
5. Inspired by and adapted from a Webinar by Norman Bodek with Kazuyoshi Hisano, Achieve Mind Blowing Innovation in the post COVID world with 3A theory. President and Profession Coach Conoway Inc.
6. John Turner . . . co-creator of the Flow System.
7. Michael Meyers.
8. For more on active listening, read LET, Leader Effectiveness Training.
9. TWI JR Manual War Manpower Commission's Bureau of training 1944.
10. Michael Meyers is speaking.
11. www.toyota-europe.com/world-of-toyota/this-is-toyota/the-toyota-way public domain
12. www.toyota-europe.com/world-of-toyota/this-is-toyota/the-toyota-way public domain
13. Correspondence from Jonathan Peyton February 2020.
14. The Red Team Handbook, Ver 9 This publication is available at https://usacac.army.mil/organizations/ufmcs-red-teaming/ and for registered All Partners Access Network users at https://community.apan.org/wg/tradoc-g2/ufmcs-red-team-central/.

15. This is an example of sensemaking.
16. CNN Video—Brooks Jackson on the New Economy, 2007.
17. Michael Meyers at Donnelly Mirrors.
18. Contributed by the late Willie Grace of Presbyterian Hospital in Albuquerque, New Mexico.
19. The quality circle is typical a cross-functional team composed of team members and/or leaders along with support members (i.e., maintenance, engineering, quality, etc.) working to solve some type of quality problem or management-sponsored improvement goal.
20. TPS, Taiichi Ohno, Productivity Press 1988.
21. Used with Permission, Begin with Trust, The first step to becoming a genuinely empowering leader by Frances X. Frei and Anne Morriss, www.linkedin.com/posts/ted-conferences_how-to-rebuild-trust-activity-6743194759902441472-sEdi

    From the HBR Magazine (May–June 2020) https://hbr.org/2020/05/begin-with-trust
22. Begin with Trust, by Frances X. Frei and Anne Morriss, From the HBR May–June 2020 Issue and from YouTube www.youtube.com/watch?v=pVeq-0dIqpk—Used with permission.
23. Protzman, Charles. The TPS Practitioner's Field Book. Productivity Press, 20160405. VitalBook file endnote 32. (Protzman 203–205), Coopers and Lybrand. Allied Signal TQ Training Course 1994.
24. Michael Meyers is speaking.
25. Michael Meyers.
26. www.leanblog.org/2006/06/looking-for-lean-quotes/
27. The Fearless Organization by Amy Edmonson, Wiley; 1 edition (November 20, 2018).
28. https://cognitive-edge.com/page/2/?s=sensemaking
29. Michael Meyers is speaking.
30. PDCA is discussed more in the Improve Business Processes section.
31. In some cases, the training may be done by a team leader or a company trainer.
32. Not sure of its applicability in larger organizations but could be applicable company sites, plants, or senior leadership team, for example.
33. www.google.com/url?q=www.forbes.com/sites/mikemyatt/2012/02/28/the-problem-with-heroic-leaders/?sh%3D79e5e29e5320&sa=D&ust=1608234427149000&usg=AOvVaw0tcURB8E5QhzbWa7jxej21
34. Assumes this is within the ordered Cynefin domain.
35. *Jishuken:* The origin of jishuken has been said to be from a Japanese statement "kanban houshiki bukachou jishu kenkyuukai," which means "kanban system department and section manager autonomous study groups." This was later shortened to jishuken, which is "self-study" and often called "autonomous study groups" in English. www.kaizen-news.com/jishuken-101/
36. Mark Jamrog, SMC Group.

Chapter 8

Implement—Skills and System Deployment via On-the-Job Development

Figure 8.1   BASICS® Lean Leadership Development Path—Implement/Check.

Source: BIG training materials.

Continuing in the Implement section of our model (see Figure 8.1), this chapter brings together the suggested coaching mindsets and behaviors, as well as many of the coinciding tools, necessary to implement at the Gemba, either on the shop floor or in the office. We cover not only some of these tools in detail but also the key indicators to measure as you implement these new practices.

> Because people make our automobiles, nothing gets started until we train and educate our people.
>
> —**Eiji Toyoda**

Coaching and Mentoring

We believe that using coaching is a form of leadership development and that combining it with continuous improvement helps integrate the people and the process. Creating these habits and a daily routine helps develop a culture of continuous improvement and will allow your organization to develop true Lean leaders. This mindset change is one of the keys to sustainability and long-term cultural change.

If your organization does not have managers ready to be good coaches, then you should consider the consultant model to get the coaching initiative started. While people can learn well from coaches, the important question is, "Are they learning correctly?" Coaching and mentoring are such integral parts of the Leadership Development Path. We must develop a good understanding of the theory and practices of coaching and mentoring. As with all the education and training topics that have been covered, there is much thought and practice surrounding coaching and mentoring. There is no one-size-fits-all *law of coaching*, but there are good practices used for creating an effective and efficient process. The following are examples:

- Ask guiding questions—employees learn and grow the most when they uncover the answers themselves.
- Ask them for their ideas.
- Recognize their accomplishments.
- Use active listening and empower them smartly.
- Show respect for other opinions by discussing them.
- Try to understand the learner's level of knowledge.
- Go to the Gemba to see what the person has learned.

We are sure that many of you reading this book can think back to a coach in your life you admired. Take a second and list those things that made them great. There is a difference between coaching and mentoring:

- Mentoring is more development-driven, looking not just at the professional's current job function but also beyond, taking a more holistic approach to career development.
- Coaching is more performance-driven, designed to improve the professional's on-the-job performance.[1]

Two distinct models exist:

- Manager as coach
- Consultant, internal or external, as mentor

A mentor is someone who helps you learn something you might not have learned or would have learned more slowly or with more difficulty versus learning it completely on your own. The most common is that of the master–apprentice relationship developed for the skilled trades and fine arts. In these areas, it was recognized that the depth of knowledge required would take the time and persistence of a mentoring-type relationship. This requirement fits the Toyota Production System (TPS) very well. On a final note, there must be a healthy tension between understanding when to coach by asking questions versus when to tell someone what to do.[2]

Coaching Example—Swimming

Let's use swimming as an analogy. Step 1, Team Member Self-Reliance (TSR), and Step 2, Improving Business Practices, would be similar to teaching someone how to swim. The teaching would involve classroom work through which the student reviews pool safety; visual charts of the freestyle stroke; some theory of how to swim fast, that is, fingers open versus closed; and some videos. At this point, it is only teaching because the student hasn't even entered the pool yet. Then the student gets a coach. The coach continues teaching around the pool but not in the water and shares their experience as they go. Sharing shows empathy and builds trust. The coach has done this before so sharing their know-how and techniques builds credibility and trust. The coach is facilitating each person as they teach and share with all the students. They coach them on their freestyle stroke on the land, show them how to breathe, and so on. Once the student is familiar and can demonstrate the skills, only then do they enter the pool. But here everything changes. It's not as easy as outside the water, and if they sink, they can drown, so there is an element of fear as with any new job. The coach starts them out with exercises and kickboards and slowly teaches them the skills. Now we have moved from teaching to training. Training includes the practice but needs a coach. The coach however is only involved until the student masters the skill, at which point they become certified. A mentor is a coach who would continue to follow the swimmer for a good portion of their career. Normally, a mentor is focused on an individual whereas, typically, a coach is focused on the performance of an overall team. A coach can become a mentor, or one could consider a mentor a longer-term individual coach.

Example of a "Bad" Coaching Moment

A friend of ours recalled a story to us when he was made assistant plant manager.[3] He was brand new to the role at the time and would complete the tasks he was told to do as he was told to do them. The newly appointed "boss of his boss" was walking around and saw that he was not busy. He came over and asked him what he was doing. He stated he had completed the task and was waiting to be told what to do next. The boss inspected the job he had done and told him he was doing a great job. However, in the future, he never expected to see him idle again.

As a result, from then on, he always made sure he was "busy" doing something whenever his boss's boss came around. He explained to us that this frustrated him because there was more emphasis being put on the perception of looking busy than on adding value.

We have found this to be a very contagious behavior that happens in most companies. When helping to relaunch a production line at a medical device company in Puerto Rico, we learned the operators would shout, "Agua, agua" (or "Water, water," in English), when a manager walked on the floor. When asked why they shouted this phrase, they explained that this is the same phrase people would yell if the police were coming. Sure enough, "Agua agua," and all the idle hands find products to look busy whenever a manager walks into the room. The worst part was during these times, people would overproduce work in process (WIP), resulting in so many parts on the line that it slowed the line down. Building WIP became a positively affirmed behavior mindset, and then people would be complimented or put down based on the amount of WIP they had at their station.

Always be mindful of the lessons you teach to those you manage, both conscious and unconscious. You may never get a second chance at a first impression when it comes to managing.

On-the-Job Development Starts with Running the Production Line

It is an important part of Skills and System Deployment for the group leader to understand how a Lean line should run and be able to read the WIP in the line. Keeping in mind that all lines are different, that is, assembly versus machining versus semi or fully automated, there are commonalities on which we can draw. The test as to whether a line is Lean or not is simple because we only have two things to look for:

1. **Idle Time**—There are many causes for idle time, that is, batching products; improper line balancing, sometimes called station balancing; or team members standing by watching machines run. Many times, people will describe these team members as lazy, but whose fault is it? We would argue it's management's responsibility 90% to 95% of the time. Why did we design jobs that allowed the team members to appear lazy? Most team members hate being idle! It makes the day drag out forever. If you see idle time, the line probably is not Lean or certainly not as Lean as it could be.
2. **Excess Inventory Anywhere in the Process**—Excess inventory is really stored labor capacity.[4] It is like old food in the bottom of your freezer. It is important to be able to learn how to "read the WIP." The idea is to compare where the WIP is located in the line versus where and how much should be there. When first implementing the system, the team leader should read the line frequently. The WIP can show immediately where problems exist in assembly lines, machining lines, or transactional processes. Lines with excess inventory are not Lean or certainly not as Lean as they could be. Most lines that have idle time also have excess inventory and vice versa.

The Old Thinking . . . Station Balancing Is World Class

Workload station balancing has been around forever. There are two components to balancing a line: people and inventory. The theory behind station balancing is that each team member has a station. The station is typically a workbench, that is, an assembler, a hostess stand at a restaurant, a machine, or a desk in an office. The team member is typically isolated and surrounded by materials and is normally sitting down. It is not unusual to find a fixture or small machine on the workstation in front of them that is required to be used a couple times during the operation. The station-balancing formula is

$$CT \text{ for each Station} = TLT \div \#TMs$$

The station's cycle time equals the total labor required to build one piece of a product produced by the cell divided by the number of team members in the cells (see Figure 8.2). If we have a process

STATION BALANCING

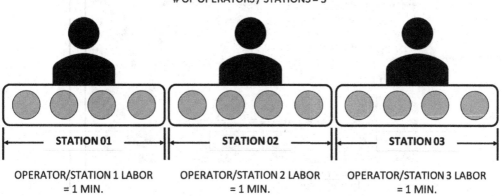

TOTAL LABOR = 3 MINs
OF OPERATORS / STATIONS = 3

| STATION 01 | STATION 02 | STATION 03 |

OPERATOR/STATION 1 LABOR = 1 MIN.　OPERATOR/STATION 2 LABOR = 1 MIN.　OPERATOR/STATION 3 LABOR = 1 MIN.

Figure 8.2　Station Balancing.

Source: BIG training materials.

in which there are 30 minutes of total labor time per unit and six people working on the line, how much work should be done by each person? The answer is

$$30 \; \textbf{minutes} \div 6 \; \textbf{people} = 5 \; \textbf{minutes} / \textbf{person}$$

This requires each person to be given exactly the same amount (5 minutes) of work, and each person, in turn, must do their fair share of the five minutes' worth of work. The goal for the manufacturing engineer is to balance each station's work as close as possible, which sometimes results at the expense of the correct flow of the product.

This is an almost impossible task because sustaining workload balancing is very difficult. Over time, everyone improves at different rates, or a new team member is introduced, which slows the line down, or a team member is absent and then the line doesn't run properly. The line can only move as fast as your slowest machine or person. Ohno described this system as swimming relay–type handoffs. In a swimming relay, the swimmer cannot leave the starting block until the prior swimmer has touched the wall.

Station-balanced lines have WIP inventory, which are called kanban squares, between each operator. WIP caps are calculated to determine the most WIP that should be in the squares. We call this system the lazy man's balance (see Figure 8.3) because the WIP is being used to balance the uneven labor times of the team members. The team member cannot start their operation until the prior team member completes the work and moves their part(s) into the kanban square. The kanban squares (see Figure 8.4) have rules:

1. The rule is that you cannot start working on a part unless there is one in the kanban square before your station.
2. You must stop working on it once you have met the WIP cap, that is, filled in the max number of parts in the kanban square.

Figure 8.5 Station balancing.

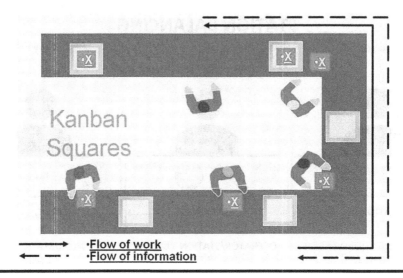

Figure 8.3 Lazy Man's Balance. Station Balancing with Kanbans in between each worker.

Source: BIG training materials.

- Total WIP in the system = 9
- 1 pc at each station and 3 pc between each station.

Figure 8.4 Kanban Squares between Each Station.

Source: BIG training materials.

This kanban-square paradigm came from a 1983 Hewlett Packard video and has been considered world class by Lean experts and very high-profile Lean certification organizations ever since. However, it was never world class for those that read up on Ohno's teachings on baton-zone line balancing, which dates back to before 1973. We call it "bumping" and have been experimenting with and using it since 1997.

Kanban squares are considered excess inventory, not standard WIP (SWIP). With this kanban-square system between each team member, we encounter idle time and excess inventory whenever we fill up or deplete the square. Remember a kanban is excess inventory, and excess inventory is evil because it hides problems. The kanban squares hide the fact the line is imbalanced. The other problem we have witnessed is that even if the WIP caps are labeled with the maximum amount allowed in the squares (which in many cases are bins or trays), team members will inevitably fill them with more than the maximum and, in many cases, as much as will physically fit in the space or area. Problems with station balanced lines include but are not limited to the following:

Figure 8.5   Station Balancing at a Popular Fast-Food Sandwich Shop.

Source: Shutterstock.

- People are not robots, and we all work and improve at different rates.
- If it's a mixed model, it is difficult to keep the labor balanced, and team members will use up all the standard SWIP, going from one product to another or at the end of a shift (drying out the line).
- Station-balanced lines are almost always sit-down lines and are up to 30% less efficient than stand-up and walking lines.

Station Balancing/Man Machine Loading Charts

Another industry standard taught by every high-profile Lean certification organization is to create man-loading or station-loading charts (see Figure 8.6). The problem with these charts is that they are symptomatic of station-balanced lines, and while they should, they seldom drive waste elimination. Instead, waste is moved from one person to another, typically disrupting the flow. In addition, most Lean experts will pad the labor times and allow a 5% to 20% or more variation in the cycle times for each team member in order to allow them to hit the number that makes them feel good. This immediately creates imbalances to the line. This tool does have its place in totally automated lines or layouts whereby team members cannot flex and are subject to isolated islands.

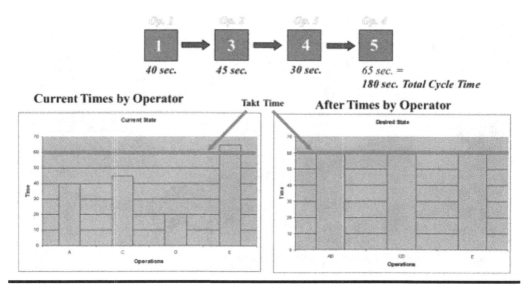

Figure 8.6 Traditional Station–Man Loading Charts.

Source: BIG training materials.

New World-Class Thinking—One-Piece Balanced Synchronized Flow (Bumping)

Part of our BASICS® model is to implement a process we call "bumping," which automatically balances the line (see Figure 8.7). This helps promote a sense of fairness among staff and generally improves department morale. To facilitate bumping we utilize a concept Ohno referred to as baton zones, or flex zones, which are areas where handoffs occur between team members. (see Figure 8.8). Bumping eliminates the need for kanban squares, results in zero WIP between the team members, automatically balances the team members across the stations and increases productivity (see Figure 8.9). When balancing the line, the product flow should never change and never go backward. Proper baton-zone balanced layouts can run with one person or 10 people, if there is enough room, and makes it easy to add, rotate and remove people on a moment's notice. To learn more about "Bumping," reference our other published book, *The BASICS® Lean Implementation Model*.

Stop-the-Line Strategy

Every team leader/group leader should have a stop-the-line strategy. This is one of the secrets to sustaining and eliminating firefighting. At what point does the problem become big enough we need to stop?

In the words of my sensei, Mark Jamrog,

> "You have to earn the right to stop the line. In any event, line stoppage of course is an essential operating element in any environment (rudimentary or advanced) as it would relate to an emergency. That said, as it would relate to 'normal' operating conditions it is a technique that is reserved for advanced and or very advanced operating environments. Stopping the line (in my experience) is a profoundly serious move and is an integral part

2nd Operator Finishes and Walks toward 1st Operator

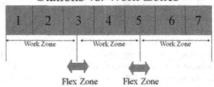

Stations vs. Work Zones

1st Operators Bumps 2nd Operator and Takes Their Piece Wherever They Are in the Process

1st Operator Returns to Start 2nd Operators Continues Building

Figure 8.7   Work Zones with Flexing (Bumping).

Source: BIG training materials.

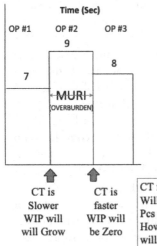

Station Balanced

Bumping

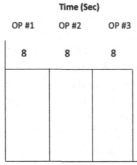

CT is Slower WIP will will Grow

CT is faster WIP will be Zero

CT for the line Will be 9 sec. Pcs per hour = 400. How much idle time will there be? How much WIP will build up in one hour?

Idle Time is absorbed by bumping so there is no WIP between operators and MURI is eliminated

CT for the line Will average 8 sec. Pcs per hour = 450 (12.5% improvement) How much idle time will there be?

Figure 8.8   Station Balancing Versus Bumping.

Source: BIG training materials.

Small Shock Line

Baseline Metrics – Station Balanced		
Operators (for two shifts)	10	
Cell Lead (for two shifts)	1.5	
Units per day 11/30 – 2/13/10	518	
Paid Minutes Per Unit includes OT	11.72	
Thru-put Time (Working days)	2.3	
Cycle Time (min – Estimated -Batch)	1.73	
Overtime #hours 1/1/10 – 2/14/10	203	
Space (sq. feet)	616	
Travel Distance (feet)	84	
WIP #	1562	
PC/person/ hour	3.2	

Baseline Product Flow

Actual After Lean Metrics June 2010 Data		
Operators (eliminated 2nd shift)	2.7	73%
Cell Lead	.9	40%
Units per day	261	49.6%
Paid Minutes Per Unit	6.6	43.5%
Thru-put Time (Working days)	.1	96%
Cycle Time (min)	1.72	9.9%
Overtime #hours	0	100%
Space (sq. feet)	558	9%
Travel Distance (feet)	42	50%
WIP #	74	95.3%
Pc/ person /per hour	12	377%

After Lean Flow

377% Increase In Pieces/Person/Hour & Eliminated Need For 2nd Shift

Figure 8.9   Results from Implementing Baton-Zone Bumping Increased the Output 49.6%.

Source: BIG training materials.

of two other advanced operating systems. Those would be the Andon system and the Standard Work system. When a team member initiates a line stop action (unless it is an emergency) the situation will be communicated to the entire line via the Andon board. That board will have a yellow section that is illuminated, announced with a unique sound, and the section number of the line in question will be (solid) highlighted. [See Figure 8.10.] If the situation is not resolved in a predetermined amount of time the line will stop. That board will have a red section that is illuminated, announced with a separate and unique sound, and the section number of the line in question will be (flashing) highlighted. The line will remain in this condition until the issue is resolved.

The second system is that of Standard Work. If the situation cannot be corrected before the product crossed into the next section of the line, the line will come to a stop automatically given the yellow status of the line. The Andon system will change as noted above. This technique ties directly into the issue of quality. That is, it will not be necessary for any team member to remember at which point they stopped work. The point of stoppage will be certainly known, as it will be the end of each standard work zone. Clearly, this discussion can get quite involved, but this brief explanation of the system (in my mind) clearly indicates why line stoppage is reserved for those advanced and very advanced operating environments. If you stop it with no plan in place to respond or escalate or update the standard it doesn't work."[5]

At Toyota, they have the famous Andon cord that any team member can pull. But pulling the cord doesn't stop the line. It takes the status Andon from green to yellow. At this point, the team leader will

Figure 8.10   Andon Board.

Source: Shutterstock.

come running to discuss the problem with the team member to understand the problem and what countermeasures need to be taken. If the problem can be corrected immediately, the team leader will return the line to green status but will record the problem and countermeasure. If it needs additional problem-solving, the team will work on it together at a later time. If the problem cannot be fixed within the takt time, the team leader will move the status to red and stop the line. At this point, the group leader will come running to help fix the problem. Stopping the line forces us to acknowledge and fix the problem. If you don't stop the line, we end up just living with the problems and continue firefighting. But we are all not Toyota. Most of us need to decide what type of problems will shut the line down.

Escalation Plans

Escalation plans document what steps are to be followed in the event a gap is discovered and how much time should pass until the next person in the chain of command is notified? The organization should have a standard operating procedure for escalation that is a key part of the group leader's job. For example, in the event an abnormality is discovered, if the team leader cannot solve it within a specified timeframe, they must be directed to escalate it to the group leader.

Escalation Example

At one company, the workers simply refused to follow the total productivity maintenance (TPM) visual board. The group leaders never escalated it, and as a result, the TPM activities were not accomplished. This is a good news/bad news story. The bad news is the TPM activities were not accomplished; the good news is, due to the visual management system, we knew it was not accomplished. In this case, no action is an action that was, in fact, rewarding the bad behaviors of the maintenance team. If the group leader doesn't care enough to follow it up, the workers are certainly not going to do it. When the consultant was on-site and approached the group leaders, they simply said they were too busy. If a team member refuses to follow their standard work, there must be a plan in place to involve the next level up and involve Human Resources (if it exists). This is what happens when there is no escalation plan in place.

A company we visited held tiered huddle meetings every day. The meetings started on the shop floor and cascaded up to senior leadership. Problems identified on the shop floor were passed on at each tier and could reach the senior leadership team within a couple of hours. We discuss tiered meetings in more detail later.

Planning and Debriefs in the Military—Brian (Ponch) Rivera

*Becoming fixated on "What happened" is a sure way to fail when our attention should be on "What's happening **now**." The introduction of the black box to the cockpits of commercial aircraft in the late 1960s provided insights to this phenomenon, as mishap cockpit crews were often heard reporting details of what happened to a central decision-maker, the captain, moments before their aircraft went out of control and crashed.*

A great example of this is Eastern Airlines Flight 401 (EA 401), during which the cockpit crew became complacent with automation while they prioritized what happened with a burned-out light-bulb over critical information such as airspeed, altitude, and downward velocity and flew a functioning L-1011 TriStar into the Florida Everglades, sadly killing 101 passengers and the crew.

A better approach, learned from EA 401, and other aircraft and high-risk industry tragedies, is to have group or team members share information with each other about what is happening now so they, individually and collectively, comprehend their environment and project the likely future state of what will happen next.

In "The Flow System," we talk about developing what is known as Level 3, Situational Awareness (SA) and/or sensemaking—critical and often overlooked prerequisites for successful decision-making in complex and dynamic situations. From my experience, the best way to build situational awareness and sensemaking capabilities is through the use of effective team planning and debriefing techniques.

Planning and debriefing or retrospectives are the bookends of what I call the Cadence of Accountability. In my former world of fighter aviation, we bucketed planning and debriefing underneath mission analysis—a component of our Human Factors or Crew Resource Management program that is foundational to team science. In fighter aviation, we discovered that effective mission analysis (planning and debriefing) improved our situational awareness, shaped our leadership skills, improved decision-making, and developed an adaptive, safe, and learning culture. Before leading effective team planning and debriefing events, one needs to define accountability.

Accountability has many definitions, but my favorite definition of accountability is one I learned from Christopher Avery, PhD, who defines accountability as the ability to recount what happened.[6] This definition will become critically important in effective debriefing techniques.

When it comes to planning, many organizational leaders view the output of planning, "The Plan," as the purpose of any planning session. This is not true. The purpose of planning is to develop teams and organizations who can cope with dynamic, changing environments. There is a quote often associated with President Dwight D. Eisenhower that captures this idea: "Plans are worthless; but planning is indispensable." Boxer Mike Tyson offers a similar view: "Everyone has a plan until they get punched in the mouth."

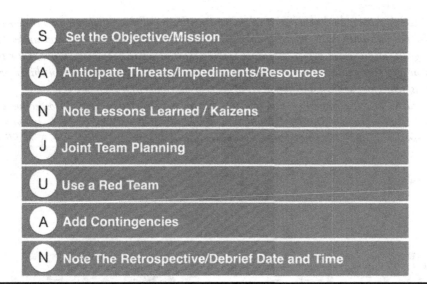

Figure 8.11   Planning Session Card.

Source: Courtesy of Brian (Ponch) Rivera, AGLX and co-creator of the Flow System.

Additionally, two axioms connect to the purpose of planning: (1) Planning should be done by those who are going to do the work, and (2) planning is fractal.

Developing a plan and handing it off to a team to execute is great if you view humans as hired hands or robots. However, if you are reading this and other books by Charles Protzman, you either hired people or were hired by people who want their talent to think and make decisions. So let me continue on fractality.

Planning is fractal. That is, it should be self-similar at all levels of the organization, from a stand-up, scrum, daily management huddle to a tiered meeting or strategy session. Anytime a decision needs to be made, or the flow of work determined, effective planning techniques are ones whereby the increased flow of information leads to a better understanding of the situation and its possible futures by all of those involved with the work. For fractality to exist, planning techniques should be simple, repeatable, and scalable. Figure 8.11 shows an example of an effective planning technique we developed live during a class in Puerto Rico.

Debriefing/Retrospectives

I came from a culture of debriefing. In fighter aviation, we debriefed to learn and improve our future individual, as well as our team performance. Similar to planning, we used a simple, scalable, and repeatable debriefing approach. The emphasis in debriefing needs to be "What happened," and not the attitudes and beliefs of what we think will improve our future.

By looking back at What Happened from multiple perspectives, we build up what is known as Level 1 and Level 2 Situational Awareness (SA).

Level 1 SA is really the ability to recognize relevant elements in our environment. For example, the colors of the cars you parked between today may not seem relevant, but I can almost guarantee you that you don't know the answers. There is a good chance that the same is happening in your day-to-day work where you and your team members are missing critical elements of your environment.

Level 2 SA is achieved when we start to see the significance of those elements on our desired objectives, goals, and outcomes. With effective debriefing, we want to make sure the team understands the objectives, goals, or outcomes before they start looking back at what happened. Why? If the team has competing or differing goals, then that makes them a group, and not a team. When this happens, the group begins debriefing against a different set of goals or outcomes and therefore is a waste.

In the SEATTLE Retrospective example (see Figure 8.12), a structured retrospective approach I developed while living in Seattle, Washington, the emphasis is on looking back at what. "What was the objective?" a key element of the Alignment and Achievement Check, the A of SEATTLE.

The S.E.A.T.T.L.E. Retrospective℠
brought to you by AGLX Consulting, LLC

Set the Time and Stage
• Who? Where? When? The retrospective is part of the plan.
• Prepare the room. A retrospective is an event, not a meeting.

Establish Psychological Safety
• Leader must display fallibility.
• Use direct language. Ask questions.

Alignment and Achievement Check
• What was the iteration objective?
• Did the team achieve the objective?

Timeline
• What happened?
• What was good? What was not so good?

Two Questions
• How did this happen? Why did this happen?
• Find the second- and third-order explanations.

Lessons Learned
• What did we learn? Who else would benefit
  from what we learned?
• Action items: Who will do what by when?

End on a High Note
• Celebrate team successes.

HIGH-PERFORMANCE TEAMING™

1-844-900-AGLX | www.aglx.consulting

Figure 8.12   Seattle Retrospective.

Source: Courtesy of Brian (Ponch) Rivera, AGLX and co-creator of the Flow System.

What happened is the key element underneath Timeline, the first T *in SEATTLE. The cadence of Accountability is focused on the what.*

    Contributed by Brian (Ponch) Rivera.

Hansei—Debrief and Time for Reflection

As we just discussed, the military has built in time for reflection after every training exercise to review what happened and what could be improved. Yet we hardly ever do this in the private sector. It is important to build time into reflecting on the outcomes of major and sometimes minor projects or problem-solving activities. This includes reflecting on both the positive and negative outcomes.

A simple debriefing technique is to review what did we learn, what did we accomplish, and what are the next steps. There is always something we could have done better. We suggest building a "lessons learned," or learning, database so that the lessons learned are captured in real time.[7] The process of reflection should always come from two perspectives: What could we have done better to improve the process, and what could I have done better to lead the team?

I[8] had a standard daily meeting during which once a week, the question was simply, "What did we learn today, and if we could have a do-over, what would it be?" While reflecting on my past managers, I consider myself very lucky to have learned from all of them. I learned how to lead from some, and some others I learned how not to lead, and I am very thankful for both.

Planning and Scheduling

The next part of Skills and System Deployment is learning and understanding the planning and scheduling systems. Since books have been written on planning and scheduling, our purpose is to only cover key points for the team leader and group leader. First, we need to make sure that in the cell, we have a plan or schedule that is visual, so everyone knows the plan and no one has to ask what the next order is to be produced. The product schedule should be posted on the line where everyone can see it: on a flipchart, whiteboard, or electronic signboard. If the schedule is just on someone's computer but not where everyone can see it, then it is not acceptable. The material status for the next order should be visible with no shortages. Planning and scheduling can result in two types of problems:

1. Inventory control problems—These are the result of a workstation that is decoupled (not part of the line) and inventory is used to connect them or when a workstation is blocked which means it is starving for parts (short inventory). Again, this is the job kanban systems perform.
2. Production ordering problems—these are problems with the order information having to do with the flow of production. These are described in detail in the book *Card Based Control Systems for Lean Work Design.*[9]

True Bottlenecks

A true bottleneck is defined as a machine that runs 24 hours a day and cannot meet the takt time. One has to manage a true bottleneck differently from an ordinary bottleneck. This means a true bottleneck should run over breaks, lunch, shift changes, and the like. It should be optimized for setup times. It must be assigned an owner to manage it. If it runs on its own, it should be connected to a system that can text a message to someone before it goes down or, in the worst case, after it goes down. Every second lost on a true bottleneck can never be recovered.

Implement Planning Rules

1. Never release an order where there is a shortage of materials. This is our number one rule! We find almost every planner violates this rule. This rule requires you to not release the order to manufacturing until we physically have the materials in-house and they are accepted by incoming quality. Most planners will violate the rule and release the order because they believe the material is coming in or is on the call-off list. The problem is the material can become unavailable to the line if it doesn't pass inspection, doesn't arrive on time, or is short. If there is not enough material in WIP, that is, sub-assembly processes that require some lead time to produce like welding or machining, then it will cause the final assembly line to shut down. This means that the order has to be pulled off the line and then skipped over until we find one that has all the materials in-house. This problem kills production, and it becomes visible when team leaders start skipping over orders on the schedule.
2. If there is a changeover, it should be part of the schedule and there should be an advance trigger[10] for the setup team.[11] The setup team should be using an external checklist, which is a list of activities to be performed in order to get ready for the next job while the current line is running. We call this external time.
3. For mixed-model assembly, think in terms of "sets" of parts. If you are filling orders that require more than one part to complete the assembly or have to ship as one "set" of parts, the planning focus should be on making and tracking sets of parts versus batches of individual parts.
4. The team leader should not have to search for the next order or materials for the next order or have to enter shortages into the system and wait for the stockroom to replace them. Everything should be delivered to the area/cell, free of packaging materials and ready to be produced. Too often, we find team leaders or group leaders trying to figure out what the next order is or what needs to be produced and then having to go to the computer to enter in material that needs to be delivered. This should all be done by the planning/production control group. The Planning Department's customer is ultimately the team leader and group leader.

Implement Planning/Scheduling Boards

A helpful way to visualize and identify what work order is next is to create a scheduling center (see Figure 8.13). This can be adopted in many different ways and will be different for all companies. One traditional way is to create a heijunka board. This is a board that will give you sequence and time of the next build. It is extremely visual and allows all team members to see where the line is running versus what was planned. The board must be both visual and accurate. Any work order that makes it into the scheduling center should adhere to all the previously stated rules of planning and scheduling.

At a company I used to work with,[12] we implemented a heijunka box for a work center. We needed a way for the water spiders to know which order was next so that they knew what materials

Figure 8.13   Scheduling Center Heijunka Board.

Source: BIG training materials.

to pick and deliver to the line. We also wanted a visual way to see if the material delivery was keeping up with the build rate of the line. After a few weeks on the line, we noticed that they were constantly behind schedule from where the heijunka box said we should be.

Instead of looking at the problem and understanding the root cause of the delay, leadership decided to get rid of the heijunka box. This hid the actual problem with material delivery but not the production lines running out of work. Getting rid of the heijunka box did not fix the problem; it just "swept it under the carpet." They weren't listening to what the box was telling them and instead chose to believe that the box just did not work for them. The moral of the story is that whatever is put in place, make sure there is a sound reason for it and that leadership supports its rollout and looks to understand the problem instead of just reacting to it.

Implement Visual Controls

Visual controls are an important part of the system deployment and the third component of visual management. They are the secret to any leader being able to dedicate 50% of their time to continuous improvement. Visual controls differ from visual displays in that they are designed to cause action. They do not necessarily force the action to occur but can provide penalties if they do not. For example, a stop sign or stoplight requires a driver to stop (see Figure 8.14). It suggests an action but does not guarantee the action. If the car doesn't stop, the driver can be penalized, for example, involved in an accident or being caught on a red-light camera and receiving a ticket. The goal is to build in standards and make defects (abnormalities) obvious.

The goal for proper visual controls allows the leader to manage the area without asking, checking, or inspecting to see if there are gaps or problems. Visual controls are of paramount importance

Figure 8.14   Visual Display.

Source: BIG training materials.

to sustaining a Lean system. Building in the ability to make the abnormal immediately obvious in all processes will highlight areas that need a quick countermeasure and then yield candidates for the Plan–Do–Check–Act cycle. It is a given in this discussion that standard work is in place, and processes are stable and capable. The more visual the process, the easier it will be to manage and sustain the process. Visual controls should be part of our standard work. This sounds easy to do but is very difficult.

Implement 5S Boards[13]

5S boards (see Figure 8.15) are visual controls that can be very helpful to the group leader. The team member's name or picture is at the top of the board and the days of the week (and sometimes week, month, or quarter) on the side. The boards can be set up several different ways. Every team member is assigned a short 5-minute-or-less task each day to complete. This can be expanded to include safety and TPM tasks as well. When the task is completed, its tag is turned over to show the complete side. The advantages of these boards are that they get all the team members in the area involved in the care and maintenance of the area, and they can be used to maintain compliance for various tasks, for example, fire extinguishers. A 5S board can be designed for self-auditing. If the person does not do their task, everyone else knows in real time. A simple walk around the area to inspect the tasks provides the audit function. We always include a card to reset the board, which is given to a different person each week.

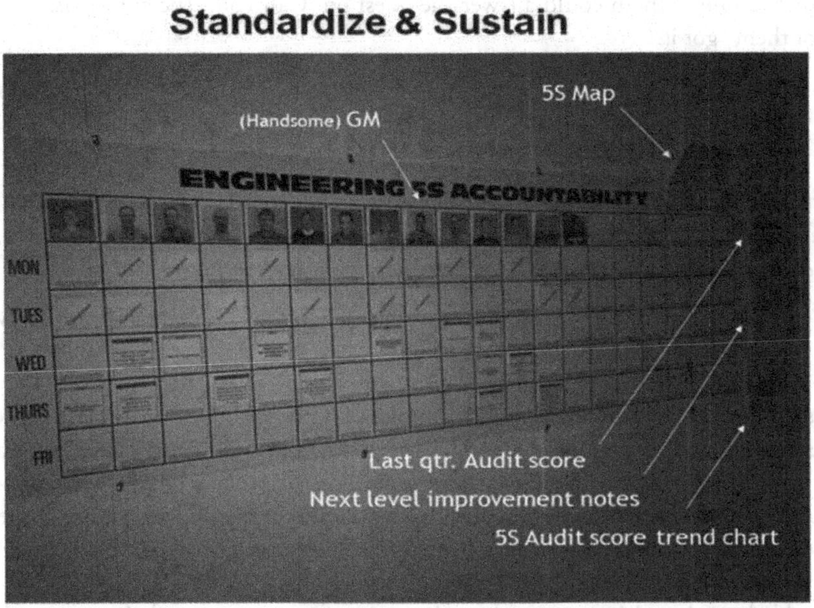

Figure 8.15   5S Board for an Engineering Department—Each person has a daily 5-minute 5S task. When it is complete, they turn the magnet over.

Source: Courtesy of Joe McNamara, president of Ttarp Industries, and BIG Archives.

Implement Hourly Line Measurement—*What We Normally Find!*

When we tour areas, we typically find the following:

■ There is no way to tell if the area is on schedule to the plan. When we ask about production information, if it exists at all, it is normally in a computer somewhere, but no one can see it. It turns into a historical report in which no root-cause analysis is done or action is taken.
■ OEE,[14] a measure of our true capacity, is based on past experience (demonstrated capacity)[15] and looks better every year as a result.
■ Standards are not updated or followed. The line generally has so many problems that it cannot even meet the "average or lower" target that has been set. So, over time, group leaders continually lower the target until they find a level the line can meet every day and keep senior leadership happy. This becomes a never-ending downward spiral. It's so bad at some plants that we literally have seen the scheduled capacity reduced by 70% or more over 5 to 10 years. This waste is all hidden and not tracked in any financials.

This reminds us of a video in a series that aired in the United Kingdom, called *Troubleshooter*. It was produced and featured the late former chairman of ICI, Sir John Harvey Jones. At a company called Sydney's Toys, Sir John was interviewing the shop floor Leadership Team (composed of the group leaders and managers) and asked them a simple question: "Who is in charge of profitability for the plant?" None of them could answer the question. Can you? The answer is: They all were! But none of them "got it."

What's a Key Performance Indicator?[16]

I often say that when you can measure what you are speaking about, and express it in numbers, you know something about it; but when you cannot measure it, when you cannot express it in numbers, your knowledge is of a meagre and unsatisfactory kind . . .

—Lord Kelvin[17]

KPI stands for key performance indicator. Examples of KPIs could be on-time delivery or fill rate, quality, headcount, and so on. These measures break down into different categories. They can be results-focused, like on-time delivery or parts per million, or process-focused, like first-pass yield (FPY) or process-cycle time. These measures can be leading or lagging indicators of the future. A lagging indicator might be sales per team member, whereby a leading indicator may be real-time output per hour.

We should always be raising our productivity target if we are constantly improving. We recommend companies implement KPIs with a focus on capturing leading process indicators. Examples could be takt time, cycle time, and percentage value added, WIP inventory, FPY, rolled-through-put yield,[18] and day-by-hour tracking, among others. We must transition our thinking to believe if we get the processes right the results will take care of themselves.

Any process-related item can be measured at some level. Measure it as a percentage or a standard number and create a graph to watch trends. In our opinion, it's critical to manually track your performance. If you want to dig deeper into the situation, you also need to check other areas to get the full picture. We believe in putting the full picture in front of the team and challenging them to achieve the targets (see Figure 8.16).

KPI	Original	Current Condition	% Improvement
Pieces Produced	191	245	28.3%
WIP (Days)	6.1	2.1	-65.4%
Product Travel	1023	270	-73.6%
Production $/SQ foot	$39	$56	43.4%
Daily Production $	$57,300	$73,500	28.3%
Production $/Employee	$2,605	$3,341	28.3%
Cycle Time (Seconds)	2143	1496	-30.2%
Lead Time (Minutes)	2958	1036	-65.0%

Figure 8.16 Key Performance Indicator Targets.

Source: BIG training materials.

The Role of KPIs[19]

Why do we need KPIs? Wouldn't it make life much easier if there were no goals or targets? What would be the result? For most of us, it would be poor performance or lackluster results. KPIs give us a challenge, and all of us have a deep-seated desire to improve and be better than the day before. Most of us are naturally competitive. It is important for all of us to constantly tap into that desire. People like to be challenged. Think about when you felt the most exhilarated or satisfied in life and it is normally when you overcame a huge challenge. Providing challenges to our team members is part of our human aspect of BASICS®. Some of us need that constant pressure or challenge to perform well every day.

Beware, You May Get What You Measure

It is really important to understand what and how you are measuring. Once a target or KPI is established, if the proper behaviors are not in place, people will try to "game" the system or "cheat" to make the target. For instance, you can game the OEE metric by using past performance versus ideal machine cycle time or by reducing the number of changeovers (increasing the batch size), thus improving your run time but increasing your inventory. This is especially important in areas like safety, where traditional KPIs should not be set as they will do the opposite of their intent. For instance, measuring lost workdays or near misses and putting rewards in place will generate the opposite of the intention. People will be afraid to report a near miss because they will get blamed or won't get their bonus or may ruin the perfect company record. For complex domains, it is impossible to prevent accidents because you are dealing with humans who always make mistakes. The best we can do is let the desired culture emerge. In the words of Gary Wong,

> [o]ur anthro-complexity view of safety is different from the traditional view held by industry leaders and executives. It has been strongly influenced and supported by the Cynefin Framework. Safety in organizations is not produced or manufactured. Safety is an emergent property of many interacting forces, such as employees, policies, incentive systems, and regulatory requirements in a complex adaptive system.[20]

Implement a Day-By-Hour Chart

The day-by-hour chart[21] (see Figure 8.17) is like a scoreboard at a stadium. It captures the plan by hour and by shift for each line, area, or department. The information is updated by the team leader in real time. If there is a variance between the plan and actual for the hour, positive or negative, the team leader or team member enters the variance, an explanation for the variance, and any containment actions or countermeasures implemented on the chart. The real value in the chart is twofold:

■ It shows the team members how they are doing against the plan.
■ It allows us to assess and fix the root cause(s) in real time for the variance so it never comes back.

There should be some type of action taken by the group leader to begin a root-cause analysis and take countermeasures to correct the variance. If the problem can be corrected right away, it is noted on the sheet. If it cannot be corrected right away, it should go to the daily management

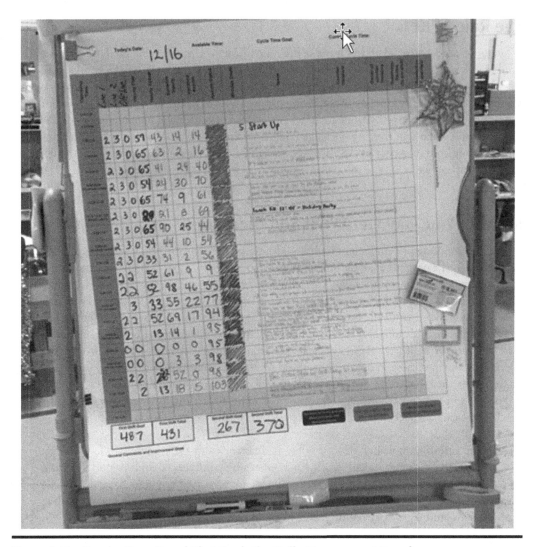

Figure 8.17 Day-by-Hour Board That Feeds the Daily Management Board.

Source: BIG training materials.

board under the appropriate heading and then have a root-cause analysis performed by the team leader or group leader. The key is to flush out all the problems in the line and make them visible. If the variance is positive, we also need to understand why.

The day-by-hour chart gives the team members something to shoot for each hour since they know from sitting in the analysis sessions that these times are achievable. When we first set up the line, we normally do not require the team leader to fill in the plan column, but we do get them used to recording the actuals each hour. Experience has told us that when we put the plan on the sheet immediately, the team members think we want them to rush in order to meet the numbers. Nothing could be further from the truth. "Quality first, the speed will come" is our mantra. We let them get used to the line and work down the learning curve, and normally a week later, we will start entering the plan by hour.

Some plants will set the targets at 80% or less of what could be achieved. This is wrong. It is important to set the day-by-hour chart plan to align with the results supported by the video analysis and job breakdowns. Reducing the plan numbers to make the team members happy does not drive continuous improvement, it sends the wrong message, is not fair to the team members, and allows supporting functions to slack.[22]

Implement a Daily Management Board

The daily management board is a daily management communication tool created for each assembly, machining, and office cell to record problems and encourage root-cause analysis and corrective action to fix a problem (see Figure 8.18). The daily management board is a communication center that covers safety, quality, delivery, inventory/ideas, and productivity. Metric development should be evolutionary and focus on what the business needs and ultimately tied to the customers within the control of the team members and support team. This approach brings accountability into the organization at all levels. It also is the beginning of developing a Goal Deployment Process[23] environment, where everyone on the shop floor sees how they contribute to the strategic goals of the business.

The board is unique in that KPIs are focused on what is important to the team members, which are tied to the goals of the organization. For example, for safety, we ask team members what they think would be good to measure and would be applicable to them. Again, it must be in their control. For delivery, did they have all the parts and tools they needed? For quality, were the bills of materials accurate? Were the drawings correct? We fill out the safety cross, which shows if we had any accidents or near misses, and then we document any unsafe conditions or behaviors or share safety observations from video audits from the day prior.

The support team and group leader are assigned to the board; the manufacturing engineer, quality engineer, buyer, and planner are all responsible for checking the board and assigning their name as the owner of the issue for their functional area. The support team responds to problems that could not be solved immediately by the team leader and provides feedback to ensure the operations run smoothly. The team members from all the different cells in a focus factory may all attend the same huddle in the morning, but they may each have their own daily management board for their individual cells. This is unique to each company. We discuss this more later as not only is this part of the Implement and Check steps, it is also part of Sustain.

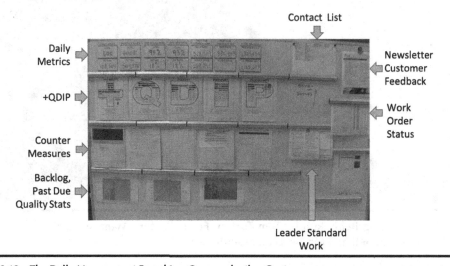

Figure 8.18 The Daily Management Board Is a Communication Center.

Source: BIG training materials.

Simple Rules for KPIs

When it comes to KPIs, it's best to keep it simple and effective. We have a list of rules to follow when it comes to creating these goals:

■ They must be within the team's sphere of influence and ability to control the KPI.
■ It must be measurable.
■ It supports and aligns with the overall organizational objectives.
■ It's attainable *yet not easily attainable.* (Provide a challenge/stretch target.)

The next step is to develop a vehicle to communicate the information. It's important that the daily management board (see Figures 8.19 and 8.20) is in the area where the work is completed. Placing them in a conference room out of sight defeats the purpose of real-time visual controls. Ideally, you will find a place close to where the work is being done and in a high-traffic area. This will make it a natural place for the team to meet and be observed regularly by anyone walking by the area. With today's technology, many people want to jump directly to monitors and computer system displays, so why would we encourage tracking the team's progress using manual graphs? (See Figure 8.21.) We do this for several reasons:

■ Manual tracking creates an emotional attachment to the data and forces each person to understand the data.
■ They are easy to update and manage, even if the computer system goes down.
■ Your team members cannot see it if it is on someone's computer, which makes it impersonal.

Figure 8.19 Meeting Being Run by Tom Turton, Focus Factory Manager Xylem Corp. Tom is also a Master Black Belt and Master Lean Practitioner.

Source: Lean Practitioner Field Book.

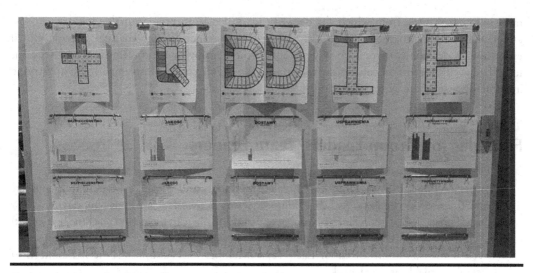

Figure 8.20 Leadership Daily Management Board.

Source: BIG training materials.

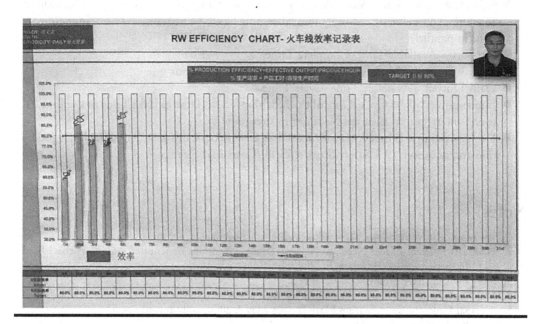

Figure 8.21 Manual Tracking. Visual Control – Helps promote System 2 thinking.

Source: BIG training materials

- It provides a vehicle to help each person understand the formula and what is necessary to improve the KPI.
- We want our leaders to spend their time at the gemba . . . not at their computers in the office!

Some companies insist on tracking their progress electronically. If it is visible to everyone and is updated in some automated fashion in real time, it's okay. However, it should only be used for more automated lines, from which the data can be pulled from programmable logic controllers and gaps can be highlighted immediately or used in conjunction with manual systems. But if everything is electronic, there is no way to capture the hour-by-hour problems and for the teams to update their progress on solving the root cause. We highly suggest implementing it and trying it manually first before ever automating.

Formulas for Group Leaders/Team Leaders

- Takt Time = Available Time ÷ Customer Demand
- Available Time = Total Time Less Breaks, Meetings, and the Like (weekly meetings are amortized across the days, e.g., 25 minutes meeting per week = 5 minutes per day)
- Cycle Time = Total Labor Time ÷ Number of Team Members (if there is no machine bottleneck)
- Cycle Time = Available Time ÷ Factory Demand
- Cycle Time = Amount of Labor Each Team Member Has Assuming Line Is Balanced (if there is no machine bottleneck)
- Number of Team Members Required = Total Labor Time÷Cycle Time
- Total Labor Time = Labor Value-Added + Labor Non Value Added Time
- Complete Time = Labor Value-Added + Labor Non Value Added + Machine Value Added + Machine Non Value Added (note that labor time has to be in addition to machine time, not done in parallel)
- Capacity = Available Time÷Complete Time
- Hourly Output = 3600 seconds÷Hour/Cycle Time in seconds
- Daily Output = Available Time÷Cycle Time
- Interruptible WIP = Cycle Time of the Machine÷Cycle Time or Takt Time of the Line. If it is non-interruptible, then double interruptible quantity.
- Kanban Sizing = (Total Amount Needed to Cover Replenishment Time [includes production and delivery] * 2 + Safety Stock + Yield)/Container Size

Notes

1. www.kent.edu/yourtrainingpartner/know-difference-between-coaching-and-mentoring
2. HBR article Every Leader Needs to Navigate These 7 Tensions by Jennifer Jordan, Michael Wade, and Elizabeth Teracino February 20, 2020.
3. Story by Andy McDermott.
4. Mark Jamrog, SMC Group.
5. Personal LinkedIn message from Mark Jamrog May 7, 2020, and LinkedIn post.
6. [pg. 48, The Responsibility Process]
7. Capturing lessons learned days later will be missing key learnings because we remember things differently over time.
8. Michael Meyers.
9. Card Based Control Systems for Lean Work Design, Thurer, Stevenson, Protzman, 2016 CRC Press.
10. Some type of Andon signal, light, sound, or card system.
11. The setup team may or may not be a dedicated team or individual and generally team members also help with the changeover.
12. Michael Meyers.
13. The first 5S board of this type to my knowledge was created by Joe McNamara in 1999.
14. OEE stands for overall equipment effectiveness.

15. For an explanation of demonstrated capacity, see The Lean Practitioner's Field Book: Proven, Practical, Profitable and Powerful Techniques for Making Lean Really Work, Productivity Press; 1 edition (April 4, 2016) Protzman, et al.
16. The term *KPI* is rapidly being replaced in many companies by the term *BPI*, or business performance indicators. This can be very confusing for some, and for that reason, we are going to use the term *KPI*. The distinction we will make is that the KPIs of a value stream or cell roll-up into BPIs. As such, we will consider KPIs to be subsets of BPIs.
17. Lord Kelvin, 1893, Lecture to the Institution of Civil Engineers, 3 May 1883 From http://zapatopi. net/kelvin/quotes.html I learned of this quote from a TEDx presentation: Quantify the unquantifiable: Tom Gilb at TEDxTrondheim, Nov 3, 2013.
18. Multiply the FPY at each station.
19. We are talking about applying KPIs within the context of the simple and complicated domains of Cynefin. KPIs don't necessarily make sense in the domain of complexity, chaos, or Aporia/Confused.
20. Gary Wong and Associates http://gswong.com/author/admin/
21. Depending on the type of work center, these charts are going to differ, and there is no one size fits all. A manufacturing line producing many parts an hour is going to differ from a machine shop where there will be some hours with no production recorded due to extensive cycle times greater than 60 minutes.
22. While we set the plan to the minimum standard achieved in the analysis (e.g., fastest times), we plan for the business at an adjusted rate based on the stretch targets in place.
23. Similar to Hoshin.

## Chapter 9

BASICS® Check by Implementing Leadership Development and Standard Work

Figure 9.1 BASICS® Lean Leadership Development Path—Implement/Check.

Source: BIG training materials.

DOI: 10.4324/9781315155227-9

> Great companies cannot be built on processes alone. But believe me, if your company has antiquated, disconnected, slow-moving processes, particularly for those that drive success in your industry, you will end up a loser.
>
> **—Lou Gerstner**[1]

The great companies in the world "out-execute" their competitors day in and day out, in the marketplace, in their manufacturing plants, in their logistics, in their inventory turns, and in just about everything they do. Rarely do great companies have a proprietary position that insulates them from the constant hand-to-hand combat of competition. If you want to out-execute your competitors, you must do the following:

- Communicate clear strategies and values.
- Align your priorities.
- Create a goal deployment plan (GDP).
- Reinforce those values in everything the leadership does—show them your back.[2]
- Allow people the freedom to act—psychological safety.
- Trust they will execute consistently within the core values—empowerment.

All organizations are filled with good people that are working really hard. The questions are, "how are their actions tied to your management objectives," and "how are those objectives tied to value for the customer?" If people are working, but it's not tied to your objectives . . . then it's just busywork. We often find teams are busy solving problems, but they might be expending their energy on solving the wrong problem(s) or ones that could just be eliminated.

The culture starts at the top with the philosophy, values, and the "real" belief system of the executive team.[3] By "real" we mean they must live their beliefs. Many companies have great values but don't live them or make decisions based on them. Leadership must understand that delivering on their customer-focused results requires true teaming with a shared mental model at the senior leadership level with a crystallized focus and daily tracking system. Ask yourself, is your company's Executive Team completely aligned on their goals and priorities, and is it laser focused on what to work on next? If the Executive Team is not aligned,[4] what can be said for their direct reports?

We view leadership as four tiers: Work Cell, Department, Plant Manager, and Corporate (see Figure 9.2). By reducing organizational layers, where it makes sense, the formal communication structure becomes more transparent and increases the ability to manage by making it less complex. Leadership needs to remove unnecessary tasks and firefighting by teaching Team Member Self-Reliance and Business Practice Improvement techniques to address the gaps in the current organizational structure. The Executive Team must clearly define the future role of the group leader and develop leader standard work and train and coach middle management on how to supervise team members effectively using their new skills and tools.

The Four Keys of Executive Leadership

1. Go and See
2. Ask Why (not who)
3. Show Respect—Challenge and build trust
4. Lead by Example—Ask yourself the following question daily: To which team member did I show respect today by challenging their knowledge and capacity?

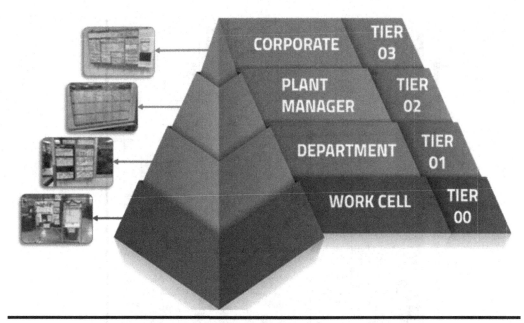

Figure 9.2 Four Tiers of Leadership: Work Cell, Department, Plant Manager, and Corporate.

Source: BIG training materials.

As a leader, please allow the team members an opportunity to expose issues and view them as an opportunity to improve a process. The Leadership Development Path is a system designed to foster participation, track improvement, assign open issues, facilitate daily planning, and develop alignment across the organization. It is intended to bring cross-functional teams together and provide a forum for quick-hitting 5- to 15-minute huddle meetings very focused on specific process-focused measures that will drive the department toward success and enable the next level up to be successful.

A team needs a leader, structure, and goals, accompanied by goal tracking systems. Additionally, a team needs a system of accountability for achieving those goals. The goals must be focused ultimately as discussed earlier on increasing value to the end customer. Generally, the team leader of the cross-functional team is somebody who has direct responsibility for goal achievement as well as the actions of the department. This doesn't mean that the team leader must govern all the team members directly, but they do have to have the ability to guide the work that is done on a daily basis.

A fully functioning system links goals using visual management combined with the GDP (see Figure 9.3) from one level of the organization to the other, focusing on leading and lagging key performance indicators (KPIs). The GDP relies on marrying process-focused goals to the results-focused goals they support. When implemented properly, one can see a direct correlation from the most senior team to the team member and all levels between (see Figure 9.4). This plan consists of our corporate goals, department goals, and process goals (see Figure 9.5). The importance of goal alignment is to make sure that all the goals and actions support the success of the level above. This alignment is key to making sure no activity is wasted on things that are not critical to the business. The GDP can also be used to intentionally set gaps based on projections in order to stay ahead of your competition.[5]

Safety,Quality,Efficiecy Machines improvement,Inventory Turn,Customer satisfation — WUXI GDP DANILO

TEAM

Ting,Forest,Alex,melania,Paolo,Daniel;Alessandro,Bruce,Claudio,Hubert,Justin

Rif.	Sub	Action Step/ Kaizen Events	Owner	Assist	Start Date	End Date (Planned Completion)	Baseline Number	Project impact	Target	Stretch target	Planned vs actual	J	F	M	A	M	J	J	A	S	O	N	D	Current Status/ Reasons / Coutner Measures
2.20	a	see action A3 for crack reduction	Ted CHEN	Mark,Alessandro,Alex	1/1/16	6/1/16	0.15%	0.10%	0.07%	0.05%	%	0.03%	0.03%	0.03%	0.02%	0.03%	0.03%	0.02%	0.01%					Discussing with R&D final result before starting in production. In week 13 test 5 code
2.3		Lumps on the mix reduction	Paolo MAGNANO	Ted,Alex,Simon,Niccolo,Joyce,Justin	1/1/16	12/31/16	0.07%	0.03%	0.05%	0.04%	%	0.07%	0.09%	0.08%	0.04%	0.04%	0.08%	0.08%	0.05%	0.05%	0.05%	0.05%	0.05%	
2.30	a	Action plan for critical code QC/R&D/Production start mix 686 and 1039 (sequency change on mix)	Paolo MAGNANO	Ted,Simon,Niccolo',Alex.	1/1/16	12/13/16	0.03%	0.01%	0.02%	0.02%	%	0.04%	0.05%	0.07%	0.02%	0.02%	0.07%	0.07%	0.02%					Result of the test was ok. Barge needs to change the group in the mix. Need approval from Barge R&D. Problem for Kifo
2.30	b	Buy raw material direct from supplier	Richard WANG	Paolo,Helen,Niccolo	1/1/16	12/13/16	0.02%	0.01%	0.01%	0.01%	%	0.03%	0.04%	0.01%	0.01%	0.01%	0.01%	0.01%	0.01%					5 Resin already arive this week but not tested. More material under evaluation.
2.30	c	compare different supplier kevlar performance	Joyce	Justin	8/1/16	12/13/16	0.01%	0.005%	0.005%	0.005%		–	–	–	–	–	–	–	0.01%					
2.30	d	cut pieces by manualfor kevlar to check the performance and need a cut machine	Justin	Joyce	8/1/16	12/13/16	0.01%	0.005%	0.005%	0.005%		–	–	–	–	–	–	–	–					
2.30	e	need a new machine to cut pieces of Kevlar	Caligiuri	Justin,Joyce	9/30/16	12/31/16																		Fix a meeting with Cali about this maybe next week
2.4	A3	Less thickness pads reduction	Paolo MAGNANO	Andy,Ted,Caligiuri	1/1/16	12/13/16	0.15%	0.10%	0.05%	0.05%	%	0.08%	0.05%	0.04%	0.02%	0.03%	0.02%	0.02%	0.01%	0.07%	0.07%	0.06%	0.05%	
2.40	a	see action A3 for less thickness pads reduction	Ted CHEN	Quality inspectors	1/1/16	6/30/16	0.15%	0.10%	0.05%	0.05%	%	0.05%	0.05%	0.04%	0.02%	0.03%	0.02%	0.02%	0.01%					This action is done but need to watch each month which is why it is yellow. This is a High Maintenance item for Paolo.
2.50		Press Overweight material reduction	Paolo MAGNANO	Andy,Alex	2/1/16	9/30/16	0.13%	0.08%	0.05%	0.05%	%	0.05%	0.04%	0.04%	0.06%	0.10%	0.07%	0.03%	0.02%	0.07%	0.06%	0.06%	0.06%	
2.50	a	Weekly systematic inspection mechanics about weigthing regulation systems	Andy	Alex ZHOU	2/1/16	9/30/16	0.04%	0.03%	0.02%	0.01%	%	0.03%	0.03%	0.04%	0.05%	0.07%	0.06%	0.02%	0.01%					This action is done but need to watch each month which is why it is yellow. This is a High Maintenance item for Paolo.
2.50	b	set evaluation system for line maintanence	Andy	Alex ZHOU	9/1/16	10/30/16	0.04%	0.03%	0.02%	0.01%														need to talk with Andy about this action
2.60		Internal cycle time reduction (weigthing, oscillator, compactor) reduction : overtime cycle	Paolo MAGNANO	Andy,Alex	2/1/16	8/31/16	0.15%	0.08%	0.07%	0.07%	%	0.14%	0.06%	0.09%	0.11%	0.15%	0.16%	0.10%	0.04%	0.09%	0.08%	0.08%	0.07%	
2.60	a	PMs - "replacement of oscillators part Sliding and blocking (press 1,2,3) restore base conditions.	Andy	Dario RICCA	2/1/16	8/31/16	0.10%	0.05%	0.05%	0.05%	%	0.14%	0.09%	0.09%	0.11%	0.15%	0.16%	0.10%	0.02%					Press #2 and #3 done and press #1 end of august
2.70		Preforming reduction	Paolo MAGNANO	Andy,Alex	2/1/16	6/1/16	0.09%	0.06%	0.04%	0.04%	%	0.04%	0.09%	0.04%	0.004%	0.005%	0.008%	0.015%	0.008%	0.05%	0.05%	0.04%	0.04%	
2.70	a	PMs 'replacement of oscillators part Sliding and blocking (press 1,2,3) restore base conditions.	Daniel YAO	Andy	2/1/16	4/30/16	0.09%	0.05%	0.04%	0.04%	%	0.04%	0.09%	0.04%	0.004%	0.005%	0.008%	0.015%	0.008%					Press #2 and #3 done and press #1 end of april.

Figure 9.3 Goal Deployment Plan with Monthly Monitoring.

Source: BIG training materials.

Rif.	Sub.	Action Step/ Kaizen Events	Owner	Assist	Start Date	End Date	Baseline Number	Project Impact	Target
2		'Quality - Scrap reduction from 1.6 to 0.7% (stretch target 0.6)		Team	1/1/16	12/31/16	1.6%	1.10%	0.70%
2.1		Broken pads reduction			1/1/16	9/1/16	0.57%	0.37%	0.30%
2.1	a	improvement of unloading of IR oven to blue box (press 1, 2 and 9) , press3 hybrid oven			1/1/16	30/04/2016	0.20%	0.07%	0.10%
2.1	b	Move code (homologation) from static oven to convective oven continuous			1/1/16	9/1/16	0.16%	0.15%	0.10%
2.1	c	New elevator after grinding			3/1/16	9/1/16	0.20%	0.15%	0.10%
2.2		Crack reduction			1/1/16	12/31/16	0.15%	0.10%	0.07%
2.2	a	cycle time changing (degasing) for NAO products QC/R&D/Production			1/1/16	6/1/16	0.04%	0.05%	0.03%
2.2	b	Introduce an Pre-Heating system on Mixing drums (press 1)			1/1/16	3/1/16	0.05%	0.03%	0.02%
2.2	c	Extention Pre-Heating for all press			12/1/16	6/1/17	0.06%	0.02%	0.02%
2.3		Lumps on the mix reduction			1/1/16	1/1/16	0.07%	0.02%	0.05%
2.3	a	Action plan for critical code QC/R&D/Production start mix 686 and 1039 (sequency change on mix)			1/1/16	6/1/16	0.05%	0.03%	0.03%
2.3	b	Buy raw material direct from supplier			1/1/16	6/1/16	0.02%	0.02%	0.02%

Figure 9.4   Goal Deployment Plan Is Managed from Both Top Down and Bottom Up.

Source: BIG training materials.

Corporate Goal Results KPI (Parent)

Process-Focused Goal KPI (Child)

Process-Based Action (Child)
This can also be an A3 (Child) if actions or solutions to root cause are not known

Rif.	Sub.	Action Step/ Kaizen Events	Owner	Assist
2		*Quality - Scrap reduction from 1.6 to 0.7% (stretch target 0.6)		Team
2.1		Broken pads reduction		
2.1	a	improvement of unloading of IR oven to blue box (press 1 , 2 and 9) , press3 hybrid oven		
2.1	b	Move code (homologation) from static oven to convective oven continuous		
2.1	c	New elevator after grinding		
2.2		Crack reduction		
2.2	a	cycle time changing (degasing) for NAO products QC/R&D/Production		
2.2	b	Introduce an Pre-Heating system on Mixing drums (press 1)		
2.2	c	Extention Pre-Heating for all press		
2.3		Lumps on the mix reduction		
2.3	a	Action plan for critical code QC/R&D/Production start mix 686 and 1039 (sequency change on mix)		
2.3	b	Buy raw material direct from supplier		

Figure 9.5 Corporate Goal, Department Goal, Process-Based Action, and Sometimes Includes Sub-Actions.

Source: BIG training materials.

During a normal workday, the leader takes on many different roles, including trainer, mentor, leader, umpire, delegator, inspirational leader, counselor, and consultant. While it's not a mandate that they be "liked" by everyone, they do need to be respected, which means a leader must be diligent, disciplined, a good communicator, and follow a routine.

Implementing Leader Standard Work

Creating and implementing "leader standard work" helps develop the routine necessary for a good leader. It is that part (or parts) of the day that can be standardized for the leader. It's providing a structure for how to become a critical thinker. Typically, the higher up in the organization, the less standardized the work becomes. Since we are focused primarily on the team leader and the group leader, whose work is primarily in the ordered part of the Cynefin Framework, we know the majority of their day can, and should, be standardized. In this domain, the process is disciplined, and people should be held accountable to follow their standard work and solve problems as they are encountered. It is then up to the team members to incorporate the necessary countermeasures, using the common problem-solving method, to either contain the problem initially or ensure the problem doesn't come back. Once problems are solved, the solutions must be documented in the standard work. The standard work is a dynamic, not stagnant, tool. It is not to remain dormant, posted on a wall or at a station, never again to be updated, just because it's laminated. This is not only how we sustain the system but continually drive improvements to the system. Team Member Self-Reliance and Improving Business Practices are at "the heart" of the system, which makes leader standard work "the brain."

In any system, if there is no standard, there is no discipline, no way to measure your progress, and no way to hold anyone accountable. Leader standard work is part of the Leadership Development Path, which provides a sustainable system to integrate, improve, and sustain changes with daily feedback to realign and solve problems as they arise. It is an hour-by-hour guide to assist the group leader and team leader carry out their roles and responsibilities during a normal shift. It is supported by pre-, during-, and post-shift checklists. The following is an example:

Pre-Shift Checklist—60 Minutes Prior to Start

- Read shift-to-shift logbook.
- Cordially greet and communicate with the team.
- Observe the physical condition of the team and address any and all concerns.
- Take attendance and report attendance—advise management of any personnel-shortage situations.
- Walk through areas and confirm checks are updated and report all problems to the appropriate group.
- Warm-up exercises—encourage teams' participation and educate them on its benefits.

During Production

- Check personal protective equipment and address any discrepancies, that is, the condition of team members' physical appearance.
- Observe any physical signs from team members during job performance.
- Ask team members how they feel and observe their behavior.

- Visually look for any safety violations, tripping hazards, 5S conditions.
- Monitor shift per group leader duties mentioned earlier and audibly listen for abnormal equipment noises and malfunctions.
- Productivity—identify and eliminate waste (*Muda*).
- Follow up with the team leader ensuring repetitive problems are counter measured.
- Observe productivity visual controls such as andon board, downtime clock, inventory, and so on; report any crisis situation and develop downtime activity plans with team leaders; and be prepared to go into backup mode if possible to bypass equipment.
- Breaks and lunch. Prepare for breaks and prepare an agenda for quality updates and make any special announcements during a break. Coordinate maintenance work and identifies problems that can be worked on during breaks. Observe attendance at break and follow up with team members on any absences.

Post-Shift

- Verify completion of shut-down procedures and notify the manager and the next shift of any shut-down problem such as safety, quality, and productivity.
- Updated shift-to-shift log—complete log covering all problems from the day with the current status.
- Input daily and monthly overtime if necessary.
- Reports—complete all required reports such as direct run, near miss, and so on.
- Attendance calendar—update attendance calendar and confirm tomorrow's attendance; communicate to those necessary.
- Confirm 5S is being met by all teams.
- Send-off—observe all teams as they go home; note any limp, pained expression, and cordially recognize each team member as they leave.

How Much of Their Time Should Be Standardized?

- 100% of team member's jobs and changeover jobs should be standardized.
- 100% of team leaders should be standardized with time allocated for problem-solving, continuous improvement, and 5S built into the standard work. We recommend starting with 10% of the time dedicated to daily improvement with a goal to get to 50%.
- 80% to 90% of the group leader's time should be defined in their leader standard work with time allocated for problem-solving, continuous improvement, and 5S built into the standard work.
- 30% to 50% of a manager's time should be defined in their leader standard work.

Implement Team Leader Standard Work

Team leader standard work (see Figures 9.6) can be normally 100% standardized. Leader standard work for the team leader and group leader should be done by the manager with consultation from the team leader and group leader, respectively. Leader standard work can take many forms depending on the company (see Figure 9.7) and should include daily improvement and updating team member standard work. We suggest the team leaders and team members be responsible

TEAM LEADER STANDARD WORK
GOAL 50% ON CONTINUE IMPROVEMENT

9 HOUR JOB					
HOUR	Operation Description (what to do)	Key Points and Quality Notes (how do it)	Reasons for Key Points (why do it)	Time	Cumulative Time
1	HANDOFF/PRE SHIFT CHECK LIST share and check daily plan with the previeus	read on the board the daily plan, change over plan, delivery plan	collect information for lead the shift	45	45
2	make sure that all the employee start the shift without stop the machine as the standard work required	walk on the machine from line 1 to line 8 and semiline, check the daily attadence, employee PPI, safety machine control, the cicle time & 5S. recheck and packaging area on the 2 SHIFT and on the 3 SHIFT ARE CONTROL BY TEAM LEADER. (check if the delivery plan are folow. check 5S and quality production and	safety: people control quality: rules follow up productivity: machine stop 5S: rules follow up	60	105
3	transfer data shift information			30	135
3	check with the team leader in each area. Make sure the schedule is to maximize piece flow.			15	150
3	break time 10 minutes			10	160
4	prepare change over plan and follow up. (RECORD ON THE VIDEO)	check the actual prodactivity line by line and plan the change over time for each line. Transfer information on the board, share information with the mechanical leader, and with the floater.	PRODUCTIVITY	60	220
6	check in the lines 1 to 7 productivity and make adjustments as needed	check the machine data on the screen, check machine scrap (on the scren is written machine scrap), check 5S, check quality of the basic pads and the finish pads. AUDIT: Check drawing with actual pads, conformity of the control plan packaging instruction, check list , MASTER	make sure all the rules are FOLLOWED	120	340
7	break time 30 min			30	370
7	AUDIT STANDARD WORK	complete the standard work audit sheet		5	375
7	(CONTINUE IMPROVEMENT)			10	385
8	CONTINUE IMPROVENT	ask to operator for improvement idea.		70	455
8	break time 10min			10	465
8	E-MANUFACTURING PROJECT	check if the confirmation paper and the display of E-MANUFACTURING have the same quantity, if not check the root cause and possible action. Check the scrap number (Lmust be the	start up the project	5	470
8	break time 10min			10	480
9	share information with the other team leader on arrival time			15	495
9	HANDOFF/POST SHIFT CHECK LIST wait the end of the shift and check the daily sheet			45	540
			Rev: Date: By:		

Figure 9.6   Team Leader Standard Work Example.

Source: BIG training materials.

for updating the standard work and then running it by the proper departments for approval and finally quality to update in the overall quality system.

Group Leader Standard Work

The group leader's job should be 80% to 90% standardized again with a goal to dedicate 50% of their time to daily improvement. The group leaders should audit the team leader's standard work daily and team member's standard work at some frequency based on the product being produced or transactions being generated each day. When the group leader starts to audit the team

| Follow-up / Notes | | Mitch | | | Mitch | | | | | | |

Daily (middle column, under Mitch)

Reason check couldn't be completed
Replace Day by Hour Sheets
Update % and Late $ in Hall
Adjust Orders on Heijunka Rack by Hour
Enter in Month By Day
Timesheets
Supervising Cells and Soliciting Ideas
Prep for QDIP Meeting
Conduct +QDIP Meeting
Order Supplies
Round Assy Cells & Shipping / Work on Countermeasures / Work on CI / Work on Safety / Lean Sheet
Check on Expedited Shipments

Daily (right column, under Mitch)

Task	Times	WK 1	WK 2	WK 3	WK 4	WK 5
Replace Day by Hour Sheets	7:00 – 7:15					
Update % and Late $ in Hall	7:15 – 7:20					
Adjust Orders on Heijunka Rack by Hour	7:20 – 7:30					
Enter in Month By Day	7:30 – 7:45					
Timesheets	8:00 – 8:15					
Supervising Cells and Soliciting Ideas	8:15 – 9:45					
Prep for QDIP Meeting	9:45 – 10					
Conduct +QDIP Meeting	10 – 10:10					
Order Supplies	10:10 – 10:30					
Round Assy Cells & Shipping / Work on Countermeasures / Work on CI / Work on Safety / Lean Sheet	10:10 – 3:30					
Check on Expedited Shipments	3:30 – 4:30					

Countermeasure Notes | **Focus Factory 2 Check** | **Assembly Cells Over view**

Reason check couldn't be completed
Safety (see reverse)
Lean Sustain (see Reverse)

	WK 1	WK 2	WK 3	WK 4	WK 5
Safety (see reverse)					
Lean Sustain (see Reverse)					

Month: **May 2011**

Monday

Safety/ TPM Check Point Details   Lean Check Point Details   **Monday**

Daily
- ❑ Make sure area is free of trip hazards
- ❑ Make sure trash is emptied in each cell
- ❑ Check scrap against scrap boards and put on scrap table
- ❑ Electrical Panels & Fire Extinguishers Unblocked
- ❑ Make sure extra parts are returned to the stockroom
- ❑ Operators wearing proper PPE

Weekly
- ❑ Check fluids in Shipping Bagger

Daily
- ❑ Make sure operators are following standard work
- ❑ Ask operators for improvement ideas
- ❑ Write down implemented ideas in Idea Tracking Book (Take before and after pictures)
- ❑ Update QDIP board with any productivity or safety issues or unsolved root causes for countermeasures

Weekly
- ❑ Film one part in 05 Cell
- ❑ Update standard work for 05 Cell
- ❑ Implement one idea in 05 Cell

Figure 9.7   Team Leader Standard Work Example.

Source: BIG training materials.

members, standard work, or the changeover team's standard work, we call this the start of the layered audit process.

Standard Work Layered Audits—CHECK

> Superb execution is not just about doing the right things. It is about doing the right things faster, better, more often, and more productively than your competitors. People respect what you (the CEO) inspect.

> —Lou Gerstner[6]

Layered audits eventually involve all levels of the organization. If the senior leadership audits it, then their team members will think it's important. This is an area where leaders need to model the behavior they are looking for within their leaders. It's also critical to create an environment where this is not optional. Part of the audit should be the frequency of how often they are revised. Standard work forms are the best method to keep track of ongoing improvements.

My boss did an informal layered audit and was looking at one of our standard work processes. He looked at me with a puzzled look on his face and made this statement: "*It's really surprising to me that with the implementation of our glass wall system [see Figure 9.8], work team meeting and all the participation we talked about, that your team couldn't make one improvement on this process in 8 months.*"

He won't even remember saying it, but it had a profound impact on me. What he was saying was standard work charts aren't a task. They are a tool to have team members participate in driving continuous improvement. Our standard work charts should reflect those improvement ideas. Taiichi Ohno said, "*Without standardization there can be no improvement.*" Needless to say, the next visit to the plant, it was the first place he wanted to look. We made one small improvement that eliminated 2 seconds of cycle time from a team member's planned cycle time. The only thing he looked for was the revision date. He wanted to see if we were using it as a tool.

Strategy to Update Standard Work

As improvements are made, changes should be documented, and standard work updated. There is always a better way to do things and all improvements need to be captured. After any improvement is made, the next step is to train the staff, across all shifts, in the new process. This is done by taking the standard work developed by the team, based on the video analysis, and communicating it to the rest of the staff. We typically do this in small groups, across shifts, and ask for their input as we go. Sometimes, it is necessary to pull the whole staff together to get everyone to agree on what steps for the standard work are going to be. Most of the time, the person's job doesn't change, just the order in which they perform the steps of the process are (see Figure 9.9).

Why Plant Leader Standard Work Is Important— Forest Sheng[7]

I experienced becoming a plant manager, in China, during a period of exponential growth. I encountered obstacles, sometimes hidden, which caused my team to be strong in will but weak in power. I was thinking, "Why is it so complex today when everything was running well yesterday?" Based on reflection, analysis, self-critiquing, listening, and feedback using continued investigation, I discovered my team was firefighting and reacting to the changes. After firefighting, they found they had lost work orders and control over almost everywhere, including people, product, process, quality, machine, material, and the like, basically everything under their leadership. Finally, we recognized the need to explore the subject of our leadership in the shop floor management system of this fast-growing business process.

One can imagine the challenges that come from an exponential growth environment. How can one leader survive? In this case, our consultant[8] guided and coached us and introduced us to leader standard work and the goal deployment plan. We were also supported by our operations director. They helped us build the standard work over 18 months with several trial runs until we achieved great results. The leader is the person who usually heads a team in a certain area or company staff level. All team members watch their backs, and the leader usually has the shadow in each team member's mind. A mature team usually has the same behavior and mindset as their leader who is developing the team to think in their methodology and execute in their way.

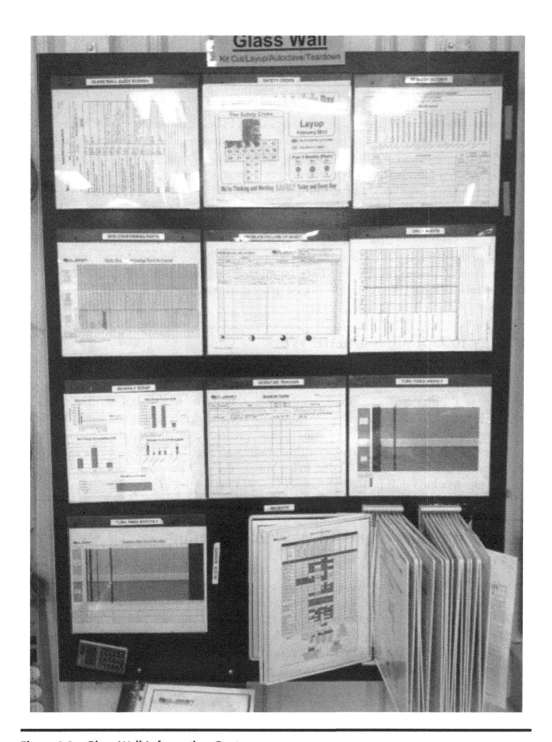

Figure 9.8 Glass Wall Information Center.

Source: BIG training materials.

Standard Work Linkage

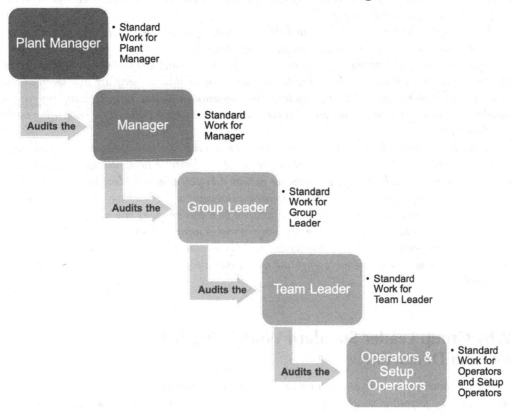

Figure 9.9   Standard Work Linkage.

Source: BIG training materials.

   For example, if the leader has a growth mindset and systems view, usually, the team will be the same as him/her. If the leader is a hands-on style, usually all team members will follow. So the leader takes the role of not only leader but also coach who can train the team and lead the team to work in a proper way to achieve high performance. The leader is not only working to improve themselves on how well the job can be done but also needs to improve how well they can organize a team to do the job. All these are dependent on the leader's leadership abilities. The leader develops themselves by developing the people.

   How can we build and sustain the leader's leadership? Standardization by building standard work for leaders has proved, for me, to be very effective. Why does leader standard work make sense? Let's go back to check . . . When a leader loses control of the team and their performance during firefighting, the leaders will lose the sequence and as a consequence forget to take care of daily, weekly, and monthly tasks. If there is no standard work, then the leader has no way to remind him/her when to proceed with the relevant work, at the required time, with the requisite people. This tends to lead to even more firefighting.

   The leader standard work structure usually includes the regular daily, weekly, and monthly tasks of the leader including subjects like team member development, problem-solving, planning and scheduling, setting goal deployment plan targets, and updating progress. I always put my standard work in my pocket and insisted my team leaders do the same. This helps remind them to proceed with a certain job at a certain time, and if for some reason they can't, we note it on the leader standard work for reflection and countermeasures later if needed.

For example, the leader is defined to hold daily management meetings (production meetings) from 9:00 a.m. to 10:00 a.m. with all operation department representatives every day. The subjects are defined to be safety first, quality always, and productivity, which are linked by goal deployment plan to the company priorities (blue chips). All topics around these subjects are also specified and quantified by each relevant KPIs. By standardizing my work in the morning, it means my team is standardized to prepare for this meeting. We have shown great progress after three years using leader standard work.

Applying leader standard work we have improved our scrap rate from 1.6% to 0.4%, efficiency from 78% to 91%, and inventory turnover rate from 3.8 to almost 14 turns, among others. Now, we continue in this way with the high performance sustained by potential risk identification in advance, fast problem-solving, with everyone working toward a common target. We have effective communication and close cooperation, which helps us run well. In fact, this company saw exponential growth in the past three years but still managed to achieve more progress using leader standard work. It should be viewed as a management tool. It can help leaders build systematic and sustainable management strategies that will change a leader from firefighting to running a high-performance area focused on daily execution.

Why Group Leader Standard Work Is Important— Melania Demartini[9]

Leader standard work, same as the team members, is really useful for planning in detail the daily activity and not forgetting the priority: Gemba walks and audits the standard work on the workshop floor. As we know, training is really important, but without an audit we can become inefficient. People like to find an excuse and always take the opportunity to change the job to the way they are thinking it should be. They think it is the right way, but standard work is really an instrument that gives to all the same the correct methods and is valued as the best time for checking safety, quality, and productivity.

For the leader it is the same. If you cover a leader position you should really think to plan your working time well in order to avoid lost time, overtime, and cover all the jobs. It's really important for supporting your team. When you first start leader standard work, it is really difficult to plan your time, but when you get used to it, you will see the benefit, and it will benefit your team successfully. It is the disciplined use of an authorized formal system. As we go up to the ladder, the plan could become weekly, monthly, quarterly, and so on, depending on the level of the organization. For example, a plant manager, same as the frontline group leader, might commit to a daily Gemba walk to touch base with the group leader in each area just to understand how the plant is running each day, what the issues are and yes, to be visible to everyone. "People respect what you, the leader, inspect."

Why Team Leader Standard Work Is Important—Justin Shang[10]

Standardization is the foundation for improvement. We use standard work for production to manage the deviation and keep the process stable. For leaders, the leader standard work can also help to improve the management deviation. I think leader standard work should be more focused on work principles and work priorities. It should define well what time to deal with which kinds of work. Using leader standard work has the following advantages:

■ *Leaders can use the standard work to build the work model for the team.*
■ *Avoid missing points in daily work.*
■ *Improve the work efficiency.*
■ *Put most important things first and try to avoid the firefighting.*
■ *Leader standard work is not static. Leaders need to review the management results and continue to make improvements.*
■ *Keep the management style consistent.*

Leader standard work allows us not to be totally dependent on the people and allows us to make sure that when positions change, other people can follow the good results.

The Value of Leader Standard Work—Eric Ren Hui[11]

Leader standard work is a Lean tool for changing behavior and Lean sustainability.

Ideally, a Lean organization's leaders lead their subordinates to eliminate wastes anywhere and anytime. However, this behavior is mostly an ideal model. In fact, Lean transformation from scratch is really hard work and a minimum 3 years of relentless commitment. Therefore, changing leaders' behavior to the ideal model runs through the entire Lean transformation process. Particularly, the successful Lean transformation entails leaders' buy-in, passion, self-participation, drive, and unwavering commitment starting from the Lean preparation, setting up Lean model line, aligning and indoctrinating Lean principles, developing Lean talents, leader standard work, to sustaining Lean culture.

Thereby, as long as the Lean model line has been equipped with Lean layouts and stations, it is crucial to start leader standard work. This enables us to embed Lean behavior on a daily basis even after the Lean team has gone. It eventually helps drive sustained Lean results while cultivating Lean leaders to help facilitate major cultural change.

■ *Role of leaders changes from 100% running lines to a combination of running lines and improving lines*
■ *Transition from the firefighting and reactive shop floor to being predictable and proactive*
■ *Ability to help sustain all lean improvement and build continuous improvement into managerial systems*
■ *Ability to provide routine standardized behaviors with repeatability and reproducibility for all leaders to adhere*
■ *Ability to drive leaders to commit to continuous improvement, developing talents and problem-solving skills*
■ *Ability to significantly support policy deployment, routine work, and problem-solving skills.*
■ *Leader standard work mainly consisting of visual management, accountability, and discipline.*

Notes

1. Who Says Elephants Can't Dance Paperback—Lou Gerstner, Harper Business; Reprint edition December 16, 2003.

2. My Leadership, The China Years, Ritsuo Shingo, 2016, Utah State University.
3. See the Leadership Roadmap by Russ Scafede.
4. Note the alignment can change based on external influences and the Executive Team has to be flexible and adaptable.
5. This is an application of the OODA (Observe–Orient–Decide–Act).
6. Who Says Elephants Can't Dance Paperback—Lou Gerstner, Harper Business; Reprint edition December 16, 2003
7. By Forest Sheng (Sheng Lin), former plant manager—29 December 2018.
8. Charles Protzman, Business Improvement Group (B.I.G.), LLC.
9. Melania Demartini—Supervisor Development Leader, ITT.
10. Justin Shang—former team leader—ITT China Wuxi Plant.
11. Used with permission—Ren Hui, Lean Sensei as BIG Chinese partner.

Chapter 10

How to Maximize Your Profitability While Developing Your Leaders

See Figure 10.1

Figure 10.1   BASICS® Lean Leadership Development Path—Implement/Check.

Source: BIG training materials.

The Goal Deployment Process

The most important use of basic policy is to aim the entire resources and efforts of the company toward a well defined target. In a general way it charts the course that the activity of the company will follow in going toward the target. Making a clear statement of the objective of the enterprise is like providing a target for a man shooting an arrow with a bow. [Figure 10.2] shows such a man who represents company management holding a bow which represents company policies and an arrow which represents the total efforts and resources of the company.

If no target is provided for management (the man), toward which company efforts and resources (the arrow) can be aimed and directed, company policies (the bow), no matter how good they may be will be utterly useless. But altogether, policies, efforts and resources and ultimate purpose to which they are to be put are all part of a single picture. Any one part has a definite intimate inter-relationship with every other part, and no one part is able to stand alone. Each demands the co-existence of the other elements in order to comprise the total picture which is the entire business enterprise.

A great advantage to be gained in a statement of the objective is the stabilizing effect it is bound to have on all features of the organization. For one thing, employees will better understand the use to which their efforts are being put in relation to the total enterprise. At the same time, the statement of the objective will build up confidence in the customers by letting them know just what they can expect from the company. Then too, the part that everyone in the company must play in relation to the attainment of the desired goal is more easily recognized because of the stated objective.[1]

We call this the Goal Deployment Process (GDP).[2]

The policies created by management must direct the efforts and the resources of the company to a defined target – The fundamental objectives of the enterprise

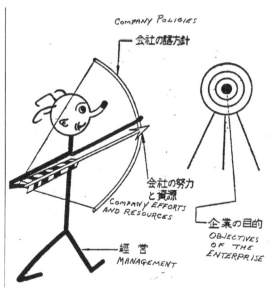

Figure 10.2 The Goal Deployment Process.

Source: CCS Industrial Management Manual, Charles Protzman Sr. & Homer Sarasohn, ©1949.

The Four Components to Maximize Efficiency, Effectiveness, and Productivity

The following are the four components that are supported by visual management, sustained by Gemba walks and watches, and linked into our strategic goals using the GDP:

1. High Efficiency
2. Zero Variation[3] in Quality—to get zero defects
3. Zero Percent (0%) Unplanned Downtime
4. Just in Time (JIT)/Pull/Synchronization

The group leader needs to focus on producing good parts in order to meet our goal of Customer First. Using this focus, we can understand where we are losing good parts in our current processes. By identifying losses in these areas, we are able to focus on and increase the percentage of good parts without overproducing. These four components, when combined with our everyday job of developing people, help us grow and develop ourselves. The end result is we meet our BASICS® fundamental principle, which is to build the lowest-cost, highest-quality product delivered JIT to our customer. This is where the BASICS® tools and the human aspect really need to be a collaborative effort. You cannot create and sustain a Lean environment without doing both.

1—High Efficiency

> *High production efficiency has been maintained by preventing the recurrence of defective products, operational mistakes, and accidents, and by incorporating workers['] ideas. All of this is possible because of the inconspicuous standard worksheet.*
>
> **—Taiichi Ohno**[4]

High efficiency means we get good parts on time at the lowest cost in the safest way possible. Notice the focus is on good parts per day. It doesn't matter how efficient we are if we are not producing *good* parts or services. It is possible, in an efficient JIT system, to produce a lot of bad parts very quickly. Therefore, the system must be effective in addition to being efficient in order to be productive. High efficiency means we are maximizing our resources to get the most output possible with those resources. This encompasses all our BASICS® tools and requires that standard work be in place for all business processes, both people and machines, and that it is continuously improved. This also means the target has to be set to drive the maximum number of parts possible. We have a saying:

> If we follow our standard work, our processes are capable, and everything is running at the correct[5] cycle time, then there is no reason why we should not hit our projected output of good parts per day.
>
> **—Charles Protzman**

Productivity, Efficiency, and Effectiveness[6]

> *Efficiency is doing the thing right. Effectiveness is doing the right thing.*
>
> **—Peter F. Drucker**

When we create standard work we strive for the best utilization of man, machine, methods, and materials (the four Ms). To do this, we must understand what it means to be productive, efficient, and effective to provide the lowest-cost, highest-quality products at the lowest cost.

Productivity

Productivity is the number of products produced in a certain amount of time with a certain amount of labor. The products could be physical products or transactional such as processing an invoice or even writing internet blogs. Productive means getting things done, outcomes reached, or goals achieved and is measured as output per unit of input (i.e., labor, equipment, and capital).

Efficiency

Efficiency is based on the energy one spends to complete the product or service as well as timing. A person has achieved efficiency when they are getting more done with the same or better accuracy in a shorter time, with less energy and better results.

Effectiveness

Effectiveness is the ability to achieve stated goals or objectives, judged in terms of both output and impact. It is the degree to which an activity or initiative is successful in achieving a specified goal. Dave Rizzardo states:

> I often would demonstrate this by pretending I was painting a wall. I was very productive in that I got the room done well within the time standard allowed. By maximizing the paint coverage with each stroke, I showed my outstanding efficiency as I continued painting with a big smile on my face. However, it turns out I am not that effective because I just learned I'm supposed to be painting the wall in the next room, not this one . . . hmmm.[7]

2—Zero Variation in Quality

If we need inspection, control plans, FMEA,[8] or even a quality organization, it is because we do not have capable processes. If our processes were truly capable, that is, zero variation to the standard, we would have zero defects. This requires a change in mindset and behaviors. The problem is we do not have capable processes. When we shoot for zero variation it is different than going after zero defects. Remember, it is the error that causes the defect. This is where the BASICS® tools and Plan–Do–Check–Act (PDCA) come into play. Going after zero variation is process-focused whereas going after zero defects is results-focused.

When we are working on sustaining, the first major problem we normally encounter is quality related. Either we did not make the right part or we did not make the right part right the first time. We all know about quality problems, and we all have them. If we have standards in place, then this means someone did not follow the standard, there is a problem with the standard, or the process is just not capable of producing good parts to the standard. Rework and scrap become the by-products, which robs us of time, good parts, and profitability. Too often, we measure scrap but not the rework, which then gets accepted and hidden.

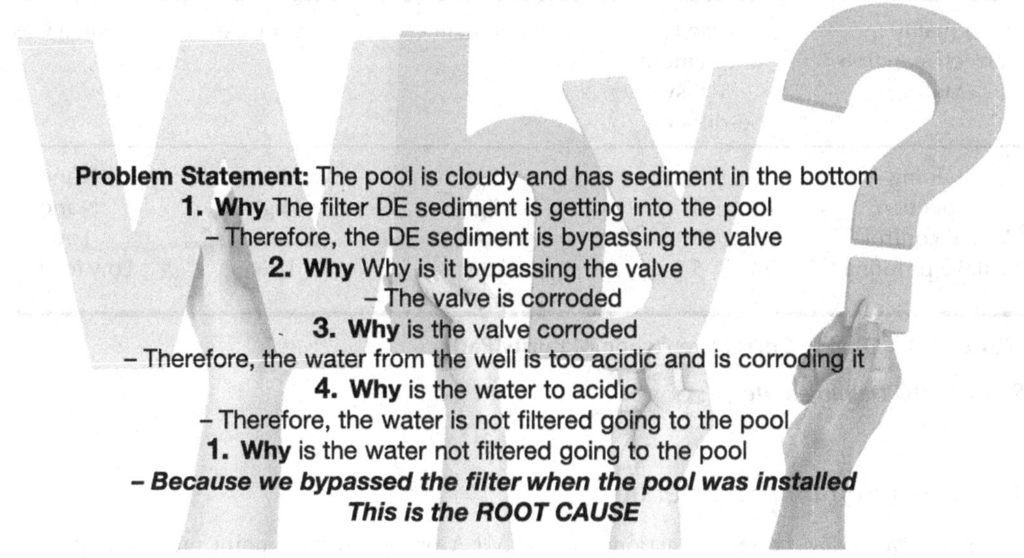

Problem Statement: The pool is cloudy and has sediment in the bottom
1. **Why** The filter DE sediment is getting into the pool
  – Therefore, the DE sediment is bypassing the valve
    2. **Why** Why is it bypassing the valve
        – The valve is corroded
          3. **Why** is the valve corroded
– Therefore, the water from the well is too acidic and is corroding it
              4. **Why** is the water to acidic
        – Therefore, the water is not filtered going to the pool
          1. **Why** is the water not filtered going to the pool
      – *Because we bypassed the filter when the pool was installed*
              This is the ROOT CAUSE

Figure 10.3   Five Whys—Real-Life Example: Pool.

Source: BIG archives.

As discussed earlier, we find that team members, instead of trying to find the real root cause, just tend to ignore the problem or "shoot from the hip" and "throw a solution at the problem."[9] This is the foundation of firefighting. For example, we all know the 5 Whys tool (see Figure 10.3), and most of us know Pareto charts, but many times we just choose not to use them. Normally, it is because we perceive that we don't have the time. This is the problem with implementing counter-measures at most companies because they can very easily turn into work-around solutions.[10] The work-around solution takes the pressure off finding the root cause and fixing the problem. This turns out to be normal human behavior backed by brain science and cognitive biases. It is impor-tant for people to believe in themselves and believe they can learn new behaviors, break the bad habits, and rise to the challenge.[11] This is where the Team Member Self-Reliance and Improving Business Practices incorporated with on-the-job development become so important.

Quality Corrective Action Maturity Path

When we find a problem in quality or anywhere for that matter, we find there is a maturity path to the steps that are taken to mistake proof an operation or process. This is also true whenever root cause corrective actions are initiated internally or by suppliers (see Figure 10.4). The first two steps below are the number one and two corrective actions we typically see from 8Ds[12] or supplier quality documentation. Steps 3 and 4 are what we should receive:

1. Train or retrain the operator
2. Add more inspection
3. Create visual controls
4. Mistake proof the problem

Quality Corrective Action Matrix	Ease to implement 1-easy 5-difficult	Maintenance	Labor Cost	Capital Cost
Training	1	High	High	None
Inspection	1	High	High	None
Visual controls	3	Low	Low	Low
Mistake proofing	5	Low	Low	Low to High

Figure 10.4   Quality Corrective Action Maturity Path.

Source: BIG training materials.

1. Train or Retrain the Operator

Whenever we review corrective actions or an FMEA or even simply point out a problem, we normally find the number one response to fix it is to provide more team member training. This response is usually taking the easy way out and is a way to ignore or throw a solution at the problem. It also creates a "blame" environment where people then begin to create excess work and time to do CYA activities.

If it really is the problem, then it begs the question; how and why aren't the team members trained properly to begin with? Is there any documentation on how they are trained? Are they certified to do the job? Are they physically capable or mentally able to do the job? If they train or retrain the person, will it fix the problem so it will never come back? We would argue that if the job is based on a human being doing it, then it will always be subject to mistakes. Humans are fallible creatures. We are at best 1 to 2 sigma based on the 6 Sigma Scale of 3.4 ppm defects.[13] The next questions are, If we say training is going to be the corrective action, can they sustain it? How will they sustain it? How frequently must the training be conducted? What if they get someone new? This means we will have to constantly check (inspect) to make sure the person is doing it properly. If so, then what does "properly" mean?

Therefore, we contend that training is a high-maintenance, high-cost proposition, which will never permanently fix the root cause because *the* people are the *root cause of the* problem. The only action which will fix this is to figure out a way to "take the person," that is, human fallibility, out of the job. We are not saying not to train or that it should not be part of the solution. We are saying that training, by itself, should never be a corrective action. Team Member Self-Reliance is the answer to most of these questions but will still not fully address team member mistakes which are inevitable.

2. Add More Inspection

Will adding inspection really fix the root cause? Inspection is the next most frequent corrective action we see. This is another easy way out for the supplier to avoid the need to really root cause the problem. Here again, if people are doing the inspection then by MSA[14] standards they are only capable of 80% to 95% quality. If this is the case, what are the chances that adding human inspection will fix the problem? Once again, this is a high-maintenance, high-cost solution. We

Sigma Level	DPMO	Percent Defective	Percentage Yield	Short Term Cpk	Long-Term Cpk
1	691462	69.%	31%	0.33	-0.17
2	308538	31%	69%	0.67	0.17
3	66807	6.7%	93.3%	1.00	0.50
4	6210	0.62%	99.38%	1.33	0.83
5	233	0.023%	99.977%	1.67	1.17
6	3.4	0.0034%	99.99966%	2.00	1.50
7	0.019	0.000019%	99.9999981%	2.33	1.83

Figure 10.5   Six Sigma Table.

Source: BIG training materials.

must pay for the person(s) doing the inspection who in many cases *may be taking apart what was just put together to inspect it*. This actually happens in real life.

Do they have the proper tools to inspect it, or is it just visual or visual using a visual display? Dr. Deming said, "You cannot inspect quality into a system." This was the point of his famous red bead demonstration.[15] So as a group leader you must realize this and, while it is not an excuse, no matter how good you are there will still be mistakes made. (See Figure 10.5.)

3. Create Visual Controls

Visual controls are the next step to mistake proofing. We *should* see this as a corrective action. The goal here is to make the mistake immediately visible. The mistake can be human or machine. How do we get the human to tell us when there is a problem? How do we get the machine to tell us when it has a problem? How do we get the machine to stop before or worst case after it makes a mistake? Visual controls are normally a relatively low-cost, low-maintenance solution. However, while this solution highlights the problem, it doesn't necessarily prevent the problem.

4. Mistake Proof/Poka Yoke the Problem

In order to mistake proof the process, we have to design the process so a mistake cannot be made or we have to implement 100% automated visual inspection (jidoka). We *should* see this as a corrective action. These solutions are all around us in products that we use every day (see Figure 10.6).

Think about it, everything your quality control (QC) Department does adds cost to the product and reduces profitability. The job of QC is not just to inspect but also to constantly think how to fix the process so we do not need inspection. We tell inspectors, Your job should be to make your job go away! Don't worry, if you can do this, trust me, we will find a new place for you in the organization. There are several types of quality-sustaining tools:

1. Daily leadership execution meetings
2. QC circles[16]

Fixture for assembly to make sure consumable bottles are placed in correct holes in tray

If cotter pin is missing, it shows up

Figure 10.6   Mistake Proofing Examples.

Source: BIG training materials.

3. Implementing rapid improvements
4. Ongoing improvement kaizen (ideas generated from team members on the front lines)
5. Point kaizen events
6. Company-chartered continuous improvement groups, BIG Idea Clubs[17]

The ultimate vehicle for sustaining, regardless of the approach, is the constant updating of the standard work and building the standard work into the quality system to capture all improvements, making it part of "muscle memory."

Control Plans

Control plans, like inspection, shouldn't be required. Their very nature says that our processes are not under control. If our processes were good, that is, zero variation, we wouldn't need inspection or control plans. But most of us do not have processes free of variation. As a result, we need control plans until we can get rid of the need for them. The control plan looks at all the things that could go wrong at each station or machine; then it looks at what documentation is in place to make sure we are making good-quality parts; then it looks at the severity of the problem and countermeasures to be taken. Team members should be aware of the control plans, and they should be posted somewhere in the area.

3—Zero Percent (0%) Unplanned Downtime and Total Productivity Maintenance (TPM)

TPM is the combination of preventative and predictive maintenance techniques. There are many books[18] written on this topic. Briefly, the idea behind TPM is the team members share in the upkeep and "own" their equipment and machines in the process. They sometimes do the simple, easy maintenance procedures like filling oil and the like and immediately notify maintenance when a big problem occurs. Maintenance is responsible for the more difficult weekly and monthly maintenance activities. Maintenance is responsible to find predictive maintenance solutions which can predict well ahead of time if there is going to be a problem.

Preventative and predictive maintenance processes should also have standard work and visual controls. These techniques become more numerous with technology but today come in mostly three forms, infrared, sonic, or vibration technologies. With the advent of industry 4.0 (the Internet of Things, or IOT) and Manufacturing Execution Systems (MESs), we now have the ability to build this sensor technology into the machines. Sensors can tell you if a motor needs lubrication or it is going to go bad before well ahead of time. This is similar to brakes squeaking on a car. They can tell you if the cubic feet per minute in a duct are too low or too high and so on. In the future, TPM checklists will be a thing of the past. Advanced technologies have been the driving force behind the growth of the manufacturing industries, and they will have a greater role to play in the industries of the future. As new technologies emerge, manufacturers will adopt them, or be forced to choose them to survive.

Overall Equipment Effectiveness (OEE)—Operational Availability (OA)

OEE stands for overall equipment effectiveness, whereas OA stands for operational availability. These two measures should be the same, but sometimes they are used differently. Both measures mean the equipment is available and working when needed. OEE was originally designed to be used to measure a single machine, normally the bottleneck, not the entire line or assembly areas. For non-bottleneck machines, we use OA because they may be idle by design for a portion of each cycle. The ideas behind both these metrics are that we need the equipment to be available when we need it to be available. JIT does not work if the equipment is down. OEE (see Figures 10.7 and 10.8) is the multiplication of three metrics that are usually measured individually. These are available time, operating rate, and quality.

Available Time

Available time is the percentage of time the machine is available during its scheduled run time. It does not include any planned downtime but does include setup times, break times, and any unplanned or unexplained downtime.

Operating Rate

The operating rate is the percentage rate at which the machine runs at the cycle time at which it was designed to run. It is not and should not be based on demonstrated cycle time or past performance.

Quality

Quality is the percentage measure of good pieces produced. If we follow the standard and we have good quality, then the next thing, which can prevent us from getting all the possible good parts, is downtime. There are two types of downtime:

1. Planned Downtime

Defects

Machine Slowed Down

Unplanned Downtime

Time Spent Making Good Parts

Overall Equipment Effectiveness (OEE) Calculator*

OEE is a measure of the value added to production through equipment.

Do not enter blue numbers. Blue numbers are preset formulas

A	Working Minutes Per Day	480	Actual time per day or per shift
B	Loading Time Per Day = Available Time (Min)	420	Actual time less time taken for meetings, breaks, lunch
C	Total Output Per Day (Good and Bad Units)	15,300	Actual output per day from day by hour chart
	Types of Downtime		
D	Setup	90	Time from last good piece to first good piece
E	Breakdowns	60	Any time equipment is stopped due to breakdown
F	Adjustments	15	Any time equipment is stopped due to adjustments
G	Total Downtime Per Day	165	(D+E+F)
H	Defects	153	# defects in total output per day from day by hour chart
I	Actual cycle time	0.0200	Measured at the machine via watch or videotape
J	Ideal cycle time	0.0160	Cycle time the machine should be running per manufacturer's specs or speeds and feeds
K	Operating Speed rate	80%	Ideal cycle time / actual cycle time (J / I))
L	Net Operating Rate	120%	[(Output per day x actual cycle time) / (loading time - downtime)] [(C x I) / (B - I)]
M	Availability Rate	61%	[(Loading time - downtime) / loading time] [(B - G) / B)]
N	Performance Rate	96%	Net operating rate x operating speed rate (L x K)
O	Quality Rate	99%	[(Total output - defects) / total output] [(C - H) / C]
P	**OEE**	**58%**	(Quality rate x performance rate x availability rate) (O x N x M)

* Based on TPM Development Program, Nakajima, Productivity Press, 1982

Figure 10.7 Overall Equipment Effectiveness.

Source: BIG training materials.

7/14/16			**Daily Report Card**			
Metric	Line 1	Line 2	Line 3	Line 4	Line 5	Line 6
Code	1423/1473	1328	1269/1411	1130/1282	1136	1351
Available Time Hrs 7:30A to 7:30A	24	24	24	24	24	24
Available Time Minutes	1440	1440	1440	1440	1440	1440
PLANNED DT - i.e. TPM or NO CUSTOMER DEMAND ONLY Minutes	0	0	0	0	0	0
Available Time Minutes	1440	1440	1440	1440	1440	1440
Theory Output Pieces (no changeovers,	15,709	17,280	19,200	23,351	21,600	25,412
Actual Output pieces	7,450	8,228	7,751	16,310	14,960	14,089
Actual Output Time Minutes	683	686	581	1006	997	798
Available Time						
Downtime (not changeover) Minutes	382	683	614	248	380	546
Downtime (not changeover) Hrs	6.4	11.4	10.2	4.1	6.3	9.1
Unexplained Downtime Minutes	347	67	202	113	58	58
Unexplained Downtime hours	5.8	1.1	3.4	1.9	1.0	1.0
Unexplained Downtime %	24%	5%	14%	8%	4%	4%
Total Downtime	12.2	12.5	13.6	6.0	7.3	10.1
Change Over						
# Setups	1	0	1	1	0	1
Setup Time Physical Minutes	20	0	35	60	0	30
Total Setup Minutes	20	0	35	60	0	30
Total Available Time Percent	48%	48%	41%	71%	70%	56%
Operating Rate						
Designed Machine Cycle Time Seconds	5.5	5	4.5	3.7	4	3.4
Mechanics's Actual Cycle Time Seconds	5.5	5	4.5	3.7	4	3.4
Operating Rate Percent	100%	100%	100%	100%	100%	100%
Quality						
Scrap Pieces	79	55	95	214	73	127
Good Parts Percentage	98.9%	99.3%	98.8%	98.7%	99.5%	99.1%
Scrap - Time Lost Minutes	7.2	4.6	7.1	13.2	4.9	7.2
OEE (avail time x oper rate x quality)	47.4%	47.6%	40.4%	69.8%	69.3%	55.4%
ITT Efficiency	64%	71%	67%	81%	88%	62%
Full Setup Time Physical BEST	10		15			10
# SW Audits	1	1	1	2	0	1
# SW Audits Changeover	0	0	0	0	0	0
# SW Audits @100%	1	1	1	2	0	1
# Layered SW Audits	0	0	0	0	0	0
# Layered SW Audits @100%	0	0	0	0	0	0
# Improvement Ideas	0	0	0	0	0	0
Day By Hour Filled Out?	yes	yes	yes	yes	yes	yes

Figure 10.8   Overall Equipment Effectiveness.

Source: BIG training materials.

2. Unplanned Downtime—There are two types of unplanned downtime:
   - Recorded
   - Unexplained

Planned Downtime

Planned downtime is required and necessary for preventative maintenance or in cases in which the line may just not have enough customer demand to keep it running. So we plan to shut the line down. Either way, we do not count this time because we only want to get the number of good parts for which we have true customer demand. Remember, the number one rule is not to overproduce.

Changeovers from one product to the next also create downtime. Changeovers, including unloading and loading parts, should have standard work and should be constantly timed and tracked.

Unplanned Recorded Downtime

Unplanned recorded downtime is the result of either not following the standard work or by machines going down unexpectedly. It can be due to missing or wrong parts, quality problems, supplier delivery problems, and the like. Our goal is to have 0% unplanned downtime. Many companies have their team members track their downtime, but the first question we ask is, How accurate is it? What are the chances they are going to capture all of it or attribute it to the correct reason for the downtime? It is best to have the machines automatically track it using their PLCs.[19]

Unexplained Downtime

This is the worst problem of all because most companies, literally, have no idea they have it. One can have it for quite a while before any symptoms ever show up, and there are no financial metrics that exist to track it. Unexplained downtime is not new, but the company's discovery of it once we point it out is almost always new and the sheer extent of it catches companies by surprise (see Figure 10.9).

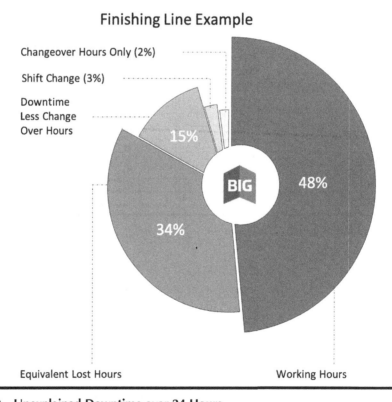

Figure 10.9   Unexplained Downtime over 24 Hours.

Source: BIG training materials.

We stumbled on this at a plant in Mexico and then in China. Their unexplained downtime turned out to be larger than all their other downtime put together. Prior to this discovery, we were primarily focused on reducing their setup time. When we ran the numbers, we found that the unexplained downtime was the equivalent of 34% of their potential output. This was an absolutely staggering number, which dwarfed their setup times. This means that if the company had 10 machines, then the equivalent of 3.4 of their machines were down 100% all day, every day. We call this a true example of what is known as the hidden factory.

This downtime can also occur if machines are not running at the proper cycle time or operating rate at which they were designed to run. In this case, we need to make sure the team members cannot slow down the machines. Many times, team members slow down machines because they are not capable of producing good parts at the designed operating rate. This can be due to a problem with the raw material or with the maintenance or upkeep of the equipment. The machine should have some type of external visual display with the actual cycle the machine is running versus the designed cycle time. This is the only way the group leader can know without having to look at the panel controls on each machine.

Unexplained downtime can be a huge loss of good parts. For instance, if a machine can make a part every 10 seconds, 360 per hour, but we slow it down to 20 seconds, then we lose 50% of our production. If this problem goes undetected, then eventually the standard will be changed to reflect the demonstrated output that will become the default capacity for the next year's planning. Once this is built into our scheduling system, the standard is reduced, and the planned output is forever less than what it should be. If our demand doubles, we will be forced to buy a new machine. What is surprising is when we hear that we don't have time to take the machine down for preventative maintenance (PM). If you work out the numbers, the machine is already down for several hours a shift regardless. What's the difference if we shut it down each day versus the entire weekend? In many cases, by adding planned downtime to do some PM, each day we may actually increase the uptime per day.

How to Calculate Unexplained Downtime

To calculate unexplained downtime, one must back into it by calculating the quantity of parts that should have been produced by the machine during the available time per shift. For example:

Step 1: Calculate "Theoretical or Installed Capacity." If we have a machine that is running at a cycle time of 5 seconds per part and assuming the team members are loading and unloading the machine within that cycle time, then the machine is capable of making 24 hours × 3600 seconds ÷ 5 seconds or 17,280 parts per day or 5,760 per shift.

Step 2: Calculate "Actual Good Parts" that were produced during the shift and multiply that by the cycle time per piece. This calculation will produce the time spent making good parts. Multiply the 10,000 parts produced by 5 seconds it equals 50,000 seconds. If we divide this by 3,600 seconds per hour it equals **13.88 hours or 57.8%** of the time producing good parts.

Step 3: Subtract the "Bad Quality Parts." Take the number of bad parts and multiply them by the cycle time per piece. For example, 500 parts are bad and scrapped. 500 parts * 5 seconds 2,500 seconds. If we take 2,500 secondsEqn003.eps 3,600 seconds = **.694 hours or 2.89%** of the time producing bad parts.

Step 4: Subtract the "Existing Recorded Downtime and any breaks, huddles, etc. where the line was planned to be down." Half of the downtime was set up related, and the other half was machine stoppages. Total reported downtime and breaks, etc. = **5 hours or 20.8%** of the time.

Step 5: Take the total time for the shift and subtract the results from Steps 1 through 4, that is, the time for good parts, setup time, and recorded downtime: 13.88 + .694 + 5 = 19.574 hours.

Step 6: "Unexplained Downtime Result." What's left is the *unexplained downtime*. 24 hours – 19.574 hours = **4.426 hours or 18.51%**

How Do You Find Unexplained Downtime?

Determining this unexplained downtime can be quite elusive. Going back to our example, let's say there was a robot putting springs into a part. When the robot cannot pick up the spring for some reason, it loses 1 second of time per occurrence. Since this was the bottleneck machine, then this lost time translates to 1/5 of a part. The robot was programmed to automatically try to pick up the spring three times before it gave up and scrapped the spring before trying another one. Now we have programmed in the loss of 3/5 of a part, but nobody really sees it or counts it. If the robot has trouble picking up the spring and then has trouble installing the spring, we could lose 6/5 (or 1 1/5) parts and the loss is completely hidden, because it normally gets added into the "cycle time." If we get a bad batch of springs and it happens 10% of the time, we will have lost 2.4 hours' worth of parts per day or 576 hours (72 eight-hour shifts) per year. The result of unexplained downtime is overwhelming, but in the moment, no one really notices it, like a slowly leaking faucet.

Normally, what we've noticed is the team members will try to fix the problem on their own. Every time they stop the machine, it results in more downtime, but they do not normally count it in their report because in their minds, it doesn't equate to "that much" time. If they stop the machine 12 times for 5 seconds, this results in a loss of 60 seconds or, in our case, 12 parts.

If the team member can't fix the problem with the robot, then they call the mechanic. Now the machine ends up being down for 18 minutes. If your company is like any company we've been to, the team member captures this instance as 15 minutes lost. Now we have three more minutes of unexplained downtime, simply due to our paradigm of rounding numbers to the nearest 0 or 5. If you have to retest a part, then you have *even more* downtime. You will never discover these issues If you do not have a day by-hour chart, with goals set to 100% of the theoretical output. The invisible time adds up exponentially.

We are also scrapping or reworking parts that were kicked out of the machine because they did not get a spring. These get counted and recorded in the scrap count but seldom converted into "lost time dollars." If the parts get reworked, then we are spending yet more time on these parts that are also not tracked but do not impact our unexplained downtime unless the rework is done on the same machine.

We cannot emphasize enough the problems created by unexplained downtime, and worse, that most companies are not aware it even exists. As a result, they end up compensating for it with additional lines, people, and equipment which the financial metrics will backup but unfortunately are wrong. It is a very expensive proposition. We must work to expose and capture downtime and identify it, explain the reasoning for it, capture the issues, and eliminate them.

4—JIT/Pull/Synchronization

JIT finishes the last of our four components. We will briefly run through some materials terminology you need to be familiar with as a group leader. To get good parts, we must have a good internal and external supply chain. The supply chain must deliver the right parts, in the right quantity, and on time. Supply chain problems can create downtime, force us to move work orders around, and

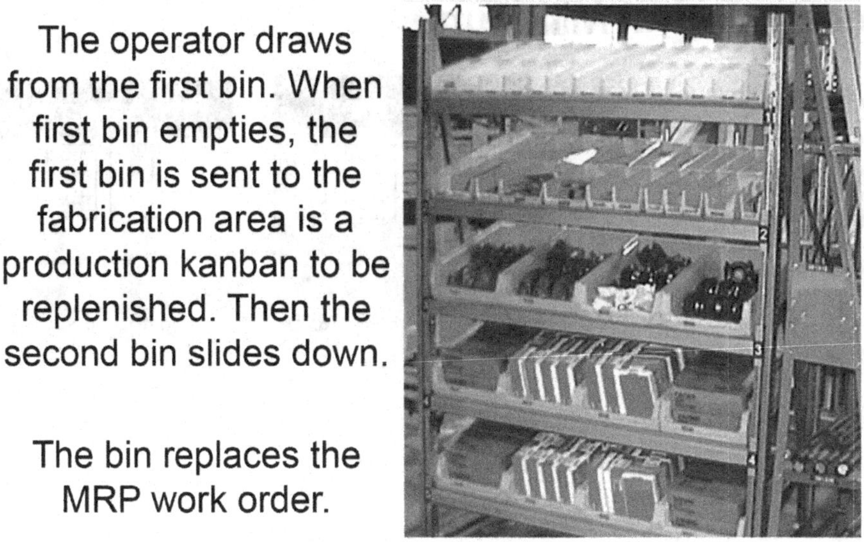

The operator draws from the first bin. When first bin empties, the first bin is sent to the fabrication area is a production kanban to be replenished. Then the second bin slides down.

The bin replaces the MRP work order.

Figure 10.10   Two-Bin Production Kanban System Example.

Source: BIG training materials.

create quality problems. Our goal is to work toward zero-excess work in process in the entire value stream. The analogy we use in our training classes is as follows: "How many of you have 3 months' worth of food lying around at home?" Everyone laughs. In some countries, the class responds that they have no inventory; they buy it fresh every day. We respond: "That is what we want in our factories . . . Fresh Parts. We want to eliminate stale, old, smelly parts."

When we ask about moving toward daily or hourly deliveries the first response is "It's impossible. . . . It would be too expensive." Yet, our entire food and perishables industry is built around just that. How can restaurants or grocery stores afford daily deliveries? One thing for sure in manufacturing is that if we had to do it, we would be doing it. JIT means we get the right part to the right place in the right quantity and quality JIT to minimize inventory and increase cash, which increases our working capital.

The most common form of JIT is a kanban[20] system that is generally using two-bin containers or in a flow-through shelf sequenced in the order of assembly (see Figure 10.10). There are mainly two types of inventory: lineside and supermarket. Lineside is the inventory on the line and the supermarket may be next to the line or in a centralized area. Ideally, both have flow-through racks that support first in, first out or earliest due date, but this is not always possible. In the beginning, the stockroom may be replenishing the supermarket, but the goal is to eventually replenish only from the supermarket and eliminate the stockroom. The goal is to get your suppliers delivering daily to your supermarket. If you get really good, you will eliminate the supermarket and deliver right to the line.

Milk Run

Whether the warehouse is next to the line or centralized it may require a milk run (see Figure 10.11). A milk run is a timed set-route run at some frequency (pitch), normally every hour, to replenish the lines using withdrawal or production ordering kanban cards and remove finished goods parts. Many times, it requires the purchase of a tugger (Figure 10.12).

Timed Internal Milk Run

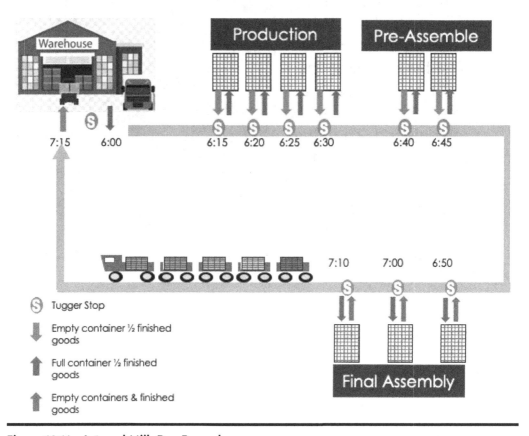

Figure 10.11   Internal Milk-Run Example.

Source: BIG training materials.

Water-Spider Process

A nonstarter in manufacturing is to use your team members to get their own parts or tools. We must keep team members working on the line because they make the money. To keep the team members at their stations, we add a position called a material handler or water spider. The water spider (see Figure 10.13) whether human or robot replenishes the parts when the bin is empty or when triggered by a kanban card. This increases productivity and efficiency in the area.

Types of Containers

There are various categories of containers:

- Recycle—Grind up and reuse.
- Reuse—Use the same container repeatedly.
- Repurpose—Figure out how to use the container in a totally different way or application.

Figure 10.12 Supermarket Tugger.

Source: BIG training materials.

Figure 10.13   Water Spider Replenishes Parts, Checks on Bill of Materials (BOM) "Special" Parts Availability, and Other Jobs as Needed.

Source: BIG training materials.

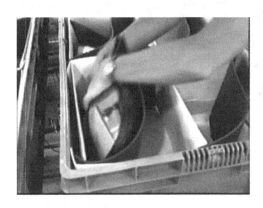

Figure 10.14 Reusable Containers—No Packaging to Remove. Lean has always been "green."

Source: BIG training materials.

Reusable containers (see Figure 10.14) are more than just friendly to the environment, they eliminate all the packaging, which used to come with the parts. Think of how much time and money are wasted each year, packaging up parts in bags, then small boxes, and then larger final shipping boxes. The receiving company also wastes time unpacking the parts. Many times, the parts end up on the line in the cardboard boxes in the plastic bags in which they were shipped. What does this do to efficiency? The first thing the team member must do is remove the parts from the box and or bag and then dispose of the rubbish. They will normally batch this task versus doing it as one-piece flow, so the line shuts down. There are companies that now have zero landfill waste. Lean is green!

Notes

1. CCS Fundamentals of Industrial Management- A textbook for The Communications Manufacturing Industry of Japan—by Charles Protzman and Homer Sarasohn—1948
2. The Goal Deployment Process is based on Hoshin Kanri.
3. CCS Fundamentals of Industrial Management- A textbook for The Communications Manufacturing Industry of Japan—by Charles Protzman and Homer Sarasohn—1948
4. www.oreilly.com/library/view/the-toyota-way/9780071392310/chapter12.html
5. Correct in this context means running to the manufacturer's designed cycle time or faster and optimum speeds and feeds for machines with maximum cutting time.
6. The TPS Practitioner's Field book, Protzman, Whiton, Kerpchar, Lewandowski, Grounds, Stenberg pgs 4–33 to 4–34, © 2016 CRC PRESS
7. Dave Rizzardo personal email correspondence 5–22–20.
8. Failure Mode Effects Analysis.
9. This has linkage back to the OODA (Observe–Orient–Decide–Act) loop. Most of us use implicit guidance and control as a default. Real problem-solving has a high energy gradient, and most people are reluctant to go down that path because we perceive it will take too much time.
10. This is the subject of another book we are working on tentatively called "Drive Thru Parking."
11. https://hbr.org/2019/01/why-open-secrets-exist-in-organizations www.uky.edu/~eushe2/Bandura/Bandura2009Locke.pdf
12. 8D is a corrective action investigation form used mainly in automotive.

13. When we conduct MSAs (measurement systems analysis tools) we have learned that only the very best team members may be 95% capable of doing the job correctly. Generally, it is in the 80% range, and this is with our average team members. So people-dependent processes are at best only capable of 80% to 95% good quality.
14. MSA is Measurement Systems Analysis.
15. https://deming.org/explore/red-bead-experiment/ Lessons from the Red Bead Experiment include the fallacy of rating people and ranking them in order of performance for next year (based on previous performance), as well as attributing the performance of the system to the performance of the "willing workers" in this simulation of an organization governed by what Dr. Deming referred to as the "prevailing system of management."
16. For more information, see The Lean Practitioner's Field Book: Proven, Practical, Profitable and Powerful Techniques for Making Lean Really Work, Productivity Press; 1 edition (April 4, 2016) Protzman, et al.
17. 40 Years, 20 Million Ideas: The Toyota Suggestion System, Yuzo Yasuda, Productivity Press, 1990.
18. The best books are written by Seiichi Nakajim.
19. PLC is a programmable logic controller that is the electronic brains of the machine.
20. *Kanban* means "signal." When one bin empties, it becomes a signal or trigger to refill it.

Chapter 11

The Organization Required to Support the Group Leader

See Figure 11.1

Development of people looks like a detour but it is actually the best shortcut.

—**Katsuaki Watanabe**[1]

Combining The BASICS® Tools & Human Aspect To Achieve Ongoing Daily Business Improvement

Figure 11.1 BASICS® Lean Leadership Development Path—Implement/Check.

Source: BIG training materials.

DOI: 10.4324/9781315155227-11

Executive Leadership

Leadership starts with the CEO and Executive Leadership Team, which becomes the driver and ultimate support team. When leaders become disconnected from the improvement activities, they lose touch with the center of where the value is created. If the CEO spends time at the gemba, on the shop floor, seeing how things really are, they begin to see the vast potential for improvements. Ironically, CBS had an Emmy Award–winning show called *Undercover Boss* in which the premise was the disguised CEO goes to the shop floor (or office) and talks to the people, gets their hands dirty, and learns what is really going on firsthand. Why does it take a television show to get leaders to the gemba? (See Figure 11.2.) If the CEO spends time at the gemba, on the shop floor, seeing how things really are, they begin to see the vast potential for improvements.

> I have taught my executive leaders to tour the shop floor every morning with their plant managers. This Walk teaches them to see the gaps and opportunities which helps them further develop their knowledge of the shop floor. I share my knowledge by asking questions and not giving the answers or telling them what to do. I always ask before I leave, "What can I do to help you?" I find when we get done my eyes have also been opened up to new ideas and opportunities. This is why we call it Continuous Leadership Development.

—**Davide Barbon**[2]

Leadership Self Evaluation/Qualities

- ❑ Shows people his/her back
  - • Humble, Modest
- ❑ Problem Solving Ability
  - • Grasping Facts
  - • Analytical
- ❑ Decisiveness
- ❑ Educate and trains subordinates
- ❑ Treat subordinates equal, clear, and fair
- ❑ Pull the best out of the people
- ❑ Motivates people
- ❑ Good listener
- ❑ Stable and solid, Never give up
- ❑ Welcomes a challenge, Confident
- ❑ Good negotiator

110 possible points

Scale/ Score:
Excellent (10), Good (8), Normal (6),
Needs Improvement (4), Inferior (2)

- ❑ Ability to integrate people, things
- ❑ Ability to see the future direction
- ❑ Be neutral
- ❑ Judgement Discernment
- ❑ Trust subordinates
- ❑ Sees the big picture
- ❑ Passion
- ❑ Calm
- ❑ Potential (be able to accept any kind of person)
- ❑ Person of breadth
- ❑ Likeable (personality)
- ❑ Dignified
- ❑ Patient
- ❑ Creative
- ❑ Entrepreneurial, Welcomes a challenge
- ❑ Intelligent
- ❑ Common sense
- ❑ Sympathetic
- ❑ Involves others
- ❑ Vigorous

100 possible points

Figure 11.2   Leadership Self-Assessment Evaluation/Qualities.

Source: Courtesy of Ritsuo Shingo—My Leadership the China Years, Ritsuo Shingo, ©2016 Utah State University.

Executives should do the following:[3]

- Set the overarching measurable goals and strive for virtually impossible yet achievable stretch targets.
- Being content is the first step toward complacency. Develop a "Kaizen Mind."[4]
- Accompany their managers and group leaders to Gemba and encourage in-depth information gathering to help root cause problems without too detailed instructions. Reinforcing that process and method is just as important as getting the result.
- When making presentations, present their problems or the bad news first.
- Don't manage problems—fix problems.
- "Failure is the mother of success."[5]

The new group leader role is a salaried position and begins with executive support and must be aligned with the company's goals, which is typically referred to as True North. This means every organizational team member[6] must have a shared mental model, which is focused on the customer and their company's role in society. The senior leadership must work as a team and be aligned around the same priorities! This does not mean "groupthink" but does mean that once we have all defined and agreed to the priorities, we should continue to execute based on this alignment knowing that in complex environments plans can and will probably need to change at any time based on outside information, unfolding circumstances, or interaction with the environment.[7] This may sound easy but are your company's executives aligned around the exact same priorities? Do they work together as an effective team toward the same True North goals? Do they provide a psychologically safe[8] environment where everyone in the organization is encouraged and expected to speak up if they agree or disagree with their boss?

A Firsthand Account by Cliff Owens

When organizational leaders begin to think about improving the operation, it can be very easy to realize there are so many opportunity areas that it can become overwhelming to the leader. The thought of "I know what needs to be done, but I don't know where to start or how to do it" then becomes the standard thought process and within a short amount of time, and leaders become disoriented and slowly drift back into their normal mode of working.

When trying to attack the multitude of areas of opportunity, we have found that the most effective way is to attempt to "dissect" the problem/opportunity area into three layers and attempt to address the area by layers to most effectively address the problem but, more important, to help create an atmosphere of sustainability.

First and foremost, we as operational excellence/lean/continuous improvement leaders need to have one single overriding priority and that is to make sure we create an environment that allows for the continuous improvement activities to continue and hopefully propagate long after we have left. One very effective method to do so is to attempt to make sure that we have addressed the following three layers of the project under focus. This requires some thoughtful planning by the leader's part however once done a couple of times, then becomes a very common way to think/understand how to approach problem-solving and continuous improvement process to create an atmosphere of sustainability. The three layers of approach are as follows:

1. The frontline operational team: Focus is to teach them "How to See," "How to Solve," and "How to Share" via the waste walks and the "Power of 15 Minutes" activities. A lot of ground can be covered using the Agile process because during the "sprints," the improvements can be identified and fixed (usually in 1-hour blocks), and this addresses the "How to See and Solve" and through the scrums, where we have them concisely report out to the group usually in 5 minutes or less, the results of the effort (How to Share) We also need to create an atmosphere of empowerment of this team, so they walk away with the knowledge and expectation of "If it is to be it is up to me/we!"

2. The leadership team: By this, I like to include the area manager/superintendent or, better yet, the plant manager. We want them to participate in the first-day activities of the workshop so they can be a part of the training piece on learning "to see," and then have them participate on the periphery for the learning "to solve" piece, so they can then start to see how the team structure is created, the problem-solving process, and the results to get a sense for what is possible in terms of the continuous improvement process. This usually translates into the plant leader wanting to stick around for the duration of the workshop (even though that wasn't the original plan) because their interest is piqued, and they want to learn even more about the process and its associated results. This helps create that atmosphere of empowerment, because it helps develop trust and a common language across multiple layers of the organization.

3. The operational support team: This team will also learn "how to see, solve, and share," but for these folks, we like to attempt to have the process as discussed in Item 1 uncover a "systemic" problem that is beyond the scope of the front line operational team's ability to address on their own. This could be because this requires input from another area, or requires needing some subject-matter experts to participate in. We then create what is called a "tiger team" to go after that issue. This usually has a longer duration, so the establishment of a regular reporting cadence helps not only to make sure roadblocks are identified and removed but also to create accountability to ensure project closure so it doesn't get forgotten.

As you can imagine, making progress on all three layers can be a tricky endeavor and doesn't always result in covering all three layers. Many times, we are only able to touch on two of the three; however, if the projects are properly scoped and planned and have the endorsement and encouragement of the leadership team, then it is likely that all three layers can be touched on in a 1-week workshop, and by doing so, a follow-up reporting process can be created such that learning continues and a method for coaching is established.

Waste Walks/The Power of 15 Minutes

To me this is one of the most important aspects of the process and requires some of the up-front investment in time during the workshops. All too often, people at all levels allow themselves to fall victim to the "that's the way we have always done it" syndrome and stop "seeing" the waste right in front of their very eyes. By taking the time on Day 1 of the workshop to conduct a very brief training and conducting the waste walks and discussing them, the curtain is opened, and then we can quickly move into the "learning to solve" step. The Power of 15 Minutes process allows the team to take immediate steps to fix those things that are annoyances to the team and allows them to get quick wins. This is what creates the ember. Leaders then need to step in to help add fuel to that ember to help it catch fire. Once the fire is burning, leadership's job is to make sure it doesn't go out . . . and then cascade the efforts to other areas of the plant.

Learning to Share

To me, this is the second-most important part of the process. Why is that? I say that because, done effectively, this is the mechanism by which a Lean leader can help to create the interest in the organization for learning more about the continuous improvement process. I call this "The Pull." To me, the effectiveness of the Lean leader is in direct relation to his ability to generate The Pull and, in order to do so, requires organizational skills and a touch of salesmanship. A requirement that I have for workshops is that we will have a 30-minute report out to senior leadership on the results of the workshop. This report-out needs to clearly describe what the problem that was addressed, the team members working on it, as well as the financial results of it. I also make sure to include a slide in the slide deck to capture comments made by team members during the daily wrap-ups on epiphanies that they may have had. This is powerful, because it demonstrates to senior leadership the impact in thinking that occurred during the week, as well as leaving a lasting expectation of the workshop participants for sustainability and enhancement of the continuous improvement process after the conclusion of the workshop. This is one, but by no means the only, method that can be used to successfully generate "The Pull."

Learning to Coach

Helping an organization become effective in the Power of 15 Minutes process and the "Learning to Share" process requires the Lean leader to coach individuals and collective organizations through the process. This can be intense and difficult for some people. This requires learning how to interpret how different individuals process information in order to reach them. It also may require "big picture" thinking in order to understand organizational objectives to translate them to continuous improvement objectives. As the process starts, the Lean leader will also need to be able to coach individuals on roadblocks they encounter along the way, which, in turn, means that the Lean leader can inadvertently be viewed as a subject-matter expert on just about everything. I recall a time when I was in the process of building a greenfield automotive components plant in the south of India. My job was to find the land, build the plant, hire the people, implement the product process and systems, and get the plant launched. Even though I interviewed and hired many people who were very well qualified for their own individual functions, they didn't know the inner workings of the company or American culture. I found that they would bring questions and problems to me asking for input, and the only way we could successfully address them was for me to become familiar with those other individual functions on my own. This forced me to learn areas of materials management, finance, human resources, and others in the local region so it could be translated to effective assimilation to the American company's way of doing things. In this way, I was developing as a leader myself, while I was coaching my team along their own leadership paths. What resulted was a successful launch of a plant and a highly effective management team.

Civil Communications Section (CCS) Leadership Lessons Still Pertinent Today

The following is paraphrased from my grandfather, Charles W. Protzman, Sr.'s 8-week CCS Industrial Management class given to Japanese senior-level executives back in 1948.[9] We believe the teachings from this CCS course and the resulting CCS manual, which was translated and taught in Japan until 1993, were foundational to the Japanese economic miracle after World War II and underlay the Toyota Way 14 principles and Dr. Deming's 14 points included in the Appendix. (See Figure 11.3.)

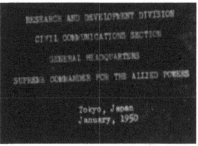

Figure 11.3   CCS Manual—Fundamentals of Industrial Management.

Source: Harvard Archives—original microfiche.

"Repeatedly, in our consideration of management principles, we have referred to coordination as one of the basic responsibilities of management. One definition of coordination, which is appropriate in the consideration of operations, is '[c]oordination is the process of bringing all the functions and operations into harmonious action for the effective achievement of the company's objectives.' You will note, in studying this definition, that it is positive. Someone has to actively do something. Actually, every management team member from the president to the foreman must bring all the functions and operations of their immediate subordinates into harmonious action. They must be able to take all the individuals who make up his subordinate group, an organization form that has been planned, and inanimate machines, tools, materials, and so on, and weld all these things into something that has unity of purpose and life.

The management of the most successful companies have learned that no matter how mechanized an industry becomes, people never become machines. To achieve the most lasting success, they must make the business something that recognizes people—something that is human. And the more complex and mechanized the business, the greater is the need for emphasis on human values.

But how is this accomplished? We will consider three specific yet closely interrelated items in our attempt to find an answer to this question. They are:

A. Leadership
B. Teamwork
C. Communication

A. Leadership

In the old days in industry, the term 'leader' was synonymous with the word 'boss.' And the 'boss' was an autocratic ruler who considered their subordinates as mere cogs in an industrial machine. The boss was supreme, and the people obeyed the dictates as automatons—frequently without even thinking for themselves. But times have changed. Management people are coming to realize that this old style 'leader' or 'boss' was not truly efficient and that this concept of management was unsound and limiting. People sometimes have to submit to autocratic domination because of economic conditions, but they do not like it and can develop a passive resistance that lowers efficiency. In time, their resentment may flare into rebellion.

One of the early causes of team members forming unions was just such a rebellion. Even today we see examples of dissension between management and the union because either one group or the other is taking an arbitrary or dictatorial stand and inevitably this is resented by the other group. And while such resentment is usually not as obvious within management groups, you can be sure that it is there, and just as strong, if the 'boss' is autocratic. After all, even supervisors (group leaders) are people.

Executive Leadership—the leadership needed to manage organizations is different from other kinds of leadership, and more exacting. Leaders in other fields can often lead through intellectual ability alone. But it's not enough for Executive Leadership. Nor is pure administrative skill. Any large organization contains examples—people who are good at getting things done themselves, and at organizing simple tasks for others, but clearly lack the golden quality of leadership. Nor is the ability to handle people enough, if other qualities are absent. True leadership in executive management demands more than intellectual ability, or the ability to handle people, or administrative ability. It requires a combination of technical skills and personal qualities that includes all three. These add up to the following personal characteristics of true Executive Leadership. He or She:

1. Is dynamic with a strong sense of personal responsibility.
2. Earns the following of the people he/she leads.
3. Is competent, adaptable, and has a strong 'feel' for people.
4. Has character and strong, consistent standards of personal conduct and business morals.

B. Teamwork

It is a natural human trait, possessed by every one of us, to want to excel. We want to personally be prominent, to achieve a position where we will stand out, where we will feel we are important, and where we are necessary. In its most exaggerated form, this trait leads us to believe we are the only one who can properly do the job and that others with whom we associate are all inferior in brains, ability, or experience. Then we become the 'indispensable worker' without whom no decisions can be made, no ideas worthy of consideration conceived, and no sound action taken.

But along with this universal trait is another that is probably equally as strong. This is the reaction any of us has in dealing with someone who considers himself that 'indispensable.' We resent the omnipotence of the decisions, and chafe because we do not have an opportunity to express our own views or show what we are capable of doing.

However, no company can afford the luxury of permitting individuals to place their own position or progress ahead of the good of the company; because when this happens, every team member who has the ambition or desire to do so will have an example and precedent to set up his or her own private goal or objective. Usually, such individual goals are purely selfish, and the result is a number of independent units or groups, each led or dominated by a strong personality, and each going its own separate way without regard to what effect it will have on other team members, or on the company. Experience has shown, over and over, that companies in which this condition exists will ultimately deteriorate and fail. This is simply one of the economic facts of life that cannot be avoided or ignored.

When an individual goes to work in a company, their first interest is in making a living. Next, they are interested in bettering their position or making a better living. The team member realizes or is made to realize by their fellow team members that their contribution to the group effort is important because unless the job is done properly, they will all be looking for another job.

But when this individual becomes the supervisor (group leader) and a part of management, he/she often fails to realize that they have assumed the obligation and accepted the responsibility of striving for certain objectives of the company. These objectives are to meet the company's customer and societal obligations for programs, schedules, quality, and costs. For success of the company, and the ultimate achievement of the personal objectives, work must primarily be for the company's objectives. These can best be accomplished through teamwork, which can be defined as follows:

> Teamwork is the work done by a number of associates, all
> subordinating personal prominence, to the efficiency of the whole.

If we consider this definition for a moment, we will see that teamwork is something that is voluntary. We cannot depend on a law or a rule that says we must have teamwork or cooperation. People must want to work together and must realize that by working together they also have the best chance of reaching their own individual objectives.

So, for full effectiveness, teamwork and cooperation must be established by the attitude and example of each management level from the president on down. It must be encouraged by the day-to-day manner in which every management team member does their work and deals with other people and must be guided by these principles which have been proved sound:

1. *Management's house must be in order.*
2. *Decisions must be understood in advance.*
3. *Workers must understand the job and opportunity must be a reality.*
4. *There must be equal opportunity for promotion from within.*
5. *Management must stay in touch and keep workers informed.*
6. *Workers need more than wages; they must be treated as people.*

C. Communications

The efficient operation of any business depends on clear, understandable, and rapid transmission of information and data (facts), instructions and orders, ideas, suggestions, comments, and complaints or grievances between all parts and levels of the company. We can call this an industrial communications system and it is the catalyst that makes leadership and teamwork effective. You will note that in defining industrial communications we say that it involves transmissions, or communication between all parts and levels. It is not just a one-way channel where the 'boss,' acting as a transmitter, broadcasts orders and instructions to their subordinates and they merely listen and obey.

Communication must be multidirectional. In the case of every team member, communications must go up the line to superiors, down the line, and sidewise to team members on the same level. These must be definite, 'recognized lines of communications' and must be properly maintained. With industrial communications, our major dependence is on people and the recognition by every team member that such communication is not only desirable but is essential. The sincere desire and effort on the part of every team member to keep all the lines of communication open and working is the secret of success. Making communications effective depends on two factors:

1. *The first is the transmission of ideas, information, or instructions in a clearly understandable form. People may be willing, but unless they are understood, the system fails. When an individual develops a good idea, they're halfway to performing a valuable service to the company, and to the individual as well.*

2. *The second consists in getting the idea put into action. The payoff comes, for both company and individual, when other people understand the idea, accept it, and help put it into effect. A scholar or a technical expert can often work up good ideas. A good salesman can sell them. The manager at the top, or the one heading for the top, should be able to do both if they are to be a real leader. The executive down the line must know the inherent art of effective presentations. They cannot go to their boss and say, 'Here's my trouble; what shall I do about it?' They must get their own answer, and present it convincingly or, begin, after a few misses, to look like the wrong manager for the job. Obviously, the individual who may have a good idea but cannot explain it might as well have a bad idea or none at all. Organization of presentation material ranks high among these principles:*

   1. *Put it down on one piece of paper.*
   2. *Determine your objectives*
   3. *Tell how you came to your conclusion.*
   4. *Tell them how they can do what your proposal will require of them.*
   5. *Show each person the opportunities your idea offers for them to fulfill some personal need or desire.*
   6. *Dramatize your presentation.*
   7. *Cultivate your speaking voice.*
   8. *Make your language a tool, not a weapon of offense.*
   9. *Do not forget there are other ways than formal presentations to put over an idea.*
   10. *With all the efforts to sell your idea, do not permit yourself to seem to be manipulating your listeners."*

Having the Proper Organizational Structure

Biologically, structure defines function. In nature this is a key to everything[10] for example a bird, an insect or a plant. If your structures are not built correctly then your functions are setting your people up for failure.

—**Roger Venegas**

This structure includes the communications networks and pathways that will mirror your organizational structure[11] (see Figure 11.4). In his book *Principles of Industrial Management*, Professor L. P. Alford suggests the maximum number of team members for most situations should be 4 to 6 but can vary up to 40 or more depending on the context,[12] structure of the work, value stream, and/or the geography. This is where an executive leader's words turn into action. Most executives will say the plant floor is the key to success. This is where the value-added work takes place, and we must support it. Do these words sound familiar? While they may be very familiar, we find it seldom translates into reality. The following items are general guidelines that are critical for the executive leader to evaluate when designing your structure to support the group leader and the shop floor:

- You view and trust the group leader as a mini plant manager who does not manage multiple shifts.
- You train them on effective communication, teamwork, coordination, and presentation skills.
- The group leader has fewer than 40 direct reports, and their team leaders have fewer than four to eight team members in a team.
- The group leader has dedicated team leaders to help manage the process.
- The group leader has hiring and firing responsibility and has been trained on how to supervise and properly document their team member interactions.

- The support teams (quality, manufacturing engineering, material planning, maintenance) report to the group leaders, which provides a rapid response to issues or improvement suggestions on the shop floor (see Figure 11.5).
- The group leader is accountable and empowered for the development and performance of the team.
- People view the group leader position as a role for which to strive.
- You coach them when they have problems and recognize them for good days.
- You don't view them as a cost that can be reduced.

TABLE 18. THE INCREASE IN THE NUMBER OF RELATIONSHIPS WITH THE INCREASE IN SUBORDINATES

Number of:										
Subordinates	1	2	3	4	5	6	7	8	9	10
Direct single relationships	1	2	3	4	5	6	7	8	9	10
Cross relationships	0	1	3	6	10	15	21	28	36	45
Direct group relationships	0	1	4	11	26 ·	57	120	247	502	1,013
Total relationships	1	4	10	21	41	78	148	283	547	1,068

Figure 11.4   The Increase in the Number of Relationships with the Increase in Subordinates (Conway's Law).

Source: The presentation of this theory has been adapted from V. A. Graicunas, "Relationship in Organization,"—L. Gulick and L. Urwick, Papers on the Science of Administration (New York: Columbia University Press, 1937).

Fast Response

Figure 11.5   Fast-Response Team Example.

Source: BIG training materials.

These are some basic questions we always ask when evaluating if the organizational structure sets up the group leader for success. If any of these bullet points are a *no*, we know there is a problem. Whether and how well the system functions depend on our human relationships. These interconnections are the most important.

We recommend aligning the organization using teams focused on the products, to the extent it makes sense. We call this a value stream organization. The group leader bears the ownership for their value stream or their potion of the overall value stream. As many functional roles as possible become a solid line to the group leader, so if the group leader has a problem, they now have the proper resources to respond which sets them up for success. This helps drive accountability because the group leader has no excuses.

The Executive Team must set the expectations and become the role model for how the rest of the organization will view this role. Ritsuo Shingo says, "Show them your back!"[13] Your team members are watching and learning from you. How the Executive Leadership Team supports their role is much more about their actions, not their words. The way the questions below are answered will determine if the Executive Team truly values the group leader position:

- Which group leader are you mentoring and developing?
- Does every group leader have a mentor?
- What is the training/coaching budget?
- Have we built it into our daily leader standard work?
- How much time out of the week is spent coaching or mentoring them?
- How many people in the group leader role have been promoted in the last 12 months?
- Do they have development plans in place? Do they know about them?
- How are they compensated compared to the same levels in engineering, quality, or materials?

This group leader position is the major linkage across the organization. They generally are leading 80% of your company's operations and results. They are the face of your company to all your internal customers. No major initiative can be successful without their active support and participation. How do we create this evolution? It's really very simple. Demonstrate to them the value this group leader position has to the Executive Team.

- Spend time with them. Teach them presentation skills and how to sell their ideas.
- Challenge them and help them develop new skills.
- Provide mentoring and coaching.
- Seek their opinion and guide them toward ongoing daily improvement for the area and themselves.
- Have their back and allow them to lead . . . even if it's not the same way you would do it.
- Publicly praise and privately provide constructive feedback.
- Provide opportunities to give them successful exposure to the Executive Team.
- Make them feel valued.

Roles and Responsibilities Matrix

We use a roles and responsibilities (R&R) sheet to define the formal organizational clarity.[14] Some people call this a RACI chart. The R&R make it very clear as to who owns what decisions in the organization (see Figure 11.6). The rule is there can only be one owner or person responsible for a decision. There can be shared owners, as well as people consulted, informed, or needed to approve, but ultimately only one owner. The format for this chart comes from a book, *Designing Organizations* by Jay Gailbraith (see Figure 11.7), and we should push decisions to the level where they should be made. If not, it will slow the decision-making process.

Roles / Decisions	Sales	Segment marketing	Insurance	Mutual funds	Marketing council	CEO	Finance	Human resources	Regional team
Product price									
Package design									
Package price									
Forecast	A	R	C	C	C	I	I	X	X
Product design									

EXHIBIT 9.1. Responsibility Chart for a Financial Services Organization.

R = Responsible
A = Approve
C = Consult
I = Inform
X = No Formal Role

Figure 11.6 Roles and Responsibilities Matrix.

Source: Designing Organizations, Jay Galbraith, John Wiley and Sons ©2002.

Tasks / Authorities **R**esponsible *(Can only have one owner!)* **A**pprove **C**onsult **I**nform **S**hares responsibility **X** - None of the above	Focus Factory Mgr	Buyer Planner Scheduler	Shipping and Receiving	Stategic Acquisition Manager	Water Spiders	Eng.	Shop Floor Team Members	Site Lead	Acctng.	Customer Service	Q.A.	Sales \ Product \ Project Manager	Shipping
1 Develop Supplier Statement of Work	C	C		R	C			A			C		
2 Create Customer RFQ				C	C					C		R	
3 Take the Sales Order										C		R	
4 Enter the Sales Order				I					I	R		I	
5 Field Customer Inquiries	C	C				C			I	R		C	
6 Develop Vendor Managed Inventory Agreeement	C	C		R	C			A	I				
7 Develop Long Term Agreements	C	C		R	C			A	I				
8 Negotiate Blanket PO	A			R				A	I				
9 Enter Blankets /VMI / LTA into system	I			R				I			I		
10 Udate approved supplier list		R		A				I	I		C		
11 Release against blankets		R					I						

Figure 11.7 Example—Roles and Responsibilities Matrix.

Source: BIG archives.

For complex decisions, which by their nature are unpredictable, we should be careful not to over-constrain the decision-making process or subjugate it to a checklist mentality. We should make sure we don't inhibit teamwork or lose sight of the informal organization and relationship interconnections. The organization needs to be able to make decisions rapidly based on an accurate assessment of their current situational awareness. This may mean that certain decisions become elastic and emerge based on environmental and human factors. As of this writing, there is a lot of new work being done in this area now by Dave Snowden and Friends.[15]

Middle Management Level—What We Normally Find

Usually when we start working with teams, the middle manager is quick to point out all the experience they have. Generally, we find they are lacking in experience instead, and are lucky if they have read even one book on Lean, been to any Lean training seminars, and so on because most companies usually stop there. Most of the time their group leaders are just thrown into the position and held accountable for the results. Why? Because this is how their leader was trained. We find that if they are trained in some way, the company doesn't require the group leader to actually apply the knowledge and facilitate change. When they fail, they are reprimanded, told they are stupid, and asked what's wrong with them and why didn't they consider this or that.

The old traditional manager was more of a "boss" barking out orders, telling the team what to do, when to do it, and how to do it. It's their way or the highway. Different situations require different types of leadership, but generally speaking, those types of leaders are usually only effective in a crisis or short time frame or when their "boss" is watching. Managers who are considered "the boss" will have higher team member turnover, lower productivity, higher absenteeism, and huge scrap rates and will stunt their team members' growth. We have often found it takes a unique individual to make an effective leader.

Middle Management Is Essential

Middle managers are considered overhead because they are an indirect cost to the organization and add no direct value to the physical product being produced. Being in an overhead position, middle managers need to contribute to their team's success so that they are delivering value with minimal waste being produced. This position is a supporting role that aids in ensuring that increasing customer-focused value-added activities are the primary focus of the organizational unit as well as addressing the developmental needs of the workforce within the same unit.

Middle management is an essential role within organizations as they are responsible for communication and coordinating daily activities across the organization. Middle management typically operates between the teams and executive levels of an organization, assuming there are teams. Middle managers play the role of being a boundary spanner, or one who facilitates interactions across departments and teams through communicating and aligning goals, coordination of activities across units, providing necessary resources when they are needed, and by developing much-needed teamwork skills for their team members.

The Group Leader and Middle Management Interaction

There are many cases where the group leader is your first and last line of defense. If they escalate an issue or a problem to middle management and do not get a response, they will stop escalating it. When that happens, you lose them, and just as important, you lose the team. Even though their position stays in place, you will force them to lose their soul and drive.

If you want your first line leaders, and the organization, to be successful, middle management must create a structured environment in which the group leader can succeed. If the Executive Team is not getting what they want, it's most likely because they haven't developed the desired organizational system. It's management's responsibility and duty to establish the roles and responsibility for the group leaders and team leaders. We often find middle management frustrated with how group leaders or team leaders perform their duties, but seldom do they truly develop the role to align it with what they want it to do.

As you develop this role as a mentor or coach, we like to have the manager of the area try to coach the group leader for a minimum of 30 minutes a day. This half-hour, or more, should be spent on the production floor reviewing their process, teaching them how to problem-solve, performing audits, reviewing the daily management boards, and doing Kata coaching routines. The ongoing development of middle management is just as important. The only way to continue developing the skills of the group leader is to continuously develop the leadership skills of the middle management team.

The group leader should be considered a mini plant manager who is responsible for safety, quality, delivery, monitoring of costs, and overall employee morale. Empowering all employees to be engaged in the production of the unit's tasks requires the inclusion of all employees in the decision-making capabilities of the unit. This means giving the employees the capability to stop the production line when they observe a potential problem or defect (the Andon cord) or safety issue. This produces an environment that is high on psychological safety which also assures full engagement of the workforce. You want people to look forward to Mondays and coming to work. Team member participation, involvement, and their ability to be part of the improvement ideas and decision-making process provide the highest level of engagement and motivation for all employees.

The Second Level of Coach

A coach is generally one level up from the learner, and the second coach is two levels up from the learner. The Leadership Development Path requires two levels of coaching. For example, the first is the group leader coaching the team leader while the second coach would be middle management or an external resource coaching the group leader in how to coach the team leader.

Scanlon Principles

Part of creating the environment required to facilitate an engaged workforce is to have an underlying belief or value system to drive the behaviors the company is looking to develop to create this new culture. Joseph Scanlon was a steelworker, union president, acting director of the Steelworkers Research Department, and guest lecturer at the Massachusetts Institute of Technology. He was the author of the Scanlon Plan, which was a gain-sharing program based on employee participation and was the precursor to many suggestion programs. Scanlon believed people were motivated by larger ideas than just the money associated with piecework. He believed they wanted to be part of a successful organization, experience pride in their work, and contribute to solving problems within the company. The Scanlon system is based on four fundamental principles and processes:[16]

1. Identity
2. Participation
3. Equity
4. Competence

1. The principle of identity is based on three assumptions:

   ■ Change is a universal given and is our only hope.
   ■ A person's performance/behavior is a consequence of how they have been treated.
   ■ Every person and organization is in the process of becoming better or worse.

   Scanlon leaders create identity through a process of education. Their curriculum includes the organization's mandate, customers, competitive challenges, and the like. Practices that support identity include the wide sharing of information including financial data "open-book management," accessible leadership, open forums, and visits to customers, suppliers, and investors. Questions about identity:

   ■ Is there a need to change?
   ■ What is the right job for me to be doing?
   ■ How do I know when I am doing the job right?

2. Participation

   Participation is not optional, it's a condition of your employment.

   — **Michael Meyers**

   Participation is defined as the opportunity, which only management can give, and the responsibility, which only employees can accept, to influence decisions in their areas of competence. Practices that support participation include employee involvement, participative management, teams, flat organizations, and suggestion systems. Questions about participation:

   ■ Do I encourage others to make decisions?
   ■ Do I take the responsibility for my decisions?

3. Equity is defined as a genuine commitment to account for the needs of all constituents including customers, investors, and employees. The process of equity is accountability. Scanlon leaders regularly report the organization's performance relative to customers', investors', and employees' needs. Practices that support equity include gain sharing, goal sharing, profit sharing, balanced scorecards, and tracking and reporting of performance results. Questions about equity:

   ■ Are the equity needs of all constituents in balance?
   ■ How do we know what organizational performances, practices, or relationships will fulfill the equity needs of all constituents?
   ■ How do we use Equity to hold ourselves and our organization accountable?

4. Competence is defined as the ability to respond to the constant demand for improvement and change. It requires a commitment to be in a state of becoming something that you never were before. Practices that support competence include training, development, job enlargement, and learning organizations. Questions about competence:

   ■ Am I willing to help others become more competent?
   ■ Am I willing to commit to make myself better every day?

Motivation

Jim Leonard writes in his blog titled Dr. *W. Edwards Deming's System of Profound Knowledge,*

> Dr. Deming wrote, "Psychology helps us to understand people, interaction between people and circumstances, interaction between a manager and his people and any system of management."[17] His philosophy for leadership rests on the belief that people are intrinsically motivated. They strive naturally for dignity, pride and joy in their work. Unfortunately, the current American management system destroys intrinsic motivation by substituting extrinsic motivators such as merit pay, sales commissions and grades in school. Thus, too many students strive for high grades, not knowledge. Too many workers strive for merit increases and high rankings, not quality or the intrinsic joy one experiences from a job well done.
>
> As it relates to motivation, is the appropriate strategy to try to motivate people? Or is it to remove barriers to their own (intrinsic) motivation? Senge wrote about how this dilemma exists in efforts to achieve the goal of continuous improvement, "which remains an elusive target for most American organizations."[18]

Senge said:

> "Motivate them. From an extrinsic perspective, the only way to get continuous improvement is to find ways to continually motivate people to improve . . . Otherwise, they will just sit there—or worse yet, slide backwards. This leads to what workers perceive as management continually raising the bar to manipulate them.
>
> . . . However, from an intrinsic perspective, there is nothing mysterious at all about continuous improvement. If left to their own devices, people will naturally look for ways to do things better. What they need is adequate information and appropriate tools. From the intrinsic perspective, people's innate curiosity and desire to experiment, if unleashed, creates an engine for improvement that can never be matched by extrinsic rewards."[19]

Von Beals, former CEO of Harley Davidson, said,

> "When you turn them loose. When they really understand that they have got the ability and can get things done; the power of that is damn near infinite. It takes longer than you like to get to that point, though once it starts it has its own momentum and you cannot stop it now."

Notes

1. https://nearyou.imeche.org/docs/default-source/South-Wales/Event-Posters/tps-lean-copy-for-imeche.pdf?sfvrsn=0
2. Davide Barbon, President, Asia-Pacific at ITT Inc.
3. Inspired by presentation by Isao Yoshino 1–29–2017 to Japan Study Mission Group.
4. Inspired by presentation by Isao Yoshino 1–29–2017 to Japan Study Mission Group.
5. Inspired by presentation by Isao Yoshino 1–29–2017 to Japan Study Mission Group.

6. We use the team member verbiage throughout the book. The team member can refer to any person in the organization or it can refer to the person working for the team leader, someone on a particular team, or someone on the shop floor depending on how it is used in context.

7. Reference to the new information source for the OODA (Observe–Orient–Decide–Act) loop.

8. Amy Edmonson.

9. This passage is titled "Leadership" by Charles W. Protzman Sr. and was delivered as part of the CCS Industrial Management course to the Japanese communications executives in 1948–1949. This is not the main focus of this book, but much of it has been incorporated at Toyota who teaches portions of this, like active quality, listening, teamwork, participation, presentation skills, and so on. See *The Lean Practitioner's Field Book* for the entire passage or visit www.biglean.com (note some of the words were changed from supervisor or boss to group leader and subordinate to team member. It was my grandfather and Homer Sarasohn that recommended Dr. Deming to the Japanese Union of Scientists and Engineers to continue teaching quality in Japan. Dr. Deming was the second choice after Walter Shewhart, who was sick at the time.

10. Roger Venegas.

11. Span of control CCS Manual, Alford Principles of Industrial Management © The Ronald Press, 1951, 1940, and Conway's Law.

12. Principles of Industrial Management, Dr. L.P. Alford, Ronald Press Co. ©1940 pg 58–59. The presentation of this theory has been adapted from V. A. Graicunas, "Relationship in Organization,"—L. Gulick and L. Urwick, Papers on the Science of Administration (New York: Columbia University Press, 1937).

13. January 2017 trip to Japan with the ADUM group.

14. Within the bounds of the complicated domain of the Cynefin framework.

15. www.youtube.com/watch?v=uKALuME8E9g

16. Joe Scanlon and Dr. Carl Frost developed time-tested practices and principles that transform an organization's culture for the highest engagement of employees in learning and effectiveness. These principles create better business practices, providing whole organization, executive learning, and networking opportunities. "I see the Scanlon Principles as allowing us to unleash the tremendous energy within the company through participation . . . to direct the beam toward the desired target through Principles of identity, to constantly keep the powerful beam in tune through equity, and to continually strengthen the beam through competence." Dwane Baumgardner, Chairman of the Board and CEO, Donnelly Corporation. www.scanlon.org/leadership-network/scanlon-principles/.

17. Deming, The New Economics for Industry, Government, Education, pg. 107–108.

18. Jim Leonard's blog titled *Dr. W. Edwards Deming's "System of Profound Knowledge"* 2012 www.jimleonardpi.com/default/assets/File/Blog%20-%20Deming's%20System%20of%20Profound%20Knowledge.pdf

19. Peter Senge, "Building Learning Organizations," Reprint from the Journal for Quality and Participation, March 1992, p. 3.

Chapter 12

BASICS® SUSTAIN through Continuous Leadership Development

Figure 12.1 BASICS® Lean Leadership Development Path—Sustain.

Source: BIG training materials.

Step 1 was to Baseline, which we covered in Team Member Self Self-Reliance, and Step 2 was to Analyze and Suggest Solutions in the BASICS®, which we did by studying how to improve business practices and suggest solutions. In Step 3, we took what we learned from Steps 1 and 2, and then we Implemented it by practicing what we learned. We checked to make sure we solved the

DOI: 10.4324/9781315155227-12

root cause (see Figure 12.1). Step 4, Sustain, combines the BASICS® Lean tools and human aspect to achieve daily business improvement with a focus on execution by Learning to Teach others which allows the improvements to Sustain (see Figure 12.2). It includes the following:

- Gemba walks and watches
- Continuously updating the standard work
- Implement leader standard work
- Daily Goal Deployment (+QDIP) process for worker engagement and participation
- Practice the Team Member Self-Reliance (TSR) and Improving Business Processes on the job and develop presentation skills
- Learners are becoming leaders; first coaches are becoming second coaches as the new skills and processes are being developed and deployed across the organization

This is how we sustain the Leadership Development Path. It is about teaching leaders how to share what they have learned (see Figure 12.3) how the steps work together. We teach them how to impart their knowledge in a humble fashion by asking thought-provoking questions and challenging their team members. We teach them about coaching moments, and we normally bring

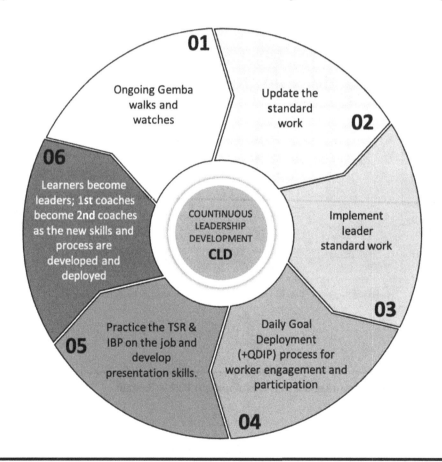

Figure 12.2   Skills and Systems Deployment (On-the-Job Development).

Source: BIG training materials.

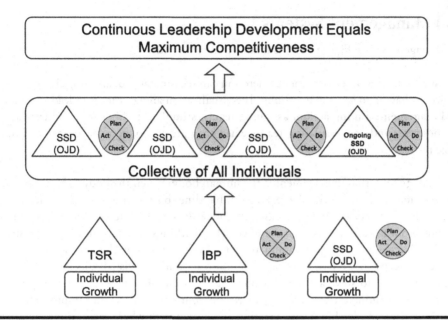

Figure 12.3 How the Steps Work Together to Achieve Maximum Competitiveness and Sustain the System.

Source: BIG training materials.

in a second coach to perform this part of the training. This second coach is the role Yoshino-san played at NUMMI. It is important to have leader standard work in place, which was discussed earlier, and visual management systems. It also requires going to the Gemba. We teach them how to implement the Leadership Development Path, which requires a new foundation starting with the interview and hiring process. We then discuss additional sustaining tools. It is interesting to note that Toyota doesn't have this fourth step because like 4S, it has hard-coded Sustain into its muscle memory, at least as far as the manufacturing side goes.

Make Sure Your Organization Is Ready

Are you prepared to uncover your dirty laundry? Some organizations are not ready and should not implement Lean. If there is no compelling need to change or fundamental dissatisfaction in how things are done today, it will not be successful. David Mann suggests in his book *Creating a Lean Culture*[1] that there are four areas on which to focus:

1. Visual Controls (visual management)
2. Leader Standard Work
3. Accountability
4. Discipline

We would propose visual controls be modified to visual management systems that have a broader context. We have already discussed accountability and discipline, which are interwoven within the Continuous Leadership Development path.

Visual Management Systems

Visual Management (see Figure 12.4) is made up of two words:

■ **Visual:** Creating an environment where you can see the status of all things in your company without having to ask any questions. The visualization allows leaders to lead.
■ **Management:** Taking action, assigning teams, stimulating thinking to address abnormal conditions, and congratulating teams when they are achieving expectations or improving the process.

The analogy for visual management is the human body. When the body has a problem, it lets you know. It may be in the form of a fever, pain, bleeding, blister, and so on, but once your body signals a problem, it needs to be taken care of right away, or it tends to get worse. Visual management is not about making pretty charts and colorful markings. The key idea behind visual management is being able to manage without having to check. It works on the universal Lean principle of manage by exception. So now the leaders do not react until the visuals dictate.

You do not have to solve all issues at once, just the ones impacting your ability to achieve your targets and eliminate the waste. This frees up your time for making improvements versus extinguishing fires. Leadership means creating an environment where each minor success breeds ongoing and eventually overall success. People want to be challenged and like to be part of a winning team.

If you want to make it important make it visual. Make it so it's easy to update, easy to see, put it in a natural area where traffic is high in the plant. We say work hard to make it simple because if you make it simple, people will follow it. As stated earlier, visual management combines 5S,

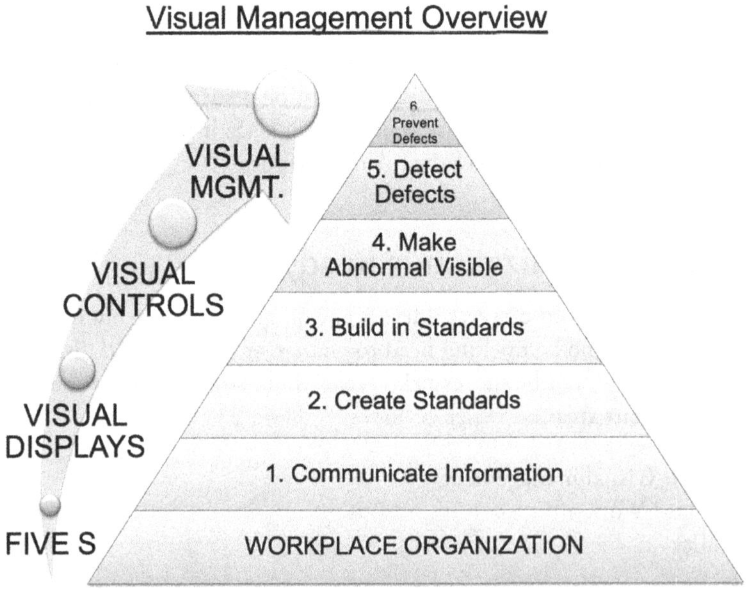

Visual Management Overview

Figure 12.4 Visual Management Overview.

Source: BIG training materials.

visual displays, visual controls, total productivity maintenance (TPM), mistake proofing, and material flow into one integrated system. Visual management should also be used for planning and scheduling, that is, heijunka (level loading) and material flow, among others. The emphasis here is on systems.

A visual management system is a department or work area that is

1. Self-explaining,
2. Self-regulating, and
3. Self-improving.

This is a system where what is supposed to happen does happen, on time, every time. If you have to ask any questions, whether shop floor or office, then there is a problem with your visual management system. When one becomes adept at visual management, one realizes the factory "talks to you." Even when it is totally silent you realize the silence speaks volumes because if the factory isn't telling you anything, and there is a good chance the area is in chaos.

When set up properly, the factory can tell you everything you want and need to know. The goal is to develop a visual management system through which anyone can enter the area and understand everything about the plant by just walking around. Some people compare visual management to a glass wall, meaning you can see through the company. The transparency is what makes it work. As a leader, ask yourself:

■ Can I walk through my area or plant without speaking a word to anybody and understand within 15 minutes where my biggest problems are?
■ Can I look at every work area and see if the team is on pace to achieve their schedule?
■ Can I see where scrap is being generated?
■ Can I see where injuries are happening?
■ Can I see, hour by hour, if the team is on pace for success for the day, and if not, why?
■ Can I see where raw material is supposed to be placed?
■ When I look at work in process (WIP) can I tell if they have the proper amount in the system, not too much and not too little?
■ Can I tell when I need to reorder more materials?
■ Can I tell if the week/month is going as planned?
■ Can I tell the team members and team leader apart?
■ Where teams are not on pace or achieving targets do you feel at ease knowing somebody will take care of it and a champion is identified to solve the problem?

As a leader, at any level, you should be able to answer each of these questions without talking to anybody. Once you develop a system in which problems are celebrated, we can highlight and fix them (see Figure 12.5).

Visual Management System Example

Visual management challenges the leaders and the team to perform to standards. The only way you can solve a problem is to realize you have a gap. For example, railroad crossings range from simple signs warning of the crossing to light systems combined with signs to gated barriers combined with lights and signs. Each example is one more level of visual management (see Figure 12.6).

Figure 12.5   Visual Control in a Traffic Visual Management System.

Source: BIG training materials.

Figure 12.6   Visual Controls—Red Light, Stop Sign, and Railroad Signal.

Source: BIG training materials.

The first case of blinking lights warns the driver to stop and check before crossing, but in reality, what will normally happen? The driver will just cross. Light systems will generally cause the driver to stop, but if they do not see anything happen, they will start to cross as nothing prevents them from doing so. The next level is adding the gates. The gates are there to try to control the driver and force them to stop. But many times, even this does not work as the drivers will go around the gates.

At each level, as we continue to add to the railroad crossing model visual management system, we are also adding mistake-proofing techniques. Mistake proofing uses both warning devices and control devices. Each of the earlier railroad crossing examples is a warning device because none actually controls the driver's behavior. As a result, we still have numerous car accidents at train crossings. The ultimate penalty, defect, is the driver losing their life. What would it take to "control" the driver? The car would need to communicate with the railroad crossing system and shut itself down prior to the railroad crossing or barriers would have to rise or platform that would allow the wheels to spin freely (like those used to test cars or motorcycles) so the car wheels spin but the car goes nowhere in order to physically prevent the car from crossing. In factories, this can be done by using conveyor stops that don't lower until the product has passed the steps required in the current station.

Make It Visual—Active Controls Versus Passive Visual Displays

Electronic dashboards can be very attractive and are useful in many situations. But in reality, they are just passive visual displays for frontline workers and may actually reduce team member engagement, becoming tools for command and control by management. Each team leader and their team should first consider active visual management (pen and whiteboard or other hands-on tools) to understand and continuously improve the flow of work and quickly spot problems. It helps to install line counters to support day-by-hour charts (see Figure 12.7). With standards and line counters in place, it is easy to determine if you are ahead or behind schedule.

By active engagement of the senses, standing in front of the daily management whiteboard in real time to solve problems, the team develops an intuitive feeling for the process. They can quickly and easily change the information gathered and displayed based on the changing needs of the process itself without asking for technical assistance. While such manual displays may seem inefficient, they promote team ownership, learning, and continuous improvement, which, in the long run, are far more valuable. We do this for several reasons:

- Easy to update
- Creates an emotional attachment to the data
- Forces the champion to understand data
- Makes sure the champion understands all the formulas to improve key performance indicators (KPIs)

We want leaders to spend time at the Gemba, not at their computers in the office behind closed doors. The following subsections describe three additional types of visual systems.

Figure 12.7 Visual Display Line Counters.

Source: BIG training materials.

1. Line of Sight—The Oba Gauge[2]

The Oba Gauge was named after a 4-foot-tall Japanese sensei named Mr. Oba. Mr. Oba insisted he have line of sight throughout the factory (or office area). This height became known as the Oba Gauge. It is also known as the 4-foot or 1.3-meter rule. Six-foot-high cubicle walls should be no higher than 3 feet in offices. This concept of line of sight was expanded in another context, which became known as value stream mapping or process flow analysis. Using these tools, we can see back to the original customer.

2. Shingo's 1–3–10 Rule for Visual Management Boards[3]

We like to use the 1–3–10 rule. The champion (management one level above or higher) has the following:

- 1 second to identify if KPI is on track. Is the team winning or losing?
- 3 seconds to identify what is causing KPI to be or not be achieved? What are the point causes and trends (i.e., Pareto, the 5 Whys, the 5W 2H, etc.)?
- 10 seconds to identify what the team is doing to correct the problem and who is managing the corrective action. Can the team see their actions tied to the trends?

(Non-Toyota Photo With Adapted Concept)

Figure 12.8   Circle—Green, Triangle—Yellow, and Cross—Red.

Source: Courtesy of Nigel Thurlow, CEO of the FLOW Consortium and co-creator of the Flow System and former Toyota Chief of Agile. Adapted from Japanese symbology and Toyota's usage.

3. The 5/20 Rule for Visual Boards

Within 5 feet, or 1.5 meters, of the board, you should only need 20 seconds to see the current state of the cell/process to determine if it is in control. If you cannot read the board from 5 feet away, then the information is too small and no one will read it. It is also useful to use the combination of color coding and symbols to guard against color blindness in order to show the immediate status of an item. At Toyota (see Figure 12.8), a triangle and a cross, a standard used company-wide, with a box to show the immediate status on boards, electronic displays, and even on A3 actions. Nigel Thurlow[4] states: "We actually just say circle, triangle and cross. As we often do not use color. That's the power of them. Color and language do not matter."

What We Normally Find

We often enjoy being asked to visit a plant. The first thing we look for is to see if the plant talks to us. Usually, the Leadership Team will tell you what they think is going on, but seldom is it really what's going on. When we see attempts at visual management, it's usually computer-generated graphs that are outdated, hidden from the Gemba, and very seldom reviewed. We normally can't find a champion identified or actionable corrective actions and trends look to be moving in the wrong direction.

What Does "The Plant Should Talk to You" Mean?

The key is to communicate information in a way that helps everyone identify a problem immediately or prevents the problem from ever happening in the first place. Think about an airport. Everything is visual, even the tarmac. Sign boards communicate the status of the flights, each gate is labeled and contains a signboard of which flights are leaving the gate and when. Restrooms, handicap areas, safety issues concerning strollers on escalators, and a speaker above saying, "Caution, the moving walkway is ending," are all visuals that interact with or talk to you. You immediately know the status of your flight and what is going on around you. Does your factory communicate to you the same way the airport does?

Benefits When the Factory or Area Talks to You It . . .

■ Surfaces problems quickly, indicates non-conformances and when help is needed
■ Reduces search time and checking by 50% or more
■ Improves safety, increases audit compliance for health safety and environmental, and increases productivity
■ Can sometimes lower insurance rates
■ Enables management by sight
■ No technical knowledge of the area needed to assess the current condition
■ Enabler for high-performance work teams
■ Reduces need for meetings to assess current situations
■ Shows if you are on target to meet requirements
■ Identifies flow, roadblocks, and controls inventory
■ Communicates real-time feedback to everyone
■ Can positively influence the behavior and attitude of team members
■ Shows everything has a place and everything is in its place
■ Customers love it!

Deviation Response System (DRS)—Is Yours Effective?

These systems do not have to be expensive and should be manual and built for human intervention. Do not fool yourselves into thinking that because you have andon systems, takt-time counters, and electronic data collection systems that you have real visual management. The management part of the system is critical.[5] Dave Rizzardo has written a white paper on what he calls the DRS system. This system has three main steps:

■ Step 1—The deviation occurs and is recognized—the goal would be to immediately recognize it.
■ Step 2—The deviation is highlighted/escalated and someone responds based on standard work.
■ Step 3—Containment and short/long-term countermeasures are put in place and removed as needed.

Do you react to abnormal conditions? If you ask a plant manager if they have a good solid visual management system, most will say they do, but very few really even know what it means, why they do it, and, most important, how to react and what to do with it when there is a problem. Ask yourself:

- Do you manage your visuals?
- Do you review your results with your leaders and team?
- Do your visual systems start to integrate other tools such as mistake proofing and TPM?

Visual Management Examples[6]

A Bias for Action

We had a client that was struggling with productivity. They had some visual systems at the area we were asked to focus on. . . . In less than 2 weeks, we were able to raise their productivity by 25% without implementing anything new or innovative . . . no new documentation, no new team members, nobody got fired . . . no new standard work for team members. What did we do? We managed the visual systems they already had in place but weren't utilizing. The system told them what to do, but nobody listened to what the process was telling them. We just worked on what the system was telling us or not telling us. We mentored the group leaders and coached the other area managers impacting this department. We asked the group leader to review the boards every hour and problem-solve any item in red immediately.

Going to the Gemba with Purpose

At another company, we worked with the plant manager on the leading indicators that impacted his plant's ability to make products. We asked him to visit the work area every 3 hours and ask questions regarding items in red. In addition to questioning the red, he was also to congratulate the team on items that were green. Essentially, we managed what the visual system was telling them. The visual system told us what the real problem was . . . the leaders of the plant only told us what they *perceived* the problem to be.

We find people love to use the word *Gemba*. . . . They say, "Go to the Gemba," but rarely are people going to "the actual place where things happen" and really taking the time to dig in and understand. Don't fall into the trap of "checking off the box" when it comes to Gemba walks. Always go to the Gemba with a purpose.

Don't Let Technology Hide Your Problems

I worked with another company whose main focus was productivity improvement and development of first-line leadership. We had been working on developing some visual management systems to help increase productivity. When I asked the operations manager about missing data on the whiteboard he said, "We are coupling that with some electronic tracking systems that show leading and lagging indicators for every batch that is produced. We no longer need the whiteboard; it's in the computer now." He said the benefit of entering the data outweighs the time of writing it on the dry-erase board we installed. I asked him how long it takes to fill out the whiteboard. He said that it's not too bad, but the hard part was following up with all the red items (area-team missed goals). We laughed a little bit at the comment and really did not discuss it.

I thought about it on my flight home and actually realized it was a very interesting comment. I came to the conclusion that one of the main reasons companies fail is because they let their visual management system fall apart. It's not that it doesn't work. It's that it works so well that teams do not like what it's telling them because they feel it creates extra work. It drives the need for focus, and oftentimes, they simply do not focus on keeping the main thing the main thing, that is, the whiteboard updated. They will slowly start removing some of the items that were put in place to highlight the issues, and the next thing you know it's in the computer and no one can see it or react to it. The actions do not get addressed because no one has time and no one can see it because now it's basically hidden . . . so, "out of sight, out of mind." Then the company reverts to the firefighting culture we all seem to love and hate so much. We believe the biggest opportunity to drive real improvements rests within visual management because it points you to where to focus attention and energy. Toyota problem-solving models do not use day-by-hour charts because they use real-time problem-solving on the floor.

Teach the "Why" . . . Don't Assume It's Known

I was once challenged to develop a visual management system for 45 molding machines, 18 assembly cells, and three plants totaling 350,000 square feet. My manager could walk the plant in 15 minutes and report to his manager the status of each of my three plants. This all had to be accomplished without the aid of a computer. That means no Excel graphs, no Excel or Word reports, it all had to be manual graphs where we would use red and green markers to highlight abnormal conditions. Red was always used to highlight where we missed goals or targets. We would update these charts every shift. We used them to drive continuous improvement.

As we developed the system it became apparent very quickly that it had to be managed daily. People need routines. We added a problem-solving open-issues sheet to every glass wall/ daily management board. The idea was that if the team missed the goal for the shift, they would document the problem and put on the corrective action, due date, and the champion. Great idea in theory. When we started this process, we had so much red we couldn't even begin to keep up and we did not follow up with the leaders regularly to manage the process.

I started to walk daily with a red marking pen and asking questions on the glass wall as to what the issue was. These often would go unanswered. I would go back to the same glass wall and ask the same question again.

One day I was writing my questions on the glass and the group leader walked up to me and asked, "Is that you writing on the glass wall?" I said yes, it is. She asked me why I did not just ask her what the daily issues were. I explained to her the vision of wanting to be able to walk and manage the plant without asking any questions. She said to me, "If I knew that you were asking the questions, I would have gladly answered timelier." As we discussed this, we openly talked about not just doing this because the plant manager requested it but doing it to help yourself drive continuous improvement every day and get out of firefighting. This was a great learning experience for her and for me as the leader.

All these visual management examples highlight the ideas behind "Leaders Developing Leaders." If the systems were to be successful, they needed leadership and guidance and personal time spent by myself and the Leadership Team. People do not naturally like to expose their dirty laundry, but if you make it a blame-free environment, people will expose their problems and feel comfortable doing so. It's the leader's job to create that culture of a blame-free environment.

One-Point Lessons

One-Point lessons are used to incorporate Lean training into the daily huddles and management routines. One-point lessons are designed to be carried out in five minutes or less. This means one to five PowerPoint slides or whiteboard instruction and then, the next day, a short quiz. If the team member successfully passes the quiz and demonstrates the skill, then they get signed off on that lesson. (See Figure 12.9.)

Daily Management Huddles Are Part of Leadership Development

Continuous leadership development is intended to bring cross-functional teams together and provide a forum for quick-hitting 5- to 15-minute meetings, or huddles, that are keenly focused on specific process-focused KPIs and sometimes includes quick one-point Lean lessons that will drive the department toward success. The intent of this meeting is not to solve all the issues but to make sure the existing, plus any new, issues, are getting the attention they need. In addition, it provides

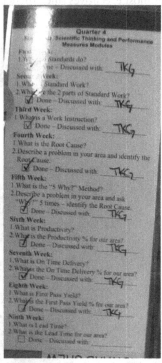

Figure 12.9   Daily Continuous Improvement and One-Point Lesson.

Source: BIG training materials.

a way to quickly escalate issues to the management team each shift. The role of management is critical to the process for the following reasons:

1. Allowing time for the meeting
2. Making sure cross-functional support or a value stream team is required to attend
3. Providing training for group leaders
4. Participating in the meeting to show you care
5. Providing coaching and mentoring to the group leader or team leader

When we implement a shop floor system, the KPI tracking is all done using manual graphs using colors to quickly identify whether teams are on track. This creates very quick visual management (see Figure 12.10). We use green if the KPI is meeting or beating the plan, yellow if within 5% of target, and red if missing by over 5%. I am sure some people are asking why with today's technology we would use manual graphs to track. By now, you should be able to answer this question.

We develop the daily management board in their area because it becomes an important communication center for the team. Ideally, you will find a place close to the cell and in a high-traffic area. This will make it a natural place for meeting and to be observed regularly. We tell companies to "focus on the process and the results will take care of themselves." This is a very difficult "leap" for most executives since there is so much pressure on short-term results.

Figure 12.10   Visual Displays.

Source: BIG training materials.

The daily management board contains KPIs and other value stream–related metrics (i.e., bookings, sales numbers, customer feedback) posted at the cell. It is important to share a quick high-level view of the health of the business to every team member. It emphasizes root-cause analysis through its Pareto sheets, which is advantageous from a Toyota Kata (coaching) standpoint when indoctrinating the concept of root-cause analysis (i.e., the 5 Whys) into your culture.

Shop Floor Daily Management Board Utilizes +QDIP. . . .

The shop floor daily management board focuses on the value-stream level as shown in Figure 12.11. Sample cell-metric calculations are shown in Figure 12.12, which should be adjusted to align with your business's exact need and strategic goal deployment. The productivity and inventory turns are typically weekly or monthly at the focus-factory level. This is particularly applicable if it is an engineered-to-order or a large-dollar build-to-order business model as day-to-day measurement is too variable and thus not meaningful. To the extent that productivity can be meaningfully measured daily at the focus-factory level, that is clearly preferred. The daily management board linkage to BASICS® Lean tools, month-by-day and day-by-hour charts, is shown in Figures 12.13 and 12.14.

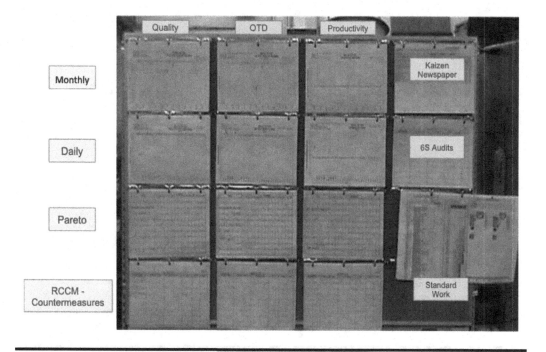

Figure 12.11   KPI Metric Board for the Work Cell Level.

Source: Used with permission from Brian Summerfield.

| | Safety | Quality | Delivery | | Cost | |
			OTD	Past Dues	Inventory	Productivity
Metric	OSHA Recordable Incidents	Total Yield	On Time Delivery to Customer Request Date	Past Dues	Turns	Productivity %
Calculation	Data - Tracked	Total Acceptable Units / Total Units Produced	Lines shipped OT to CRD / Total lines shipped	Data - Tracked	COS / Total Inventory	Total Conversion Cost (*less materials*) / Total Sales
Data Required	Recorded incidents	Daily Defects	Lines Shipped OT to CRD	Number of Lines Past Due	Total Cost of Sales	Total Conversion Cost (*less materials*)
		Daily Total Units Produced	Daily Total Lines Shipped	Total Past Due $	Total Inventory	Total Sales
Goal	0	98%	98%	0	4.5	TBD (lower)

Daily — Weekly or Monthly

Figure 12.12 Cell-Metric Calculations.

Source: BIG archives.

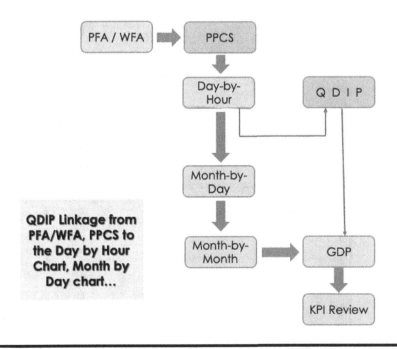

Figure 12.13 Leadership Development Board Linkage to BASICS® Tools and Month-by-Day and Day-by-Hour Charts.

Source: BIG training materials.

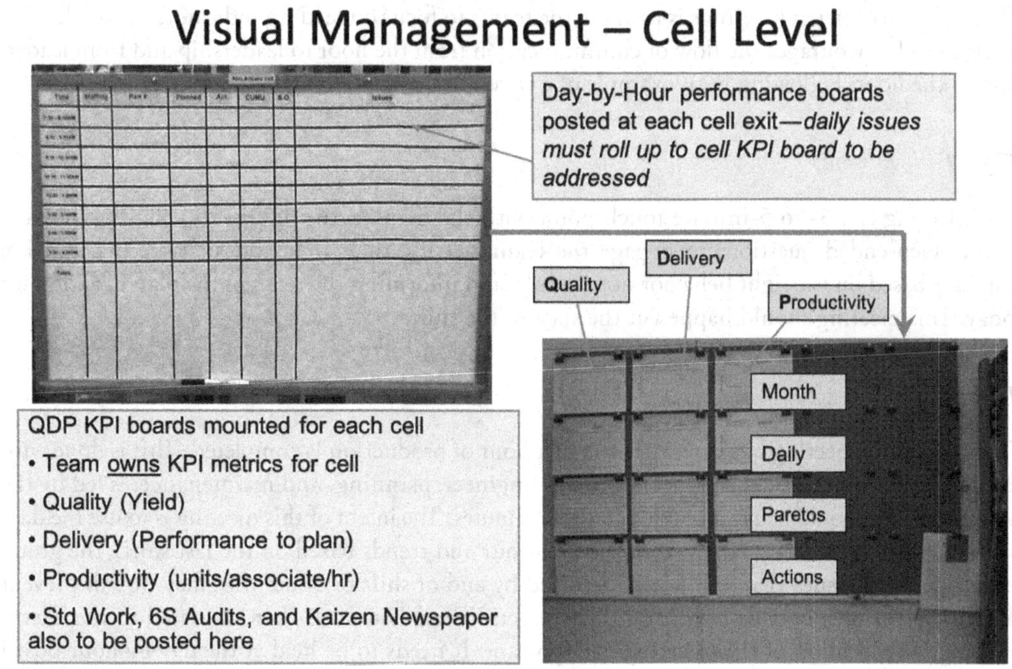

Visual Management – Cell Level

Day-by-Hour performance boards posted at each cell exit—*daily issues must roll up to cell KPI board to be addressed*

Quality

Delivery

Productivity

Month

Daily

Paretos

Actions

QDP KPI boards mounted for each cell

• Team <u>owns</u> KPI metrics for cell

• Quality (Yield)

• Delivery (Performance to plan)

• Productivity (units/associate/hr)

• Std Work, 6S Audits, and Kaizen Newspaper also to be posted here

Figure 12.14 KPI Linkage Day-by-Hour Chart to Leadership Development Board for the Work Cell Level.

Source: Used with permission from Brian Summerfield.

Tiered Meetings Concept

Think of tiered meetings as the governance element of an operating system. It enables accountability (a core element needed for sustainment and driving culture) and culture change through the following principles:

1. Focus on the process.
2. Empowerment and engagement of those who do the work.
3. Standard work is in place and updated regularly.

   ■ Operators
   ■ Supervisors
   ■ Engineers (quality and manufacturing)
   ■ Managers

4. Follow Shingo's 1–3–10 rule.
5. Implement visual management everywhere.
6. Use Gemba walks to link elements of the operating system together.
7. Utilize simple problem-solving as issues or trends arise with a focus on using the scientific method.
8. Quick escalation of bad news or misses to metrics.

The structure of tiered meetings is to allow the teams to focus on leading indicators at each level of leadership. It encourages the flow of communication from the floor to leadership and from leadership to the floor. Following is an example of a tiered stand-up meeting structure.

Tier 1

This meeting is a 3- to 5-minute touch point with the manufacturing line or cell. The intent is to use open-ended questions to engage the team, getting their input on an issue, recognizing someone based on the right behavior not a result, and informing the team of the plan of action for today. This meeting should happen at the start of the shift.

Tier 2

This 10-minute meeting happens after the first hour of production is completed. This is done with the core team, Mechanical Engineer, Quality Engineer, planning, and maintenance; is led by the supervisor; and should be no more than 5 to 10 minutes. The intent of this meeting is to use the day-by-hour board to identify issues from the first hour and trends based on the last shift. The group leader identifies issues that will not be resolved by end of shift or issues that may or will prevent the shift team members from hitting their targets. These issues are then escalated to the Tier 3 meeting. The location of this meeting is important. It needs to be held at the day-by-hour board location so the actions can be tracked and the team knows their priorities. This will also allow the area leaders to follow up with coaching or resources when the leader performs their Gemba walks.

Tier 3

This 10-minute meeting happens daily and focuses on the daily trends based on the summary of all shifts' performance utilizing the month-by-day chart. The team is managing the daily trends to ensure that the weekly targets are being achieved. The attendees are the same as Tier 2 but with the addition of the area manager. Daily trends that cannot be corrected by the end of the week are escalated to Tier 4. The escalation may be an awareness, or it may be an ask for additional support needed to resolve the issue.

Tier 4

This 5-minute meeting happens weekly with the area managers to include the engineering manager, quality manager, maintenance manager, and planning manager. Functional directors may attend to listen and observe at this meeting. This meeting is led by the operations director, and the focus is to look at weekly trends that may impact the monthly performance of the site. The issues are prioritized for alignment on resources and actions are tracked to ensure issues are being resolved and understood. This is also when managers may adjust their standard work regarding where their Gemba walks will take place and their theme. Issues that will impact the month are escalated to Tier 5, and decisions on priorities and support allocation are then shared with Tier 3.

Tier 5

This 30-minute meeting happens monthly with the directors and managers. The site's monthly performance and trends are reviewed. This meeting is led by the site director or plant manager.

The issues are prioritized for alignment on resources and actions are tracked to ensure issues are being resolved and understood. This is when directors may adjust their standard work regarding where their Gemba walks will occur along with the theme. Issues that will impact the quarter are escalated to Tier 6, and decisions on priorities and support allocation are also then shared with Tier 4.

Tier 6

This 30-minute meeting is held monthly by the divisional leader. The site directors, quality directors, and finance directors, along with the divisional leaders' direct reports, all attend. The focus of this meeting is understanding the constraints or themes the division is facing, what to prioritize, and if additional resources need to be reallocated to resolve issues. The information and decisions are then cascaded to Tier 5.

The key thing to remember is that a red metric is the result of a process that is not yielding the desired outcome. How a leader reacts to this will drive the culture. If the leader casts blame on people, does not help the team see the real issue(s), and does not help their approach on solving problems, the teams will shut down and no longer bring up issues or even assist in helping to resolve the issue. If the leader focuses on the process at the right level, then the team will respond with engagement. Remember, all outcomes are the consequence of a process. It is nearly impossible for even good people to consistently produce ideal results with a poor process both inside and outside the organization. There is a natural tendency to blame the people involved when something goes wrong or is less than ideal when in reality, the vast majority of the time the issue is management's fault due to allowing an imperfect process. If you blame the people, you will never find the root cause.

Visual Management Is a Sustaining Tool

Companies read about visual management, often decide it's a good idea, and off they go. But they never really understand that it makes the leaders feel vulnerable because the plant becomes more transparent by exposing issues and showing their weak points. It takes a strong confident leader to expose their faults and weaknesses. The most important part of the Leadership Development Path process is developing the leadership capabilities that enable the ability to sustain the improvement made. The lack of clear visualization of KPIs allows the deviation of the actual condition and target condition to go unnoticed. When you first begin the process, you will find problems that have been occurring for a long time, but teams have become oblivious to them. They just deal with them. This is the boiled frog syndrome at work.

For example, we have a client for whom we were piloting the production line, which had three models. One of the models took 30% longer than the other two. This problem went unnoticed for over 3 years. When we started measuring actual time to target time and reviewing variation during the Leadership Development Path huddle, an engineer was assigned to evaluate the problem. In 2 days, the root cause was identified, and in 3 days, the problem was solved. The issue was that the variant model specification did not allow for the same ease of operation as the other two. This issue has been traced back to when this variant was implemented 3 years earlier.

This issue had cost the company $150,000 in lost production, and it only took 2 hours to identify the root cause and 4 hours of work to solve the problem. This is a great example of how visual management combined with Plan–Do–Check–Act (PDCA) is the cure for firefighting! This is also a great example of how much money companies leave on the table. The water was lowered and the rocks exposed, and the team reacted quickly once the system was in place. Once the easy problems are solved, it becomes harder, so you need a visual management system in place to make it easier to show results.

Going to the Gemba—One Cannot Fix a Problem at Their Desk

At one company, the leader pores over report after report, using their newly learned MBA skills to analyze their spreadsheets to identify and isolate the problems. They create a PowerPoint deck 3 inches thick and develop a host of solutions to fix the problems without ever going to see the problem firsthand. Is it a wonder why the problems never seem to get fixed?

One cannot fix a problem sitting at their desk and just looking at reports. Reports are only history with trends that can be useful but are many times misused or misunderstood. Figures don't lie, but liars do figures. We have seen the prettiest A3s in the world, lots of charts, Paretos, pie graphs, bar graphs, and so on that contained useless information, sometimes not even remotely related to the problem at hand.

The only way to fix a problem is to go to the source and watch. Only by watching and or doing the job yourself can we truly discover the root cause of the problem? If you have been in your job for over a year, then you must come to a pivotal realization. You are a boiled frog! You have to get outside the system, pretend you are looking down on it from above, and see what's really happening. There is a saying: Today's problems come from yesterday's solutions. All the solutions you have put in place yesterday are creating the problems you have today. You are to blame, not your team members.

Gemba Watch Versus Gemba Walks—Go and Watch

We were at a winery in Santorini, Greece, with Ritsuo Shingo.[7] He noticed they had several inspectors, and Ritsuo asked what seemed like a simple question: "Why do you have so many inspectors?" The manager looked at him like he was crazy and said, "We have to have inspectors. Their job is to make sure that no foreign particles get into the bottles."

The workers would pick up four bottles and hold them up in the air against a lighted backdrop to see if the bottles were clean. Ritsuo-san just sat there and spent almost 2 hours watching, and then he started to ask some more simple questions. Then he went to the machine and "got his hands dirty." He climbed the ladder (he was 69 years old at the time) and inspected the top of the machine (see Figure 12.15). He asked why the lid to the machine was off as this could allow particles into the machine. He also inspected the packaging and found problems there. When all was said and done, he found several problems and their root causes and suggested solutions. Implementing these solutions would eliminate the need for the inspectors. He explained by getting control over the process the results take care of themselves. This has always been his guiding philosophy. Ritsuo-san summed it all up by saying, "Gemba walks should be changed to Gemba watches!"

It is important that the management level guide the teams on a regular basis through their feedback and coaching. Without feedback, we cannot build on our strengths and work on our

Figure 12.15   Ritsuo Shingo—Santorini Winery Tour.

Source: Used with Permission from Ritsuo Shingo—Lean Leadership Institute Santorini Trip August 2017.

gaps. *Genchi genbutsu* translates "to go and see" and refers to the management tactic of spending a good amount of time at the Gemba or place of reality. Toyota chairman Fujio Cho said about going to the Gemba, "Go see—ask why—show respect."[8] Katie Anderson stated, "Mr. Yoshino said management at Toyota goes to the floor to show the team members they care."[9]

Mike Rother[10] suggests that, in addition to the previously mentioned three common aspects, the Gemba walk should focus on how people are working. This means "focusing on their pattern of thinking or acting which they utilize as they improve and strive for their goals." This involves four steps:

1. It should be used systemwide.
2. It should be suitable for any goal or problem.[11]
3. It should be based on the scientific method.
4. It should include structured practice routines for beginners.

This approach is described in detail in his books and videos which can be found on his Kata website.

Leadership Development Walks

The term *Gemba walk*, which we now refer to as Leadership Development Walk, has many meanings today and takes on various forms at every company. Gemba walks have really lost their original purpose in many factories. They range from just walking through areas to check on the daily management boards, if they even exist, to speaking with team leaders or group leaders and the like. There are books written on them, but everyone has their own opinion on them. In our case, if you go to the floor (or office) it is a walk to the Gemba. Gemba is where the action is going on. The common three aspects are to watch, eliminate waste, and learn. We conduct different types of walks which can be separate or combined and are not an inclusive list. They include the following:

1. Waste walks during which we look for waste
2. Process walks during which we look at each workstation, along with the tools and materials used, to see what could go wrong and how to improve or mistake proof.
3. Daily management walks during which the manager should be able to look at the daily management board and know immediately if there is a problem. Depending on the severity of the problem, the manager may leave a note to be answered by the team leader or group leader (to see if they are managing the board), or they may use an urgent problem/gap on the board as a coaching moment to further develop their team leader's thinking.

Waste Walk

A waste walk is a type of Gemba walk used to teach others Learning to See. This was what is called the Ohno circle (see Figure 12.16), during which Taiichi Ohno would make his managers stand in a circle he outlined on the floor. Waste walks offer a way to continually improve our ability to see waste in the process. Ritsuo Shingo says, "You should not just watch their hands but also eyes and then ask why?" This concept dates back to Frank Gilbreth's motion-study process.

Taking a small group of your team members along as you continuously perform these daily walks will not only coach and improve the team member's ability to see waste but will improve the plant's ability to continuously improve. These walks are centered on the Eight Wastes and require a leader with the knowledge and skill "to see" in order to be effective. That leader must coach and train the other team members and then allow them to identify and ultimately reduce the waste that is being found.

Process Walk (Watch)

This is a Learning to See and Solve walk. The first question we always ask on a process walk is, What is the standard? If there is no standard, then we have an immediate gap, and it means we need to do a job breakdown and develop the standard work. If there is a standard, then we should be looking to see the actual condition. Are we meeting the standard? This is why creating and improving standards is part of TSR. You can see how TSR now helps sustain the improvements.

Daily Management Walk (Watch)

This is a Learning to Share walk. This walk reviews the daily management board. This is where we use Shingo's 1–3–10 tool. Are we ahead or behind schedule? Both are problems. If we are behind, we need to understand why and remember the problem is not the person. If we are ahead, we need

Figure 12.16 Ohno Circle—Managers would spend many hours, sometimes over a shift or more, until they saw the waste Ohno wanted them to see.

Source: Source Unknown.

to understand if we are following the standard. If we are and have figured out a way to better it, then we need to update the standard work to include the improvement.

The bottom line on it all is the Gemba walk should be focused on teaching, coaching, and driving ongoing improvement toward your targets. This means you need to understand the gaps between where you are now and your target and then experiment using small PDAC cycles to overcome the gaps. Typical Gemba walk questions encourage problem-solving, teaching, and developing your people the following:

■ Problem identification—finding a gap or deviation from the standard
■ Problem solving—watching and listening. One must touch and get their hands dirty.
■ Team—team leader and management coaching on how to watch and discover the root cause
■ What improvements the team is working on now. Then we need to understand how and where they are in the problem-solving process. We need to understand the target they are shooting for compared to the baseline and if they have identified the root cause. The most important thing is to make sure they are not just throwing solutions at the problem.

Ritsuo Shingo[12] says, "You cannot manage the floor or office area or fix a problem without going to the Gemba, floor, or office, to determine what is really going on." When he was president of Sichuan Toyota, China, he personally walked the entire property, prior to building their new facility, in order to find the root cause of a problem with a stream and related drainage that would have seriously impacted the plant. If he hadn't walked the property, he would have never discovered the problem. You cannot manage a plant from your office. Gemba watches are an important component of the Leadership Development Path and a sustaining mechanism if done properly. However, there must be visual displays and controls in place. If not, it just becomes another walk or tour of the floor.

Notes

1. Creating a Lean Culture, David Mann, Productivity Press 2010.
2. The Lean Practitioner's Field Book: Proven, Practical, Profitable and Powerful Techniques for Making Lean Really Work, Productivity Press; 1 edition (April 4, 2016) Protzman, et al.
3. This is not an inclusive list.
4. Nigel Thurlow is CEO of the Flow Consortium, co-creator of the Flow System, and former Chief of Agile at Toyota.
5. Dave Rizzardo white paper personal correspondence 5–26–2020.
6. Michael Meyers.
7. Ritsuo Shingo taught at the Lean Leadership Institute (LLI) conference, August 2017, hosted by George Trachilis in Santorini, Greece.
8. www.lean.org/shook/DisplayObject.cfm?o=1843
9. Personal correspondence with Katie Anderson 5/7/2020.
10. www-personal.umich.edu/~mrother/Homepage.html
11. Within the complicated or simple domain of Cynefin.
12. Ritsuo Shingo taught at the Lean Leadership Institute (LLI) conference, August 2017, hosted by George Trachilis in Santorini, Greece.

Chapter 13

Secrets to Sustaining

Figure 13.1 BASICS® Lean Leadership Development Path.

Source: BIG training materials.

Our Leadership Development Plan (see Figure 13.1) is not meant to compete with the Toyota House but works in conjunction with it and is in harmony with both Toyota's philosophy[1] and Deming's 14 Points.[2] It requires constant attention to and helps develop a learning organization, supported by people development, promotion from within, succession planning, and the infrastructure, that is, "hard" tools mainly led by standard work. Remember, if there is no standard work, there can be no evidence of sustained improvement.

DOI: 10.4324/9781315155227-13

Let the Needs Drive the Process[3]

I had just started a new job and was talking to one of the group leaders for a particular production line. I asked him what I thought was a pretty basic question, and the following was our dialog over the next several days on the production floor. Each dialog was only 5 minutes per day.

Day 1

MIKE: Hi, Kevin, how is our scrap doing?

KEVIN: Pretty good.

MIKE: What is pretty good?

KEVIN: We did not make many bad parts.

MIKE: I am going to ask you the same question tomorrow, and can you please tell me how many good pieces we made how many bad pieces we made, the percent of good and bad?

KEVIN: Certainly.

Day 2

MIKE: Hi, Kevin, how is our scrap today?

KEVIN: We made 520 pieces with 65 bad for an 87% good, and scrap dollars were $4,875.

MIKE: Thank you, Kevin. Is that considered to be good or bad?

KEVIN: It's the first time I really looked at it like that, but I think it would be bad.

MIKE: Do you know what our biggest scrap issue was?

KEVEN: No, not really. I didn't look into it.

MIKE: Tomorrow do you think you could add that to the conversation?

KEVIN: Sure.

MIKE: Thank you and look forward to our 10-minute talk tomorrow.

Day 3

MIKE: Hi, Kevin. How was our scrap today?

KEVIN: We made 600 pieces with 60 bad for a 90% good, and scrap dollars were $4,500.

MIKE: Thank you, Kevin. What was our largest defect?

KEVIN: Out biggest scrap issue was bubbles on Line 7.

MIKE: Wow, thanks, Kevin. Was this a good or bad day?

KEVIN: I am not really sure.

MIKE: It's a good day because we are starting to understand where to put out attention. When we talk tomorrow can you also let me know what obstacles you are working on to reduce the bubbles?

Day 4

MIKE: Hi, Kevin. How was our scrap today?

KEVIN: We made 620 pieces with 55 bad for a 91% good, and scrap dollars were $4,125.

MIKE: Thank you, Kevin. What was our largest defect?

KEVIN: Out biggest scrap issue was bubbles on Line 7, and we realized our temperatures were running below specification.

MIKE: That's very interesting. Can we go see how we monitor the temperatures?

KEVIN: Certainly.

MIKE: How do the team members know the spec?

KEVIN: It's in the book.

MIKE: Can we identify the spec by color coding the temp gages so it's really easy to understand what the spec is?

KEVIN: Yes we can.

MIKE: Make sure we get the team members involved and train them properly and we can start communicating the performance to the team.

Day 5

On Day 5 we developed our first daily management huddle (see Figure 13.2) with a whiteboard that was placed line side so the team members could be engaged and be part of the process. This board had two key performance indicators (KPIs) that the team managed with Kevin being the leader. The board consisted of three levels of tracking:

■ Run chart to track daily performance
■ Pareto analysis to show top issues
■ Plan–Do–Check–Act (PDCA) charts

These charts were all *filled out manually,* and our 15-minute meeting took place every day for 3 weeks until we had completed initial development of our daily management board. After that, we cascaded it to the other 45 other work cells. We developed the foundation for the system in a very short time by asking the leaders very basic questions. This provided a kind of script for the group leader and gave them questions they would be asked that set the foundation for what their role should be. The boards became more complex with additional data but only what was required to move forward.

We were putting in a new system, but nobody realized it other than me. In their minds, they were just simply doing something to answer questions and drive improvements and get participation from a cross-functional team. The boards weren't put out just to implement a tool. They were established to lead the department, manage the process, and begin cross-functional teaming between the groups. It's a subtle difference, but the impact is huge.

One thing I will never forget is that Kevin and I would have our meeting every day at the same time at the same place. All of a sudden, other people started joining because they were interested in what we were doing and wanted to be part of "this" even though they did not know what "this" was. We did not name it, we did not schedule it, we did not establish roles, and we let the needs

Figure 13.2 Shop Floor Daily Management Board/Communication Center.

Source: BIG training materials.

drive the process. I remember looking over my shoulder one day and noticed we had 15 to 18 people as part of the meeting with none of them required to come. One day, the chief financial officer and the president of the global division were visiting, and they all engaged in watching our handwritten charts and our handwritten corrective actions that drive real improvements with real participation by a cross-functional team that was engaged in their process. It all started with a simple question and the initial realization that we did not even have the system in place to answer a very basic question: "Hi, Kevin, how is our scrap doing?"

Just having all the data doesn't mean you have a system. This company had numerous scrap reports housed in a computer that nobody looked at and certainly nobody reacted to. The president of the division and I went to dinner in the evening, and I still find the conversation interesting. He asked me how, in just a few short weeks, I was able to get all that participation. I told him that all people want to participate, they all want to do better, and they all want to see the results of their effort. He asked me why we do not post electronic information. I told him that I believed there is a place in manufacturing for computers. Manufacturing Electronic Systems (MES) and the Internet of Things (IoT 4.0) play a role in feeding the PLC (programmable logic control) information to the computer and video monitors. These data can help us ensure equipment is not only running but is also running at the right speeds, feeds, and so on. We can use these systems for predictive maintenance by putting vibration or sonic sensors on motors, blowers, and the like.

But for shop floor visual management, we need these systems to be visible to all. We insist that the KPI tracking is performed using manual graphs, with standardized coded colors, to quickly identify in real time if teams are on track (see Figure 13.3). This creates a very quick visual system that is green if the KPI is beating the plan, yellow if it is within 5% of target, and red if it is missing by over 5%.

Lean thinking has been around a long time, and almost all manufacturing people have been exposed to Lean to varying degrees. During my experience, I learned that not only was I developing others but that I was also learning every day and developing myself at the same time by putting these systems in place. I have been very lucky to work in this type of environment at Donnelly Corporation under mentors like Russ Scafede, who was past General Manager/Vice President of Toyota Motor Manufacturing Power Train Donnelly Corporation. We made a huge cultural transformation under Russ and others[4] into what was considered to be world class by our customers and third-party Lean experts who were completing worldwide benchmarking studies. We were also featured in an SME video.[5]

I grew up in this environment, was part of the evolution, and always consider myself very fortunate. Just because you worked in a Lean environment doesn't make you an expert. What it does do is help separate people who know Lean from those who say they do. It helps you understand that there is a difference between theory and actual application. It also helps you appreciate the journey we took, how difficult it was, and how much we learned without even knowing it.

Lean wasn't some special project; it was just how we did our job. We were expected to become a team as production group leaders. We did not even talk about it much or use all the buzzwords. Although we understood the vocabulary, we were mostly charged with the actual implementation. The implementation was what was important, not the theory, although we were taught the theory. I haven't worked at that company for years now but often rely on that foundation.

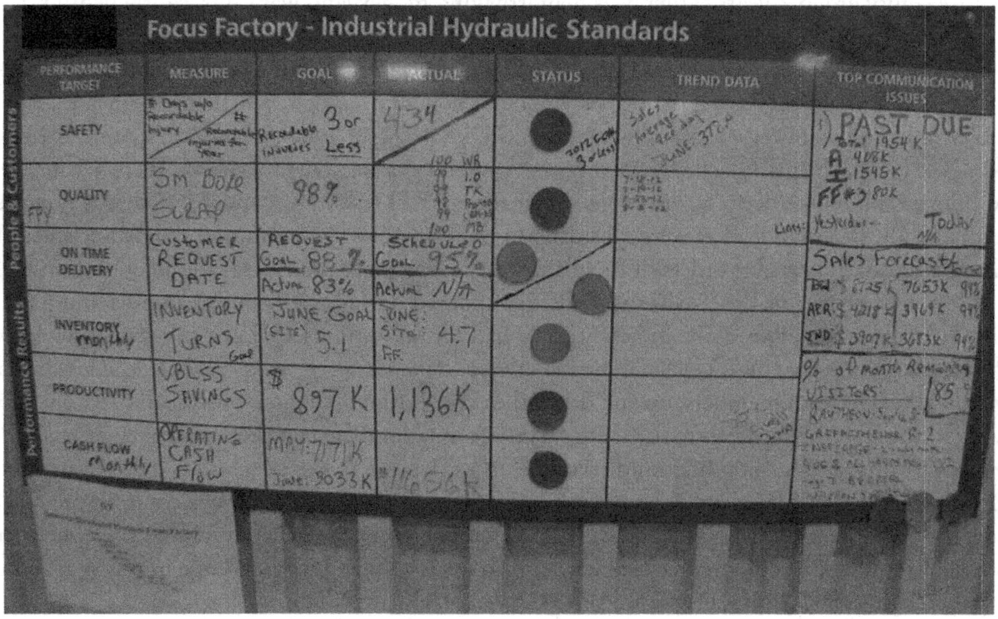

Figure 13.3　High-Level KPI Tracking.

Source: BIG training materials.

Treat People as People

The following is quoted directly from an article in *Inc. Magazine*, titled "The Wisdom of Peter Drucker from A to Z":

> For more than 60 years, Drucker preached that workers are assets not liabilities, and should be treated with respect. . . . Drucker reimagined the organization as a human community and the job of management as preparing people to perform and then getting out of their way. That attitude wasn't just nice. Given that knowledge skills are more portable than manual ones, it was also smart. "The management of knowledge workers should be based on the assumption that the corporation needs them more than they need the corporation.[6]

Why Companies Fail[7]

Most companies I have seen fail in the last 15 years fall into three categories regarding this transformation:

- They are "Lean theory–based" and really struggle to implement anything.
- They use the Lean tools to cut costs and survive the month or year.
- They don't have a true compelling need to change.

I visited a company recently, and early on in my visit, the plant manager showed me his Bronze or Gold Lean certificate, I forget which one it was. This company had been purchased from a private equity group 2 years earlier, was hemorrhaging money, and was significantly behind their turnaround plan. We discussed the plant and the challenges they were facing. Again, he made me aware of his Lean expertise while sitting in his conference room. I always give people the benefit of the doubt when they tell me how much they know and point to all their certificates, but I prefer to let the plant tell me about their real skill, knowledge, leadership abilities, and expertise. Needless to say, the plant lacked anything that resembled a Lean organization. There was broken equipment, oil on the floor, no visual management, no KPI tracking, standard work was nonexistent, and all the group leaders were all sitting in their offices when we toured the plant. Schedule changes and skipping over orders in the plant were taking place hourly due to material shortages.

Person after person I met with over the day spouted out all the Lean buzzwords and used a vocabulary that would lead one to believe they had formal training on Lean subjects. They knew the words like *Gemba*, *pull*, *takt time*, *kaizen*, *andon*, *standard work*, *waste walks*, and *kanban*. The more I talked to team members, up and down the organization, the more I was stumped as to why, with all the training on Lean tools, there was no correlation between the words they were speaking and reality on the shop floor and in their offices. I came to the conclusion that the inability to implement was embedded in the system several layers deep. What I always try to figure out is why the plant manager, a really smart, very knowledgeable, experienced guy, often knew where the problems were but he couldn't harness his team to focus or turn his knowledge into actual action to even begin transforming his plant.

This is not only the only example. The same story could be written countless times. The failure in most companies is not the knowledge they hold or the certifications they have been awarded, but the ability, courage, leadership, and systems necessary to take their knowledge and persistence to create a culture that thrives on application of both the technical tools and the human aspect.

Beware of Multitasking

This waste is encountered when someone is trying to multitask (see Figure 13.4). Do you think you are good at multitasking? Most of us believe we are, but in reality, no human is good at it. The definition of multitasking is trying to do two distinct tasks at the exact same time. An example is texting and driving. Based on Weinberg's table,[8] you are either not keeping your eyes on the road or your phone 20% of the time. This is why people slow down or swerve when they are texting and driving or even talking on their cell. Another is texting while someone is talking to you.

Most of us have a list of action items that are all due right away. It's impossible! Stop trying to do it! Pick one at a time, get it done, and check it off then go to the next one. As a group leader, you must be able to prioritize your actions and make sure your team's actions are tied to tangible objectives. To be clear, if you start a task and are forced to wait for some reason, then, by all means, go on to the next task.

Combining the Scrum Kanban Board and Lean

You can avoid context switching waste by using kanban boards that are a tool used by scrum teams. The scrum kanban board is simple to use and helps enforce the discipline to work on only one task at a time. You will see better and faster results by solving one problem at a time, which is tied to a measurable result.

This doesn't mean the organization cannot work on more than one action at a time, but it means the resources must exist so that each team can start and finish the action before moving to the next, that is, one-piece flow. If there is a point at which you have to wait for an action, then another action can be started until the wait time is completed. However, there should be a date when it should be completed, that is, placing an order for a part. We have introduced these boards (see Figure 13.5) to facilitate individuals and teams working in administrative areas, including

Number of Tasks	% of Time on Each
1	100
2	40
3	20
4	10
5	5
more than 5	random

Figure 13.4 Impact of Context Switching—Trying to Do Things at the Same Time, Like Texting and Driving.

Source: Quality Software Management: Systems Thinking, Gerald M. Weinberg, Dorset House (September 1, 1991) Slide courtesy of Nigel Thurlow—CEO of the Flow System Scrum The Toyota Way ©2017 and the Flow System Training ©2019—used with permission.

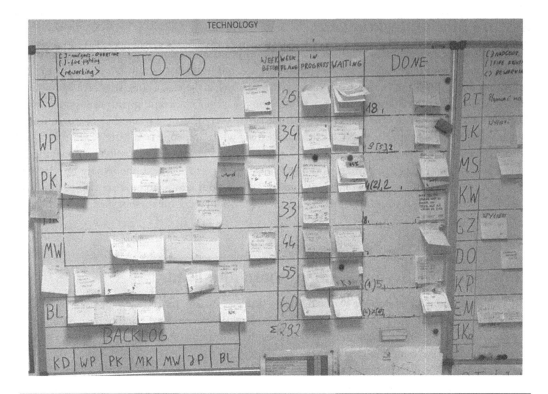

Figure 13.5 Research and Development Scrum Kanban Board.

Source: BIG training materials.

sales and engineering that are outside of the traditional software context, to help stop multitasking and significantly improve productivity. Seeing and eliminating waste becomes how everyone in the organization does business. The kanban board is a logical extension of visual management (*Mieruka* in Japanese). In order to make sense of our environment, we must change our behaviors utilizing 4S/5S.

Visualizing Our Backlog

Leaning out our process for greater quality and the application of the scrum framework tools can help provide the platform to level the office workload and convert batching to one-piece flow by making our work visible and identify issues/wastes in the process. This early detection will allow for greater agility. Whereas Lean focuses on building the product correctly, agility focuses on building the right product, and incorporating scrum will allow empirical planning with feedback mechanisms early in the process rather than at the end of a long cycle of work. By changing our behaviors and Leaning out our process, we can adapt to change requirements and facilitate the use of an Andon system to halt the line and fix the problem in real time. This can provide true agility.[9]

We implemented this scrum kanban board system at a company in southern Maryland, which became a big success. In the past, the administration team always found themselves being reprioritized by the leadership. We installed some rules with the kanban board implementation. When a new task came along from management, they simply said, "Okay, put it where you think it belongs on my board. If you are changing my priorities, it's okay, but the other tasks will be a bit delayed without committing additional resources." This made the process visible and forced everyone to think about each task and is it really adding value to the end customer. It also showed management the workload on each team member.

What Does Leadership Commitment Mean?

We always talk about leadership's role in sustaining and that leaders must be committed, but we started discussing what that really means. We think it means not just knowing but participating in and practicing the following:

- Exhibit teamwork and trust at the senior leadership level.
- Live and make decisions based on your company's values.
- One-piece flow—drive it always even if you can't attain it.
- Set your personal standards high and always strive for perfection, knowing it is never possible.
- Role model the desired behaviors. Your actions are always being watched more than your words.
- Use active listening; ask for and thank people for feedback. When asked, provide constructive feedback, both positive and negative.
- Create the feedback loops so you know what you need to know not what people think you want to hear.
- Learn and understand that just-in-time is philosophical and that jidoka is paramount to sustaining and successfully meeting customer commitments at the lowest cost.
- Develop your team members during your Gemba walks.

Sphere of Influence

Sphere of influence is key when it comes to sustaining. One can only sustain and continue to improve what one has direct control over. Outside your span of control, we are dependent on influencing others. This is where our verbal and written presentation skills become important. One must be able to build a business case for the ideas and improvements in order to get people behind them, get them approved, and get them implemented. One technique we use for this is to meet with all stakeholders individually to get their feedback, objections, and buy-in, before calling a meeting to get the idea, improvement, funding, and so on approved. Proposal A3s work well for this. If you can learn and understand each individual's objections ahead of time and overcome them, then the final meeting becomes a rubber stamp of approval.

People Need Challenges

People need to be led and leadership needs to lead while being inspiring to those they are leading. People pick leaders who can take them somewhere they couldn't go by themselves. One way to do this is to challenge your team every day with a problem and then provide a framework within which to work. The framework sets boundaries and makes sure the problem is within their scope and ability to solve. Encourage them to try to solve one problem at a time. This is one way to motivate your team members to build a culture of continuous improvement.

Notes

1. See the Appendix—Toyota's Philosophy. See the Appendix for the Toyota 4 Steps, 5 Precepts, and 14 Principles.
2. See the Appendix for Deming's 14 points.
3. Michael Meyers
4. Art Smalley, Bill Constantino.
5. SME Manufacturing Insights Series, Mapping Your Value Stream, 2001.
6. www.inc.com/articles/2009/11/drucker.html, © 2009, by Leigh Buchanan, Editor at Large INC. magazine.
7. Michael Meyers.
8. Inspired by Nigel Thurlow, CEO of the Flow Consortium, co-creator of the Flow System, and former Chief of Agile at Toyota.
9. www.scrumguides.org/

Chapter 14

Sustaining—The New Hiring Process and Expectations

Origins of the HR Movement at Toyota

See Figure 14.1

Figure 14.1   BASICS® Lean Leadership Development Path—Sustain.

Source: BIG training materials.

DOI: 10.4324/9781315155227-14

Ohno stated in his book JIT for Today and Tomorrow—Toyota's founding chairman Toyoda Kiichiro issued a postwar challenge to the Japanese auto industry to catch up with America within three years or lose all chance of survival. It can be said that resistance to just-in-time began at that very point. However, just-in-time and jidoka (autonomation) steadily permeated the organization in the early 1960s and continued to do so throughout the period of rapid growth. They were implemented gradually, with commitment to the principles serving as the background for establishing such manufacturing practices as

1. Making one worker responsible for several processes
2. Dramatically reducing setup times for presses
3. Rethinking the transport and withdrawal of goods. The function of kanban as information was steadily adopted between the production processes.[1]

It is thought that during this time when Human Resources (HR) at Toyota started down this path. The following is from correspondence from Mr. Isao Yoshino:[2]

You asked about who was a kind of organizer of HR at Toyota, just like Taiichi Ohno on TPS [Toyota Production System]. It is true that the function of Human Relations or Human Development has been believed to be important at Toyota. But I do not think we used to have any specific executives in that area like Ohno on TPS or Nemoto on Hoshin Kanri. Our top management, starting from Kiichiro Toyota all the way through Eiji Toyoda, are very much eager to develop people, probably more than any other companies in Japan. Top management has put "people development" as one of the first priority items at Toyota for a long time. Toyota's motto of "Good Products, Good Thinking" is based on the concept of "show respect" to people. Also, one of the most important roles of senior managers has been to "develop subordinates." TPS promoted by Ohno was targeted primarily to the manufacturing segment. Hoshin Kanri promoted by Nemoto was primarily focused on senior managers. But the concept of developing subordinates is considered to be the main role of all the managers who have subordinates to develop. So, if I am asked who is the big pillar in Human Relations or Human Development, I would say it would be "all the managers who have subordinates working for them."

HR's New Role

In HR's new role, the interview process morphs to find people that can work as a team, take ownership and be accountable, suggest improvements, and have a bias for action.[3] People who share and pass on their knowledge should be the type of people you are using to build your organization. People who use their knowledge for self-preservation and importance are the type of people your company is better off without, even if they are sometimes the smartest person in the room. Companies may have to filter hundreds of candidates to get one person who can work and thrive in this new environment.

Every leader should be evaluated by their manager and HR on how well they develop their people. Most organizations are still utilizing the old style: very subjective team member employee performance evaluation systems. It is not unusual for subjectivity to creep in based on personalities and to have responses tainted with cognitive bias. The biggest mistake many companies make is to have their annual review processes all come due at the end of the year. This creates havoc and poor review cycles. It is best to use a hire date or monthly alphabet system to level load the reviews.

In the new system, the evaluation should include their progress on meeting their objective goals, living the company values, and include a professional growth plan outlining the team member's aspirations and what position they might be seeking in the next 1 to 3 years. The manager and team member should each complete a copy of the evaluation, meet to assess where they agree and disagree, and then together explore the gaps. Once the gaps are discussed and agreed on, the team member should record the actions they plan on implementing over the next year to overcome the gaps. This then becomes their development plan. Some organizations formally document this development plan after the discussions are concluded and review it several times during the year. Informal team member evaluations should be ongoing as part of the everyday coaching, monthly goal deployment plan reviews, and not be a surprise during the formal annual review process.

The Foundation—Developing Yourself through Others

The group leader's role here is a bit of a paradox. Assuming the building is not burning down, when a team member comes with a problem to the team leader or the team leader to the group leader and so on, the leader, depending on context, does not necessarily provide the answer. The role of the leader should be to turn this into a coaching moment and ask guiding questions to encourage the team member to think. This is how one turns followers into leaders. The Executive Team's role is to teach and role model this behavior which can be a huge culture shift at some companies. This chapter will walk through this process by using Plan–Do–Check–Act (PDCA) and the problem-solving tools we use to teach team members to begin their learning journey.

The role of the group leader is to pass on their accumulated knowledge, skills, and abilities to their teams. Passing on their knowledge will help your company progress much faster because you will have people with enhanced knowledge driving you forward. Development comes from a variety of sources including but not limited to the following:

1. Leadership coaching and mentoring
2. Skills and system development—experience and practice
3. External training and coaching
4. Reading, research, and subject-matter videos

People who can offer different opinions or different techniques that will stretch your current paradigms and often lead to a better outcome.

Company-Wide Training Plan/Academy

HR should be responsible for training people not only on teamwork and interpersonal skills but also on the skills necessary to run the business. While HR is not teaching the team members to run the machines, they are working with the group leaders on their cross-training tables to make sure team members and leaders get the training they need to run the machines as well as to advance and grow. HR can create a training academy to oversee and teach the necessary interpersonal and technical skills but need the line personnel to do the training. Toyota instructs on the job implicitly so they cannot tell you in words what they are doing, not even in Japanese.[4]

Orientation Training

Remember your first day at a new company? How did it go? Everyone remembers their first day on a new job. Were you welcomed by the group leader? Did the group leader follow up with you throughout the day? Did the group leader ask you for feedback before they left? Did you feel challenged with the learning that took place? What did you tell their family? The group leader and HR should be able to echo the voice of the team member when they're asked these questions. Too often the new hire is thrown into the process and is randomly assigned someone to train them.

The orientation program at most organizations is focused on the wrong goals. Most orientation programs range from a 1-hour to a 1-day session with the HR department to discuss benefits, company policies, cultural or legal norms, and expectations from the organization. There are very few programs that stress the organizational operating system with a real goal of orienting the person to their role in the larger operational systems of the organization. We have seen some programs in which there is a self-paced slideshow, online reading, or webinar that covers a fairly extensive overview of the organization; however, there are problems with this approach. One is the fact that using a video has a low-retention rate, and next, these presentations are rarely at the level needed to help clarify the individuals' standard work expectations.

A comprehensive orientation program is shared in some of the stories below and should be a part of the theory of education and training. Orientation training needs should be delivered by the group leaders or management. They should focus on the company's customers, philosophy, values, and operational systems required to design, develop, and manufacture its products and/or services provided to its customers. The operating procedures are usually documented in some type of operation manual or handbook. New team members need to be introduced to the nomenclature of the organization. Every organization has a bevy of acronyms and terms specific to the organization or the industry. An orientation to these terms and acronyms can be a great benefit when a person is just starting their job.

Once standard work is in place, it is important when hiring people to communicate the expectations during the initial interview process that all team members are expected to follow standard work and contribute daily improvement ideas. We must spend time with our workers to teach them they can still critically think while doing standard work. Good judgment and critical thinking will always be part of any business.

Promotion from within

What is the difference between bringing people in from the outside vs. promoting from within? In the United States, prior to the mid-1990s, companies used to primarily promote from within. Job-hopping was even considered detrimental to your career. Then everything changed, and all of a sudden, if you were in your job longer than 2 or 3 years, something was "wrong with you." This can have a big impact, or bias, on how companies approach developing people whom they feel are going to leave in less than 3 years.

Promoting from within provides an apprenticeship-type path, prepares workers to be team leaders whereby they can learn the business from the ground up, and fosters company loyalty.

There used to be an expectation that one would move from apprentice (team member) to journeyman (group leader) and then foreman (operations or plant manager). This process normally took 10 years or more to get to be a team leader and another several years before supervisor and then foreman. Trade unions used to provide much of these skills. If you were going to hire people for life, what kind of changes would you make to your hiring or on-boarding process?

However, if the company only promotes from within, it needs a way to get new information into their system. Toyota used to do this with what was called the Big Idea Club.[5] This club was made up of high achievers for improvement suggestions who were awarded the opportunity on their own time to work on teams that explored and researched the next new "thing" to come along, things like the introduction of the personal computer, MRP I&II and enterprise resource planning systems, among others. These teams became study groups that, over the course of 6 months to a year, would come back to the CEO with a recommendation on how to proceed with the new technology or concept. So there needs to be a balance in the organization so that it doesn't turn into a closed-minded system.

Upgrade/UpLevel the Organization

Once we define the new vision for the organization, we need to review the organization chart and look to see if we have the right people on the bus and in the right seats. This is the start of succession planning. During our coaching of leaders, we teach them that there is also a selfish reason to develop your people. If you don't develop your people, then there is no one to take your place, which means you can't move up in the organization.

Part of the goal of ongoing leadership coaching is to continue to help each team member evolve and increase their skill sets and problem-solving mindset as well as living the company's values through their behaviors. We suggest reviewing the organization every 6 to 12 months because as the vision evolves, we have to constantly ask ourselves if we have the right people in place to take us to the next level. If not, what do we need to do to develop them?

This does not mean that the responsibility for developing people is totally on the company. Part of the process is training each person on the team that they need to be the best they can be first. This means looking for ways they can help understand where the weaknesses are in their behaviors and skill sets and look for ways they can self-improve. Every employee should know what the plan is for their development over the next 1 to 3 years. As companies move more toward scrum culture and teaming organizations, this assessment may become more team-based versus individual-based. Even so, the individual and the company both share in their ongoing development responsibility.

High Turnover Can Be a Symptom of Poor Development

Generally, turnover is an executive leadership problem, not a first-line leadership problem. When you have a high level of turnover, it cannot simply be brushed under the rug; you need to take a step back and honestly understand why people do not want to stay. We might not like what we find out but if you truly want to know, it's easy enough to find out. People don't always leave companies; sometimes, they leave their managers.[6] There is a huge cost to turnover that organizations never seem to understand or calculate.

I was sitting in a strategic planning meeting with a client where one of the goals was to reduce the recruitment cost from $500,000 to $400,000. While I was observing, I found it interesting that the majority of the discussion resulted in actions that were centered on reducing the cost, yet the root cause of the cost was never discussed. There was no discussion around development plans, training, education, forums for participation, performance management, or trying to understand why people were leaving. When I investigated, I found some team members left the organization because they did not feel challenged to develop. Just replacing somebody won't fix this issue. If this company had taken 50% of the dollars spent on recruiting and used them to fund true people development opportunities, they would have naturally reduced turnover and recruiting costs[7] and at the same time started getting the results they desired. The constant churn of people only exacerbates your problems.

HR Should Provide the Guidance and Tools

In the application of the change equation, the organization must identify the major departments that will aid in helping combat the resistance to change. Many times, we find that organizations are reactionary and immediately put employees straight to work with no formal standard training. This will add an extra layer of complexity for the individual and the organization. One way to mitigate these levels of complexity is to train people in real time. Utilizing on-the-job development, supported by standard work, combined with providing a psychologically safe environment allows them to fail and learn quickly.

Companies can start by developing an organizational structure that supports their value streams whereby their teams have alignment on goals and actions. Then companies must create standard work for repeatable processes and work standards for processes where steps can be standardized but times for each step may vary. Every team member should have and know their standard work, which is imperative to sustaining Lean across all levels of the organization. HR or another designated department should be coordinating and working to ensure the following for our team members:

- They have been trained properly with ongoing feedback.
- They know what they are building and how it fits into the overall product.
- They know who their top customers are and how they use and service the product.
- They know what and where it is used in the final product.
- They know the importance of what and why they are doing it for the company and the customer.
- They are being developed and challenged and are engaged every day.
- They participate in Gemba watches.
- They are working in a problem-solving team resulting from the tiered meetings or some type of continuous improvement activity. Some companies still refer to these teams as quality circles, especially in Japan.
- They have been provided a structured and psychologically safe environment where all team members can be successful.

We have mentioned several times how important it is to create a safe-to-fail culture. This is how to start to develop trust and teamwork, which in turn helps motivate your team members. The goal is to create a safe-to-fail culture, with leader's intent, where team members have a purpose with a clear line of sight to the customer and control over their destiny. Things to consider:

1. Foster trust and teamwork.
2. Reward innovation and continuous improvement.
3. Develop an environment where healthy conflict and active listening thrives.
4. Promote out-of-the-box thinking. Get outside the system!
5. Invest funding and time in developing your team members. Developing people is paradoxically a shortcut to growing the business.
6. Have goal setting be collaborative between team members, the team leader, and the group leader. Give timely feedback with the intent to develop the whole person.
7. Give people the opportunity to influence others' success.
8. Celebrate failures or close calls/near misses to provide opportunities to learn.
9. Communicate, communicate, communicate.

Compensation

HR and Finance need to take a new view on compensation moving forward. The goal for this system is to get to the point where you can pay your people significantly more than the market rate but have significantly fewer people than your competitors. Companies also should factor in full-time trainers overseen by HR. We normally implement a bonus system so team members can share in the gains. It may take several years to get to this point, but the bonus should be based on the overall performance of the organization.

Toyota's Hiring Process

Compare your hiring process and orientation to Toyota's. Many people talk about how exceptional Toyota team members are, but what goes into hiring those team members? Toyota has a different approach when it comes to hiring new team members. Most companies just try to find bodies to fill positions . . . not at Toyota.

Since most companies are not Toyota, they may not be able to afford to adapt or have the time to implement this type of hiring process, nor are we saying this is the only way it can or should be done. However, we are presenting some real-life examples to give you a different perspective and maybe provide some ideas for thought. Think as you read through the following, contributed by Tracey Richardson,[8] as to how you might consider changing or adapting your interview process?

Tracey and Ernie Richardson write in their book The Toyota Engagement Equation:

> I went through Toyota's hiring process when I applied for a position at Toyota Motor Manufacturing Kentucky where they were constructing their new plant. Everyone knows hiring processes evolve over time due to our ever-changing world and market. At that time (1986–1988), Toyota was building their first plant in North America, so it took a little time to build a structure capable of 540,000+ cars a year output. Today, HR has since evolved but the competencies Toyota looks for in people and future leaders haven't changed.

Tracey shared,

> I went through a battery of tests in the beginning and over the years have realized they
> were looking for specific competencies in people. Assessors were present during the
> hiring process who were analyzing behaviors and actions of all potential hires as we
> went through various tests and exercises. The hiring process I went through functioned
> almost like a sifter. You start out a large rock at the top and only the granules of sand
> make it to an interview. There were probably seven sifters to pass through to be consid-
> ered a Toyota team member. If you made it, this was something to be proud of and it
> helped you to be better than you were the day before.

As a trainer myself now, this is something I still hold on to today. None of us are experts. We
all should be learning and so we should look for this same quality in our team members and new
hires. Perhaps a couple of questions we should ask is:

■ "Is this a person able to be developed?"
■ "Do they demonstrate a willingness and ability to learn?"
■ "Can they be a leader in 3–5 years and more?"

Human Resources created its policy management so all team members understood expectations from the interview process, on-boarding, training, then on to job expectations. Everyone was
on-boarded as a temporary team member, and it took 3 months before ever getting to the floor.
During the on-boarding process HR was determining what competencies they wanted. It took
over 1.5 years at that time to meet the full expectations of the hiring process. There were 2 days of
simulated production for the interviewee to give ideas on how it could be done better. I was tested
on how well I could listen, analyze, and offer improvements. I remember being asked numerous
times, "What do you think, Tracey, how would you do it differently?"

I was offered a production team member position as one of the initial 1,500 hires in early 1988
out of 150,000 applicants. All hires at that time were on a 6-month trial period wearing colored
armbands leading up to the 6-month mark. Team member MK hourly production workers have
to go through an 18- to 24-month program including course curriculum gates to be considered
for a full-time hire. If there is attrition, it is now on the temporary side versus a full-time team
member (very low attribution), allowing a potential team member to grasp the situation on the
expectations of a team member at Toyota. It can take several years (5+) to reach current top pay as
a full-time team member.

We all had to unlearn some conditioned norms and think differently. The beauty of being a
Toyota team member is that your thoughts and ideas matter. They were important for the best-
known method at the moment to be created (standardized work), until we changed it together.

Toyota never had a standard without accountability—you signed off on it and created it with
your team. If you wrote standards without accountability, it just became a suggestion for people
to follow. If there isn't a known standard that the team members were part of creating (engaging
them in the work), then it's difficult to have correct action if the standard isn't being followed.

At non-Toyota companies many people see standard work as a deterrent, but no one ever stifled
my thinking. It was the exact opposite. You learned that your job is to contribute to your own job
security through seeing abnormality and improving the current situation.

Prior to becoming a team leader, I had to undergo learning a core curriculum and fulfill specific expectations. The expectations included lots of role-playing, creating, and thinking through

the A3/PDCA process, and bringing the Toyota Way values to life. At that time administering the Myers–Briggs® MBTI tool allowed each individual to understand their particular type as well as learning the 15 other preference types.

As a group leader, or any other leader in management, I was responsible for spending 50% of the time to develop people. Even the president is on the floor 50% of the day if they are onsite. Over the years HR has created everything that supports it. Mr. Fujio Cho[9] always made servant leadership very tangible in his actions. He did frequent Gemba walks grasping the current situations ensuring we could always measure to a known standard and see our gaps. Mr. Cho never told anyone what to do—he always asked. "How can I help? What do you need from me?" He was always about asking questions about a process versus blaming a person. It all comes down to people's ability to listen and have empathy for what people go through and not make assumptions and opinions. Go to the Gemba and talk to the person.

One time Ernie Richardson (my husband) shut the entire Assembly plant down due to a mechanical problem in Powertrain for over 4 hours at thousands of dollars per minute. He was concerned when he heard Mr. Cho was coming to see him. Mr. Cho shook his hand, thanked him for bringing attention to this problem so a permanent countermeasure could be developed.

Toyota has a culture of putting people and their personal development first. HR created this understanding vertically and horizontally setting expectations at every level:

- Do you have the best interest of the company at heart?
- Does the company have the best interest of the team member at heart?

We always had expectations of growth. True North—Customer First, highest quality in shortest time to the Customer is True North. . . . Every person should be able to measure their performance, by person, then team, then bigger team. Everyone knew their gaps—we even displayed them on our team production boards and people appreciated having the cross-training matrixes to show our current state at all times. A lot of people asked me if I was upset that they were tracking my progress and putting it on display publicly. "My question is, how can you not track it?" At Toyota it was a cultural norm to show the processes we used to get great results as a team and as a company.

There were five competencies, as I learned later, that Toyota looked for in people. These are also the competencies I recommend you look for if you want to develop a more robust hiring process.

- *Listening skills*—I think this one is deceptively simple. What I mean is: How effective are we at really listening, and how do we know this? Have you ever tried the simple exercise of listening to someone for two minutes and then trying to paraphrase back to them what they said? This sounds easy, but try it. Our first instinct is to share our opinion, or to come up with a rebuttal in our minds before someone is even finished talking. This hinders us from truly listening. I remember during my hiring process, we were doing exercises and the assessors were watching for the folks who were truly able to listen and absorb new information.
- *Problem-solving skills*—The ability to solve problems as an organization is crucial. This is what allows any organization to achieve long-term growth and sustainability. Being able to see abnormality at a glance is so key. I can remember for one portion of the tests going through a 2-day (12 hours each day) simulation of the type of work that we would be doing on the line (this can be simulated for non-manufacturing as well), placing us in a work cell that had various problems. We would do the work and be asked every hour how we would improve the work, layout, and area among any other possibilities we saw. Could we see abnormalities and come up with our own ideas to make things better?

■ *Teamwork*—How well did we work with others? This competency is often downplayed as a given, but it was/is a significant component rooted deeply with the Toyota Way. Every team member at Toyota is an essential part of the team. In one hiring exercise we were put with other people into groups of twelve who we hadn't previously met who were also going through the hiring process. We were given a problem and asked to solve it "as a team." Our assessors were looking for personality traits, our responses to ideas offered up by others, and our general attitude and demeanor throughout the exercise. They wanted to see if we could work effectively with people who had different personalities.

■ *Initiative*—This one often sparks an interesting conversation, depending on the industry. How do you define "initiative" exactly? In my case, Toyota was looking for someone who would go above and beyond in terms of creating ideas for improvement, ways to work smarter not harder, and understanding that value-added work is essential for future job security. So it wasn't necessarily about staying late or working up a sweat the focus was on capability development (and the team member's desire and ability to develop oneself). And more than this, the hiring process was about finding people who felt and could be empowered to "think" without needing massive amounts of prodding or incentives.

■ *Leadership*—This one is hugely important if you're interested in "growing" leaders internally. I was a perfect example of a "homegrown" leader at Toyota. I started out on the line and through great coaching, was developed in the other competencies above following Toyota Way values. I worked up from hourly to salary in seven years witnessing the leadership above me "walking the walk" and learning how to do this myself. This was all grounded in the idea of respecting people's ability to think, building this respect for learning by doing, problem solving, and improving into our daily work. We also had to show specific qualities/competencies before we were chosen for pre-promotion classes. Within the hiring process we were made a mock leader in an organization and asked to handle specific issues that arose. We were instructed to ask questions and grasp the situation. How we did this was what we were assessed on. Our ability to see facts and not make assumptions was noted along with our ability to see people as the most important asset of an organization and lead from that principle.

At Toyota, many things that were just a given, would be considered by most companies needing to take to make this transformation, as major steps from an HR policy management point of view. Could you imagine your companies investing 3 to 4 months in the onboarding process, then another 3 months after hire of training and workouts and then another 2 years as a temporary worker and then more training to become a team member.

The trainers would always push you past what you thought you were capable of doing; every day questioning you on your thinking. Toyota developed me in ways I ever dreamed possible. As Mr. Cho taught us, you must always pass your knowledge to the next generation, and I still do that and I haven't been a team member for many years."

> Tracey summed it up by saying that Toyota is a company that develops people who just happen to make cars.

> The preceding section was contributed by Tracey Richardson.

Notes

1. Just in Time for Today and Tomorrow, Ohno, Productivity Press, 1988 pg 6.
2. Email correspondence from Isao Yoshino 4–23–2020.
3. For more on this see the books *Toyota Talent* and *Toyota Culture*.
4. Matthais Holweg -The genealogy of lean production, Journal of Operations Management Volume 25, Issue 2, March 2007, pg. 420–437.
5. 40 Years, 20 Million Ideas: The Toyota Suggestion System, Yuzo Yasuda, Productivity Press, 1990.
6. Forbes Aug 4, 2015, 08:21 am EDT—People Leave Managers, Not Companies, Victor LipmanFormer Contributor—based on Gallup data.
7. Michael Meyers speaking.
8. Conversation with Tracey Richardson, author of the Toyota Engagement Equation 4–20–2020.
9. Fujio Chō served as Chairman of the Board and Representative Director of Toyota Motor Corporation from June 2006 to June 2013 https://en.wikipedia.org/wiki/Fujio_Cho

Chapter 15

Sustain—Managing the Change

Figure 15.1   BASICS® Lean Leadership Development Path—Sustain—Leaders Developing Leaders.

Source: BIG training materials.

Step 1 of our BASICS® Leadership Development Path was to "**B**aseline," which we covered in team member Self Reliance. Step 2 was to "**A**nalyze" and "**S**uggest Solutions," which we did by studying how to improve business practices and suggest solutions. In Step 3, we took what we learned from Steps 1 and 2 and then we "**I**mplemented" by practicing what we learned. We then "**C**hecked" to make sure we solved the root cause and learned how to share with others. Step 4 was "**S**ustain" (see Figure 15.1), whereby we combined the BASICS® Lean tools and human aspect to achieve daily business improvement with a focus on execution by Learning to Teach others, which

DOI: 10.4324/9781315155227-15

allows the improvements to sustain over time. In order to implement and follow the Leadership Development Path, we need to overcome the resistance to change that is ever present. This chapter discusses some of the tools and theory we use when we implement change.

The Change Equation

We all resist change; it is our basic human nature. Some changes, however, are easier to accept than others. If you've ever noticed, change that agrees with our way of thinking is accepted easier, but we truly resist changes we consider as negative. If people around you don't buy into the changes and consider them as negative, what does that convey for your chances of sustainment and long-term success? Sustaining is the hardest part of any change. Why is it so hard? Well, it all starts with the change equation and a compelling need to change.

The Change Equation—Compelling Need to Change—The Why?

The change equation[1] is (see figure 15.2):

$$C \times V \times N \times S > R_{change}.$$

Compelling Need to Change × Vision × Next Steps × Sustain must be greater than the Resistance to Change

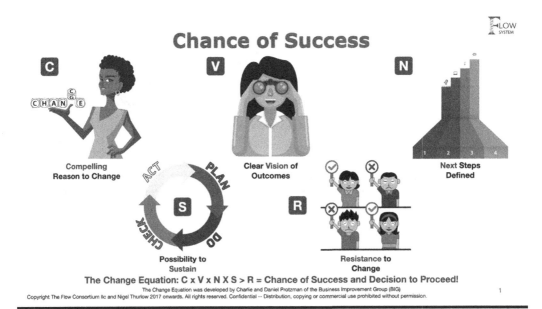

Figure 15.2   Change Equation

Source: Graphics courtesy of Nigel Thurlow, CEO of the FLOW Consortium, co-creator of the Flow System, and former Chief of Agile for Toyota. ©2021. Charles Protzman BIG Training Materials ©1997.

The first questions we always ask are, Do you/does the organization have a truly compelling reason to change? What is it? Can you quantify it? Can you rally your organization around it? In the long run, suffice it to say if you do not have a compelling need from the start, which is greater than the resistance to change, you will not be successful. Language is important, and in this case, the word *compelling* is intentional because it is much stronger than the word *dissatisfaction*. One can be dissatisfied and never overcome the resistance to change; they will always slide backward.

The compelling reason to change may be equated to the *"Why?"*. Why do we want to change? What are the factors affecting the *"Why?"* Is this a reactionary or a proactive compelling reason to change? If we are just reacting, we probably don't really have a compelling need to change, and if we do it probably won't sustain.

If your **C** (compelling reason to change) isn't truly compelling enough, then there's no way you can overcome the resistance to change. Remember, this is a multiplication equation, which means if the C becomes zero, the whole equation fails.

Vision—The What?

The next step is to brainstorm the **V** (vision). This combines the purpose of the company with the social responsibility, focus, and direction we intend to pursue. The vision includes desired behaviors, physical factory, or area appearance, along with expected business results, and helps us focus and prioritize our resources. It can also include the culture you would like to create. The Vision provides the *"What."* What are we trying to change?

Next Steps—The How?

The vision (see Figure 15.3) leads us to our *"How,"* our next steps. *"How"* will we execute the *"What"* and at the same time answer the *"Why"* questions along the way? You need to understand where you are now, what we call situational awareness, in order to figure out if your next steps are taking you toward your vision and your True North. We then start to plan the next steps to take, our goal is to continually move closer and closer toward our vision.

Figure 15.3 Dream Goals and Targets.

Source: Unknown.

The next steps will involve implementing the intended strategy,[2] plans, or actions necessary to close the gaps between where we are now and our vision. By grouping the collection of these prioritized actions, we create the goal deployment plan.

There is no way to know for sure how someone is influencing the culture, and the traditional antiquated company surveys are full of cognitive bias. They do not truly provide what leaders need to know about their culture; in fact, many of these surveys blind leaders to the gaps that are obvious to employees, sort of like in the "Emperor's New Clothes."

Culture fits in the complex domain within the Cynefin framework created by Dave Snowden. As Ritsuo Shingo reminds us, companies don't have culture—culture comes from people and is influenced by people's interactions and leadership's behaviors. In order for companies to respond in a complex environment, they need to be aware of their situation and the environment around them. In complexity, one needs to be able to gather as much information as possible about the present and conduct multiple parallel probes to look for patterns, amplify enabling constraints, and be cognizant of weak signals. The Flow System[3] includes a great overview of complexity along with the other DNA components of distributed leadership and team science.

One of the tools which can help change the culture is called SenseMaker®,

> . . . which is a form of distributed ethnography that helps the leader with situational awareness. That is, do we really have psychological safety? SenseMaker® (see Figure 15.4) offers a unique way of collecting narratives (observations, experiences, or stories) from your employees in a way that you can better understand your company culture so that you can nudge it in a direction most favorable for your objectives (see Figure 15.5).

Ultimately, the culture emerges over time based on the behaviors of the executive leadership team, the flow of communications, and the development of formal and informal networks resulting from the organizational design.

Figure 15.4 SenseMaker™.

Source: https://sensemaker.cognitive-edge.com/sensemaker-for-research/ Used with permission.

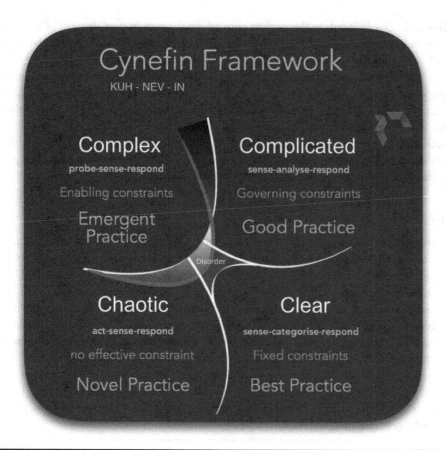

Figure 15.5   Cynefin Framework—Nonliminal Version.

Source: www.cognitive-edge.com Used with permission.

We listed in the endnotes several books that can help guide you on this journey.[4] Since culture falls generally in Dave Snowden's Cyenfin domain[5] of Complexity, there is no guarantee that following these books will necessarily change your culture, but together, these books offer some great ideas for how to move forward and to start nudging your culture in the direction you want it to go. According to David Mann,[6] accountability and discipline are two of the components necessary to sustain Lean. These books do a good job of addressing ideas for accountability and discipline. Dave Snowden also offers a tool called SenseMaker®, which allows organizations an alternative to traditional employee and safety surveys that tend to provide ambiguous results with little or no follow-up actions.

In the words of Michael Cheveldave[7] from Cognitive Edge,

One can map a culture using SenseMaker® . . . in effect a set of narrative landscapes/cluster patterns that are reflective of the unique attributes of a culture for a team, department, division, company, or an enterprise. Then taking actions informed by Cynefin one can increase their potential to stimulate a pattern shift preferably in a desirable direction vs. an undesirable one. So you shape a culture from where it's at and in a direction that leverages the dispositionality and propensities of the system as a whole.

This is the classic "work in the present with where the system is at" instead of working with an ideal state of where you would like it to be. This also is how you work with the "adjacent possibles" that Dave Snowden speaks about frequently.

SenseMaker®[8] uses narratives, that is, stories from your workforce and customers, to give you a complete picture of your culture through the lens of complexity that can be used to baseline and track the progress of your cultural directional changes. Altogether, this is the "vector theory of change." In short, SenseMaker® gives you the complexity equivalent of key performance indicators (KPIs) but in the form of patterns of which you can only be partially aware and which have varying degrees of clarity (i.e., the patterns may be weak/strong, obscure, and most often vague).

Sustain

The last step in the change equation is sustain, whereby we challenge the leadership to figure out how they are going to sustain in this new environment and manage all this change. In order to sustain, we must always be improving.[9] This means ongoing Plan–Do–Check–Act (PDCA) and quality circle activities and looking for ways to accept and create new products, services, and processes. Sustain requires "continuous improvement" and constant monitoring of our environment.

The key is to realize that sustaining isn't a separate step; instead, it's doing all the Leadership Development Path steps to the fullest. Sustainment isn't a separate concept or set of tools; instead, it is implementing the system and providing training with accountability and discipline woven throughout.

In order to sustain, one has to ensure that the new systems get built into muscle memory and become part of the fabric of the organization. Companies must develop their people in order to create a problem-solving culture and make sure systems are in place to problem-solve and update the standard work on an ongoing basis.

Resistance to Change

The idea behind the change equation is that if any of these letters are zero the company will not overcome the resistance to change. Toyota has somehow managed to sustain and continually improve its culture since the 1950s, which is truly a testament to its deep-seated beliefs, perseverance, and determination. A company can unfortunately lose the "Lean culture" very easily and quickly. The new system is very fragile until both the tools and the human aspect are firmly embedded into the organization starting at the top and built into "muscle memory."

We have seen companies lose the culture they worked so hard to build, sometimes overnight, simply with the change of president/CEO/CFO who wasn't cognizant of or didn't adapt to or understand the vision of the new environment, and instead created a negative impact that reinforced the resistance to change. In some cases, they stopped developing their people, lost the tools-influence, stopped videoing, stopped acting on fact, and reverted to a shoot-from-the-hip culture or even went back to batching. In the end, if you don't sustain it, then it ultimately points back to you or the company not having a true compelling need to change.

Are You a Change Agent?[10]

When you recognize you need to change, do you consider yourself a change agent? Some people are "naturals" when it comes to leading change. Are you ready to make the change or want to help others change? Do you have a compelling need to change? Being a change agent is probably one of the most difficult and yet most important jobs in any organization. The first rule of a change agent, however, is to survive.

Take meaningful steps in the implementation of the changes necessary and work to develop others around you to help in this journey. Follow the tools listed in both this book as well as *The BASICS® Implementation Model*. When we say the first rule is to survive, what we mean is that you can't make the change if you are quite literally no longer "there." Be careful of the stands you make against people or the organization and know that sometimes the hill you're standing on and guarding may be the hill you metaphorically die on if you're not mindful and careful of how you implement these changes.

The Victim and Resistance to Change[11]

Many times, we find ourselves in conversations with those who can only come up with excuses as to why things *cannot* be done. This is referred to as the victim syndrome. Most of the time the person doesn't even realize they have fallen in this trap. The victim, like Eeyore from *Winnie the Pooh*,[12] tends to have a cloud over their head all the time and, no matter the effort, will find something to complain about. We have found there are two main types of resistance to change: rational and irrational.

Rational resistance to change is normally backed by logical argument, justification, or a reward that can bring about the change. If it's rational resistance and one can solve the objections, the resistance will vanish. Change can be viewed as threatening or opportunistic. People can accept lots of positive change very rapidly. People need to see what's in it for them if they accept the change, so you must figure out how to present your idea as positive and an opportunity in order to lower the energy gradient to the resistance.

Irrational or unjustified resistance is usually visible based on an individual's behavior. In his book *Me Change? Not Now, Not Ever!*[13] Jerald Young, PhD, describes irrational resistance as an emotional-based resistance to change. He states that "rational resistance presents a problem to be *solved*, where emotion based resistance presents a problem to be *dissolved*."

Many times, people aren't aware that there is something emotional behind their objections. Irrational resistance tends to only be visible through behaviors and the posing of what seem like ongoing rational objections that, even after solving them, just result in more objections. One must discover the root of the emotional objection and then work to overcome it. The problem is that it could take years of analysis for the person to realize what is behind the objection. This resistance may take the following forms with fear or threat being the major drivers:[14]

- Fear toward the unknown
- Fear of being passed over or no longer needed
- Fear regarding the personal failure
- Fear of being labeled as incompetent
- Fear of loss of control over the situation
- Threat to personal values, principles, or philosophy
- Threat of a possible change in the status

This type of resistance can be in the form of covert or overt activity. Typically, in the beginning, it will be overt and then switch to covert, whereby it eventually ends up being very passive-aggressive.

Why Is the Leadership Development Path So Difficult to Sustain?

Until a leader comprehends and understands the new Continuous Leadership Development paradigm, human nature is always fighting against you. As humans we seemed to be programmed or conditioned to do the following:

- We think batching is always the best way and most efficient way to do anything. We will go to any lengths to protect our ability to batch. It's really batching that makes you a robot, not Lean.
- We always want to take the easiest way out—whatever will be the least stressful and least amount of work or least amount of thinking. Thinking is extra work, and the brain tries to protect us from this. We already have too many things going on and too many problems. Our brain doesn't want another one it has to cope with.
- We default to what Boyd calls "implicit guidance and control." We at first want to ignore the problem, and then we tend to take the intuitive, almost subconscious actions, when we first encounter problems, especially emergencies.
- If we can't ignore it, then we love to just throw a solution at the problem so it goes away, by any means necessary. Our brain always wants to take the path of least resistance. We do this even at the risk of the problem coming back and creating rework. This is because the rework to the problem is in the future, and we really do not want to think about that now. This also happens with KPIs. We want to meet them the easiest way possible sometimes using shortcuts or gaming the system.
- We all love to be the hero of the day/month/quarter, and we are rewarded for it with accolades, team member of the month, and career promotions. We all hate to admit it, and as much as we complain about it, we love to firefight and be the one recognized by all so as to say, "I fixed the problem." Again, it doesn't matter that we created a problem for next month by pulling in all of next month's shipments to this month or that we end up with a bunch of rework. After all, we can always find someone or something else to blame. Then we get to fix it and be the hero again. We not only like to work around the system, but we are also excellent at it. Why, because we all know it is too difficult to change the formal system. That would be extra work and our minds won't allow it.
- Do not reward work-arounds! If the old hero of the day and work-around culture prevails, Lean will fail. When we work around a problem, we do not solve it, so ultimately it comes back. Lean will only sustain in cultures that learn to address root causes and fix problems with the goal that they never come back.
- We love to complain about it but not fix it. Complaining is easy. If we have to fix it, we throw the solution at it. Imagine if nothing ever went wrong. What would we talk about?
- We never have time to do it right the first time, but we always seem to have time to rework it later (and complain about it). We like—no, we love—to blame someone else or something else. It's not our fault, and blaming is the easy way out. If I can blame someone, I do not have to fix it. We all like to blame external causes, which is characteristic of non-systemic thinking.
- We do not have time. This is one of the number one excuses. Again, our brain is trying to protect us from even thinking about one more thing to do. The human mind is just naturally always working against Lean, one-piece flow, PDCA, and standard work.

Organization Change Takes Over 20 Years for Toyota and Never Ends

Use Your Authority to Encourage Them.

—Taiichi Ohno[15]

If you read Ohno's writings and those about him, one can see he truly cared for the team members on the line, and this is where his respect for humanity was evident. However, these passages support the notion that top management must change its way of thinking and behaving. They must be persistent, stay the course, make an unwavering commitment, and show strong support for Lean to be successful. This means that the traditional system on which top management has relied so long must change. You must question everything all the time.

> In the beginning, everyone resisted kanban because it seemed to contradict conventional wisdom. Therefore, I had to experiment with kanban within my own sphere of authority. Of course, we tried to avoid interfering with the regular work going on. . . . In 1962, I was named manager of the main plant. Only then was kanban implemented in forging and casting, making it a company-wide system at last. It took 10 years to establish kanban at the Toyota Motor Company. Although it sounds like a long time, I think it was natural because we were breaking in totally new concepts. It was, nonetheless, a valuable experience.
>
> To make kanban understood throughout the company, we had to involve everyone. If the manager of the production department understood it while the workers did not, kanban would not have worked. At the foreman level, people seemed quite lost because they were learning something totally different from conventional practice. I could yell at a foreman under my jurisdiction, but not at a foreman from the neighboring department. Thus, getting people in every corner of the plant to understand naturally took a long time.
>
> Based on my experiences in the production plant, I know that in the beginning, people tended to resist change, whether large or small, making the atmosphere not conducive to implementing change. However, if the employees were frantic, we were crazy! In the end, we forced our way through and persuaded the others. The whole process of developing the Toyota Production System took place this way. . . . When I was—rather forcefully—urging foremen in the production plant to understand kanban, my boss received a considerable number of complaints. They voiced the feeling that this fellow Ohno was doing something utterly ridiculous and should be stopped . . . From the late 1940s to the early 1960s, with everyone in opposition, it was called the abominable Ohno Production System. People refused to call it the Toyota Production System. When I confirmed the validity of the system and tried to implement it, everyone objected vehemently. To overcome this resistance, I had to quarrel and fight. And since the numbers were against me, I had no choice—I went crazy." . . . During this period, Toyota's top manager was a man of great vision who, without a word, left the operation entirely to me. . . . This must have put the top manager in a difficult position at times, but even then he must have trusted me. I was not told to stop and for this I am grateful.

. . . It is often said that while pursuing our goal with manic devotion in the production plant or research lab, we begin to lose zeal because the surroundings become too comfortable or familiar. This is untrue. Organizational leaders must comprehend factors such as inner and outer environmental changes and the demands and directions of the times. Based on these factors, the corporation must indicate what must be done from the top down. In the production plant, from the bottom up, employees must propose ways to improve human relations, increase productivity and ultimately reduce costs through improvements to their own workplaces. I believe it is this harmony and discord, the magnified effect between the top-down and bottom-up styles that cause insanity in the minds of people working there.

In 1962, kanban was adopted company-wide; it had earned its recognition. After that, we entered a high-growth period—the timing was excellent. I think the gradual spread of kanban made possible the strong production yield. While in charge of the assembly line, I applied the just-in time system there.

—**Taiichi Ohno**[16]

There is always a better way! By sticking with his new system, Ohno eventually introduced it company-wide, even though it was not a smooth transition. If the Toyota leadership had not supported Ohno, the system we know as kanban probably would not exist. Ohno now is considered the father of the TPS.

Notes

1. Leveraging TPS in Healthcare, Transforming Your Enterprise into a High Quality Patient Care Delivery System, Protzman, Mayzell, Kerpchar, ©2011, CRC Press.
2. There are new tools available to plan strategies called Wardley Maps that also help along with Cynefin and OODA (Observe–Orient–Decide–Act) to understand situational awareness.
3. The Flow System, Nigel Thurlow, John Turner, Brain Rivera © 2020 University of North Texas.
4. The first book is called *Turn the Ship Around* by David Marquette, who is a nationally recognized speaker. This book is summarized on Amazon as follows: "As the Captain of a nuclear submarine, David Marquette created Intent-based Leadership. He discusses in his book his personal transformation and true story of turning followers into leaders." The next book is called The Oz Principles by Roger Connors, Tom Smith, and Craig Hickman. The authors define accountability as a personal choice to rise above one's circumstances and demonstrate the ownership necessary for achieving the desired results—to See It, Own It, Solve It, and Do It. When you do not take accountability you become the victim and everything is someone or something else's fault. This book details how people and organizations, armed with attitudes of accountability, can overcome the obstacles, excuses and biases that keep them from getting the results they want." The last book is called Influencer,# The New Science of Leading Change by Joseph Grenny et al. ©2013 by VitalSmarts LLC. In the book Mr. Grenny states that *"[l]eadership calls for changing people's behavior. Influencers are those leaders who understand how to create rapid, profound, and sustainable behavior change. There are three keys to influence influencers to do three things better than others. They are clearer about the results they want to achieve and how they will measure them. They focus on a small number of vital behaviors that will help them achieve those results. They determine change by amassing six sources of influence that both motivate and enable the vital behaviors."*
5. Cynefin by David John Snowden, who is a Welsh management consultant and researcher in the field of knowledge management and the application of complexity science. SenseMaker is a trademark of Cognitive Edge® www.cogntive-edge.com Snowden, D. (2010) *Naturalizing Sensemaking* in Mosier and Fischer *Informed by Knowledge: Expert Performance in Complex Situation* p 223–234

Mark A. Snowden, (2017) Cynefin (Chapter 4) in de Savigny, D., Blanchet, K., Adam, T. (2017) Applied Systems Thinking for Health Systems Research—a methodological handbook. Open University Press, Milton Keynes. www.amazon.com/Cynefin-Weaving-Sense-Making-Fabric-World-ebook/dp/B08LZKDCYM/ref=sr_1_3?dchild=1&keywords=cynefin&qid=1606673455&s=digital-text&sr=1-3

6. Creating a Lean Culture, David Mann, Productivity Press 2010.
7. Personal Correspondence with permission Michael Cheveldave at Cognitive Edge 12–28–20—cognitive-edge.com
8. David John Snowden is a Welsh Management Consultant and researcher in the field of knowledge management and the application of complexity science. Sensemaker is a trademark of Coginitve Edge® www.cogntive-edge.com.
9. John Boyd, in his papers "Destruction and Creation," 1976, and "The Conceptual Spiral," 1992, called this the conceptual spiral of destruction and creation. We must always be questioning, analyzing the present, and looking for ways to get outside our systems in order to synthesize or create the new paradigms.
10. Joel Barker discusses this in much detail in his paradigm video series.
11. Reasons for Resistance to Change, https://managementstudyguide.com/reasons-for-resistance-to-change.htm
12. Winnie the Pooh, AA Milne, 1926.
13. Me? Change? Not Now. Not Ever! How to Dissolve Hard-Core Resistance to Change in the Workplace Paperback—March 31, 2003, Center for Stable Change (March 31, 2003).
14. Reasons for Resistance to Change, https://managementstudyguide.com/reasons-for-resistance-to-change.htm
15. Ohno, T. Toyota Production System: Beyond Large-Scale Production Original Japanese Version. Cambridge, MA: Productivity Press (English translation), 1978 pg. 55–57.
16. Taiichi Ohno, Setsuo Mito, Just-in-Time for Today and Tomorrow (New York: Productivity Press), 1988 pg. 96–97.

Chapter 16

Becoming a New Team Member

Figure 16.1 BASICS® Lean Leadership Development Path—Continuously Developing Yourself Through Others to Achieve Competitive Advantage While Maximizing Profitability

Source: BIG Training Materials

The Leadership Development Path (see Figure 16.1) is supported by Human Resources' (HR's) new role and is the beginning of developing our team members into leaders. Developing yourself and your people is an often overlooked and underdeveloped skill in most organizations, which is exactly the opposite of what it should be. It is not uncommon to find people who do not want to hire someone "better" than themselves or who lack the confidence to share information about their job because they are afraid that if they share what they know, they won't be needed anymore.

DOI: 10.4324/9781315155227-16   **259**

Knowledge should be shared, easily accessible, and not used to create self-importance or to hold a company hostage. A person's knowledge should be used to improve the entire organization. The story below is about a colleague of ours, Mike Riley. Mike highlights his personal journey which we felt was a wonderful overall summary for this book.

The Journey—Contributed by Mike Riley[1]

For Toyota, it's not about hiring a body, it's about hiring the right body. Toyota invests a lot of time, effort, and money into the hiring process to reduce the risk of introducing the wrong person into the company's environment. My journey to being hired at the Toyota plant in Indiana took 2 years to complete, and I am happy to report it was successful.

First, Toyota coming into the Indiana area was a huge deal. Everyone wanted to work for them, and they were positioning themselves geographically where people from Indiana, Illinois, and Kentucky were going to be competing for jobs! I can remember the radio ads for the company playing all over the area as the plant was getting closer to being completed. Toyota received about 100,000-plus applications for about 3,000 jobs. There were a lot of nearby surrounding rural communities excited to see such a well-paying company move into the area.

I'll give you an idea of the impact the hiring process had on the company I was working for at that time which was going to be a couple of hundred feet from Toyota's door. They were trying to find assembly line team members and were offering to pay them minimum wage, which was in the single digits at that time. Compare this to what Toyota was offering, which to my recollection was in the range of $15 an hour to start in the production areas. Eventually, there came a time when I saw a local sheriff escort a person in their prison orange clothing to an interview to try to get a job on work release at the company at which I was working. We had one leader who worked during the day and returned to the local jail at night. It was a shock to my system to suddenly see our quality of applicants for the jobs change so drastically.

When the Toyota plant was announced to be built near us in Indiana, I remember feeling like I wasn't truly ready to give my current administration position up, so I continued with my current company. But while the Toyota building was being constructed, I had an interaction with my boss that changed my mind. He had called me into his office for my annual review, and I remember thinking that this was going to be great, because I was wearing many hats. I was managing the warehouse and doing additional import/export duties, sales, and accrual reporting as part of the business coordinator position. I was also supporting the company's staff with troubleshooting PC issues. I was doing the work previously done by four other individuals. It was therefore a real shock to my system to have my boss tell me that he was having a hard time justifying a cost-of-living raise, about 2% for me because I did not work overtime. Wait, what?

As I sat in the chair, dumbfounded, it appeared, by his face, that he had finally decided to toss me a 1% bone; I remember being really outraged about this as I left the office. I thought, I am doing all these job functions, keeping up with my work and excelling, saving the company a lot of money, and I was already driving an hour each way at a salaried rate. It was then that the adage came true for me: People do not leave companies, they leave managers. By the way, that company ended up closing that location a few years after I left.

That night, I decided to apply to Toyota, and it was one of the best decisions of my life. I guess, in retrospect, I should thank that manager someday. I knew I was applying to Toyota just to get my foot in the door with the hopes of working my way up in the organization. At my current company, it had taken me 5 years to work my way up from assembler to office assistant in the engineering offices and finally to a supervisory position with direct reports in the warehouse. I was in my mid-20s at this point.

While my old company shipped and received products from various locations around the world, there's something a little more—impressive? awe-inspiring? humbling?—about working for a company that comes with the global stature that the Toyota name carries. Of course, you do not really realize the scope of this until you step foot on-site and see the sheer size of its operation. I think, at the time, it was a mile walk across the building in one direction and very humbling.

Like with any other company, my first step was starting out with a simple application. I remember it seemed like the wait took forever to get a call back, but months later, when I did, I was ecstatic. However, I was to learn this was not going to be the typical employment screening. I was told to report to an assessment center for the next phase of the process, which would take about 4 hours to complete. The test site turned out to be an old school the company had rented from the city. I took a lengthy paper test full of the favorite situational questions that everyone loves, and then I was moved to another room. Here, an assessor gave me directions to assemble a simple light circuit and told me that he would be back in a few minutes. I was given a few minutes to study the work and try the assembly out and then had to mentally formulate how I would teach this to someone. About 5 minutes later, an assessor walked into my cubicle area and sat down, and it was game on. My time with the assessor took about 10 minutes, during which time I conveyed to him how to assemble the circuit, demonstrated the assembly process, and then had him try it with me. I did not know it at the time, but this was part of an assessment utilized to qualify someone as a team leader. When this was all done, I had no indication as to how I had performed or if I would hear back. I was told if I had done well, I would hear back from someone on the next steps.

A few months went by and then the next call came. Surely I was going to be hired if they were calling me, but no, it was another assessment. This time, I had to report for a day of work, on a Saturday, for a full 8 hours. What was this? The job, however, was too good to pass up, so off I went. When I arrived back at the assessment center, I spent the day being ushered through some work-simulation environments.

I remember that one of the rooms consisted of multiple large panels stationed on each side of the candidates with a step-down between them. One panel had pegs on it; the other panel also had pegs and tire rims of various shapes and sizes. We were told that there were a number of manifests on the empty panel and that our job was to take the correct rims from one panel, put them in the correct order on the blank panel, and ensure that they were aligned correctly to where the manifest said the valve stems should be placed. The rims weighed between 5 and 15 pounds each, and we were told we were not being judged by how many we completed, but it still did not stop me from moving as fast as I could because I wanted that job.

After the allotted time had passed, we were told to stop. Then the instructor surprised me. He handed out some paper with a survey related to the process and then asked us to tell him how we could improve it. Not knowing about Toyota's continuous improvement philosophy, I genuinely thought that they wanted to know how to improve that process, not even thinking we were still being assessed on our ability to creatively think, suggest ideas, and see how we would fit Toyota's culture.

The day continued with more testing. Another test that day related to wire harnesses. We had the manifests again and had to plug in the wire harness plugs correctly to the corresponding receptacle and ensure we did the quality check that went with the assembly, in this case, a "push–pull–push" test to make sure that wire wouldn't disengage from the harness. Again, I did not think much of it, but once at the company, you realize how critical something like this can be when you're dealing with airbags. There were several other assessments to round out the day, and then again, I was told that the company would be in contact if I was selected to move forward. Months passed again.

This time, I was finally there, an interview! I showed up for an interview and was ushered into a conference room by two gentlemen, and this was a pretty typical interview, from what I remember: Tell us about yourself, why do you want to work here, and so on. I must have answered everything correctly because I was next sent off-site for a drug test, which consisted of a hair sample, rather than a urine test. Additionally, I was put through a physical assessment and hearing test. Then I waited. Again. And waited.

It would be many more months before I finally got the call to report to work, but I did get the call. I remember being very humbled, knowing the number of people that I must be competing against in order to qualify for a ground-floor position at the company.

From here, the experience continued to get interesting. I was hired into a class, I think there were probably 20 to 30 of us at the time, and I say class because it was a full 2 weeks of sitting in a classroom getting training before we set foot into a process on the production line. We were oriented to the company, its culture and its values, and items that more directly impacted us as teammates. The idea was to provide us everything we needed to be successful, both at work *and* at home. Toyota knew that if we weren't happy at home, we weren't going to be successful at work. While Toyota never discouraged unionization, the company strove to give us everything we needed or wanted (within reason) to make having a union pointless.

Classes covered Toyota history, including how Toyota was born from a loom factory, how the Toyota Production System (TPS) methodology arrived at Toyota after World War II, how the grocery store model in the United States was critical to the invention of kanbans, and more, including just-in-time (JIT), kanbans, poka yokes, and quality and how the production line would operate, among other things.

The classwork covered items that we'd need, such as payroll and benefits, perks such as local businesses that would offer us discounts because we were team members, and discussion about being able to purchase a vehicle at team member pricing, but then also how to budget yourself so you did not exceed your means and go crazy with the higher pay rates most of us were earning. This meant learning about BOB. BOB stands for Balance on Base—meaning, do not count on the overtime or bonuses or the like; balance on your base pay rate. Phones were not allowed on the production line or on a person's body on the production line. Phones were to be kept in the break area in your lunch bag. Usage was only during break times.

Each production line had its own break area set up to a standard with equipment: microwaves, paraffin wax baths, protective equipment storage, tables, chairs, and so on. All equipment was taped off and 5S'd. There were no shelves or places to gather papers in the break area—the only place to put your lunch bag was across two bars that acted as a shelf, but there was no flat surface between them—engineering control to eliminate clutter! Standard work was to place chairs on top of tables when leaving the break area. Teammates were allowed to have only Toyota-approved water bottles on the production line during shift. No soda, tea, flavored drinks, and the like.

As part of the class and before we could set foot in a process as a teammate, we had to have our uniforms ordered, which was part of this process as well. Toyota allowed only certain colors and styles to be worn in the plant, with small variations depending on departments only (such as welding and paint). Everyone had to wear head protection—such as a ball cap with a plastic insert, a bump cap, or a hard hat, depending on where the teammate worked. Additionally, each shirt was monogrammed with the teammate's first name, and each component of the uniform was also monogrammed with the Toyota logo. If you were working in an area where the vehicle was painted already, such as assembly, you had to wear a Toyota belt (which was monogrammed and had a Velcro clasp so it did not scratch any painted surfaces) to cover the pants' button, and all shirt buttons could only be plastic.

Everything was designed to prevent scratches and defects when teammates were working on the vehicles. We were allotted so many points that we could allocate how we wished to spend in the Toyota team store, and then if we wanted to, we could buy more clothes with our own money or via payroll deduction. The team store was on-site and had Toyota-branded polo shirts, T-shirts, button-down shirts, navy Docker pants, khaki Docker pants, Toyota jackets, parkas, water bottles, watches, steel-toed shoes, and more, in both men's and women's designs.

This last bit included a work simulation with Lego® blocks on an actual miniature moving production line set up in the offices. The production line was complete with stack lights for Andons that would stop the line. The simulation was designed such that several of us took on various assembly roles in the plant, at different stations. One person built axles, one built frames, and so on. We were able to try several variations on working production that taught us the benefits of batch versus one-piece flow and that we had an ability to stop the production line with an Andon pull, and you know what, it was actually *okay* to do this. You were *not* to pass a quality defect to another process on the production line without pulling an Andon to have a team leader assist. If the team leader did not arrive in time, the line was to stop until a leader arrived to take over the situation.

We were taught that team members shouldn't fix defects but allow the team leader to tackle those issues. That was designed to keep the team member focused on production and operating within the standard work of the process. If the team member deviated from the standard to attempt to fix a defect, the team member had the potential to cause more defects, and then it could become a punitive issue if the defect caused was a serious safety or quality issue; after all, someone wasn't following the standard work. Calling a team leader allowed the leader to handle the defect and keep the line moving.

Often, team leaders fixed defects while the line was moving, having various repair stations set up at multiple locations on the production line, complete with battery tools, taps, dies, and more. A team leader was allowed to handle no more than two defects at a time, and this was done with visual management. A team leader had a "defect magnet" with their name and line number on it, and if they were making one repair, and another Andon alarmed, they could stick their magnet to the vehicle carrier and then walk away to answer another Andon. This allowed others to know that a leader knew that this vehicle had an issue and was in the process of either having it fixed or documenting the issue to be fixed after the vehicle was driven off the production line.

Toyota then revised this process just a bit once we got to the shop floor, and we learned that each team member had a "defect magnet" that was attached to their helmet and that if they had a defect, they were to place the magnet as close to the defect as possible and pull the Andon. If the leader did not arrive before the vehicle was going to leave the process, the team member released the Andon and then signaled again, allowing the vehicle to pass one more process before finally stopping the line altogether if the leader still did not arrive.

We had no requirement of any kind to learn or complete A3s. I finally learned about them in depth when the economy turned down and they had selected me as a trainer. There were some quality circle teams that did them outside of production, but again, this was only voluntary, not a requirement. I knew and had practiced 5 Whys, and we taught how to create a perfect flip chart, which entailed the details of an "ask A3" to present to leadership, line side, when there was a problem.

Another surprise for us was that for 2 hours a day, we were going to be paid to exercise. During our classroom weeks, we toured the assembly plant and to be honest, the jobs looked easy. As we walked the plant, no one appeared to be in a hurry, and everyone had plenty of time to do the job. What we quickly learned was that this was the result of a lot of hard work and practice. Personally, my first months on the production line, I found my hands would go to sleep when I was on the phone at night because my elbows would swell. I also tore the bottom out of six pairs of Docker pants in the first 3 months (fortunately, these were part of my Toyota uniform and they replaced them for me).

The exercising was done to condition us to the rigors of work at the Toyota plant. The company had usually five to six exercise professionals on hand at any given time. The 2 hours we were in the room alternated between cardio and strength training one day and aerobics and work simulation the next day. Our progress was monitored, and we had to pass the class in order to be deemed capable of working on the floor. I can tell you I lost 20 pounds during the exercise regimen, which lasted 3 months.

The work simulation area in the exercise room was set up with a variety of stations that simulated various assembly processes in the plant. One station had metal plates with threaded studs welded to them that were mounted vertical, horizontal, and overhead, and the teammate practiced grabbing nuts, installing them into the pneumatic tool, and then installing them to the plate without cross-threading the nut. There was a design to even these body mechanics, as you were to grab the nuts with one hand and put the nut into the tool without lowering the tool but keeping it close to the threaded stud—this reduced the time it took to install the nut since you were loading it really close to the install location.

There was a mock door with a weather strip that team members would practice installing and removing to get hands used to pressing on the harder rubber, among others. The idea was to minimize the aches and pains and cramps that a team member would go through. After all, we may have to install six nuts on 80 vehicles every 2 hours, just in one process. When we rotated to the next process after 2 hours, we might be installing those weather strips in the doors and installing more nuts and bolts. Like I said, the processes looked easy, but assembly was another matter entirely.

During this period, we were given time at the end of the shift in order to ice our muscles from the day's work. The exercise time would have a cooler of bagged ice that we were required to use at the end of the shift. Additionally, each team area on the production lines was equipped with a hot wax bath that we were told to use prior to shift, to heat our hands and fingers and limber them up. At this point, you may realize that I have 6 more hours in the workday outside of the two I was spending exercising. These 6 hours were spent training in a process.

When I first arrived on the assembly line, I was greeted by my group leader. I was given two green vinyl stickers to place on either side of my bump cap, and for the next couple of months, my peers would refer to us as "green dots." The green dots were visual management to let anyone know that I was a new team member to the company, that I was in training, and so on. This was so if I did something not quite right, they knew it was probably because I was new.

After this, I received a tour of the production line with the group leader. The tour covered each process with a brief description and required personal protective equipment (PPE), where the eye-wash stations were located, where the spill kits were located, and where to go for evacuation issues. I was then introduced to my team leader, who showed me around specifically to the processes I would be working at, typically four to five processes that we rotated every 2 hours. I had a target to learn my process within a month, combined with the 2 hours' exercise each day, and a weekly goal that was similar to being able to produce the process at 150% of takt time within a certain time period, 125% of takt time, and finally 100% of takt time. I was then taken to a process and introduced to another teammate. For the first 2 hours, I was just to watch the teammate build the process while I followed along with the process standard work, located in a binder attached to a rack in the process.

As the teammate built the vehicle, this gave us a chance for small talk and for me as a new teammate the chance to develop a comfort level with my peer and the process. As I followed along in the standard work, I could see the major step that the teammate was performing, the key points related to that step to perform it successfully, and then the reasons for those key points which explained why that was important and/or what consequences could arise from not performing the function as indicated. Additionally, the standard work had pictures of the areas being discussed so I could locate them visually on the vehicle, a work combination chart that showed a vehicle outline that was numbered with where the teammate was supposed to be operating for each step and a graphical representation of how long each step should take along with a visual representation of the PPE required. Overall, it was good to be able to take the time to watch someone perform the work I would need to learn. There are subtle things that a person still learns in the process, such as watching a teammate use both hands to perform the process. Believe it or not, realizing that you have two hands and then trying to develop the coordination to use them in tandem for the processes can be very difficult! I also learned what the trainer identified as the more difficult or easier parts of the process and then simply learning about their experiences over time.

One thing that was very relevant here is that I would learn through practice and observation because it wasn't really a formal rule or practice. When I became a team leader everyone was taught and expected to perform the process in the same manner and meet the same safety, quality, and takt and cycle time requirements, regardless of gender, age, and the like.

Another important requirement for managing in the system was having equal standards and no exceptions. Yet, there are still team members that simply excel at one particular job over another that may produce fewer defects or have fewer installation difficulties or better technical coordination or that are more skilled and effective at training over others. The reasons behind this can be many, such as simply coordination, dexterity, or an aptitude of technical things and having the ability to explain them. So the team leader is smart to place them with these team members to begin their learning as this helps them meet the requirements effectively and on pace. As a new teammate gains ground on learning the process, then is the time to start to rotate them through different jobs in order for them to spend time with other teammates in the job. This gives those teammates the opportunity to develop as a team, also as trainers, and for me, as the new teammate, to get to know them further and increase my comfort level.

HR played no role in training. The skills matrix was left up to the team leader, and the team leader identified gaps and set up training to close them and with our training plan. For training, the team leader did none of it unless they were covering for an associate. The team members trained each other based on the standard work of the process. Regardless of age or gender, the expectation was the same everywhere in the plant. There were no adjustments for these things related to line speed and the like. Tools and jigs could be developed to help out, but the expectation to produce high-quality vehicles, safely, in the correct takt time was standard. I have worked with recent high school graduates on the same team as I had 60-year-old teammates.

As my training progressed, I was introduced at a staggered pace to two more processes so that I was building at one pace in the first process, another pace at the second, and another in the third process while exercising for 2 hours a day. Routinely, the team leader would check in as other functions were performed to observe my progress and to speak to my trainers for their opinions and insight as well. While I built and practiced, the other teammate's role gradually shifted from building and quality control to primarily quality control and 5S. So, for the person doing the training, this can be a little more difficult to start, as you are responsible for your own quality and that of the person you are training. If this became too much of a struggle for some reason, it was simply the expectation to pull an Andon and ask a team leader to help or to stop the line for a moment to catch up.

I would start out by building a certain portion of the process, whichever part of the process the trainer felt like I could build to start and they could finish the process on time and still be able to check the quality of my build and theirs. There are different mental methodologies and approaches applied depending on the process and trainer. However, as I picked up speed, I would gain more process elements to build and practice. Once I could build an entire vehicle, the trainer would follow along as I built and checked the vehicle quality and shifted to more of an observer role while I practiced, offering further suggestions and insights based on a more "outside view" of the process. It should be noted that while I was in the training phase, if one of my teammates was out on vacation or sick leave, my team leader stepped in to train me and observe as they always had to know all the team's processes to cover them for events such as this.

Once I was deemed proficient at the process by the team leader and my trainer, I was given a couple of hours off-line to document the standard work in my own personal process book, in my own handwriting (no computers on the production line). This took a good deal of time to complete, but it was an important part of the process as I was recording each major step and quality check, key point, and the reasons for them in writing and at the same time, committing them to memory. When I built the process, then the actions came more naturally and I was less likely to miss a step or create an issue.

When my personal book was completed for the process, the team leader told the group leader that I was ready to be certified. The group leader would then randomly show up when I was building the process to audit me, following my standard work, and asking questions as I went ensuring that I could build at least 10 vehicles in a row and meet the process takt and cycle times. Until the group leader showed up, which could be even days later, I always built the process with a trainer to quality check me.

These steps were followed for each process I was trained on until I knew all the processes for the team. I learned that my primary job was to be on time to work, build the process per the standard, and ensure quality. When the production line stopped, be it for mechanical reasons or whatnot, my responsibility shifted to review the quality of my last several vehicles built and then to ensure that the line was 5S'd. There was always something to do to keep busy.

To train for new models and new plant start-ups, demo vehicle bodies were set up, and parts allocated for teammates to train off the main line and practice installing parts. This was critical for process changes or updates. We all got to try and see what it would be like to install parts on the vehicle before going into production so we could identify any possible bottlenecks or issues ahead of time and work through them. Teammates were required to review the standard work and were audited and signed off on in the static build area by their team leader before being allowed to build the new process.

As you can see from my journey, literally months and years of assessment and investment is involved in selecting a teammate that will fit the culture of the company, that is intelligent, a problem-solver, and engaged, and shows potential for development: a teammate who will care about the work they are doing and will take pride in it and not be content to just do the job, collect a check, and go home, a teammate who wants to be proud of the company that they work for and will give 110% each and every day.

My Journey to Becoming a Team Leader at Toyota

The plan I had when I decided to leave my last job was to get hired at Toyota and get promoted—real detailed, right? That's kind of how it worked at any other organization I was at though, including the global company I had just worked for—there wasn't a real detailed method of promotion or rules around it. As an example, I actually applied for a position as an assistant to the president of the site I was working and was asked if I wanted to do import/export and sales reporting functions (including accruals) as that person was resigning. It should be noted that at this time, I had *no* experience in any of that. If you wanted to be promoted, you applied for the position and interviewed; if you were good at interviewing and good at your previous role, you got the job. Easy, right? Based on my previous experience then, that was my thought process when I got hired at Toyota and began my time as a teammate. It only took me 5 years at my last company to work into management; therefore, I should be able to do that again with no problem!

It came as a surprise to me after I got there to learn that Toyota restricted team members from applying for new positions or transfers. Once hired, a team member had to work in their current position for a time, at least a year, before being eligible to apply for promotion or even laterally move to another area of the plant, unless an injury was involved—safety first. Later, I would reflect on this and realize that this was a great policy as it gave me time to acclimate to the company and how it operated, to allow the company culture to ingrain itself within me, and it also provided time to build relationships and "street cred" with my peers as I learned processes and could demonstrate that I could capably build them with high quality. However, upon learning I had time to kill before I could even apply for a promotion, I needed to set my mind to other tasks.

There is a dedicated process to becoming a team leader. When a position became available, I had to fill out an interest form to apply and see if my group leader would sign off to recommend me. Then I had to interview for the role with leadership and pass the team leader test with a score high enough overall to get put into the "pool" of candidates. We had to hope for an opening within the time frame the "pool" was valid. If it doesn't happen, you have to decide if you want to go through the process again the next time the team leader "pool" is taking applicants to fill vacancies that the company sees forthcoming. What I am going to relay in the following paragraphs is not only this process but also the things I did to prepare for those steps and the little extras I tried to make myself successful for the process. Others may have done things differently, or not at all for that matter, but this was my path and the learnings and insight I gained. Most of the people put into the "pool" were selected for positions because management typically had an idea of how many new leaders they would need based on their knowledge of upcoming promotions and movement of group leaders and/or new opportunities that were going to open up based on model expansion, line changes based on model changes, leaders going to rotate to off-line roles (such as Kaizen or Training Departments) and attrition.

Having explored the process steps for becoming a team leader, I decided to go about setting myself up for success when the time came to make my move. I needed data, and the best source of information I had was my peers, some of which had obviously been there longer than me. So while I performed as a production teammate, I worked to deepen or build relationships with my peers by helping them where I could in their processes, if my time permitted. Typically, I knew the processes that surrounded me as most of a team's processes were usually co-located near each other, and if they finished closer to the process takt time and I was in a comfortable place, I could jump in and do a few of the next process' elements to give that teammate a chance for a quick drink of water. As a small side note, a team's processes were spread out among a production line if ergonomic issues needed to be considered. For example, I had processes that were underneath the vehicle as it traveled overhead, so I had to be able to work inside or next to the vehicle to give my arms and back a rest. These processes may not have been next to my other ones based on how the line was physically constructed. Processes were built to be at least 80% of takt time to allow for flex such as line speed changes, but occasionally a process was tighter due to vehicle-ordered options.

As a result of my focus on relationships, my peers became increasingly comfortable with me and opened up to me about what they thought and saw in our leaders and processes. Frankly, a lot of teammates will give you this information straight from when you walk in the door and join their line. The adage about one mistake erasing a thousand "atta-boys" is true just about anywhere, and people are eager to talk about their frustrations. There was also a lot of learning and insight to be gained in listening to what they had to say and how they said it so that when I became a team leader, I could anticipate responses, concerns, and issues and be ready with a mitigating plan or course of action to address the teammate's concerns. I really got into a team-mate's head in this manner.

I interacted with them every day, and even though we had processes to build, all teammates are typically very in tune with what their leaders are doing to support them, or not, as the case may be. I listened to complaints and compliments that my peers would pay to their leadership in casual conversation with me and made mental notes of this. From observation and discussion with my peers, some of the typical complaints were "my team leader just stands around," "my team leader only builds the easy processes on our team," and "my team leader doesn't know all of the jobs, yet." Yes, even at Toyota, the grass is always greener on the other side. Regardless, I could then question whether I agreed with the opinion being expressed. What would I do if I were the leader? This was also good training for how the minds of my peers worked and what they would be thinking if I was the leader. I would use this skill to build connections with my teammates later!

From what I saw and felt, and combined with information from my peers, I had a couple of good leaders whom I could observe as mentors and at least one goofball, but that was just his leadership style and how he connected. When time permitted between processes and vehicles, I was able to observe behaviors of the leaders in my area and mentally noted good or bad and why. I silently questioned if this aligned with what I thought a leader should be, did this person represent the values and principles that Toyota expected to be displayed and practiced, and how would I do it differently if I were in the position.

Hearing this, you may be thinking, "Why would I want to emulate this process? Why is Toyota considered the best if this is the culture?" As a teammate, I had those thoughts also, but remember, there are two sides to every coin, and the perspective can change when you become a leader. Not every directive to a team leader by the group leader or every scrap of information regarding what the team leader has planned is for public consumption; there are business decisions that may affect the actions of others that the teammate is not yet privy. So, when considering the earlier issues that a teammate had with their leader, it's important to remember that from a team-mate perspective, it may seem like the grass is always greener on the other side, as the expression goes, and that their leader is just "standing around."

As another example, I can often remember when I was assembling the cars thinking that we needed more teammates and that this was a stressful, difficult process; however, when I became a team leader and was told in no uncertain terms that there were no more resources coming, I accepted it and began to problem-solve other ways to a solution and was honest with my team—more hands were not coming to fix this, so what were we going to do? Eventually, someone would come up with a solution or change to the process, be it an improvement to the tooling or technique or swapping another part to a different process to make a particular element workable (remember the 80% of takt for flex?).

Frankly, there were some leaders like this; when the line ran smoothly, they either just did not have what it took to be a self-starter and keep busy or had taken the job for other personal reasons that did not match up to supporting the teammate the way it should be done. When I became a trainer during the 2009 economic issues that caused a slowdown in production, I heard stories in my classes about leaders not performing as they should.

The *last* thing a teammate wants to see while they are working hard, sweating on the production line, is their leader laughing and joking and standing around between repairs, instead of cleaning the line and filling parts so that they are working also. The teammate–team leader relationship is symbiotic—when the teammate is working because the line is running smoothly, the team leader should be supporting them by keeping things clean and stocked so that the teammate doesn't need to worry about this when their 2 hours' building is over and they are ready to rotate to the next process or go home. There were just some leaders who never understood this or had simply become complacent over time, in my opinion, and needed a refresher about what the job was supposed to be. I bet some of this defies all the notions you have heard about Toyota, doesn't it? Like any company, it has problems; it's just all in the way that the problems are handled. Remember, Toyota practices TPS, which involves continuous improvement, not once-and-done improvement.

I took these observations to heart and set myself to *not* exhibiting them when I became a team leader as the leaders that fell victim to these practices were *not* well respected. At the same time, I was helping my friends out and listening to their thoughts. I was able to work in some networking with those who had gone through the team leader evaluation process. While the process steps were public knowledge, it was a well-guarded secret about what questions might be asked of a candidate, since those who did not get picked for the "pool" or did not make it out of the "pool" did not want to give you an edge over them, but those who made it through the process were often great sources of information.

The interview questions were behavior-based, meaning that there was no resume review but the questions were more situational in nature because the leadership panel you were interviewing with (HR and group leaders) wanted to see how you would treat others, how you would handle pressure, how you would develop your teammates, how you would problem-solve, and so on. The questions were along the lines of "Tell me about a time you did not get along with a peer. Tell me what the situation/problem was, what was the task/what was your role in it, what activity was taken, and what was the result. Oh, and what could you have done to change it, or would you have done differently?" or "Tell me about a process improvement you have made," or "Tell me about a time you had to coach and mentor a peer."

There was another acronym for how to answer the questions during the interview that I cannot recall, but the STAR (Situation, Task, Activity, Result) technique is similar, and it was important to answer in that order to properly explain your answer in a clear way, to demonstrate that you can think clearly and critically under pressure, and to demonstrate that you can follow standard work. Additionally, the leaders were also looking for your ability to self-reflect, recognize missteps, and your ability to internalize and learn from them. The company knows you're going to make mistakes, they want to know what you're going to do about it to grow.

As the interview progressed and you answered the questions from the standardized question sheet, the leaders in the room graded you on each answer. The grading criteria was the Toyota standard "O" or "Δ" or an "**X**," and each one was worth a certain number of points. The teammate in the process had no idea what or how they were being graded by each leader. I had three group leaders and an HR representative in my interview, and if a glance at the score sheet was spied, I had no idea what it meant or if I was doing well.

Before you got to the interview, however, your group leader needed to sign off on you meeting the requirements for promotion eligibility, essentially sponsoring you for promotion. The requirements included items such as being safe, high quality, ability to meet time in your processes, attitude, no disciplinary actions above coaching, and no attendance issues, amongst others. No group leader, therefore, was going to put their signature to paper for a teammate to be promoted and assume that responsibility lightly lest they become known to their leaders for poorly developing their future leaders or for not being able to recognize teammates who were not up to the Toyota standard.

When I communicated my interest in being a team leader to my group leader, I also asked for opportunities to learn, and one of my learnings was that I should ensure that I model the behaviors that Toyota wanted in a team member. These characteristics are basic items and should be expected of all managers, but as I have grown in age and organizational responsibility, I realize now truly why this was spelled out—because these behaviors are not taught, practiced, or adhered to in a lot of cases and a successful organization starts and ends with the right team members. For me at Toyota, attitudes and behaviors that were expectations to model meant when I was on the clock, there was no standing around if the line stopped. I needed to be checking my current and last vehicles' quality, stocking my empty parts as needed, performing 5S on the line in my process and underflow racks, reviewing my training manual and standard work, and, lastly, performing 5S on the line as a whole and break areas if time was still available, and yes, I have cleaned out many a microwave, scraped wax off many a paraffin bath in my break areas, and swept entire production lines with the push brooms—as a teammate and as a team leader as well.

Additionally, although it really shouldn't need to be spelled out, this meant being on time to work consistently, wearing the correct PPE and being safe, helping others and maintaining a professional attitude, constructively working through any conflicts I might have with my peers, suggesting ideas to improve my process, area, and the company.

To demonstrate leadership and engagement, I suggested a lot of improvement ideas both verbally and using kaizen improvement sheets, and although I tried to always submit quality ideas, whether they were implemented or not was not my overarching goal. It was the fact that I was observing my processes and surroundings and trying to improve our work life. It also meant that I had to work with my peers on two shifts to try to gain buy-in and support, so I was able to practice consensus building and teamwork and influencing without authority. Another question that I was asked in my interview process was, "Tell me about a time you had to convince one of your peers to believe in your idea or point of view."

Each day, a team leader leads the daily stretch routine while the group leader reads communication line-side. The communication consisted of relevant topics from the previous shifts, such as safety and quality issues, process changes, company-wide general communications, and other announcements. After the 6-minute stretch, the teams broke up and the team leaders briefly touched base with their teammates related to team-specific concerns or issues, maybe a deeper dive into the safety or quality issue brought up by the group leader for a few minutes prior to line start. The daily stretch was also something I led to show leadership that I was engaged and not nervous about being in front of others and that I took safety seriously.

Finally, little by little, my team leader would teach me pieces of the role or functions of the practical job. I would come in with my team leader 30 minutes early and learn the pre-shift setup tasks, paid and with group leader approval. These included making sure that all areas of the line were stocked with parts so that production could start, filling all fluids in various processes, calibrating torque wrenches, and documenting the readings—sending any wrenches that did not meet spec to quality for adjustment and recertification, reading the shift-to-shift communication, making sure all of the Andon lights functioned by pulling the cables and triggering the light and alarm, making sure that the paraffin bath had wax in it, ensuring that repair stations in my area had the tools required, and helping create a daily process rotation schedule for my peers, although my team leader would review and approve and/or change to ensure that it was fair so that team-mates wouldn't complain about one of their own doing this if they did not like the schedule and documenting that the pre-shift checks had been done and signing my name to it on the team leader standard work.

Team leaders are required to be a half-hour early for start-up tasks and may need to stay 10 minutes after shift to wrap up. This is planned daily overtime for this role. Occasionally and rarely, team leaders were allowed to leave a few minutes before the end of a shift to mitigate the overtime incurred. The amount of overtime to work on any given day was mandatory and communicated halfway through the shift and depended on how production was running. Additionally, if a part was delayed but would be arriving from a local supplier, overtime may be used to recover any lost production due to the delay. Overtime was delivered in terms of six-tenths of an hour; therefore, the overtime call could be for as little as .6 of an hour (6 minutes), 1.5 hours, up to a maximum of 2 hours a day per shift, or anywhere between.

It was during this time that the word came to us that management was opening up the team leader "pool" for new applicants. If I recall correctly, applications were taken for several weeks. Afterward, there was usually another several-week gap, and then the process started. All in all, I think it was more than a month and a half before I actually found out the results and that I had made it into the pool. Of course, it was a giant weight off my shoulders, but now came another grueling period of waiting to find out if there was a vacancy and whether I was going to be selected to actually be a team leader.

It was kind of an interesting process at this point because we often found out that we were selected when a random new teammate showed up at our line one day. We'd have to speculate if someone resigned, was being transferred, or was promoted and if this was their backfill. Except for resignations, a teammate was not moved to another area or promoted until their backfill was hired, trained, and in place working on the line. It wasn't fair to the team to just simply pull a teammate and expect the team leader to pick up the slack and forgo other parts of the role to build production while the teammate trained. This shorted the team their support.

When my replacement showed up to the line and trained and they were certified to a Level 4 and could perform a process or two independently with no oversight, which took about a month, we had an extra body for a few hours, and I would be let off of the line to help team lead with supervision, to get practice answering Andons and dealing with teammate process issues. However, it was a very rare condition that a person selected to be a team leader became one in the same production area where they were a teammate. When it was time for the transition, a newly minted team leader would be moved to another production line, or sometimes another production plant; we had two assembly plants onsite. Moving a new team lead to another location where no one knew them was very essential to success. It was a very difficult task to lead people who have become your friends as teammates; suddenly transitioning to a leadership role in which you would be responsible for them might make it difficult for them to see me in a different light and respect the position of authority I now held. Dropping a team leader into a position where they weren't seen as a friend first was a great boon to their success.

I can remember my transition like it was yesterday; the learnings came fast and furious and thinking back on them I sometimes still get a chuckle. As much as I thought I was ready, there was still so much to learn. When I was moved to my new line, I would team lead for a couple of hours and train in a process to learn my team's jobs.

One of the first things a team leader needs to do is to learn their team's processes in order to build a relationship with their new teammates and to gain their respect. A team leader who did not budget their time to do this right away often found themselves struggling with their teammates and their peers because when the time came to cover a gap due to vacation, sickness, or injury and they couldn't do their part to build their own process and cover their own gap, they were frowned on by their peers. So I knew to set myself to this task right away and worked with my new peers to make sure that when I was scheduling myself to train in a process that there would be enough support on the line to answer Andons.

As important as it was to pick up your processes safely, quickly, and with high quality, it was important to give a few hours to your team-leading duties as well. This gives some of your peers a chance to go off the line to work on improvement projects or updates to standard work and the like. So during my first week as a team leader on my new line during this period, I observed that all the flow racks in my areas were sitting over the edge of the line by about 6 inches. We only had about 3.5 feet between the racks and the vehicles, and the teammates were pulling the racks up closer to the vehicles and out of their standard location. So I would go along and push them back into place to 5S my area and thought I was also removing a safety hazard for my teammates. It did not take long for me to get called out by one of my new teammates for making adjustments to processes while not even knowing them yet. That was a bit like getting hit in the forehead with a hammer and took the wind right out of my sails. I look back at this as my first "aha" moment as a team leader. A few learnings I can remember from this simple occurrence:

1. Calm down—I was excited and needed to dial it down a little.
2. Take my time and do not rush to make a big impression—see Learning 1.
3. Get to know the teammates better first. It turns out that my predecessor was passive, not very active in improving the area, and was therefore more complacent than I was, being shiny and new, so these teammates and I were going to need an adjustment period.
4. Ask questions—The teammates were actually adjusting the racks closer to reduce walk time, and the standard had not been adjusted from my predecessor—what I really needed to do was simply retape the rack locations on the floor. Well, I guess everyone has to start somewhere.

One of my next learnings ties back into my statement earlier that even though as a teammate we are building processes, we're typically in tune with what our leaders are doing to support us, or not, as the case may be. I was supporting the production line a few weeks later and had a problem with a teammate's build—I believe it was a quality issue. I remember asking the teammate about it and getting some type of answer that I just thought was a ridiculous excuse. I did not call the teammate on it, but it wasn't about an hour later that I had a visit from my group leader. We got the opportunity to discuss the importance of body language as apparently, when my teammate had responded to me, I had rolled my eyes and another teammate had seen it from 15 feet away and decided to say something. Alrighty then, two more learnings: the importance of body language and keeping facial features in control—check. This is pretty important, as a teammate can really learn to push your buttons in some cases, but as a team leader, you need to remain calm and neutral. Nothing is personal, even though sometimes it may seem like it, and second, teammates can observe anything at great distances—check.

Problem-solving was a typical function of the team leader as well. team leaders most commonly engaged in either full-blown practical problem-solving on their own shift, having cross-shift discussions with the team leader's counterpart, or facilitating discussions between teammates from opposing shifts. Several different types of scenarios could present themselves on a daily basis. Most common were the following:

1. A teammate submits a kaizen improvement sheet to the team leader to improve their process. The team leader would review this personally with the teammate to understand what they were wanting to improve and why. If I, as the team leader, liked it, I would have to leave it for review for the opposing shift leader and team. Then came the face-to-face discussion with the other team leader to discuss questions and concerns to try to come to consensus with each other, and/or to try to figure out to get the teammates into a consensus state either for or against it. The kaizen sheet would need to be signed by all teammates and leaders either for or against the idea and, if against, why.

2. Whenever there was a quality issue on the line, if it was serious enough, it would merit a flip chart to be done. A flip chart was manually written out in marker with the A3 problem-solving steps. The team leader would need to meet with the teammate that caused the quality issue after shift and run through the steps, documenting everything from the date of occurrence, the problem statement to describe what occurred, the location it occurred, the location in the standard work, who was involved, and so on; then through a 5 Whys problem-solving to implement a containment immediately; and then a countermeasure within a week's time. This flip chart, along with any others in the plant, was then reviewed on a daily walk by plant leadership with the group leader of the line.

When I got to Toyota, there were things I hadn't done before that I suddenly needed to learn. I needed to learn to use a variety of tools and Toyota had a certification program for different sets of tools: hand tools, power tools, welding, and electricity, and there was a visual representation on the back of each person's bump cap in the form of stickers: A, B, C, or D, and each letter stood for a particular class of tools you were permitted to use.

I was expected to build flow racks to deliver parts, for example. They use a material called Creform (which is a type of pipe); it goes together with brackets and screws, and you cut pipe to length with a bandsaw and put rollers on and taper them to angle the right direction, but have you ever built a flow rack before? Neither had I. There's no class, except to be certified to use the tools. You go design in your head what it should look like and then put it on a piece of paper so you can remember your dimensions, and then you might talk to a team leader in the Kaizen Department who could advise you, but you were typically left to build your own racks. The people in Kaizen Department could help if they had a minute to spare and typically had to help if the build required complex parts such as automation, heat, or air. But the point of this is that there isn't a manual. You go, you do. If it doesn't work as designed, what are you going to do differently and try again? Do you have a resource on your team that is mechanically inclined that can help? There was no team of subject matter experts, black belts, MBAs, industrial engineers, or anyone else coming to your aid—just you and your team of former farmers, bankers, sales clerks, mechanics, recent graduates, grandfathers, mothers, microbiologists, etc. And you know what? We solved it and got the job done. It's a powerful thing.

Additionally, I had to learn how to change out tooling or adjust settings on both air and impact tools. Toyota used Atlas Copco–branded tools and as situations presented themselves, I learned about adjusting the air pressure on the tool, how to oil the tool properly, how to calibrate the tools, how to run and set up a poka yoke, and the like. Even though there were tooling specialists who could be used for support, they were infrequent, and most of the learning came from peers and informal training when the job needed to be done. We crafted balancers and tracks to hang tools above us and used pieces of PVC to create tool holders on carts. As I recall, eventually, standard work and a class were put together, as it was recognized by the tooling specialists that everyone was learning through trial and error or unwritten knowledge and that our lives could be easier if a process was established.

This was also how you typically learned about being a team leader and were trained. A bit of desire, ambition, and intuitiveness to learn about the role while you're a teammate, and then it was on the job by your new team leader peers and through experiences and trial and error. You had to be good enough to observe the good and bad, eliminate the bad, and humble enough to be open to always learning from whatever was thrown your way. An experience arises and someone has to be willing to rise up and meet it head-on, good, bad, or ugly, and learn how they could have done it better next time.

There wasn't much formality to it that I remember; one day I was building as a teammate, went home for the weekend, and then returned to a new production line and was a team leader. There was leader standard work in the form of a checklist of what to do before shift when you arrived and after shift before you left. You checked the boxes and signed your name after you performed the task. To boil the job down succinctly, it was support production to keep the line moving and producing with high quality, to ensure everyone is safe, and to improve the processes to make them efficient and remove waste, all while supporting your teammates.

What I eventually came to realize is that all the teammates wanted was to know that while they were working, the team leader wasn't getting away with murder, so to speak. So when they built vehicles, I answered andons quickly and efficiently, I fixed any defects that came my way, I filled their parts up, and I cleaned and cleaned and cleaned. I could build all our processes and understand any difficulties from their perspective. I listened to their concerns and ideas intently and with genuine interest and acted quickly and efficiently to improve life for them to the best of my ability. When they sweated, I sweated. In short, I empathize (not sympathize), and in return, they did their jobs well and built quality vehicles safely and in time so that we all kept our jobs and the plant kept going. I occasionally jumped into a process and let a teammate go do an improvement or perform some 5S, which also earned me more respect as they saw I wasn't afraid to dive into a process and give them a different task to do so that they remained engaged.

Toyota will tell you that being a team leader is probably the toughest job at the plant. This is because the role expectations involve you not only being an advocate for your teammates to leadership but also supporting leadership's decisions, policies, and procedures to the teammates, regardless of your agreement with them or not. Essentially, a team leader always operates in the middle ground and must remain a neutral party. A team leader has no authority to discipline a teammate, issue corrective action, or write a teammate up. Therefore, it's up to a team leader to get the teammates to continue to follow policy and procedure and be safe while remaining neutral and having no disciplinary authority. I can remember a lot of times coaching teammates and reminding them that I wanted to be their friend, but I am their leader first, so they needed to follow this rule or policy or procedure. If a situation kept recurring, my role was to escalate to the group leader to handle it, and when I would, I would tell the teammate that I understood they may not agree with this rule or policy but that they would need to discuss it with the group leader and that until it was changed, this is what I required of them.

Throughout what I have relayed so far, I hope that you are realizing that while a lot of work and thought went into my preparation to try and become a successful team leader, it still wasn't just because I was a good teammate that I was selected for the role. Yes, I had to model ideal teammate behaviors, but there was an application in which I had to be recommended by my group leader, an in-depth behavior-based interview to pass, and the testing I took during my hiring as a teammate in which I demonstrated my ability to gain commitment from a peer and educate them on standard work. I had to be the right teammate for the job. Often times as I have worked at different companies, my observations have led me to conclude that many people were promoted to roles and responsibilities that weren't a good fit for them simply because they had been a good teammate or a good manager, and the like, and this was the criterion for elevating them instead of there being a true evaluation process to be considered for that next-level role.

Once per quarter, the president of the company communicated via recorded message to all team members in all areas of the plant, on all shifts. This was the QBRC, quarterly business review communication. This communication covered everything from market conditions to awards being received to legislation that would affect us and other newsworthy items. This was a planned half hour of communication and was in addition to our 6-minute stretch and communication, and production targets for the day were adjusted to accommodate.

Fluid, Shifting Structure

Another learning that is more role-related is that a person considering being a team leader should realize that about half of their time, 6 months a year, should be planned as being on line still building vehicles. If a person's motivation to seek promotion in trying to become a team leader is thinking that they will get to be off-line, not building, most of the time, they have another thing coming to them.

The reason for the planning of half your time being on line building as a team leader is because of many reasons—the most common being simply bathroom breaks during the shift while the production line is running, teammate vacations, and teammate sickness. If you have four teammates on your team, and each teammate has earned 3 weeks of vacation a year, there's 12 weeks of a team leader's time consumed by building a process. A linear line cannot move if there's no one in the process to build, so part of your role as support for the teammate is to cover during these periods.

Injuries are another story altogether. Just because a teammate gets injured and told they are going to be restricted from building on the line for several weeks doesn't mean Toyota goes right out and replaces them. The team leader steps in to build the process while the teammate is out. Until the teammate is out for a period of a couple of months, Toyota typically doesn't start the replacement process, and even then, it may be that the replacement is a new teammate and needs to be hired, oriented, trained, and so on. I can remember building on the line for at least 6 months for an injured teammate several times over the course of my career, and that did not include the vacations I was going to need to cover for the rest of my teammates.

This brings up an important point to consider. I have worked in different organizations, and at least one of those has implemented a team leader and group leader structure. During this implementation, one of the most senior leaders in my part of the organization imparted to me that the primary role of the team leader was to develop the teammates and that if there were gaps in the staffing due to a vacancy as listed earlier, then the team leader wasn't doing the job of developing the teammate and that this needed to be problem-solved. His solution was that the group leader should be dropping down to assume the team leader role and fulfilling that obligation.

Being a former team leader and actually seeing the process work, I can tell you in no uncertain terms that the primary role of the team leader is to keep production moving first, whether you're in manufacturing, health care, or some other industry. This is simply practical to keep the bills paid and the lights on—if you do not produce, you'll find yourself out of business and the only developing getting done is honing interview skills. Do not misunderstand; this isn't saying that the teammates aren't important or do not need development; succession planning should always be on a leader's mind and strategy. I am simply stating that there is a priority that must be followed in any situation, and if a team leader has to cover a vacancy to keep production flowing, teammate development halts. The key to note is that this is temporary. If a team leader finds that there is never time to develop their teammates because they are always in production, then this does need to be problem-solved and required staffing analyzed.

Back to Toyota: From my observations and experiences, when a team leader is having to build on line to cover a gap, sometimes the group leader must drop into a team leader function; however, this is more a rarity than a common occurrence. In the Toyota leadership design, teammates, team leaders, group leaders, and even assistant managers typically exist in a cascading leadership structure. So, what does that mean and why is it good?

Typically, a production line runs with one team leader per four teammates. I have seen this as high as five or six but never eight like I have read about or been told about in other organizations and industries. I am not sure where these people get their numbers related to this statistic when they try to adopt this structure and budget for staffing, and then they tell me it's based on Toyota. Now, let's run through a few what-if scenarios so that I can illustrate how I have seen this system work:

- **Scenario:** I am one team leader out of four on a production line and have a vacancy due to sudden unplanned illness. I have to drop to be a teammate to cover the vacancy; Team Leaders 2 and 3 of the four team leaders on the production line simply absorb coverage of my team as part of their own duties, and my team remains supported with full parts and Andons getting answered. This is a lateral shift, I would say.
- **Scenario:** My teammate is still not back from their illness the next night, and another teammate seems to have caught the flu also and will be out. Two team leaders of the four, have to cover for vacancies and drop to teammates. At this point, there are several choices possible based on what I have seen:
  - The other two team leaders may split the line to ensure coverage is maintained, calling for their group leader to assist if there are too many Andons to handle.
  - Before a group leader assumes a team leader role, they will typically call across to neighboring production lines to see if a team leader can be borrowed. Team leaders will be capable of answering Andons, making repairs, filling parts, and cleaning. Support won't typically extend much beyond that as the primary focus is the production for the night. If the borrowed team leader runs into a situation that is foreign and they do not know what to do, they will
    - call for one of the remaining team leaders on the line via radio for assistance or the group leader.
    - stop the line in order to have a conversation with the teammate in process, the team leader building on the line as a teammate, the group leader, or other team leader, in order to understand what has to happen with the Andon to support it sufficiently.
- **Scenario:** My teammate is still not back from their illness on the third night, and two other teammates seem to have caught the flu and will be out. There is only one team leader of the four to support all the teammates on line by answering Andons, filling parts, covering for bathroom breaks, cleaning, and so on.

Choices

The group leader will typically call across to neighboring production lines to see if a team leader can be borrowed. The team leader will be capable of answering Andons, making repairs, filling parts, and cleaning. Support won't typically extend much beyond that as the primary focus is the product for the night.

1. The group leader may triage their duties to tackle only the utmost important items and split them with the team leader duties to ensure his teams remain supported by answering Andons and keeping the line moving
2. The group leader may stay primarily in their role, have the one remaining team leader run the line, and, if they get overwhelmed, call for the group leader's assistance.
3. The group leader may utilize a more unorthodox approach as well:
   a. Other departments in the facility might support building a process with two team-mates, supported by a light-duty teammate to act as a quality check. Two teammates will quickly learn half a process each, and then each vehicle will be checked by the light-duty impromptu quality inspector.
   b. The process in (a) has also been applied to a group leader or two, splitting the process, in which case, the assistant manager will come to the production area to act as the line's group leader
4. As you can see from the examples I have outlined, that I have personally seen, a fluid leadership structure of cascades is very beneficial to allowing production to continue to flow and to produce vehicles safely while maintaining high quality. The flexibility this structure provides allows for myriad situations to be handled and teammates to still remain supported.

Now, let's look at an example scenario going the other direction:

■ **Scenario:** My line has four team leaders, and my group leader calls out sick for the night.

1. The assistant manager can appoint a team leader to step up temporarily. This team leader, while performing their functions, acts as a point person for group leader tasks that arise during the shift, that can include the following:

   a. Attending the assistant manager and group leader meeting prior to shift and leading the 6-minute communication with the teammates at the start of the shift
   b. Investigating quality issues that crop up once a vehicle has left the production line
   c. Providing communication to the next shift's group leader about the shift and any relevant safety, quality, cost, delivery, or teammate issues
   d. Managing the leaders on the line; if another line needs to borrow a leader to continue to run, can this be supported? By whom?

2. Or the assistant manager can simply assume the role of the group leader temporarily.

These types of situations are pretty common on a daily basis. With an assembly plant the size of a Toyota plant that has thousands of teammates across multiple shifts, these types of challenges should be expected. The structure that is designed to support this may not always look neat and tidy as I have illustrated earlier, but it gets the job done as designed: to limp production along temporarily and maintaining the same production standards as if there were no gaps in teammates or leaders.

The New Thinking Culture

Companies do not have cultures. . . . People make up the culture.

—**Ritsuo Shingo**[2]

We must invest time in continuous training of our people in order to create a sustainable improvement-based culture. I once asked Ritsuo Shingo what HR's role was at Toyota. He said HR should play a huge role in creating the kaizen culture starting from the job-posting process. HR should make it part of their interview and orientation, and actively support the culture change. They should help facilitate, support, and drive the Lean culture and continuous learning organization. The BASICS® Lean Leadership Development Path will help you create this sustainable culture focused on delivering on our customer's expectations.

Ten Rules to Live By—

1. Keep it simple
2. Know and respect your people—challenge them. People work best in teams of four to six persons.
3. Create a culture of problem-solving.
4. Lead by example.
5. Learn to see the waste.
6. Create and sustain flow—Ask yourself, How do I make it an assembly line or as close as possible (JIT)?
7. Know your processes, their cycle times, and where the bottleneck is located. Know how to check the process—does it have a process capability (Cpk) of 2 or better?
8. Make everything visual. Make people fill in charts by hand.
9. Build in quality—Fix problems at their source so they never come back; eliminate the need for inspection!
10. Build continuous improvement into the system (culture) every day—daily kaizen!

Hansei—Reflection/Conclusion[3]

My grandfather, Charles W. Protzman Sr. ended the CCS training with the following story, which we thought was a fitting ending for this book.

> When a Japanese farmer plants his wheat, he arranges the field so there is symmetry and organization. Every row has a definite relationship to every other row and to the field. But he does not merely go out and plant the wheat among the rice stubble in mud and water. He knows if he did this the grain would not grow—there could be no harvest. Before he plants his wheat he must prepare the ground. He must provide for draining away the excess water and cultivate the ground so the seed will take root and grow. He must get rid of the rice stubble and weed. But when he begins preparing the ground he has a plan in mind. As he prepares it, the rows where the wheat will be planted take shape.
>
> Then when he plants the wheat it grows in accordance with his plans, because he has done two things. First, he has prepared the ground to receive the seed and provide the food for growth. Second, he has made all his preparations according to a plan so the results will be what he wants.
>
> In this course we have been provided the fundamentals for planning, and the things that you need to assure your crop or harvest as industrial managers. But, like the farmer,

you must first prepare the ground so your crop will grow. Your ground is the people who make up the company. You, as executives, your subordinates, and the workers, must be prepared to receive the ideas and plans, and each must contribute to the taking root and growing of the crop. It is up to you to be sure that you prepare yourselves and your people by study, analysis, training, example, and the application of sound principles so that you can be assured of the final Customer harvest of improved quality and lower costs delivered just-in-time.

The Authors Would Like to Leave You with This Ultimate Challenge . . .

We say the goal of Lean is to create a culture where 80% of your ideas come from the shop floor or office and then we implement 96% of them. This is what we call daily kaizen. Can your existing culture support this? If not, there is still work to do. Remember, having no problem is the biggest problem.

No matter how much you have improved, there is still room for more. Dr. Shigeo Shingo used to do an exercise with his P-course classes. He would wet a towel and pass it around the class, having each person squeeze it. Toward the end, each student could still squeeze out a drop of water. This was a great analogy for finding waste.

The other example we like to use is small improvements. Every once in a while, you will get a big one, but the goal is small, incremental improvements every day. We use snow for analogy. Each snowflake may seem insignificant, but eventually, they turn into inches (centimeters) and then feet (meters) of snow. Each idea on its own may seem insignificant, but eventually, we create a snowstorm.

We sincerely hope this book helps you unleash the ideas and engagement of those who do the work while giving you a good, granular, structured approach to implementing the BASICS® of ongoing Lean improvements.

A Bunch of Turkeys[4]

An enterprising turkey led the flock to a field and, with demonstration and instruction, taught them how to fly. All afternoon they enjoyed soaring, flying, and the thrill of seeing new vistas. Each one remarked what a wonderful new skill set they had acquired.

AFTER THE MEETING WAS OVER, ALL THE TURKEYS WALKED HOME.

Notes

1. For everything you are about to read, I would like to provide the caveat that this is based solely on my personal experience and observations during my time at a particular Toyota plant. This may or may not be common among other facilities. Others in my positions may have different views and may have had different experiences that shaped their views and opinions. I would encourage the reader to take these experiences of mine and to be able to learn from them, but do not stop reading about the Toyota experience from others at varying facilities. There will always be some nugget of valuable information to be gained from each of our observations.
2. Ritsuo Shingo taught at the Lean Leadership Institute (LLI) conference, August 2017, hosted by George Trachilis in Santorini, Greece.
3. CCS Industrial Management Manual, Charles Protzman Sr., Homer Sarasohn, 1949.
4. Story told by Charles Protzman's sensei, Mark Jamrog, SMC Group.

Appendix

Sakichi Toyoda's Five Main Principles[1]

1. Always be faithful to your duties, thereby contributing to the company and to the overall good
2. Always be studious and creative, striving to stay ahead of the times
3. Always be practical and avoid frivolousness
4. Always strive to build a homelike atmosphere at work that is warm and friendly
5. Always have respect for the existence of a higher spiritual being, and remember to be grateful at all times

Toyota's Philosophy[2]

1. Customer First
2. People are our most valuable resource.
3. Kaizen (activities that cause improvement).

   a. Create a learning organization
   b. Create a problem-solving environment
   c. Surface problems quickly with swift solutions and counter measures.
   d. Standard work—(there cannot be improvement without a standard in place).

4. Go and see.

   a. Shop floor focus.
   b. Everyone in the organization is a resource that supports the floor (Gemba).
   c. Build and encourage a supportive culture.

Toyota 4P's[3]

Toyota developed the 4P model, which includes the following:

1. Philosophy: The philosophy sets the foundation for all the other principles. According to this, leaders of the company see it as a vehicle adding values to the customers, society, community, and associates. It goes back to its founders Sakichi Toyoda and his son Kiichiro

Toyoda, who wanted to help farmworkers in interior Japan, including his own mother, by inventing automatic power looms.

2. Process: When you stick to the right processes, you get right results; Toyota leaders have learned this through mentorship and experience.
3. People/Partners: Right people and partners by training and challenging to grow. Creating a challenging environment that challenges its people to think critically, learn, and grow.
4. Problem-Solving: Everyone faces problems whether they like it or not. But problems will return unless they are analyzed to remove the root cause. There is always an opportunity in problem-solving to figure out what causes a problem and to solve it from its root cause. Everyone in Toyota has a fair chance of sharing their learning with others facing similar problems so the company can improve.

Toyota Five Precepts[4]

"The Toyoda Precepts are five tenets that can be traced back to the convictions of Sakichi Toyoda, the founder of Toyoda Automatic Loom Works, Ltd. Originating from a period of rapid expansion for the Toyoda company, the precepts were compiled by his son Kiichiro and members of the Toyoda management, who sought to educate and unite a workforce around core principles. Announced on October 30, 1935, the fifth anniversary of Sakichi's death, these moral standards became the official guidelines for all Toyoda operations."

1. Always be faithful to your duties, thereby contributing to the Company and to the overall good.
2. Always be studious and creative, striving to stay ahead of the times.
3. Always be practical and avoid frivolousness.
4. Always strive to build a homelike atmosphere at work that is warm and friendly.
5. Always have respect for spiritual matters, and remember to be grateful at all times.

14 Principles of the Toyota Way[5]

Following is the Leadership Development Path and where the 14 principles fit:

Principle 1—"Base your management decisions on a long-term philosophy, even at the expense of short-term financial goals."
Principle 2—"Create a continuous process flow to bring problems to the surface."
Principle 3—"Use 'pull' systems to avoid overproduction."
Principle 4—"Level out the workload (work like the tortoise, not the hare)."
Principle 5—"Build a culture of stopping to fix problems, to get quality right the first time."
Principle 6—"Standardized tasks and processes are the foundation for continuous improvement and employee empowerment."
Principle 7—"Use visual controls so no problems are hidden."
Principle 8—"Use only reliable, thoroughly tested technology that serves your people and process."
Principle 9—"Grow leaders who thoroughly understand the work, live the philosophy, and teach it to others."

Principle 10—"Develop exceptional people and teams who follow your company's philosophy."

Principle 11—"Respect your extended network of partners and suppliers by challenging them and helping them improve."

Principle 12—"Go and see for yourself to thoroughly understand the situation."

Principle 13—"Make decisions slowly by consensus, thoroughly considering all options; implement decisions rapidly."

Principle 14—"Become a learning organization through relentless reflection and continuous improvement."

Ohno's 10 Precepts[6]

Ohno is also known for his "Ten Precepts" to think and act to win:

1. You are a cost. First reduce waste.
2. First say, "I can do it." And try before everything.
3. The workplace is a teacher. You can find answers only in the workplace.
4. Do anything immediately. Starting something right now is the only way to win.
5. Once you start something, persevere with it. Do not give up until you finish it.
6. Explain difficult things in an easy-to-understand manner. Repeat things that are easy to understand.
7. Waste is hidden. Do not hide it. Make problems visible.
8. Valueless motions are equal to shortening one's life.
9. Re-improve what was improved for further improvement.
10. Wisdom is given equally to everybody. The point is whether one can exercise it.

Ohno's Method (Very Much Like Plan–Do–Check–Act)[7]

Mentally force yourself into tight spots (something like a gun to the head concentrates the mind).

1. Think hard; systematically observe reality.
2. Generate ideas; find and implement wise, ingenious, low-cost solutions.
3. Derive personal pleasure from accomplishing kaizen.
4. Develop all peoples' capabilities to accomplish Steps 1 through 4. Everyone learns kaizen by doing it. Managers and staff learn to support workers, proposing only big-step improvements. They learn not to control self-functioning workers.

HUMAN-BASED DESCRIPTION OF THE TOYOTA PRODUCTION SYSTEM WITH OHNO'S METHOD

Problem Visibility

Kaizen Problems

Look carefully; think hard
↓
Minimize all waste
↓
Gain satisfaction by overall improvements
↓
Develop everyone's capabilities (mentor team)
↓
Develop flexibility (ability to quickly and easily respond to changes)
↓
Long-term survival

Dr. Deming's 14 Points[8]

1. Create constancy of purpose toward improvement of product and service, with the aim to become competitive, stay in business, and provide jobs.
2. Adopt the new philosophy. We are in a new economic age. Western management must awaken to the challenge, must learn their responsibilities, and must take on leadership for change.
3. Cease dependence on inspection to achieve quality. Eliminate the need for massive inspection by building quality into the product in the first place.
4. End the practice of awarding business on the basis of a price tag. Instead, minimize total cost. Move toward a single supplier for any one item, on a long-term relationship of loyalty and trust.
5. Improve constantly and forever the system of production and service to improve quality and productivity and thus constantly decrease costs.
6. Institute training on the job.
7. Institute leadership. The aim of supervision should be to help people and machines and gadgets do a better job. Supervision of management is in need of overhaul, as well as supervision of production workers.
8. Drive out fear, so everyone may work effectively for the company.
9. Break down barriers between departments. People in research, design, sales, and production must work as a team, in order to foresee problems of production and usage that may be encountered with the product or service.
10. Eliminate slogans, exhortations, and targets for the workforce asking for zero defects and new levels of productivity. Such exhortations only create adversarial relationships, as the bulk of the causes of low quality and low productivity belong to the system and thus lie beyond the power of the workforce.
11. (a) Eliminate work standards (quotas) on the factory floor. Substitute with leadership. (b) Eliminate management by objectives (MBO). Eliminate management by numbers and numerical goals. Instead substitute with leadership.
12. (a) Remove barriers that rob the hourly worker of their right to pride of workmanship. The responsibility of supervisors must be changed from sheer numbers to quality. (b) Remove

barriers that rob people in management and in engineering of their right to pride of workmanship. This means, inter alia, abolishment of the annual or merit rating and of MBO.

13. Institute a vigorous program of education and self-improvement.

14. Put everybody in the company to work to accomplish the transformation. The transformation is everybody's job.

Notes

1. Extreme Toyota, Osono, Shimizu, Takeuchi, Wiley, 2008 pg 90.
2. Speech by Gary Convis to MWCC, 2008 annual meeting.
3. The Toyota Way, Jeffrey Liker, McGraw-Hill Education; (c)2003.
4. www.toyota-myanmar.com/about-toyota/toyota-traditions/company/toyoda-precepts-the-base-of-the-global-vision Toyoda Precepts: The base of the Global Vision Toyoda Precepts: The base of the Global Vision released on April 2012 www.toyota-global.com/company/history_of_toyota/75years/data/conditions/precepts/index.html
5. The Toyota Way, Jeffrey Liker, McGraw-Hill Education; (c)2003.
6. www.linkedin.com/pulse/what-every-lean-coach-should-know-teach-ohnos-trachilis-p-eng-/ www.youtube.com/watch?v=d24gUrF2RoU Matt Amezawa, Former Chief Executive Officer at Toyota Motor Manufacturing Kentucky, Inc. shares what Taiichi Ohno expected from his employees Oct 12, 2019 Lean Leadership Institute.
7. www.ame.org/sites/default/files/target_articles/02-18-1-Ohnos_Method.pdf
8. Deming, W. Edwards. *Out of The Crisis*, MIT Press 2000 pg. 23–24. https://deming.org/explore/fourteen-points/

Index

Note: Page numbers in *italic* indicate a figure on the corresponding page.

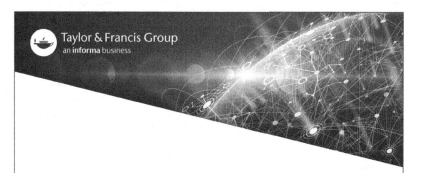